Populism and Democracy

Populism and Democracy

Sascha Hardt, Aalt Willem Heringa and
Hoai-Thu Nguyen

eleven
international publishing

Published, sold and distributed by Eleven International Publishing
P.O. Box 85576
2508 CG The Hague
The Netherlands
Tel.: +31 70 33 070 33
Fax: +31 70 33 070 30
e-mail: sales@elevenpub.nl
www.elevenpub.com

Sold and distributed in USA and Canada
Independent Publishers Group
814 N. Franklin Street
Chicago, IL 60610
USA
Order Placement: (800) 888-4741
Fax: (312) 337-5985
orders@ipgbook.com
www.ipgbook.com

Eleven International Publishing is an imprint of Boom uitgevers Den Haag.

ISBN 978-94-9094-723-1
ISBN 978-90-5454-669-6 (E-book)

Table of Contents

List of Abbreviations

A3-P1	Article 3 of the First Protocol to the European Convention on Human Rights
AFC	Austrian Federal Constitutional Law [Austria – *Bundes-Verfassungsgesetz*]
AfD	Alternative for Germany [Germany – *Alternative Für Deutschland*]
AK	Justice and Development Party [Turkey – *Adalet ve Kalkınma Partisi*]
ANO	Action of Dissatisfied Citizens [Czech Republic – *Akce nespokojených občanů*]
AWS	Solidarity Electoral Action [Poland – *Akcja Wyborcza Solidarność*]
B-VG	Federal Constitutional Law [Austria – *Bundes-Verfassungsgesetz*]
CJA	Code of Administrative Justice [France – *Code de justice administrative*]
CNL	National Liberation Committee [Italy – *Comitato di Liberazione Nazionale*]
CSM (France)	High Council for the Judiciary [France – *Conseil Supérieur de la Magistrature*]
CSM (Italy)	High Council of the Judiciary [Italy – *Consiglio Superiore della Magistratura*]
DL	The Left [Germany – *Die Linke*] (DL)
ENA	National School of Administration [France – *Ecole Nationale d'Administration*]
ECHR	European Convention on Human Rights
ECtHR	European Court of Human Rights
EU	European Union
FN	National Front [France – *Front national*]
FPÖ	Freedom Party [Austria – *Freiheitliche Partei Österreichs*]
Fr. Constit.	French Constitution [France – *Constitution française du 4 octobre 1958*]
GDPR	EU General Data Protection Regulation
HZDS	Movement for a Democratic Slovakia [Slovakia – *Hnutie za demokratické Slovensko*]
IDEA	International Institute for Democracy and Electoral Assistance
KRS	National Council of the Judiciary [Poland – *Krajowa Rada Sądownictwa*]
LFI	La France Insoumise [France]
LOPP	Political Parties Law [Spain – *Ley Orgánica 6/2002, Partidos Políticos*]
LOREG	General Electoral System Law [Spain – *Ley Orgánica 5/1985, Régimen Electoral General*]
LOTC	Constitucional Tribunal Law [Spain – *Ley Orgánica 2/1979, Tribunal Constitucional*]
MSZP	Hungarian Socialist Party [Hungary – *Magyar Szocialista Párt*]
NATO	North Atlantic Treaty Organization
ND	New Democracy [Greece – *Νέα Δημοκρατία*, Nea Dimokratia]
NetzDG	German Network Enforcement Act [Germany – *Netzdurchsetzunggesetz*]
NSF	National Salvation Front [Romania – *Frontul Salvării Na□ionale*]
ÖVP	Austrian People's Party [Austria – *Die neue Volkspartei*]
PiS	Law and Justice [Poland – *Prawo i Sprawiedliwość*]
PSD	Social Democratic Party [Romania – *Partidul Social Democrat*]
PVV	Dutch Freedom Party [the Netherlands – *Partij voor de Vrijheid*]
QPC	Priority question of constitutionality [France – *question prioritaire de constitutionnalité*]
RI	Intermediate Sphere
RN	National Rally [France – *Rassemblement National* (formerly National Front – *Front National*)]
RoP NA	Rules of Procedure of the National Assembly [France]
RoP S	Rules of Procedure of the Senate [France]
SC	Spanish Constitution [Spain – *Constitución Española*]

SD	Sweden Democrats [Sweden – *Sverigedemokraterna*]
SMER-SD	Direction-Social Democracy [Slovakia – *Smer – sociálna demokracia*]
SP	Socialist Party [the Netherlands – *Socialistische Partij*]
SPÖ	Social Democratic Party of Austria [Austria – *Sozialdemokratische Partei Österreichs*]
SVP	Swiss People's Party [Switzerland – *Schweizerische Volkspartei*]
UKIP	UK Independence Party [the United Kingdom]
VfGG	Constitutional Court Act [Austria – *Verfassungsgerichtshofgesetz* 1953]

PREFACE

Are liberal democracies in decline? If they are under threat by what is commonly called populism, what can and should they do to defend their essential features? What are those features? These are the main themes of the questions raised in this volume. We sought to bring together authors from different disciplines, i.e. political science and (constitutional) law and asked them to either reflect on a general aspect of these issues, or to describe in a country report how populism plays out in their respective country and to assess the effectiveness of its constitutional system in protecting basic liberal democratic values.

The book is made up of two parts. The first part discusses general aspects of populism, of which we selected four, preceded by an introductory chapter, *A Populist Age*, which sets the scene and defines the scope of the book and the contributions. The first of the subsequent four general contributions relates to the changing role of political parties. The second contribution provides a more specific focus on the nature of populist movements and their political agendas. The third contribution discusses the relationship between populism and social media. And the fourth chapter debates the relationship between referenda and democratic constitutionalism.

The second part of the book consists of seven country reports and one regional report analyzing the success or failure of national constitutional safeguards against populism. Apart from a regional report on East-Central Europe, the other countries under scrutiny are Austria, France, Greece, Hungary, Italy, Spain, the United Kingdom, Indonesia and the Philippines. The pictures painted in these articles are diverse, het highly interesting and relevant from a comparative perspective. We see similar problems with different solutions; similar solutions to different problems – and a plethora of nuances that show how closely success or failure of populism is connected to political culture and constitutional design.

We do not try to summarize each contribution here – that would not do them justice. The best way to satisfy your curiosity is to read them one by one. However, in the concluding chapter we try not only to provide a general analysis but also to discover best practices and workable solutions to remedy the dilemmas described in the various chapters, and to fix constitutional flaws identified there. The question we faced in writing the conclusion was less whether liberal democracy is under threat and whether finding remedies to protect them is necessary; this seems obvious if one believes, as we do, in the values of liberal democracies. The difficult questions are what to do, how to do it, and how to learn from each other. In particular, the question we ask ourselves was how, in the name of combatting undemocratic populist movements, not to accidentally undermine liberal democracy ourselves by stepping in too harshly.

Evidently, we are aware that much more research and analysis has to be done in order to be able to arrive at a full understanding of all the variations, nuances and pros and cons of suggested remedies and solutions. Nonetheless we hope that this book, together with the accompanying monograph by Sascha Hardt, as well as our conference on the topic in April 2020 will stimulate and contribute to efforts to protect the idea of liberal democracy throughout world.

We would like to express our gratitude to all the authors who contributed their expertise. We also thank our assistants Sarah Sørensen and Giulia Bonazzi for their excellent work in putting together the present volume.

This book is part of a project entitled 'Protecting Liberal Democracy in a Populist Era' (Bescherming van de liberale constitutie in een populistisch tijdperk). This project has been generously funded by the Fonds Staatsman Thorbecke of the KNAW (Statesman Thorbecke Fund of the Royal Netherlands Academy of Arts and Sciences). More information about this fund can be found on the following website: https://www.knaw.nl/en/awards/funds/thorbecke-fund. The output of the project, which was started in 2018, consists of the present edited volume, a conference (on 24 April 2020 in the Maastricht University Campus in Brussels), and a monograph written by Sascha Hardt.

Sascha Hardt, Aalt Willem Heringa, Hoai-Thu Nguyen

Maastricht, The Netherlands, February 2020

Part I: Populism and Democracy

Introduction: A Populist Age

*Sascha Hardt**

1 Introduction

The present volume is entitled "Populism and Democracy" and its outlook is as wide as this title suggests. This book brings together accounts from a range of countries in Europe and beyond, whose experience with populism differ as widely as their constitutional tradition. It attempts to combine a view of populism as a global phenomenon, affecting the very fabric of democratic governance all over the world, with specific national and regional contexts. In doing so, it aims to incorporate the different perspectives necessary to understand populism: how it has led to 'democratic backsliding' in many countries, how it presents a systemic threat in others, and why some democracies seem better able than others to cope with the populist threat.

In their contributions, the authors of the various chapters of this volume focus on those aspects of populism which are most relevant in the context of their respective country and scholarly discipline. The focus therefore necessarily differs between countries on the basis of the different respective national experience and the particular character and perception of populist observed there, and between legal scholars and political scientists, whose analytical tools and perspectives on a multi-faceted phenomenon as populism often differ considerably. The largest section of the chapter is therefore devoted to tracing various accounts of what populism *is*, and to arriving at a workable understanding of the concept (section 3). On the basis thereof and after some interim qualifications (section 4), I will offer a justification of the idea underlying this volume, namely that populism, even if there is little consensus on many aspects of this phenomenon, constitutes a threat to democracy (section 5).

2 What do we mean by populism?

"We are seemingly living in populist times" reads the opening statement of a comprehensive account of populism as an increasingly global phenomenon in early 21st century politics by political scientist Benjamin Moffit.[1] But are we? On the one hand,

---

* Assistant professor of comparative constitutional law at Maastricht University and a fellow of the Montesquieu Institute Maastricht.

1 B Moffitt, *The global rise of populism: performance, political style, and representation (Stanford University Press 2016) 1.*

Moffit's claim is far from new, given that prominent scholars have described populism as "a spectre [that] is haunting the world" as far back as 1969,[2] which may cast some doubt on whether politics today is indeed more populist than it used to be fifty years ago. On the other hand, what does populism mean in the first place? Indeed, despite – or perhaps because of – the abundance of literature, scholarly and journalistic, on the theme of populism that has accumulated over the years, it remains an essentially contested concept.[3]

3 Giving up Cinderella

Allegations of being populist, leading populist campaigns, or engaging in populist tactics have been voiced against political parties, movements, and individual players from all parts of the globe and the political spectrum. From Latin American socialists like Hugo Chavez to right-wing authoritarian hardliners like Rodrigo Duterte in the Philippines, from the Brexit Leave campaign to Emmanuel Macron's pro-European *La République en Marche*, from the Italian political nihilist Beppe Grillo to Germany's no-nonsense centrist conservative chancellor Angela Merkel. If trying to find meaningful common denominators between all these is a sensible exercise at all, it is at least is not an easy one.

The fact that the word is very often used not as a political classifier at all but merely as a political fighting term – applied, no less, to players from the entire range of the political spectrum, left to right, by their opponents – has called the overall analytical usefulness of the term into question.[4] As an additional complication, no political organization or movement since the late nineteenth century[5] has self-identified as 'populist'.[6] Hence, while for other concepts that are in themselves similarly elusive – think of socialism or fascism – a description of the concept can, with a degree of certainty and consensus, be

2 G Ionescu and E Gellner, 'Introduction'. in G Ionescu and E Gellner (eds), *Populism: its meanings and national characteristics* (The Nature of human society series, Weidenfeld & Nicolson 1970) 1.

3 C Mudde and C Rovira Kaltwasser, *Populism: a very short introduction* (Oxford University Press 2017) 2.

4 K Weyland, Populism: A Political-Strategic Approach. in C Rovira Kaltwasser and others (eds), *The Oxford Handbook of Populism* (Oxford University Press 2017) 51.

5 The 19th century Russian movement of the народники (*narodniki*) and their ideology of народничество (*narodnichestvo*) are commonly translated as 'populists' and 'populism'. The movement strived for a form of "peasant socialism" on the basis of the cooperative lifestyle of the rural population and is sometimes described as a forebear of the Bolshevik revolutionary movement. Cf. A Pedler, 'Going to the People. The Russian Narodniki in 1874-5' [1927] 6 *The Slavonic and East European Review* 130. In the United States, the People's Party (also called Populist Party) was a relatively short-lived political party formed on the basis of grass-roots farmers' movements at the end of the 19th century. Cf. P A Taggart, *Populism* (Open University Press 2000), 27 *et seq.*

6 At least not in earnest. Of course, politicians accused of populism often try to capitalise on the vagueness of the term, such as the former leader of the French extreme-right party Front National, who claimed: "Populism precisely is taking into account the people's opinion. Have people the right, in a democracy, to hold an opinion? If that is the case, then yes, I am a populist." Quoted in B Stanley, 'The thin ideology of populism' [2008] 13(1) *Journal of Political Ideologies* 101.

derived from the self-image and the objective features of the organization or movement in question, no sensible definition of populism in the twenty-first century is likely to come from the populists themselves.[7] Accordingly, anyone using the concept in a consistent manner will have to fall back on an external definition, of which there may never be a debate-ending, conclusive one.

Many attempts to solve the problem of populism once and for all have delivered results worth considering, but ultimately failed. In the ironic words of Isaiah Berlin, the study of populism suffers from a "Cinderella complex":

> by which I mean the following: that there exists a shoe – the word 'populism' – for which somewhere there exists a foot. There are all kinds of feet which it *nearly* fits, but we must not be trapped by these nearly fitting feet. The prince is always wandering about with the shoe; and somewhere, we feel sure, there awaits a limb called pure populism. This is the nucleus of populism, its essence. All other populisms are derivations from it and variations of it, but somewhere there lurks true populism, which may have lasted only six months, or in only one place...That is the Platonic ideal of populism, all the others being dilutions or perversions of it.[8]

Why, then, should we care using the concept of populism in a study dealing with (the failing of) constitutional defences of liberal democracy? Why is it relevant whether we can attribute legal changes that constitute a deterioration of liberal constitutional democracy to a phenomenon called populism? If the term is meaningless, or so over-inclusive that it has no analytical value whatsoever, this would be a futile exercise. But as Moffit correctly points out, the tendency in the literature of using the term 'populism' to refer to many different things and the seemingly endless debate about its meaning and definition can be read in either of two ways: either, we could conclude that 'populism' is a hollow notion, of little more use than as a derisive term for politicians we do not like. Alternatively, we may also conclude that part of the reason for all the attention and debate devoted to the definition of 'populism' is that it is an extremely difficult, yet important one,[9] crucial to understanding early 21st century politics and, as I am going to argue, constitutional developments.

The decision to engage with the concept of populism instead of discarding it for its ambiguity rests on the sentiment now very common among scholars of both political

---

7 This point, valid to this date, has already been made by M Canovan, *Populism* (Harcourt Brace Jovanovich 1981) 5 *et seq.*

8 As quoted by J B Allcock, ''Populism': A Brief Biography' [1971] 5(3) *Sociology* 371 endnote 34; also, in part, M Canovan, *Populism* (Harcourt Brace Jovanovich 1981) 7.

9 Cf. B Moffitt, *The global rise of populism: performance, political style, and representation* (Stanford University Press 2016) 11.

science and law, as well as among general observers of current events, that we *do* live in populist times, that populism is a meaningful concept, that it actually is on the rise in the early 21st century, and that the very diverse but increasingly successful group of political players subsumed under the umbrella of populism by a plethora of loosely convergent definitions has a profound impact on both national and global politics. To understand this impact does not require establishing what Isaiah Berlin called "the Platonic ideal of populism." We do not need to identify Cinderella, or at least we can absolve her from unworkable standards of purity.

3.1 *A workable understanding of populism*

What is required, instead, is a workable approximation – an understanding of 'populism' which contains a set of criteria encompassing enough to capture instances of populism from different parts of the political spectrum and from different parts of the world, operating in diverse socio-economic circumstances and different constitutional contexts. At the same time, these criteria must be sufficiently narrow and exclusive to tell populism from non-populism. Lastly, the criteria used to identify populism should relate to politically and legally relevant characteristics and behaviour. This is far from easy, since displaying a 'common touch' seems to be a central instrument of communication for many politicians described as populist. In effect they stand out by certain types of public demeanour – countless examples spring to mind: Rodrigo Duterte's lustful use of expletives, Hugo Chavez's characteristic track suits and call-in shows, Boris Johnson personally serving hot tea to journalists outside his private residence, or Dutch party leader Thierry Baudet posting nude pictures of himself on social media. Of course, such behaviour is 'political', because it carries the anti-elitist message that is common to many populist actors. But while it may have a certain indicative value and is clearly part of many populists' charismatic appeal and strategy, it should not constitute a sufficient criterion for populism – after all, establishing a 'connection' with voters is something all politicians running for elected office must do, and arguably many political actors not structurally labelled 'populist' have gone to similar extremes in times of campaigning, with varying degrees of success.

What, then, is a set of criteria that satisfies these demands without becoming Cinderella's shoe? The political scientist Jan-Werner Müller has proposed an elegantly thin definition which may well be up to the task. In his small but impactful volume 'What is Populism',[10] Müller proposes two main characteristics that mark populism: anti-elitism and anti-pluralism. In the following, I will reflect on these two characteristics in turn, briefly tracing Müller's argument why they should constitute not merely signifiers but

10 J-W Müller, *What is Populism?* (University of Pennsylvania Press 2016).

conditiones sine quibus non populism, effectively allowing us to categorize political actors and movements as populist or non-populist in a sufficiently clear manner.

3.1.1 Anti-elitism

In a democracy, it is common for members of the opposition, who seek to replace those currently in government, to portray the latter as representative of a status quo that is somehow deficient and in need of change. Parties and political groups argue that their specific cause is neglected, that their particular clientele is disadvantaged by current government policy, and that their programme is much better suited to address the challenges faced by society than the old recipes of the incumbents.

This type of discourse is, of course, utterly normal in a democracy. Even if we imagine a situation where power has been in the hands of one political camp for a very long time, the opposition's campaign for change in both personnel and policy is not anti-elitist in the sense that is meant here. Populist anti-elitism goes beyond criticism of policy and political opponents; it is usually directed against the system as such, i.e. against the legal and institutional framework that govern democratic processes and constrain unfettered majoritarianism. Often, such anti-elitism comes in the guise of a campaign in favour of democracy, for instance when populists lament the alleged lack of democratic legitimacy of an unelected judiciary or press for the holding of plebiscites with the power to override legislation or force elected legislatures to behave in line with the populist agenda.[11] Indeed, the populist habit of presenting anti-elitist agendas, often directed against legal institutions tasked with the preservation of constitutionalism, as essentially *democratic* projects is one of the most dangerous and destabilising features of contemporary populism.[12]

Where populist politicians are not in power yet, they portray themselves as standing up to an oppressive elite that governs without actual democratic legitimacy or even directly against the popular will. In a representative democracy whose technical function is not in doubt – election results are not manipulated, and voters not coerced – this requires an argumentative twist that explains the allegedly oppressive status quo. Think of the argument that *all* established parties are part of a 'cartel', degrading the electorate – the sovereign people! – to a powerless flock by lack of an electable alternative to represent the actual will of the people. Variations of what is essentially the same argument refer to the power of an alleged 'deep state' or the scheming of powerful hostile individuals, the media, clandestine groups, or foreign powers that dominate the state and prevent it from enacting the popular will.

Populist anti-elitism conjures a narrative of victimhood, in which the populists and their political causes are kept low not least by rigid social rules of political correctness.

---

11 On the populist demand for direct democracy, see section 4 below.

12 Cf. W Sadurski, *Poland's constitutional breakdown* (Oxford University Press 2019) 8.

Decrying alleged thought control or social prohibitions enacted by a hegemonic political opponent are common tropes of populist discourse. In this vein, the Dutch Forum for Democracy (*Forum voor Democratie*) recently set up an online reporting tool for victims of leftist indoctrination in schools.[13] This 'underdog' narrative is an integral part of populist political strategy. Interestingly, it remains so even where populists have managed to gain power, win majorities in parliaments and occupy the highest executive offices. In this respect, Müller correctly observes that the "conventional wisdom" that the appeal of populist parties will dwindle once they are in power and have become part of the elite themselves, is manifestly false:

> The notional that populists in power are bound to fail one way or another is comforting. It is also an illusion. For one thing, while populist parties do indeed protest against elites, this does not mean that populism in government will become contradictory. First of all, all failures of populists in government can still be blamed on elites acting behind the scenes, whether at home or abroad [...]. Many populist victors continue to behave like victims; majorities act like mistreated minorities.[14]

With regard to populist anti-elitism, one must also notice that neither populist leaders nor their voter clientele necessarily originate in or belong to lower classes of society or socio-economically underprivileged groups. In fact, while some populist leaders base much of their moral appeal and claim to representativeness of the 'ordinary people' on their humble origins (Recep Tayyip Erdoğan is one example[15]), there are equally many examples of politicians commonly referred to as populist whose background lies squarely within the social and economic elite (Donald Trump and Boris Johnson are obvious cases). In many cases, also the electoral base of populist politicians and parties is found not so much in precarious and lower-class *milieus* but rather among economically stable middle and even upper middle class strata of society. Income seems to be a less predictive factor for populist leanings than the divide between cosmopolitan and traditional

13 Nos nieuws online, 'Onderwijs en politiek vallen hard over meldpunt indoctrinatie' (NOS Nieuws Online, 27 March 2019) https://nos.nl/artikel/2277889-onderwijs-en-politiek-vallen-hard-over-meldpunt-indoctrinatie.html accessed 5 February 2020.

14 J-W Müller, *What is Populism?* (University of Pennsylvania Press 2016) 41-42.

15 In the words of Müller, "Recep Tayyip Erdoğan has [...] presented himself as a plucky underdog; he would always be the street fighter from Istanbul's tough neighbourhood of Kasımpaşa, bravely confronting the old Kemalist establishment of the Turkish Republic – even long after he had begun to concentrate all political, economic, and cultural power in his own hands.", J-W Müller, *What is Populism?* (University of Pennsylvania Press 2016) 42.

lifestyles, often coinciding with a divide between urban and rural areas; another (weaker) indicator is the level of education, with the highly educated slightly less likely to vote for a populist party.[16]

Populist anti-elitism thus has relatively little to do with any objectively determinable placement of either the populists or their voter base in non-elite segments of society; instead, it is closely connected to the populist vision of the antithesis of the elite, the pure and uncorrupted people whom they claim to represent. To a very large extent, anti-elitist rhetoric serves as a primer for those who identify themselves as members of 'the people' in moral terms. It is also 'the people' – defined by populists in an exclusionary manner as including the ethnic, religious, or cultural majority and in any event in sharp contrast to the corrupted elites and any outsiders – on whom populists rely to justify their political projects and render them as essentially *democratic* endeavours. Hence, anti-elitism is both a necessary (but by itself insufficient) identification criterion for populism and an essential operative part of populist political strategy.

3.1.2 Anti-pluralism

In the words of Margaret Canovan, "[p]opulism is not just a reaction against power structures but an appeal to a recognized authority. Populists claim legitimacy on the grounds that they speak for the people: that is to say, they claim to represent the democratic sovereign, not a sectional interest such as an economic class."[17] Populists make a claim to *exclusive* representation: they are the only ones representing the true people and whoever is not represented by them is excluded from that very notion. Consequently, their cause and agenda – regardless of its concrete content in a given instance of populism – is the only valid one, which makes populists inherently anti-pluralist.[18]

Evidence of this anti-pluralism abounds in political rhetoric – think of the Finnish *Perussuomalaiset* (True Finns) party, which already carries the exclusionary nature of its representative claim in its name. Other examples include sympathizers of the German extreme-right PEGIDA movement and the allied party *Alternative Für Deutschland* (Alternative for Germany, AfD) famously hijacking the slogan of East German demonstrators in 1989, "We are the people!", or members of the Dutch Freedom Party (*Partij voor de Vrijheid*, PVV) repeatedly denying that parliamentarians of other parties

16 For an analysis of the electoral base of the German AfD, see C Koppetsch, *Die Gesellschaft des Zorns: Rechtspopulismus im globalen Zeitalter* (1st edn, X-Texte zu Kultur und Gesellschaft 2019) 104 *et seq*; similar findings regarding Brexit-supporters and voters for UKIP are presented in D Goodhart, *The road to somewhere: the populist revolt and the future of politics* (Hurst & Company 2017).

17 M Canovan, 'Trust the People! Populism and the Two Faces of Democracy' [1999] 47(1) *Political Studies* 4.

18 J-W Müller, *What is Populism?* (University of Pennsylvania Press 2016) 20.

and parliament itself represent the Dutch people at all.[19] Where populists are in power, their rejection of pluralism often manifests itself in projects of legislative reform and constitutional amendment that weaken the institutions tasked with maintaining open political competition and a level playing field, for instance through packing or otherwise silencing constitutional courts, limiting the freedom of the press, or even wholescale constitutional replacement (see section 4 below). While it is true that the latter activities are not essential to populism – it is possible that a populist government would refrain from undoing the institutional basis of democracy – experience shows (as many of the chapters of this volume will demonstrate) that such restraint is unlikely. It would also be at odds with the intrinsic logic of populism. If you are convinced that your will is identical with that of the people, if your ambition is to give effect to the latter, and if, at some point, you dispose of the necessary majorities to permanently remove legal and institutional stumbling stones – why should you not do so? Especially if these barriers are erected by interests you identify as illegitimate and *hostile*.[20] What makes populism fundamentally dangerous for democracy is that it does not acknowledge the legitimacy of the democratic other.

However, it is necessary to remind ourselves that prioritizing the needs of "Joe the Plumber" or any other convenient rendering of 'the common people' does not automatically constitute populism, where it does not reject pluralism and does not deny the legitimate existence of other interests in society, be it interests one finds unimportant, disagrees with, or abhors. The necessary condition for populism lies in its claim to speak for 'the people' exclusively. It helps that this term has no clear meaning and is open to interpretation. Canovan notes that the "claim to speak for 'the people' is far from straightforward, for the term is ambiguous and populists tend to be adept at exploiting its rhetorical possibilities."[21] This, lastly, makes the populist claim to exclusive representation of the entire people unfalsifiable – those who fall outside of the populist definition of 'the people' deserve no representation as they are not, in fact, members of the polity. Müller quotes Donald Trump giving bringing this aspect of populist thinking to the point: "the only important thing is the unification of the people – because the other people don't mean anything."[22]

19 Various instances of this are on record, see for instance the speech of Marjolein Faber, member of the First Chamber, repeatedly speaking of "fake representatives of the people" in a "fake parliament", First Chamber, parliamentary year 2015/16, 4th session, 13 October 2015, written transcript available at https://www.eerstekamer.nl/verslag/20151013/verslag accessed on 4 February 2020.

20 Cf. C Mouffe, The 'end of politics' and the challenge of right-wing populism. in F Panizza (ed), *Populism and the Mirror of Democracy* (Verso 2005) 59.

21 M Canovan, 'Trust the People! Populism and the Two Faces of Democracy' [1999] 47(1) *Political Studies* 5.

22 As quoted in J-W Müller, *What is Populism?* (University of Pennsylvania Press 2016) 22.

4 Some qualifications

The above analysis results in a thin and simple definition, using only two *conditiones sine quibus non*, for populism: anti-elitism and anti-pluralism. As I argued earlier, these criteria allow us to mark populists from non-populists with sufficient clarity. But while this allows us to tell whether a political actor is a populist, it does not say much more. It hardly says anything about the programmatic content of a given populist movements.

I will argue below that populism bears an inherent threat to democracy. However, this does not mean that it cannot have any positive connotations at all or that it is not capable of advancing any defensible causes; depending on context, history, and motive, populism can indeed have all the qualities highlighted by those scholars who give a much more positive account of the phenomenon. On an abstract level, some have argued that populism is a necessary component of democracy, because it fulfils the task of intellectually constructing a people, to which democracy necessarily refers.[23] In much more practical terms, it also cannot be denied that policies of populist politicians have, at times, served as a counter-balance or a corrective to excesses experienced in systems favouring unfettered economic liberalism – see for instance the often applauded efforts of economic redistribution during the early years of Hugo Chavez's government in Venezuela.[24]

Indeed, it is in particular the Latin American perspective on populism that makes us hesitate to see populism as a synonym for, or a political strategy employed by, authoritarian movements. While in Europe the term 'populism' carries a predominantly right-wing and authoritarian connotation, this is not the case in Latin America. As a result, scholars tend to use the term as a descriptor for certain political *techniques*. As Tom Daly notes for Brazil: "Populism as a term does have some utility in the attempt to capture the growing strength of a particular technology of political messaging and governance in Brazil, and to compare these developments with the rise of populism elsewhere. However, the Brazilian context also emphasises that, when used as the dominant analytical lens, it can impede a fuller appreciation of a complex reality."[25]

These limitations should be kept in mind when discussing populism. Nevertheless, they do not seem to impede the validity of our thin definition, nor the legitimacy of emphasising the threat of populism to democracy, as many of the contributions to this book do.

---

23 E Laclau, *On populist reason* (Verso 2005) 169.

24 B Moffitt, *The global rise of populism: performance, political style, and representation* (Stanford University Press 2016) 138.

25 T G Daly, 'Populism, Elitism and Democratic Decay in Brazil: Understanding the rise of Jair Bolsonaro' (*International Society of Public Law Conference, Hong Kong, 2018*) 1.

5 Populism as a threat to democracy

5.1 No populist democracy

Is it correct to speak of populism as a threat to democracy? Answering this question does not only require a definition of populism and an idea of what populists do when in power, but, prior to that, some clarification of the concept of democracy. This is true, in particular, as the populist self-image is one of radical democracy: some scholars speak of "populist democracy", marked by the emphasis on a direct, unmediated relationship between governed and governing, thus a rejection of parliamentarianism and institutions limiting the power of government legitimized by the popular will.[26] If we are to accept this, populism does not threaten but rather epitomize democracy in a certain sense. However, this is not particularly useful: first, it ignores all notions of constitutionalism, the necessity for systemic stability and prevention of abuse. For as we noted earlier, the relationship between populists and the people they claim to represent is circular and exclusionary, enabling populists to construct the popular will in any manner that suits them. This, however, is not merely a *kind* of democracy we do not usually mean when debating modern concepts of government; as a matter of fact, it does live up to the principle of democracy at all, which at the very least should contain some guarantee that the electorate can change its mind, and, as a result, replace its leaders in a peaceful manner as a matter of course – this is the most minimalist definition of democracy.[27] The populist vision of democracy, however, emphasises merely the enthronement of leaders by an electoral majority that is equated with the popular will. It does not, however, envisage future transfers of powers to opposing political forces, since the populist logic does not allow for legitimate opposition. Therefore, "populist democracy" is at best a one-off constituent democratic act but cannot be a sustainable form of government.

For a meaningful debate of the relation between populism and democracy, then, we should assume a base line of *constitutional* democracy. This implies the limitation of power, crucially including the power of momentary majorities, and the presence of legal institutions to safeguard the perpetuation of these limitations – the rule of law. Stable democracies also require mechanisms protecting individuals and social groups from exclusion (not least from exclusion from the notion of 'the people'), making functioning safeguards for minority rights essential. Lastly, popular will-formation and government accountability requires that citizens are able to freely form a political opinion. Hence, ancillary freedoms – a free media, freedom of speech and assembly, and associated liberties – are indispensable, too. Debating whether populism poses a threat to democracy is only useful against this backdrop of constitutionalism.

26 N Urbinati, 'Democracy and Populism' [1998] 5(1) *Constellations* 116.

27 J-W Müller, *What is Populism?* (University of Pennsylvania Press 2016) 55.

5.2 Populist government as an anti-constitutional project

Being anti-pluralist, populists reject institutions and legal rules that limit the implementation of their vision of radical, unfettered majoritarian democracy. It does therefore not surprise that populist politics knows a number of recurring themes as well as legal or political moves that can be observed wherever populists operate. For instance, one of the most frequent demands made by populists (in particular while still in an opposition role) is that for referenda and other forms of direct democracy. Referenda do, of course, not necessarily work against constitutionalism – in many countries, they form a fixed part of the constitutional system, perhaps most notably Switzerland, where it is relatively easy for popular initiatives to call a referendum whose result is of constitutional rank.[28] However, especially where referenda are not anchored both in the constitution and in the political tradition of the polity in question, they bear a very high potential for eroding the system of representative democracy otherwise in place.[29]

Once in power, many populist governments have engaged in projects that either weaken existing constitutional safeguards, or that amend or even replace the constitution entirely, establishing an entirely new constitutional system which no longer meets the standards of constitutional democracy referred to above. Some pertinent examples of such projects are discussed in the various chapters of this book, taking a closer look from a national perspective. By way of illustration, it will therefore suffice here to mention some well-known examples, such as the effective neutralisation of the Hungarian constitutional court by the government of Viktor Orbán after winning a supermajority in parliament, by lowering the age of retirement of members of the court and subsequently 'packing' it with sympathizers. This move was soon after followed by the enactment of a new constitution.[30] Other examples include the recent reforms of the Polish Constitutional Tribunal,[31] and the amendment of the Turkish constitution to introduce a presidential system in which the head of states holds extensive powers over the judiciary.[32]

---

28 For an overview of the role of referenda in the Swiss constitutional and political system, see A H Trechsel and H Kriesi, Switzerland: the referendum and initiative as a centrepiece of the political system. in M Gallager and P V Uleri (eds), *The Referendum Experience in Europe* (Springer 1996).

29 Cf. the contribution by İlker Gökhan Şen to the present volume.

30 G Halmai, A Coup Against Constitutional Democracy: The Case of Hungary. in M A Graber and S Levinson and M Tushnet (eds), *Constitutional Democracy in Crisis?* (Oxford Constitutions of the World 2018) 240. For the concept of 'court packing', see also L Chennamaneni, 'Towards a Concept of Court-Packing' (2019) available at https://papers.ssrn.com/sol3/papers.cfm?abstract_id=3496986.

31 See W Sadurski, *Poland's constitutional breakdown* (Chapter III The remaking of the Constitutional Tribunal Oxford University Press 2019).

32 Z Yılmaz and B S Turner, 'Turkey's deepening authoritarianism and the fall of electoral democracy' [2019] 46(5) *British Journal of Middle Eastern Studies*. For a wider picture on populism in Turkey, see S E Aytaç and E Elçi, Populism in Turkey. in D Stockemer (ed), *Populism around the world* (Springer 2019).

This is not to say that populist governments *necessarily* behave in this way or that all is lost once populists reach government (the effects of this very much depend on the constitutional system in question, as well as the strength of the supporting majorities). It also does not mean that populists generally pursue (or if they do, succeed in) a radical turn to authoritarianism; many populist movements may not even be congruent with notions of authoritarianism at all. What can safely be claimed on the basis of observation, however, is a tendency of populist governments to foster the erosion of constitutionalism, usually through smaller, incremental changes in legislation[33] (which, by the way, is always preceded and certainly closely connected to a demise of standards of political communication and culture) This phenomenon – variably referred to as 'democratic erosion', 'democratic decay', 'constitutional backsliding', etc. – has become a global occurrence:

> Bad ideas can spread as rapidly as good ones through many of the same mechanisms. Democratic erosion is one example of this.
> Erosion is the main form of democratic political decline across Latin America, Eastern Europe, Russia, and Asia. In sheer numbers, a larger number of countries have suffered declines in democratic quality than have undergone some form of democratic collapse. Scholars of comparative politics have been observing incremental regression in a wide range of countries, including Russia, Hungary, Poland, Thailand, Turkey, Ukraine, Venezuela, and many others.

While the causes for such regression are diverse, global populism is one of them. It is therefore no understatement, much less defamatory, to refer to populism as a threat to democracy. This threat results directly from the anti-pluralist nature of populism. Democracy presupposes, accepts, and in fact demands the existence of political adversaries with equally legitimate standing in the arena of public discourse and electoral choice. This is the democratic process, which populism uses, but ultimately seeks to undermine.

6 CONCLUSION

Populism is an elusive concept, but mainly so because many attempts to capture it attempt a precise description – which necessary varies between the many different instances of populism – which is unnecessary for a debate on the question whether populism is harmful to democracy, and if so, how harm can be prevented. What is

33 T Ginsburg and A Z Huq, *How to save a constitutional democracy* (The University of Chicago Press 2018) 72 *et seq.*

needed instead is a workable, thin definition, which must serve two functions: first, it must allow us to distinguish populism from non-populism with sufficient clarity. Second, it must consist of criteria that are relevant to a legal-political debate, i.e. it must focus on the political and legislative content of populism, not appearance. These requirements are met by the definition offered by Jan-Werner Müller, which can be condensed to two main criteria, i.e. anti-elitism and anti-pluralism. Populists raise a claim that they *exclusively* represent the morally pure people against a corrupted elite and against outsiders. This exclusionary concept of 'the people', based on populists own moral notions and standards, and the claim to exclusive representation, leads to the rejection of central values of constitutional democracy. In particular, populists deny the legitimacy of democratic opposition (since they represent the will of the people, which is the only legitimate instance) and thereby democratic pluralism as such. It follows from this logic of populism, that it tends to reject institutions and legal rules that stand in the way of unfettered majoritarian democracy, including parliamentarianism and constitutional limit on government power. When in power, constitutional governments can therefore be expected to undo the legal and constitutional safeguards that entrench constitutional democracy.

Rise of Populist Parties and Decline of People's Parties: Loss of Parties as a Guarantor of the Consolidation of Democracy?

Hans-Joachim Lauth[*] *and Christoph Mohamad-Klotzbach*[**]

1 Introduction

Parties are at the heart of representative democracy. They are essential for the democratic process, because they transform societal demands into political programs, try to find majorities and to implement them when they are in power. The linkage between voters and governments under conditions of mass democracy has been organized primarily through the institutionalization of political parties. Without parties, a representative democracy and thus democracy in our time is not viable at all. They make a significant contribution to the integration of political participation, mobilize voters, and create acceptance for government decisions and, last but not least, provide the relevant reservoir for the recruitment of political personnel. Some way or other, the meaning and functions of political parties are outlined in numerous basic literature on political systems.[1]

But when we take note of the studies of political parties in Europe, we recognise that parties as key institutions of democracy are increasingly challenged. For some time now, parties have almost become synonymous with democracy crises. They are accused of

---

* *Dr. Hans-Joachim Lauth* is Professor for Comparative Politics and German Government at the Institute for Political Science and Sociology University of Würzburg since 2008. He received his PhD at the University of Mainz in 1991. In 2002 he finished his second book (*Habilitation*) about democratic theory and measuring democracy. His current topics of research concern democracy informal institutions rule of law and separation of powers (accountability) civil society local self-regulation and comparative methods.

** *Dr. Christoph Mohamad-Klotzbach* is Researcher at the Institute of Political Science and Sociology at the University of Würzburg and General Coordinator of the DFG Research Unit "LoSAM" (FOR 2757). He has written his PhD thesis on the measurement of cleavage systems in democracies. His research interests lie in the following areas: voting behaviour, political culture, democracy research, stateness.

1 R Gunther and L Diamond, *Political parties and democracies* (Johns Hopkins University Press 2001); P Mair, *Party System Change: Approaches and Interpretations* (Clarendon Press 1997); P Mair, Populist Democracy vs Party Democracy. in Y Mény and Y Surel (eds), *Democracies and the Populist Challenge* (Palgrave 2002); A Ware, *Political Parties and Party Systems* (Oxford University Press 1996); R Wildenmann, The Problematic of Party Government. in FG Castles and R Wildenmann (eds), *Visions and Realities of Party Government* (de Gruyter 1986).

incompetence, abuse of political power (party state/Parteienstaat) and lack of contact with the population.[2] This alienation is often evidenced by two strong indicators: a decline in party membership and a loss of trust in parties. Both together contribute to the decline in voter turnout.

Specifically, such processes find their expression in the so-called decline of the people's popular parties or 'Volksparteien'. The exact meaning of such a party type is still in discussion and it is used partially synonymous with the terms 'mass party' or 'catch all party'.[3] But while mass parties are based on a largely homogenous constituency, catch all parties do not have a fixed ideological standpoint. This, however, exists with popular parties – such as Christian Democratic or Social Democratic parties. Even if programmatic adjustments and changes have taken place over time, they consider themselves part of a programmatic party family.

The discussion of party decline already exists for a longer time.[4] What is new, however, is the widespread and growing emergence of mostly right-wing populist parties, especially in the last decade. What does this development mean? Is it to be understood as a strengthening of the party system or does it accelerate the decline of the democratic party system and ultimately endanger the consolidation of democracy by attacking the heart of democratic processes? This is a key question because radical-right populism can be seen as the "major foe [,] of contemporary liberal democracy" because it "underpin[s] *liberal* democracy".[5]

We understand the consolidation of democracies as a two-dimensional concept. The first dimension is the *quality of democracy*. How does the decline of people's parties and the rise of populist radical right parties impact the quality of democracy?

Our second dimension of consolidation would be the *stability of democracy*. How do the aforementioned developments impact the stability of democracies? This question relates to aspects of political support for the democratic systems, especially related to trust in the political institutions like parliaments, governments and parties in general.[6]

---

2 HH von Arnim, *Volksparteien ohne Volk. Das Versagen der Politik* (Bertelsmann 2009).

3 Ignazi, for example, referred to mass parties: The idea of party decline is strongly related to the type of the *mass party*. Its power is strongly related to mass membership. See: P Ignazi, 'The Crisis of Parties and the Rise of New Political Parties' [1996] 2(4) *Party Politics* 550.

4 ibid; P Mair, *Party System Change: Approaches and Interpretations* (Clarendon Press 1997); RS Katz and P Mair, 'Changing Models of Party Organization and Party Democracy: The Emergence of the Cartel Party' [1995] 1(1) *Party Politics* 5.

5 TS Pappas, 'Populists in Power' [2019] 30 (2) *Journal of Democracy* 70 (emphasis in the original).

6 D Easton, 'A Re-Assessment of the Concept of Political Support' [1975] 5(4) *British Journal of Political Science* 435; D Fuchs The Political Culture Paradigm. in RJ Dalton and HD Klingemann (eds), *The Oxford Handbook of Political Behavior* (Oxford University Press 2007); P Norris, Introduction: The Growth of Critical Citizens? in P Norris (ed), *Critical Citizens: Global Support for Democratic Governance* (Oxford University Press 1999); P Norris, *Democratic Deficit: Critical Citizens Revisited* (Cambridge University Press 2011); SJ Pharr and RD Putnam (eds), *Disaffected Democracies: What's Troubling the Trilateral Countries?* (Princeton University Press 2000).

As people's parties we understand (mainly) the conservative and Christian-democratic parties dominant in the post-war period in the right-wing camp as well as socialist and social-democratic parties in the left spectrum. In investigating the decline of the people's parties, it must also be clarified whether only populist parties have entered the gap or whether other parties have also made use of this space (see France). Then we analyse the empirical findings and look at the interactive effects inside the party system. Our understanding of populist parties is based on Mudde's working definition of populism.[7] This position is different to the understanding of popular democracy, which Mair presents: "populist democracy primarily tends towards partyless democracy"[8]; "At a very general level, [...] populist democracy may be understood as *popular democracy without parties*".[9] The transformation, we observe, is not the shift to a partyless democracy, but to a party system with an increasing share of populist parties. We understand the party system as an interdependent space in which the actors influence each other.

These interactions inside the party system were analysed in the last decade of the 20th century, when the crises of parties became a topic of research, which points specifically to the falling identification of voters with parties. This was accompanied by declining party membership numbers and a weakening of the historical linkages between parties and interest groups such as trade unions. The decline in social ties and representation was accompanied by their increasing importance within state institutions. These developments were explicitly captured by the theorem of the "cartel party", which emphasised the interest of parties and their functionaries in state functions and resources.[10] To what extent this only concerned individual findings or characterised the general development of the party spectrum remains a topic of academic debate.[11]

Another transformation was indicated by Mair with the conception of a 'partyless democracy'.[12] Both developments – cartel party and partyless democracy – could be understood as an opportunity structure or invitation for populist parties. "In other words, the decline of the parties' representation function invites populist reactions in

---

7 Cas Mudde understands the term populism as a 'thin' ideology that can be defined as 'an ideology that considers society to be ultimately separated into two homogenous and antagonistic groups – 'the pure people' versus the 'corrupt elite', and which argues that politics should be an expression of the volonté générale (general will) of the people'. See: C Mudde, 'The Populist Zeitgeist' [2004] 39 *Government and Opposition* 543.
In a similar way, Müller stresses furthermore the anti-pluralistic alignment of populism. See: JW Müller, *What is Populism?* (University of Pennsylvania Press 2016).

8 P Mair, Populist Democracy vs. Party Democracy. in Y Mény and Y Surel (eds), *Democracies and the Populist Challenge* (Palgrave Macmillan 2002) 89.

9 P Mair, Populist Democracy vs. Party Democracy. in Y Mény and Y Surel (eds), *Democracies and the Populist Challenge* (Palgrave Macmillan 2002) 91 (emphasis in the original version).

10 RS Katz and P Mair, 'The cartel party thesis: A reinstatement' [2009] 7(4) *Perspectives on Politics* 753.

11 ibid.

12 P Mair, Populist Democracy vs Party Democracy. in Y Mény and Y Surel (eds), *Democracies and the Populist Challenge* (Palgrave 2002).

the traditional sense".[13] Concerning the dynamics of party systems, it should be noted, however, that parties reflect these discussions and take them into account in their own positioning.

The cases of our study are the 28 member states of the European Union, for which we tried to gather data concerning all our indicators. For some indicators, we use data from 1900 to 2019, and concerning others we have shorter periods of investigation. In the following, we look at the further course of party-specific developments in order to analyse the result in relation to right-wing populist parties. Hereby we will discuss, whether we find support for the positive view of Kriesi:

> I would like to suggest that populism is a productive force that may serve as the catalyst for a profound realignment of West European party systems – a realignment that brings the West European party systems more in line with the transformed conflict structures of West European societies.[14]

We do this with a systematic investigation of the principal functions of parties (as expressed at the beginning): representation, integration, recruitment, and coalition building. Also, we are interested in the party type of "populist party" which should differ from other parties, because populists are against parties in particular.[15] They don't like intermediary organisation between the people and the decision makers and prefer a more direct linkage of masses to elites. If this is right, we should expect that the new challengers may revolt against the party system as such.

2 DEMOCRATIC CONSOLIDATION AND DEMOCRATIC REGRESSION

In order to precisely determine the effects of the change in party systems on the consolidation of democracy and the loss of its quality, it is necessary to clarify the concepts of democratic consolidation and democratic regression.[16]

Göbel argues that *democratic consolidation* "starts right after democratisation and paradoxically only ends with a regime breakdown".[17] On the contrary, Merkel[18] –

13 H Kriesi, 'The populist challenge' [2014] 37(2) *West European Politics* 371.

14 ibid 361.

15 G Pasquino, Populism and Democracy. in D Albertazzi and D McDonnell (eds), *Twenty-First Century Populism. The Spectre of Western European Democracy* (Palgrave 2008) 21.

16 Schedler uses the term authoritarian regression as a synonym of our term democratic regression, i.e. the transformation of a democratic regime into an authoritarian regime. See: A Schedler, 'How should we study democratic consolidation?' [1998] 5(4) *Democratization* 2.

17 C Göbel, 'Authoritarian Consolidation' [2011] 10 *European Political Science* 181.

18 W Merkel, 'The consolidation of post-autocratic democracies: A multi-level model' [1998] 5(3) *Democratization* 36.

following Schmitter[19] – writes that the phases of democratisation and consolidation overlap. It is therefore the phase, in which democracy becomes and stays (!) "the only game in town".[20] This is the case when "all relevant actors act according to the rules set up by the democratic institutions".[21] The political elite – and in our case the political parties – therefore have to act within democratic borders to gain power in the political system. As Merkel suggests, "the behaviour of the actors (especially the political elite) is the deciding factor in democratic consolidation".[22] They are the key drivers that have an impact on the functioning of the institutions and on the attitudes of the general public towards democracy.

We use the term *democratic regression*[23] as a synonym for processes of democratic erosion,[24] democratic backsliding[25] or democratic deconsolidation.[26] This concept describes processes "in which countries experience veiled and incremental regressions towards authoritarian rule".[27]

In our understanding both democratic consolidation and democratic regression can be seen as a multi-level model. Both processes can happen on the *macro-level* (quality of democracy), the *meso-level* (degree of fragmentation and polarisation, existence of anti-system parties) and the *micro-level* (diffuse support of democracy). On the macro-level, countries could be distinguished as "functioning democracies" or "deficient democracies".[28] For our purpose, we have to look at the developments over time, because the literature suggests that there is a decline of the quality of democracy because of the rise of populist parties.

On the meso-level, elections and the party systems come into the focus. Following Merkel's considerations on the development of the party system as part of the representative consolidation, we look at the following key indicators: fragmentation,

---

19 PC Schmitter, 'The Consolidation of Political Democracy in Southern Europe (and Latin America)' (Unpublished paper, Florence, 1985).

20 JJ Linz and AC Stepan, 'Toward Consolidated Democracies' [1996] 7 (2) *Journal of Democracy* 16.

21 W Merkel, 'The consolidation of post-autocratic democracies: A multi-level model' [1998] 5(3) *Democratization* 37.

22 ibid.

23 G Erdmann and M Kneuer (eds), *Regression of Democracy?* (VS Verlag für Sozialwissenschaften 2011).

24 A Schedler, 'How should we study democratic consolidation?' [1998] 5(4) *Democratization* 8.

25 V Mechkova and A Lührmann and SI Lindberg, 'How much Democratic Backsliding?' [2017] 28 *Journal of Democracy* 162; P Norris, 'Is Western Democracy Backsliding? Diagnosing the risks' [2017] *Journal of Democracy: Online Exchange on "Democracy Deconsolidation"* 1; E Lust and D Waldner, 'Theories of Democratic Change. Phase 1: Theories of Democratic Backsliding' (2015) USAID Working Papers Series https://www.usaid.gov/sites/default/files/documents/2496/Theories%20of%20Democratic%20Change%20Phase%201-Democratic%20Backsliding.pdf accessed 21 September 2019.

26 RS Foa and Y Mounk, 'The Signs of Deconsolidation' [2017] 28 *Journal of Democracy* 5; P Howe, 'Eroding Norms and Democratic Deconsolidation' [2017] 38 *Journal of Democracy* 15.

27 A Schedler, 'How should we study democratic consolidation?' [1998] 5(4) *Democratization* 8.

28 HJ Lauth, *Demokratie und Demokratiemessung: Eine konzeptionelle Grundlegung für den interkulturellen Vergleich* (Springer VS 2004); M Kneuer and HJ Lauth, Parteien und Parteiensysteme in der Vergleichenden Politikwissenschaft. in HJ Lauth and M Kneuer and G Pickel (eds), *Handbuch Vergleichende Politikwissenschaft* (Springer VS 2016).

polarisation and anti-system parties.[29] Schmitter argues that party systems can remain unconsolidated for some time and that this should have not a strong effect on the overall consolidation process.[30] We will discuss this argument, because party systems can enter periods of transformation, in which new parties enter the field of electoral competition, present new ideas and bring in new public demands, which will result in a higher degree of fragmentation and polarisation, but in the end after the termination of the transformation period the party system will be stabilised anew at a higher level of integration.

On the micro-level, which refers to the political culture inside of a political regime, we follow several scholars who argue that consolidation should also happen on the level of the mass public.[31] We include measures of trust in political institutions (government, parliament, political parties, and politicians), which range at a lower level than the general support of democracy. This is important because we can see if people support those institutions, which should be responsible for taking political action on the one hand, and be responsive to the demands of the people on the other hand. Lastly, we add some thoughts on polarisation on the mass level, especially concerning partisans, which have an impact on the strategies of party elites and also impact the public discourse.

---

29 W Merkel, 'The consolidation of post-autocratic democracies: A multi-level model' [1998] 5(3) *Democratization* 50-53.

30 PC Schmitter, Parties are not what they once were. in L Diamond and R Gunther (eds), *Political Parties and Democracy* (Johns Hopkins University Press 2001).

31 L Diamond, *Developing Democracy. Toward Consolidation* (The Johns Hopkins University Press 1999); W Merkel, 'The consolidation of post-autocratic democracies: A multi-level model' [1998] 5(3) *Democratization*; A Schedler, 'How should we study democratic consolidation?' [1998] 5(4) *Democratization.*

Table 1 Indicators of democratic consolidation and democratic regression

	Democratic consolidation	**Democratic regression**
Macro-level		
Quality of Democracy (DeMax)	functioning democracy	deficient democracy
Quality of the intermediate sphere (DeMax)	functioning	deficient
Meso-level		
Fragmentation (fragmentation index by Laakso/Taagepera)*	Low (< 3) or moderate (3-5)	High (> 5)
Polarisation (polarisation index by Dalton 2008)	Low or moderate	High
Anti-system parties (CHES)	None	opposition or government parties
Micro-level		
Trust in political institutions: parliament, parties, politicians (ESS)	Strong (4-6)	Weak (1-3)
Polarisation of general public and partisans	Low or moderate	High

Source: own compilation on the basis of Merkel, Diamond, Kneuer and Lauth.**

* M Laakso and T Rein, '"Effective" Number of Parties: A Measure with Application to West Europe' [1979] 12 *Comparative Political Studies* 3.

** W Merkel, 'The consolidation of post-autocratic democracies: A multi-level model' [1998] 5(3) *Democratization*; L Diamond, *Developing Democracy. Toward Consolidation* (The Johns Hopkins University Press 1999) 69; M Kneuer and HJ Lauth, Parteien und Parteiensysteme in der Vergleichenden Politikwissenschaft. in HJ Lauth and M Kneuer and G Pickel (eds), *Handbuch Vergleichende Politikwissenschaft* (Springer VS 2016).

Since this paper is concerned with populist parties in democratic regimes, we leave the authoritarian regimes aside. The debate concerning the rise of populist parties in democratic regimes lead in two directions:

- The *pessimistic* version would be that populist parties may lead or are already a sign of democratic regression. In this case, populist parties want to change the political order of the democratic regime and their rise will lead to a hybridisation of the political regime or potentially towards a democratic breakdown.
- The *optimistic* version would be that populist parties may lead to more political alternatives and therefore resuscitate the political competition between status quo parties and challenger parties.[32] They should bring back those people into politics,

32 H Kriesi, 'The populist challenge' [2014] 37(2) *West European Politics*.

who are frustrated by the behaviour of the governing parties, which are responsible for whatever status quo the democratic regimes may have. They bring back those that feel that politics is not responsive anymore but serves a small group of people and not the society as a whole. This would encourage the established parties to sharpen their political swords again and help to regain some fresh air into the political system.

3 Some Key Empirical Observations

3.1 Macro-level change: quality of democracy and the intermediate sphere

If we measure in the EU member states we generally receive a positive picture. The average has improved since World War II and especially after the great transition after 1989. The quality of democracy is at a remarkable level and reached its highest level so far in 2012 (0.84 of 1); after that it drops slightly to 0.8 in 2017. Although there seems to be a slight overall decline, the quality of democracy in the European Union still stays on a very high level.[33]

The same applies to the regulation of the Intermediate Sphere (RI), which includes intermediate organisations like political parties, associations and civil society. Parties should be structured in such a way that they are able to articulate, select and bundle social interests, in order to communicate them to governmental decision-making instances and, at the same time, to allow for a feedback effect. The aim is the most inclusive possible representation of citizens' preferences. Furthermore, a democratic system of mediation has to have sufficient openness, such that certain interests are not systematically filtered out, but rather have the opportunity to be made visible. Finally, we have to mention the control function that organised interests discharge vis-à-vis the government.

In this democratic institution, the crisis of the parties cannot be shown as a general trend. We find deviating findings, however, in Hungary and Poland as well as in Bulgaria and Romania.

---

33 The data are from the democracy matrix project, which uses selected indicators of V-Dem, to assess the quality of democracy. See: Democracy Matrix, 'Democracy Matrix' (*Democracy Matrix*) https://www.democracymatrix.com accessed 22 September 2019. The definition of democracy is based on the dimensions of political freedom, political equality, and political and legal control and, on the other, distinguishes between five essential institutions that cut across the dimensions (procedures of decision, regulation of the intermediate sphere, public communication, guarantee of rights, and rules settlement and implementation). See: HJ Lauth, *Demokratie und Demokratiemessung: Eine konzeptionelle Grundlegung für den interkulturellen Vergleich* (Springer VS 2004).

Fig. 1 The quality of democracy and the regulation of the intermediate sphere (RI) in Europe, 1900-2017; the context measure includes informal institutions.[34]

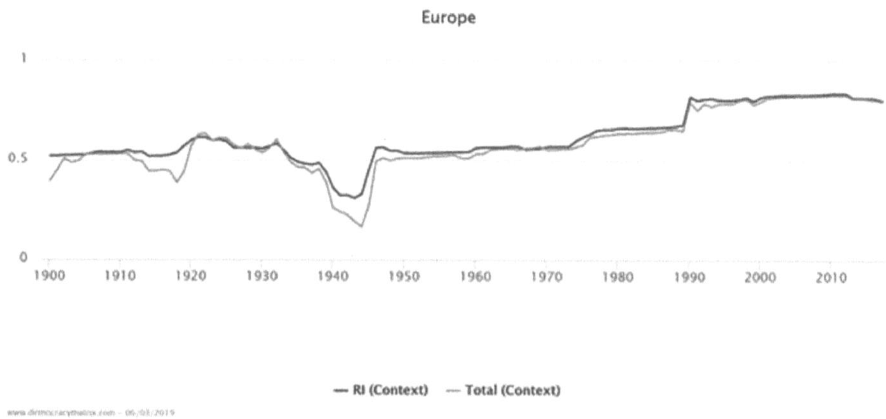

When we turn to the more specific developments of the EU member states, we can see varying trends between 1945 and 2017 (see Fig. 2). In most of the EU member states we see fully consolidated democracies, i.e. democratic regimes, which are classified as working democracies by the Democracy Matrix for a minimum of 20 years in a row. Besides Western European countries (Austria, Belgium, Denmark, Finland, France, Germany, Ireland, Italy, Luxembourg, Netherlands, Portugal, Sweden, Spain, United Kingdom), we also see some Eastern European countries which are classified as working democracies since 1989/1990 (Czech Republic, Estonia, Lithuania, Poland).

Additionally, we also see some countries in Eastern Europe that could be classified as deficient democracies for more than 20 years (Bulgaria, Cyprus, Croatia, Hungary, Latvia, Romania, Slovakia). Hungary is a special case, because it had been classified as a working democracy for 19 years between 1990 and 2009, hence it could be described as a success story, which ended in 2010.

34 Source: Democracy Matrix, 'Country Graph' (*Democracy Matrix*) https://www.democracymatrix.com/online-analysis/country#/01-Europe/total_index_context accessed 22 September 2019.

Fig. 2 Trends in democratic quality in the EU member states, 1945-2017; Source: Democracy Matrix 2019;[35] own calculations.

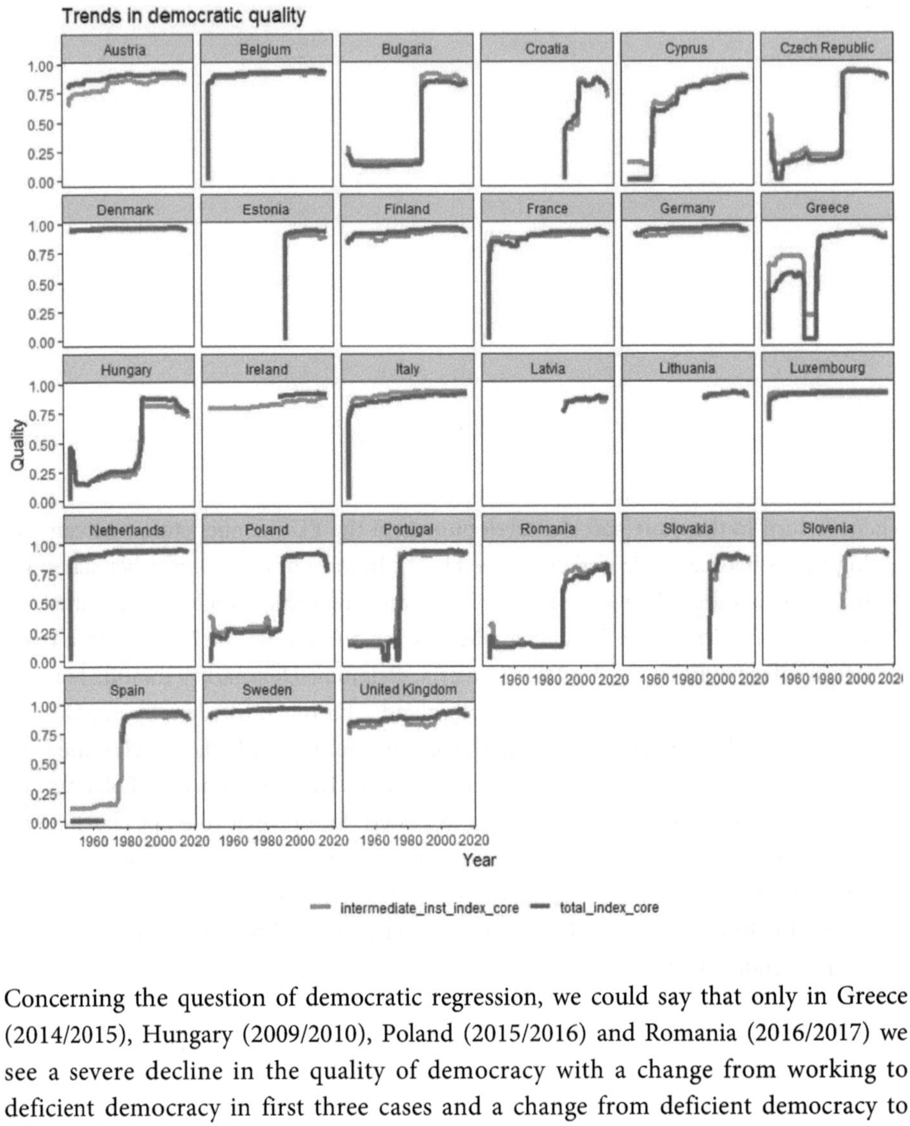

Concerning the question of democratic regression, we could say that only in Greece (2014/2015), Hungary (2009/2010), Poland (2015/2016) and Romania (2016/2017) we see a severe decline in the quality of democracy with a change from working to deficient democracy in first three cases and a change from deficient democracy to hybrid regime the in case of Romania. As Table 2 below shows, we can see that we have populist parties in Hungary and Poland which came into power just before the decline of the quality of democracy was measured. In both countries, the decline of the quality of democracy could be linked with decisions of the populist governments. Only in

35 Democracy Matrix, 'Democracy Matrix' (*Democracy Matrix*) https://www.democracymatrix.com accessed 22 September 2019.

Greece the decline of democratic quality was measured before Syriza came to power. But in fact, Syriza did not change this situation and Greece is still seen as a deficient democracy.

Table 2 Populist parties and democratic regression 2010-2017

Country	Period of democratic regression	Populist parties	Role of populist parties
Greece	2014/2015	Syriza (left), ANEL (Eurosceptic), DIKKI (left)	Syriza as governing party since 2015
Hungary	2010-2017	FIDESZ (right), MIÉP (right)	FIDESZ as governing party since 2010 (re-elected in 2014 and 2018)
Poland	2016-2017	PiS (right), Kukiz'15 (right), LPR (right), SRP (eurosceptic)	PiS as governing party since 2015
Romania	2017	PRM (right), PRU (right), PPDD	Opposition parties, but not in parliament

Source: populist parties = Rooduijn and others.*

* M Rooduijn and others, 'The Populist: An Overview of Populist, Far Right, Far Right, Far Left and Eurosceptic Parties in Europe' (The Populist, 2019) http://www.popu-list.org accessed 10 July 2019.

3.2 *Meso-level change: Voter turnout and the development of party systems*

3.2.1 Voter turnout

Another often-mentioned indicator is voter turnout in national elections. We use data from the International Institute for Democracy and Electoral Assistance (IDEA), which collects information concerning voter turnout all around the world. In Figure 3 we see patterns of voter turnout in 30 European countries. In Belgium, Denmark and Luxembourg, we find continuously high ratings of voter turnout, whereby Belgium and Luxembourg both have compulsory voting. Cyprus also had compulsory voting until 2017, but it showed a decline of voter turnout before the decision to abolish it. None of the other countries practice compulsory voting; they show some different patterns.

Concerning the Western countries, we can see that there is a general decline of voter turnout in Austria, Finland, France, Germany, Greece, Iceland, Ireland, Italy, Netherlands, Portugal and Switzerland. In a few countries like Malta, Sweden and United Kingdom, we can see a rise in voter turnout in the last elections. This holds also true for Austria, Germany, the Netherlands and Switzerland. For Eastern Europe it becomes clear, that most countries in the region experienced a massive decline in voter turnout (e.g. Bulgaria, the Czech Republic, Latvia, Lithuania, Poland, Romania, Slovakia and Slovenia). Only Estonia and Hungary show a somewhat stable pattern with little fluctuations.

But what do these trends tell us? Again, it is difficult to understand the findings appropriately. We can see that turnout rates declined overall in Europe since the 1940s. But while some countries still have a higher turnout rate between 70 and 80 percent (e.g. Germany, Denmark or Norway), other countries show a crushing decline (e.g. France or Portugal as well as the OME-countries). While the decline in France could be linked to the party system, this is less convincing in Portugal. Too many other factors are relevant to explain voter turnout. At a first glance, a higher participation or a rising voter turnout is not interconnected with strong populist parties as the example of France can illustrate, where another party has demonstrated a strong increase.

Fig. 3 Voter turnout in Europe, between the 1940s and the 2010s; Source: International IDEA;[36] own presentation.

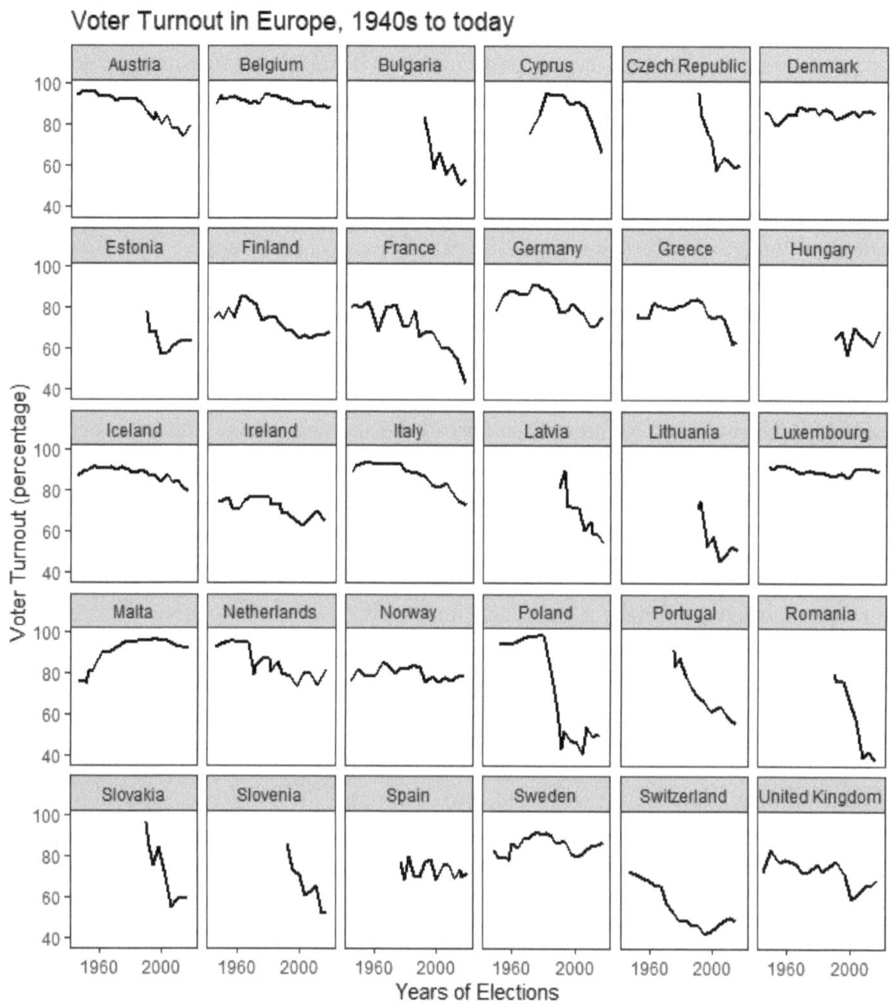

36 International IDEA, 'Voter Turnout Database' (*International IDEA*) https://www.idea.int/data-tools/data/voter-turnout accessed 22 September 2019. There have been elections under the communist regime, but they have not been free. But they are counted in the data which explains the drop in 1989. See for elections in the polish communist period G Sakwa and M Crouch, 'Sejm Elections in Communist Poland: An Overview and a Reappraisal' [1978] 8(4) *British Journal of Political Science* 403.

3.2.2 Party membership

Since the 1990s we can find several studies that look systematically at the development of party membership figures in European democracies.[37] Their findings suggest different things. First, several studies show, that on the level of general party membership in a country – measured through the percentage of party members of the electorate (member/electorate ratio) – there is a decline of party membership in most of the west and east European countries since the 1960s. There are a few exceptions, which depend on the time period under study and the case selection. Second, the decline of party membership shows different patterns with some countries showing more decline while others only medium or small trends of decline. Third, looking at the party level, Kölln for example shows that some parties – actually like the German Greens – show an increase in the member/electorate ratio and also in absolute member numbers.[38] Additionally, the rise of new pop-up parties like "La République en Marche" in France also lead to the mobilization of voters and partisans.

The decline gives cause for concern. On the one hand, the linkages with citizens are weakening and reservoirs for recruitment are also becoming smaller. On the other hand, these shifts and party membership might lead to transformations of the mass parties or people's parties to different party types, e.g. the cartel party. If you consider only the organisational capacity of parties, these findings might lead to the conclusion that membership should not be seen as a key indicator of party organisational capacity;[39] the financial reserves of many parties have improved.

3.2.3 Decline of people's parties and rise of populist parties

Another issue is the decline of the so called people's parties, which can be seen as the two or three major parties in each country that had been successful in attracting the majority of voters for a long time on the one hand, and dominated the political competition on the other hand (see above). Figure 4 looks at the vote shares of people's parties and populist parties (right & left) on the national level between 1945 and 2019 (see Appendix 1 for party classifications) in several EU member states.

The data shows that in Western Europe there is a decline of these established parties in Austria, Belgium, Denmark, Finland, France, Germany, Greece, Ireland, Italy, the

37 RS Katz and others, 'The membership of political parties in European democracies, 1960-1990' [1992] 22 *European Journal of Political Research* 329; P Mair and I van Biezen, 'Party Membership in Twenty European Democracies, 1980-2000'[2001] 7(1) *Party Politics* 5; I van Biezen and P Mair and T Poguntke, 'Going, Going, . . . Gone? The Decline of Party Membership in Contemporary Europe' [2012] 51(1) *European Journal of Political Research* 24; E van Haute (ed), *Party Membership in Europe: Explorations into the Anthills of Party Politics* (Université de Bruxelles 2011); E van Haute and P Emilien and V Sierens, 'Assessing Party Membership Figures: The MAPP Dataset' [2018] 17(3) *European Political Science* 366.

38 AK Kölln, 'Party membership in Europe: Testing party-level explanations of decline' [2016] 22(4) *Party Politics* 465.

39 I van Biezen and P Mair and T Poguntke, 'Going, Going, . . . Gone? The Decline of Party Membership in Contemporary Europe' [2012] 51(1) *European Journal of Political Research*).

Netherlands, Norway, Spain, Switzerland and UK. In Sweden we can see some ups and downs over the years. In Portugal, the decline has not been very strong. In Eastern Europe, we can see different trends. In Croatia and Estonia there is a rise of the people's parties, while in Bulgaria, the Czech Republic, Hungary, Poland and Slovakia, there is a slight decline.

Fig. 4 Vote share of populist and people's parties in EU member states 1945-2019; own calculation based on Rooduijn and others and Nordsieck.[40]

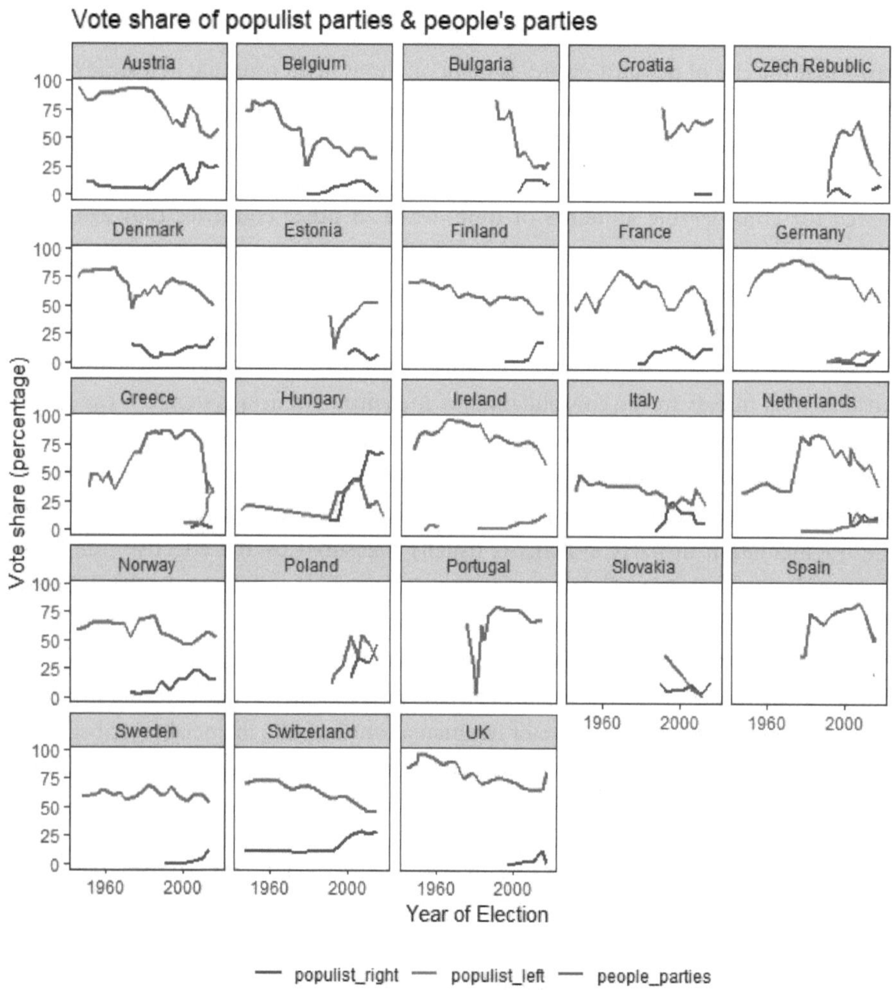

40 M Rooduijn and others, 'The Populist: An Overview of Populist, Far Right, Far Right, Far Left and Eurosceptic Parties in Europe' (The Populist, 2019) http://www.popu-list.org accessed 10 July 2019; W Nordsieck, *Parties and Elections in Europe. Parliamentary Elections and Governments since 1945, European Parliament Elections, Political Orientation and History of Parties* (2nd edn, Books on Demand 2018).

Concerning the rise of populist parties, we can see that in every country except Portugal, we can measure a rise of populist parties both from the right and/or the left. The latter are only present in Germany,[41] Greece, Ireland, the Netherlands and Spain, while right-wing populist parties can be found in nearly all countries (except Ireland, Portugal and Spain).[42] In Greece, Hungary, Poland and Slovakia, these left- and right-wing populist parties had become stronger than the established people's parties.

As a general pattern we can observe that populist parties seem to function as the populist pendants of the people's parties, in most cases the rise of populist parties corresponds with a decline of the people's parties and vice versa. This observation also shows that the rise of populist parties is not a one-way street resulting in a steady rise of these parties, but it can be seen as a competition between the established status quo parties and the new challenger parties. We can also see that in some countries such as Austria, Denmark, Norway, France, Netherlands and Switzerland, these parties have existed for considerable amounts of time, while in other countries they are a new phenomenon.

3.2.4 Fragmentation of the party systems

Merkel mentions that democratic systems "with a high fragmentation index are considered as threats to the consolidation of the entire political system".[43] The threats are not only the fragmentation of the party system, but the degree of polarisation, weak government coalitions and unexpected alternations in governments. The higher the degree of fragmentation, the lower the chance to build stable government coalitions. The fragmentation of party systems is usually measured by the effective number of parties.[44] In Figure 5 we used data by the ParlGov database to look at the developments of party system fragmentation in the 28 EU member states between 1945 and 2019.[45]

The data shows some interesting patterns. Of the three young southern democracies (Portugal, Spain and Greece), only Portugal still has a low degree of fragmentation. Spain and Greece experienced an increase of fragmentation since the financial crisis beginning in 2007/2008. The rest of the third wave democracies experienced a decline of

41 Rooduijn and others are classifying the Left (Die Linke) as a populist party. We don't really agree on this decision, but we will stay with their decision for the moment to use the data consistently. See: M Rooduijn and others, 'The Populist: An Overview of Populist, Far Right, Far Right, Far Left and Eurosceptic Parties in Europe' (The Populist, 2019) http://www.popu-list.org accessed 10 July 2019.

42 After the last parliamentary elections in Spain, a national right-wing populist party also exists in this country with the election of Vox.

43 W Merkel, 'The consolidation of post-autocratic democracies: A multi-level model' [1998] 5(3) *Democratization* 52.

44 M Laakso and T Rein, '"Effective" Number of Parties: A Measure with Application to West Europe' [1979] 12 *Comparative Political Studies*.

45 H Döring and P Manow, 'Parliaments and governments database: Information on parties, elections and cabinets in modern democracies. Development version' (ParlGov) http://www.parlgov.org accessed 22 September 2019.

fragmentation (Croatia, Estonia, Hungary, Poland, Romania), an increase (Bulgaria, Czech Republic, Lithuania), and fluctuations (Latvia, Slovakia, Slovenia). In Western Europe we can see increases of fragmentation in all countries except Malta (stable) and France (fluctuations). The highest fragmentation can be seen in Belgium, where we have the highest value of fragmentation in 2019 (11.0). These trends show, that in most of the European countries there is an increase in party system fragmentation. This corresponds to the findings that the old established people's parties are in decline in the European countries.

When we look at the four countries which experienced a decline in quality of democracy, we can see an increase of fragmentation only in Greece, while all other countries (Hungary, Poland, and Romania) experienced a decrease of party system fragmentation since the 1990s. A decline of fragmentation does not automatically lead to an increase in democratic consolidation. If we consider the rise of fragmentation in Western European party systems, it is not – as Schmitter mentioned[46] – as problematic as expected in transformation research. One should, however, be aware that it certainly makes a difference whether such processes take place in established or young democracies. This finding corresponds to a more elaborate study of Wang, who looked at the effect of party polarisation and party fractionalization on the level of democracy.[47] He confirmed that party polarisation and the level of democracy shows a positive relationship, whereas the degree of fractionalization has no effect on the level of democracy.

46 PC Schmitter, Parties are not what they once were. in L Diamond and R Gunther (eds), *Political Parties and Democracy* (Johns Hopkins University Press 2001).

47 CH Wang, 'The Effects of Party Fractionalization and Party Polarization on Democracy' [2014] 20(5) *Party Politics* 687.

Fig. 5 Effective number of parties (vote share), 1945-2019; source: ParlGov data.[48]

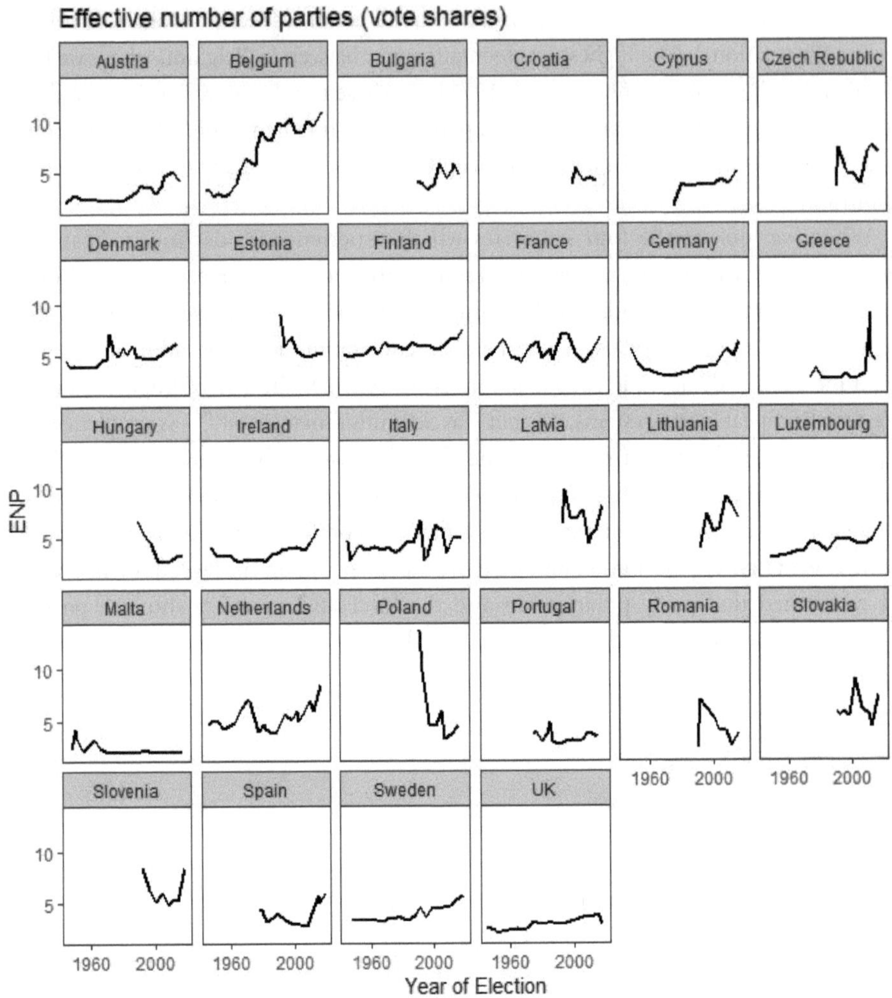

48 H Döring and P Manow, 'Parliaments and governments database: Information on parties, elections and cabinets in modern democracies. Development version' (ParlGov) http://www.parlgov.org accessed 22 September 2019.

3.2.5 Polarisation of party systems

Next, we want to discuss the relationship of party system polarisation and the rise of populist parties and ask: Do these parties increase party system polarisation?[49] We again use data from the ParlGov dataset on elections, which refers to Dalton's measurement of party system polarisation.[50] Figure 6 shows that party system polarisation is on a moderate level in nearly all countries. However, in some countries such as Belgium, Denmark or Norway we can see a continuous increase in polarisation over the decades. In other countries such as Ireland, Germany, Luxembourg or Sweden there is a rise of polarisation since the 1970s/1980s, especially in the last years. In Greece and Romania we can see a rise in polarisation in the last elections, whereas in Hungary (fluctuations) and Poland (decrease) there are different empirical observations.

---

49 Abedi studied the impact of party system polarisation on the rise of *anti-political-establishment parties*. See: A Abedi, 'Challenges to Established Parties: The Effects of Party System Features on the Electoral Fortunes of Anti-Political-Establishment Parties' [2002] 41(4) *European Journal of Political Research* 551; A Schedler, 'Anti-Political-Establishment Parties' [1996] 2(3) *Party Politics* 291.
His study shows that these populist challenger parties "generally profit from a close positioning of the establishment parties on the left-right scale." See: A Abedi, 'Challenges to Established Parties: The Effects of Party System Features on the Electoral Fortunes of Anti-Political-Establishment Parties' [2002] 41(4) *European Journal of Political Research* 551.
On the other hand, there is no evidence that party system polarisation in general leads to an increase of populist parties. See: A Abedi, 'Challenges to Established Parties: The Effects of Party System Features on the Electoral Fortunes of Anti-Political-Establishment Parties' [2002] 41(4) *European Journal of Political Research* 570.

50 RJ Dalton, 'The Quantity and the Quality of Party Systems: Party System Polarization, Its Measurement, and Its Consequences' [2008] 41 *Comparative Political Studies* 899.

Fig. 6 Party system polarisation (votes) in EU countries 1900-2019; Source: ParlGov data;[51] own calculations.

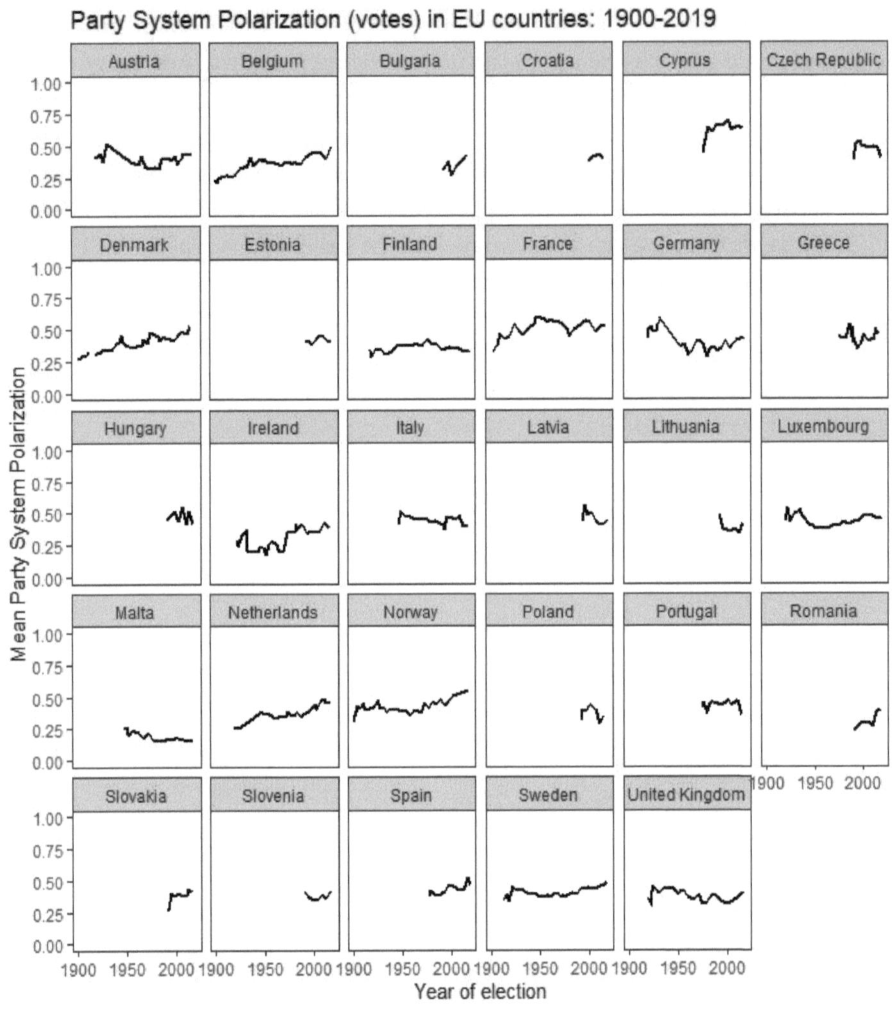

It also seems that neither polarisation nor depolarisation are really connected to the quality of democracy or the rise of populist parties. Therefore, we should also analyse the ideological divergence of the political parties. In Figure 7 we can see that parties like the PiS (Poland), FIDESZ (Hungary), the Sweden Democrats ((SD) Sweden) or Lega Nord (Italy) position themselves clearly on the pole preferring traditional, authoritarian

51 H Döring and P Manow, 'Parliaments and governments database: Information on parties, elections and cabinets in modern democracies. Development version' (ParlGov) http://www.parlgov.org accessed 22 September 2019.

and/or nationalist positions (TAN) of the socio-cultural axis, whereas they diverge concerning the economic ideology. In all the cases right-wing populist parties amplify the degree of polarisation. Only in the UK we can find two clearly distinguishable groups of parties. On the one side there are the Tories and UKIP, on the other side there is Labour, the Liberal Democrats and the Greens. In Germany, there are also both groups, but the gap between the SPD and the two Union parties (CDU, CSU) is not as big as the two opponent parties in the UK. In Greece, Syriza plays the left alternative on both dimensions, whereas the right alternative is occupied by the New Democracy (ND), which won the last elections in 2019 (European Union 2019).

Fig. 7 Ideological divergence in EU member states around 2017; Source: Polk and others 2017;[52] own calculations.

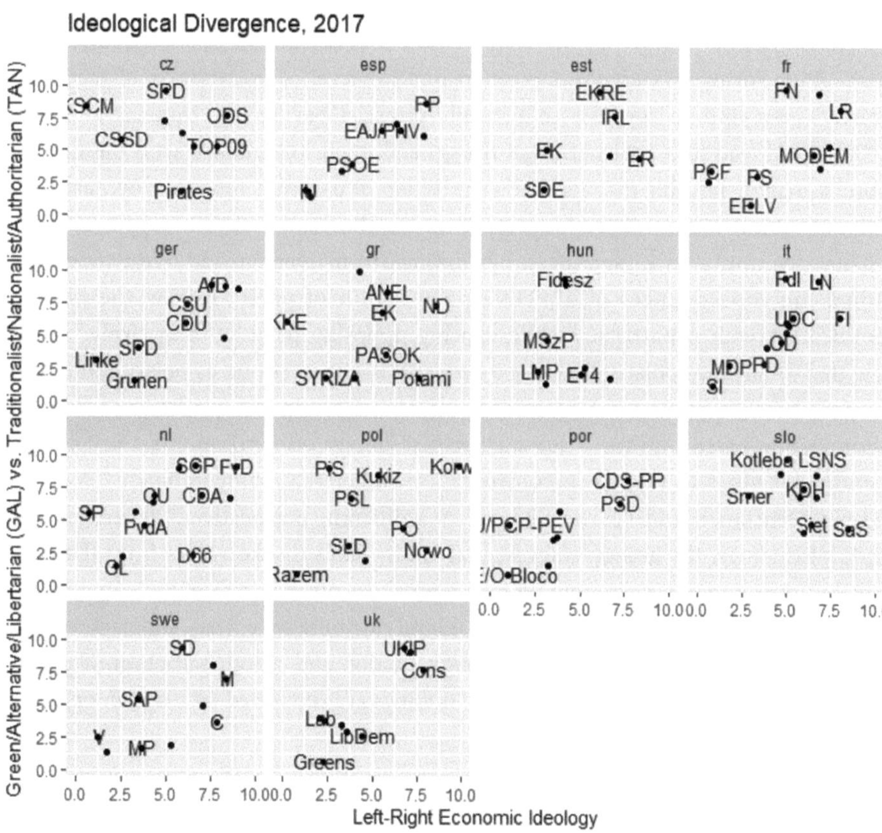

52 J Polk and others, 'Explaining the salience of anti-elitism and reducing political corruption for political parties in Europe with the 2014 Chapel Hill Expert Survey data' [2017] 4(1) *Research and Politics* 1.

3.2.6 The polarisation of partisans

We already looked at the polarisation of the party systems in EU member states. Since political parties and citizens are intertwined, we also observe the polarisation of the society in general. Several studies have looked at this issue out of different perspectives. We are going to summarise some of their key findings and discuss the implications for our research questions.

Ezrow and others. studies the relationship between voter polarisation, the level of partisanship and the support for extremist parties.[53] Based on CSES data they studied 21 established European and Anglo-American democracies and 10 post-communist democracies. They show that "extreme parties receive electoral support when electorates are polarized and their attachments to political parties are weak".[54] The lower the degree of party attachment, the more likely it will be that polarised voters support parties at the extreme poles of the ideological spectrum.

Silva showed in a study on the Netherlands, that the rise of populist radical right parties (Pim Fortuyn, Geert Wilders) increased the level of polarisation of the Dutch public.[55] This finding suggests that visible populist parties can impact the public discourse and lead to a polarisation of the general public. Combined with the findings before, it may be possible that also the polarisation of partisans increases, because these parties are going to use strategies to strengthen the attachment of their supporters.

This assumption is underscored by findings from Iyengar and Westwood, who studied the consequences of affective polarisation of partisans, i.e. the positive identification with copartisans, while viewing opposing partisans negatively.[56] They show that a) affective polarisation based on party is just as strong as polarisation based on race; b) that partisan discrimination against opposing partisans exceeds discrimination based on race. They suggest that "increased partisan affect provides an incentive for elites to engage in confrontation rather than cooperation".[57] A recent study by Druckman and Levendusky shows a different perspective.[58] Based on their empirical findings, the authors suggest that "individuals dislike voters from the other party, but they harbour even more animus toward the other party's elites." Again, these findings underscore the importance one should attribute to parties and especially to politicians. This shows how important personalisation and emotionalization of politics has become in the last decades. Most of the findings are supported by research on voters

---

53 L Ezrow and M Tavits and J Homola, 'Voter Polarization, Strength of Partisanship, and Support for Extremist Parties' [2014] 47(11) *Comparative Political Studies* 1558.

54 ibid 1574.

55 BC Silva, 'Populist Radical Right Parties and Mass Polarization in the Netherlands' [2018] 10(2) *European Political Science Review* 219.

56 S Iyengar and SJ Westwood, 'Fear and Loathing across Party Lines: New Evidence on Group Polarization' [2015] 59(3) *American Journal of Political Science* 691.

57 ibid 690.

58 JN Druckman and MS Levendusky, 'What Do We Measure When We Measure Affective Polarization?' [2019] 83(1) *Public Opinion Quarterly* 114.

and party sympathisers in the USA.[59] Especially those with extreme partisan attitudes show a higher degree of perceived polarisation.[60]

What are the consequences of this affective polarisation of partisans and society? Jacobson showed in several studies that these deepening partisan divisions in the United States are a key explanatory factor for divided governments, policy stalemates and institutional gridlocks.[61] The effects are, however, more profound concerning political culture. A friend/enemy-thinking is intensified, which does not correspond to the democratic competition thought. It undermines social integration and complicates the search for compromise.

3.2.7 Anti-system parties

Both Merkel and Diamond argue that anti-system parties jeopardise the consolidation of democracy.[62] Since the idea of anti-system parties emerged in the 1960s through Sartori,[63] the concept has been discussed more extensively in comparative politics and various typologies concerning anti-systemness have been established.[64] Often, this position is understood as the rejection of democracy and the rule of law.

59 Lupu studied the relationship of party polarisation and mass partisanship in the United States. His study revealed several key results. See: N Lupu, 'Party Polarization and Mass Partisanship: A Comparative Perspective' [2015] 37(2) *Political Behavior* 331.
First, citizens in polarised systems also perceive their parties to be more polarised. Second, perceiving party polarisation makes people more likely to be partisan. Third, citizens become more partisan as they perceive polarisation increasing. Lelkes on the other hand, distinguishes four manifestations of polarisation (ideological consistency, ideological divergence, perceived polarisation, affective polarisation) which he also studied on US data. He shows, too, that in the United States the perceptions of polarisation have increased. But he argues, that this development is especially partisan driven. Partisans have become – compared to the general public – more ideological diverged and consistent over time. See: Y Lelkes, 'Mass Polarization: Manifestations and Measurements' [2016] 80(S1) *Public Opinion Quarterly* 392.

60 J Westfall and others, 'Perceiving Political Polarization in the United States: Party Identity Strength and Attitude Extremity Exacerbate the Perceived Partisan Divide' [2015] 10(2) *Perspectives on Psychological Science* 145.
Lauka and others investigate mass partisan polarisation through cross-country comparisons. They constructed a new index on mass partisan polarisation which is "based on the support and rejection of the political parties by the public". See: A Lauka and J McCoy and RB Firat, 'Mass Partisan Polarization: Measuring a Relational Concept' [2018] 62(1) *American Behavioral Scientist* 107.

61 GC Jacobson, 'Partisan Polarization in American Politics: A Background Paper' [2013] 43(4) *Presidential Studies Quarterly* 688; GC Jacobson, 'Polarization, Gridlock, and Presidential Campaign Politics in 2016' [2016] 667(1) *The ANNALS of the American Academy of Political and Social Science* 226.

62 W Merkel, 'The consolidation of post-autocratic democracies: A multi-level model' [1998] 5(3) *Democratization*; L Diamond, *Developing Democracy. Toward Consolidation* (The Johns Hopkins University Press 1999).

63 G Sartori, European Political Parties: The Case of Polarized Pluralism. in J LaPalombara and M Weiner and L Binder (eds) *Political Parties and Political Development* (Princeton University Press 1966); G Sartori, *Parties and Party Systems: A Framework for Analysis* (Cambridge University Press 1976).

64 G Capoccia, 'Anti-System Parties: A Conceptual Reassessment' [2002] 14(1) *Journal of Theoretical Politics* 9; M Zulianello, 'Anti-System Parties Revisited: Concept Formation and Guidelines for Empirical Research' [2018] 53(4) *Government and Opposition* 653.

Following Zulianello, who investigates parties in Greece, Italy and Hungary, only Jobbik (Hungary) could be seen as a clear anti-system party.[65] The Northern League (Italy) had been an anti-system party during the first Italian Republic, while it changed its ideology and strategy in the Second Republic.[66] It seems that the anti-system parties from the left and the right play only a marginal role in the political systems of the EU member states. However, in addition to this strict anti-system type, another anti-position has now established itself, which is more difficult to measure. Populist parties reject the current form of liberal representative democracy, which is accused of taking only the interests of the elite into account. The aspiration is for a largely institutionally uncontrolled form of democracy that more strongly embraces the 'will of the people'. If such an uncontrolled idea of democracy is accompanied by a crude understanding of the rule of law without a comprehensive free judiciary, without minority protection and with restrictions on media rights, then the borderline to anti-system parties is fluid.

3.3 *Micro-level change: Trust in parties, politicians and parliaments*

One of the key mantras we can find here throughout scholarship and in the public discourse is the decline of trust in political institutions, especially in political parties. Putnam and others[67] show that there is a decline of trust in politicians in 12 of 13 trilateral countries[68] between the 1960s and 1990s. Dalton, using data for different western countries between the 1950s and late 1990s, argues that there "is clear evidence of a general erosion in support for politicians and government in most advanced industrial democracies".[69] Based on data from the Eurobarometer surveys 1997 to 2009, Norris showed that there is no general decline of trust in parliaments and political parties.[70] During her observed period only the United Kingdom and Portugal showed a greater decline in trust in both institutions. Most of the countries "experienced trendless fluctuations" in trust in parliaments and political parties.[71]

---

65 M Zulianello, 'Anti-System Parties Revisited: Concept Formation and Guidelines for Empirical Research' [2018] 53(4) *Government and Opposition* 671-673.

66 M Zulianello, 'Anti-System Parties Revisited: Concept Formation and Guidelines for Empirical Research' [2018] 53(4) *Government and Opposition* 673-675.

67 RD Putnam and SJ Pharr and RJ Dalton, Introduction: What's Troubling the Trilateral Democracies? in SJ Pharr and RD Putnam (eds), *Disaffected Democracies. What's Troubling the Trilateral Countries?* (Princeton University Press 2000) 14-16.

68 The term trilateral countries is connected to a cooperative forum of Western Europe, Japan and North America since the 1970s. One of the most popular publications of the Trilateral Commission had been the Report on the Crisis of Democracy by Crozier and others. See: M Crozier and SP Huntington and J Watanuki, *The Crisis of Democracy: Report on the Governability of Democracies to the Trilateral Commission* (New York University Press 1975).

69 RJ Dalton, *Democratic Challenges, Democratic Choices. The Erosion of Political Support in Advanced Industrial Democracies* (Oxford University Press 2004) 28-30.

70 P Norris, *Democratic Deficit: Critical Citizens Revisited* (Cambridge University Press 2011) 72-77.

71 ibid 73.

Since the findings do not fully coincide and new data are available in the meantime, we want to look at trust in three key institutions of the democratic political system: parliaments, parties and politicians. All three can be seen "as genuinely political institutions" that can be distinguished from "non-political or 'order' institutions" such as the legal system or the police.[72] When we relate to the crisis theses or pessimistic version, then we should see a continuous decline of trust in all three institutions throughout the period under investigation.

For our analysis we use data from the rounds 1 to 8 of the European Social Survey, that had been collected between 2002 and 2016 via face-to-face CAPI interviews in all participating countries.[73] We use the following survey question for all three institutions:

> Using this card, please tell me on a score of 0-10 how much you personally trust each of the institutions I read out. 0 means you do not trust an institution at all, and 10 means you have complete trust. Firstly [...] political parties / politicians / parliaments?

Figure 8 shows the different trend patterns concerning trust in *political parties* between 2004 and 2016. Firstly, we can see, that trust in political parties ranges between 0 and 6 points on the 10 point scale. This means, that trust in parties ranges at the lower end of trust in institutions. Some countries show higher trust ratings between 4 to 6 points (e.g. CH, DK, FI, NL, SE), while others show really low ratings between 0 to 3 points (e.g. BG, HR, IT, PL, PO).

Concerning the decline-hypothesis we can see that only Cyprus, Denmark, France, Greece and Croatia show a continuous decline of trust. Most of the countries, however, show a rise in trust in the last years, e.g. Austria, Czechia, Germany, Spain (after a period of decline), Great Britain, Hungary, Ireland, Lithuania, Poland and Portugal. The other countries show patterns of smaller ups and downs on different levels of trust. This means, that both patterns (decline & rise) can be observed, but the rising tendency prevails.

Analysing trust in *politicians*, we can see similar patterns as with trust in parties (See Fig. A1 in Appendix 1). Nearly the same countries show a continuous decline of trust (e.g. Cyprus, Denmark, Greece, Croatia, France and Slovakia), while other countries show a rise of trust in the last years (e.g. Austria, Czechia, Germany, Hungary, Lithuania, Poland or Portugal).

---

72 P Kotzian, 'Conditional trust: The role of individual and system-level features for trust and confidence in institutions' [2011] 5 *Comparative Governance and Politics* 38.

73 European Social Survey Cumulative File, ESS 1-8 (2018). Data file edition 1.0. NSD - Norwegian Centre for Research Data, Norway - Data Archive and distributor of ESS data for ESS ERIC. doi:10.21338/NSD-ESS-CUMULATIVE.

Fig. 8 Trust in parties in Europe (2002-2016); Data: ESS[74] Round 1-8; mean scores; missings excluded; some countries had been surveyed not in every round on this topic.

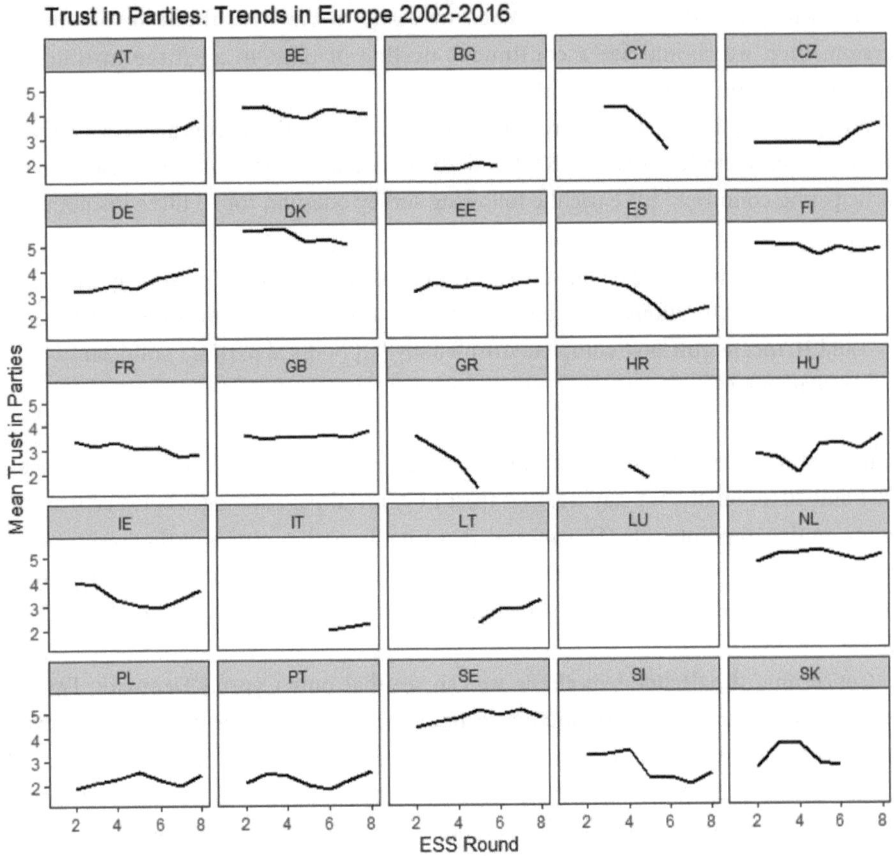

What about the trust in *parliaments*, the key institutions where parties and politicians act in a representative democracy besides government? First of all, we can see that trust in parliaments shows a higher mean score in some countries than parties and politicians. Continually high trust can be measured in Denmark, Finland and Sweden, which ranges between mean scores around 6. We also have some countries with low trust scores, e.g. Bulgaria or Croatia. A decline in trust in parliaments can be observed in Cyprus, France, Greece, Croatia, Italy and Slovakia. Again, we can see that a variety of countries

74 European Social Survey Cumulative File, ESS 1-8 (2018). Data file edition 1.0. NSD - Norwegian Centre for Research Data, Norway - Data Archive and distributor of ESS data for ESS ERIC. doi:10.21338/NSD-ESS-CUMULATIVE.

experienced a rise in trust, such as Czechia, Germany, Great Britain, Hungary, Ireland, Lithuania, Poland and Portugal.

Fig. 9 Trust in parliaments in Europe (2002-2016); Data: ESS Round 1-8;[75] mean scores; missings excluded; some countries had been surveyed not in every round on this topic.

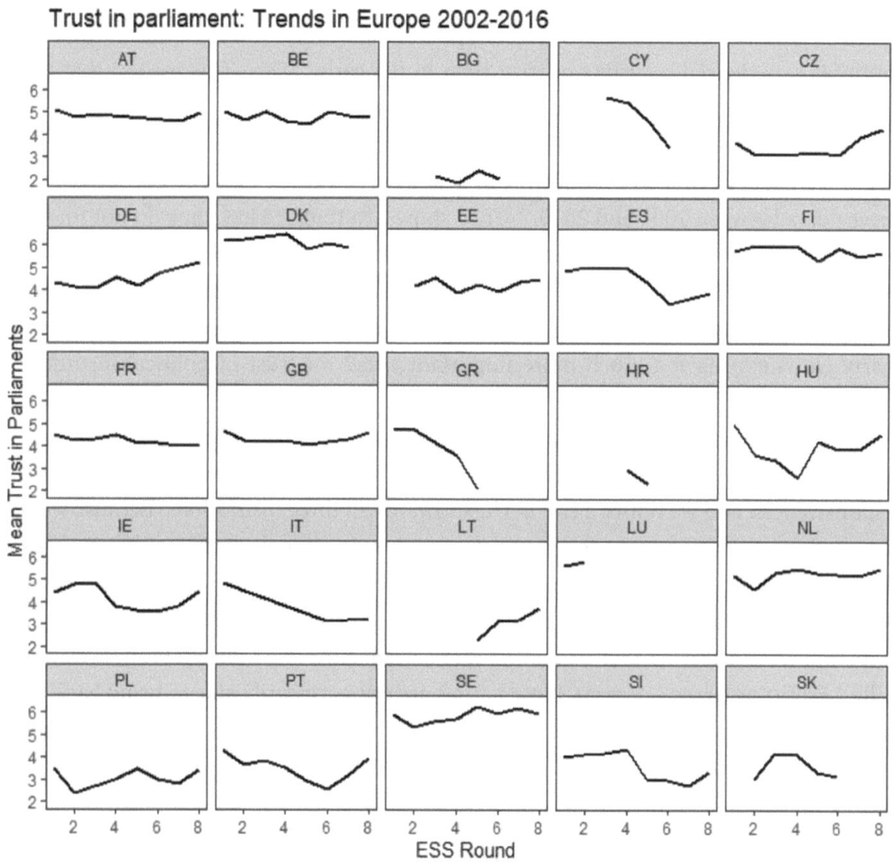

When we look at all three objects of interest, it is possible to find some relationships between trust in parties, politicians, and parliaments. In some countries we can see a stagnation with little ups and downs in trust. In others we see a pattern of decline in all three institutions, whereas the broadest group of countries show again a rise in trust. Therefore, the findings cannot confirm the decline-hypothesis. Even if the highest

75 European Social Survey Cumulative File, ESS 1-8 (2018). Data file edition 1.0. NSD - Norwegian Centre for Research Data, Norway - Data Archive and distributor of ESS data for ESS ERIC. doi:10.21338/NSD-ESS-CUMULATIVE.

values are only around six points (out of 10), this should not give cause for concern. Democratic rule does not require unlimited trust, especially when actors are in play. Rather, democratic rule always faces a certain degree of mistrust, as the various mechanisms of control in democracies show.

The values for the consolidation of democracy are problematic if they are permanently at a low level (between 1 and 3 points) and also show a downward trend. Additionally, our findings suggest that in both Great Britain and Portugal the decline in trust has reversed compared to the findings of Norris.[76] At the same time now more countries experienced a decline of trust than in the early 2000s. This means, that there is both a positive and a negative message included in the data.

What about the relationship between party membership, closeness to a political party and trust? Hooghe and Kern studied this relationship on the basis of European Social Survey data between 2002 and 2010.[77] They show two things: First, they do not find any empirical relationship between the decline of party membership and political trust. Second, feelings of closeness towards a political party are much stronger positively related with political trust. This means, affective orientations towards specific parties (party closeness) have a much more important effect for trust in political institutions than the structural indicator of party membership.

What do we find, if we link trust and populist parties? Could it be that the rise of new or old anti-establishment parties (left, centre, right) should serve as an indicator of system responsiveness, and we notice a rise in trust towards all three institutions. Because we did not check each party system for populist parties, it is difficult to assert that such new players lead to more trust in parties, politicians, and parliaments. Only in the case of Hungary there is a clear positive relationship between rise in trust and a strong populist party. But we can also see that, e.g. in Denmark (Danish People's Party), France (National Rally / Front) or Greece (Syriza), these parties are not necessarily able to bring back trust in these institutions. Likewise, the long-standing rule of the right-wing populist PiS in Poland has not led to a significant increase in trust; it remains at a low level.

4 Consequences for and Strategies Inside the Party Systems

Do right-wing populist parties strengthen or weaken the consolidation of democracy? Our answer is differentiated. Such parties increase interest in politics and in political participation. So far, they tend to integrate marginal voters into the political process. At the same time, they build on an understanding of politics that is at least unwieldy of democracy by deepening polarisation and promoting unrealistic expectations – such as

76 P Norris, *Democratic Deficit: Critical Citizens Revisited* (Cambridge University Press 2011).

77 M Hooghe and A Kern, 'Party membership and closeness and the development of trust in political institutions: An analysis of the European Social Survey, 2002-2010' [2015] 21(6) *Party Politics* 944.

a homogeneous will of the people – that can lead to disappointment later on. For the dynamics of the party system, this means a reduction in the coalition space, although this is not necessarily the case, and an expansion of the space for controversial issues, which now include the dispute over the appropriate forms of democracy itself. This can be turned around productively and also offers the people's parties the opportunity to strengthen their position in the political discourse again.

Populist parties partly have their origins in social movements or have close relations with them (e.g. AfD and Pegida in Germany). But despite their aversion to parties, populists have formed parties, and apart from financial interests, the institutional context was certainly decisive in this, as Roberts emphasises: "Pressures for party building are especially pronounced in Europe, where parliamentary institutions preclude strictly plebiscitarian path to executive office".[78] Right-wing populist parties are internally structured in a strictly hierarchical way, demanding allegiance to the leading person and a high degree of party discipline towards the party leadership.[79] In this way, they are not a school of democracy.

How is this rise of populist parties to be judged with regard to the functioning of democracy? What does this mean for the democratic process and especially for the party systems?

The first task is to determine the dynamics of recent developments. A central aspect here is the increase in polarisation that occurs primarily between populist parties and 'traditional' parties, especially at the level of party activists. A priori, polarisation is not undemocratic per se and the European democracies have previously experienced a period of stronger polarisation in the 1960s and 70s (at that time between left and right). The decisive question here is whether the polarisation is taking place within the democratic continuum or has already taken on the anti-systemic traits that we experienced in Germany during the Weimar Republic. Furthermore, the kind of polarisation must be defined in more detail, assuming that (most) right-wing populist parties are not anti-democratic but favour a different understanding of democracy. What has the empirical analysis shown?

The empirical findings in this realm are not spectacular. The rise of polarisation in the Netherlands and in Norway should not threaten democracy. It is in some way astonishing that the data do not accentuate the polarisation in Hungary or, even more, in Poland, where we could observe strong manifestations against the anti-democratic reforms of the government. Therefore, it is possible, that we have a data problem. Polarisation should be measured better on the level of party activists and sympathizers and not by analysing

---

78 K Roberts, Populism and Political Parties. in CK Kaltwasser and others (eds), *Oxford Handbook of Populism* (Oxford University Press 2017) 297.

79 However, this does not apply in all countries, as the example of the AfD in Germany shows. Within a few years, the leadership there was replaced twice at party conferences.

party programs. Additionally, the polarisation of political discourses should be included in the research.

Against this background, it can be said that with right-wing populist enlargement it has become more difficult to increase the integration performance of parties. Political communication between citizens, and between them and politicians, has become rougher. Emotions are gaining weight, rational discourse is becoming more difficult in the context of fake news and hate speech.[80]

On this basis, we discuss the importance of fragmentation also for coalition formation. In addition to increasing polarisation, there is also a growing fragmentation of party systems in many European countries. In hardly any country one party can govern alone and only in a few a coalition of two still finds a majority. In most cases, multi-party coalitions form the government. The stronger the share of right-wing populist parties in parliament, the more difficult it is to form a majority if they are not considered capable of forming a coalition. This can lead to a situation where the coalition conditions make it necessary to seek compromise and the contours of the governing parties become blurred. This in turn plays into the cards of right-wing populists, who have long claimed that all other parties are the same.

4.1 *Different reaction patterns to right wing populist parties*

Party systems are characterised by the fact that they are interactive and self-referential reference systems. Changes in one party affect others. For example, the orientation of large popular parties towards the centre has opened up new groups of voters to them, but at the same time it has thinned out the right-wing spectrum, into which right-wing populist parties have been able to push. It is possible that the general tendency towards the centre of left-wing and right-wing popular parties has even intensified the pointed demand in the left-wing and right-wing electoral segments. At the very least, it has led to the election activation of those sections of the population who had not yet decided to 'protest'.

80 G Rico and M Guinjoan and E Anduiza, 'The Emotional Underpinnings of Populism: How Anger and Fear Affect Populist Attitudes' [2017] 34(4) *Swiss Political Science Review* 444; R Wodak, *The Politics of Fear. What Right-Wing Populist Discourses Mean* (Sage 2015).

Another systematic aspect of party systems concerns the programmatic orientation of the parties in combination with coalition building. The spread of right-wing populist programmatic and their parliamentary anchoring require a positioning of the other parties. This happened in different ways. We can see at least three different strategies, which mirrors the fundamental reaction of parties to right wing populist parties:[81]

- *Alignment and coalition.* In the first and most frequent case, other parties are willing to share some programmatic agenda items and form joint government coalitions. This has happened among others in Austria, Norway, Italy, Slovakia and Switzerland, the latter being a special case in the ongoing oversized government coalition. In others, bourgeois minority governments have been tolerated by right-wing populist parties (longer-term in Denmark, short-term in the NL 2010-12 by the PVV). In all cases, this led to a programmatic rapprochement with the right-wing populist program, especially in migration and refugee policy. Such coalitions between people's parties and populist parties are, however, fragile in principle, since in some policy areas (such as legal policy and EU policy) there is little overlap.
- *Confrontation and exclusion.* A second strategy is strict confrontation, which intends to isolate or ban populist parties. A coalition is strictly rejected. The right-wing populist program is argumentatively rejected or largely ignored. France or the minority government in Sweden (2014-2018) are examples of this position.
- *Confrontation and convergence of content.* The third strategy is quite similar. A coalition is strictly rejected and the contentious dispute is sought. However, in some programmatic points – such as refugee policy – the governments are approaching right-wing populist positions (as could be observed in Germany and in Sweden in the recent years).

The second and third strategies are similar and can also be understood as two variants of a strategy, which aims to isolate populist parties either by ignoring or partially copying them. This means only a selective shift towards the right-wing program, overall, because other positions are retained, this increases party-political polarisation. In the first strategy, however, a general shift to the right can be observed, at least in Europe, when dealing with right-wing populism. Both strategies have been widely successful in the

81 Downs argues that responses to extremism work along two dimensions. "The first being the pole between engagement and disengagement and the second being the pole between militancy and accommodation. This produces a fourfold typology of ban/isolate, co-opt, ignore, or collaborate". See: W Downs, *Political Extremism in Democracies: Combating Intolerance* (Palgrave Macmillan 2012); CR Kaltwasser and P Taggart, 'Dealing with populists in government: a framework for analysis' [2016] 23(2) *Democratization* 210.
Similar Mudde and Rovira Kaltwasser: "In this regard, it is possible to identify four general strategies: isolation, confrontation, adaptation, and socialization." See: C Mudde and CR Kaltwasser, Populism: corrective *and* threat to democracy. in C Mudde and CR Kaltwasser (eds), *Populism in Europe and the Americas. Threat or Corrective for Democracy?* (Cambridge University Press 2012) 213.

sense that right-wing populist parties were held off power.[82] It was not successful, however, in the target to minimise populist parties. This failing can be demonstrated regarding both principal strategies: confrontation (National Front / Rally in France) and cooperation (Freedom Party of Austria).

If a populist party still belongs to the democratic family, it seems paradoxical to favour the strategy of ban or isolation. It is something of an attempt to beat the populists with their own weapons as Mudde and Rovira Kaltwasser underscored:

> It is worth noting that this reaction is quite similar to the populist language, since it assumes that the political world should be seen as a moral battle, which is (almost) impossible to solve through democratic channels.[83]

Cooperation or even co-optation does likewise not always work, especially when populist are strongly ideologically oriented. In such cases – like in Austria – a cooperation can deepen the societal polarisation. In the long run perhaps processes of political socialisation could generate the best solution. This means that populist parties could be comprehensively integrated into the democratic process and can also assume offices. Not necessarily the responsibility associated with these offices, but the practice of democratic procedures may result in their political integration. We have some experiences in the EU-Parliament, when parliamentarians regularly take part in parliamentary activities; one example of populist parties could be the Danish DF (Dansk Folkeparti).

The situation is different when (right-wing) populists are alone or dominant in power.[84] Within the party system, polarisation is intensifying (as in Poland) and right-wing extremist parties feel encouraged (as in Hungary). The competitive conditions for other parties are deteriorating due to the restriction of the free press. Since right-wing populist parties have strong patronage characteristics, they can damage the democratic image of parties. Since right-wing populist governments also strive to limit the separation of powers and undermine legal control, they noticeably weaken the quality of democracy. Deficient democracy in illiberal and/or delegative forms or in combination is emerging.[85] In these cases, the ruling party also fulfils the recruiting function, but with the sole aim of filling as many state positions as possible with its members and sympathizers. Qualification is secondary.[86] It is still unclear whether this loss of democratic quality was possible because both countries were still little consolidated democracies or

---

82 Different is the Italian case, where the radical rejection of the mainstream parties still takes place in the electoral channel.

83 CR Kaltwasser and P Taggart, 'Dealing with populists in government: a framework for analysis' [2016] 23 (2) *Democratization* 213.

84 TS Pappas, 'Populists in Power' [2019] 30 (2) *Journal of Democracy* 70 (emphasis in the original).

85 M Bogaards, 'De-democratiation in Hungary: diffusely defective democracy' [2018] 25(8) *Democratization* 1481.

86 See the results of measuring democracy for the respective countries at: Democracy Matrix (n 35).

whether the same effects can also occur in established democracies. The USA is a case of particular interest here.

4.2 *Reasons for the emergence of populist parties*

Even if it does not explicitly concern our guiding question, we also want to discuss reasons for the changes in the European party systems. This helps us to understand the persistence of the changes and to sound out possible room for manoeuvre.

Firstly, we have to emphasise internal factors, which we have observed inside the party system and which have fostered the rise of populist parties. Merkel and Zürn focus in their argumentation on the representation gap:

> The emerging new cleavage can be explained by a representation gap left by the mainstream parties in European party systems. In the last two or three decades, a growing number of citizens have emerged who do not feel represented – economically, discursively, or culturally – by the established parties.[87]

Beside the internal reason, secondly, numerous external factors were discussed, which caused the change of the party systems in Europe – the decline in people's parties and the rise of right-wing populist parties. In the field of political sociology, the differentiation of societies and the loss of ties were pointed out. In general, the increasing force of globalization, which led the shaping of political action from parliaments to the executive, was emphasised. This became clear when the financial crisis had to be resolved, which at the European level was primarily based on executive cooperation. These remarks intend to make it clear that the parties and party systems had already been in a significant fluctuation even before the right-wing populist wave of recent years.

Having all these transformations in mind, restoring the status quo ante is not realistic. It is not a question of whether the people's parties have not learned from their mistakes and can now do better again. Surely there are numerous efforts and improvements in these fields. But this alone is not enough. The decisive factor is the differentiation of the electorate in terms of content.[88] While in earlier decades the people's parties were still able to bundle the majority of individual demands into a coherent party program, this is less and less possible. This creates dissatisfaction among voters, who always only find offers from parties with which they are only more or less satisfied. This dissatisfaction is also a reason for the electoral success of right-wing populist parties. However, these

---

87 W Merkel and M Zürn, Conclusion: The defects of cosmopolitan and communitarian democracy. in P de Wilde and others (eds), *The Struggle over Borders. A political Sociology of Cosmopolitanism and Communitarianism* (Cambridge University Press 2019) 164.

88 P Ignazi, 'The Crisis of Parties and the Rise of New Political Parties' [1996] 2(4) *Party Politics* 556.

voters are also united by a more homogeneous view of the world, which links them to the right-wing populist parties (back to the sixties). These parties can reinforce these worldviews, but they are not their inventors.

If the cleavage assumptions made with the populist parties are correct, then we should expect and find a correspondence of the party programmatic with the attitudes of the citizens.[89] Thus not only the party landscape has changed, but also the electorate. This statement is important because – if it is true – a longer existence of right-wing populist parties can be assumed. This assumption is even more valid in the young democracies in Central Europe, where hardly any party system has been able to establish itself to date. Here we can discuss, whether a new cleavage exists, which will find its expression in party systems.[90]

5 Conclusion

Party systems have profoundly changed in many European countries, but this does not yet jeopardise the foundations of democracy everywhere. The quality of democracy declines in such countries where right-wing populist parties are in power and dominate the political systems for the longer term (as in Hungary and in Poland). The problem of democracy is less associated with the dominance of a populist party itself than with its radical right-wing orientation. This is a major cause for concern. The decline of the quality of democracies is not noticeable in countries, where such parties are in the opposition, although it leads to a stronger debate about the appropriate notions of democracy, its institutions and its values.[91] This debate is to be welcomed as it can lead to a deeper understanding of democracy. Democracy is not inherited and thus kept alive, but in the constant confrontation with its achievements, limits and merits. The decline of the people's parties had begun long before the rise of the right-wing populist parties. Their at least partial transformation into cartel parties has itself contributed to the promotion of populist parties. The new challenge should therefore also be seen as an

89 If we take up the criteria of the institutionalization of parties by Harmel and others., then many right-wing populist parties in Europe can already be regarded as institutionalized. See: R Harmel and L Svåsand and HL Mjelde, *Institutionalisation (and de-institutionalisation) of right-wing protest parties: the progress parties in Denmark and Norway* (Rowman & Littlefield 2018); K Weissenbach and SU Bukow, 'Travelling concepts of party institutionalization? A comparative perspective' [2019] 13 *Zeitschrift für Vergleichende Politikwissenschaft* 157.

90 H Kriesi, 'The populist challenge' [2014] 37(2) *West European Politics*; W Merkel and M Zürn, Conclusion: The defects of cosmopolitan and communitarian democracy. in P de Wilde and others (eds), *The Struggle over Borders. A political Sociology of Cosmopolitanism and Communitarianism* (Cambridge University Press 2019).

91 This observation should make it clear that the strong anti-democratic interpretation of Müller, which is specifically justified by the antipluralist orientation of populist parties, is somewhat overdrawn. See: C Mudde, 'The Populist Zeitgeist' [2004] 39 *Government and Opposition* 543.

opportunity to regain general trust in the key actors of democracy. Whether these must then still be people's parties in the classical sense is then a secondary question.

The people's parties face multiple tasks with an almost paradoxical orientation. They must combine differentiated programmatic offers with the power of integration. So, they must differ significantly and form coalitions at the same time. They must take the right-wing populist debate seriously and still minimise it. The two left-wing populist parties in Europe (Syriza in Greece and Podemos in Spain) have quickly shown integrative movements that can revive democracy. This will not be so easy with right-wing populist parties. Nevertheless, this is necessary and should be possible, if the people's parties consider only their own mistakes, which have contributed to the crisis of the parties. "If weak parties are aiding the success of populism, then (re)building stronger parties is imperative".[92] This might also be the medicine to keep representative politics as party-based politics alive and does not lead to a structural transformation of the democratic polities.[93]

92 M Bogaards, 'Lessons from Brexit to Trump: Populism Is What Happens When Political Parties Lose Control' [2017] 11(4) *Zeitschrift für Vergleichende Politikwissenschaft* 516.

93 S Tormey, *The end of representative politics* (Polity Press 2015).

Populist Parties Under Scrutiny – One Common Vision or a Scattered Agenda?

*Tjitske Akkerman**

1 Introduction

Although populism tends to be identified as the driving force behind the autocratization processes that can be witnessed, among others, in Hungary, it is far from clear that Orbán's 'illiberal democracy' is an ideal for all populist parties and movements in Europe. Populism is a thin ideology that considers society to be separated in two antagonistic groups, the 'pure' people and the 'corrupt' elite.[1] This is a broad concept that covers parties among the political spectrum from the far left to the far right and some in between. Moreover, liberal principles may be more respected by populist parties in vested democracies in Western Europe than in Eastern Europe.

This chapter presents an analysis of the policy agendas of three right-wing and three left-wing populist parties in Western Europe to assess their commitment to liberal principles. The populist parties under scrutiny are: the German parties *Die Linke* and the *Alternative für Deutschland*, the French parties *France Insoumise* and *Rassemblement National*, and the Dutch *Socialist Party* and the *Party for Freedom*. Principles of liberal democracy that will be central to the analysis are the protection of the rights of individuals and minorities and the legislative and juridical constraints of executive power. The results indicate that the agendas of left-wing and right-wing populist parties in Western Europe diverge substantially regarding the liberal protection of individual and minority rights, but do not contain clearly distinct ideas about checks and balances. Moreover, the agendas between right-wing populist parties differ gradually and cannot be put neatly in one pigeonhole.

---

* Tjitske Akkerman is a former faculty member and continuing researcher affiliated with the Department of Political Science at the University of Amsterdam. Her research focuses on democratic theory and on populist radical right parties. Her publications have among others appeared in *Political Studies, West European Politics, Party Politics, Journalism, Journal of Political Ideologies, Government and Opposition, Patterns of Prejudice, Acta Politica.* She is the editor of *Radical Right-Wing Populist Parties in Western Europe. Into the mainstream?* (2016) with S.L. de Lange and M. Rooduijn.

1 C Mudde and C Rovira Kaltwasser, *Populism: A Very Short Introduction* (Oxford University Press 2017) 5-6.

2 Liberal Democracy

Liberal democracy is based on the principle that it is important to protect individuals and minorities against the tyranny of the state and the tyranny of majorities. The protection of individual and minority rights is achieved through constitutionally protected civil liberties on the one hand and through executive and legislative constraints that limit the use of executive power on the other hand. Democracy is not one-dimensional. Liberal features should be distinguished from other qualities of democracy such as the opportunities for citizens to elect representatives or to participate in political processes.[2] Liberal democracy implies that executive power and the power of a majority should be restrained in order to protect the freedom of individuals and minorities. Other types of democracy prioritize other democratic values. Electoral democracy centers on the question how rulers are chosen and how responsiveness and accountability of rulers to citizens can be best guaranteed. Another type of democracy, the participatory model, values above all the opportunities for citizens to engage directly in political debate, agenda-setting and decision-making. Liberal democracy does not focus on how rulers are chosen or how citizens participate, but is most concerned about limiting the power of elected rulers once they are in office or the power of the majority when citizens govern directly. When liberal features such as judicial and legislative constraints have been diminished, a regime still may have some democratic features. To illustrate this, the 'illiberal democracy' that has been produced in the laboratory of Prime Minister Victor Orbán in Hungary after Fidesz won a majority in parliament in 2010, may still be called a democracy.[3] Orbán has rewritten the constitution and erased checks and balances by replacing staff. All fifteen of the Constitutional Court's current members have been appointed since Fidesz's rise to power. Public broadcasting and the national news agency were subsumed under the authority of a new government-dominated body.[4]

---

2 T Akkerman, *Democratie: de grondslagen van het moderne idee* (Het Spinhuis, 1997); D Held, *Models of Democracy* (3rd edn, Polity 2006); J Teorell and others, 'Measuring Electoral Democracy with V-Dem Data: Introducing a New Polyarchy Index' (2016) V-Dem Working Paper 2016/25, https://papers.ssrn.com/sol3/papers.cfm?abstract_id=2740935 accessed 01 February 2020.

3 It should be noted that Orbán does not use the term 'liberal' in the classical sense, but broadens the term to include progressive ideas about family life, gender and sexuality. See: MF Plattner 'Illiberal Democracy and the Struggle on the Right' [2019] 30(1) *Journal of Democracy* 5.

4 P Krekó and Z Enyedi, 'Explaining Eastern Europe: Orbán's Laboratory of Illiberalism' [2018] 29(3) *Journal of Democracy* 39.

The quality of democracy in Hungary has declined substantially since 2010. Yet, even though the electoral process is hampered in Hungary due to government control of media and civil organizations, the outcome of elections is not rigged in advance. Illiberal as it may be, it can still be called an electoral democracy, be it a highly diminished or defect one.[5]

It is important to note that definitions of liberal democracy tend to include features that are considered basic for democracy, such as free and fair elections, as well as typical liberal elements such as the protection of individual and minority rights. In this chapter, the focus will be on the elements of the liberal dimension only: the protection of individual and minority rights and the judicial and legislative limits of executive power.

3 Populism in Established Democracies

Democracies worldwide are subject to erosion. Populist movements and parties tend to be regarded as the main culprits behind this decline. In Europe the process of autocratization is most apparent in Eastern Europe. The governments of the populist parties *Fidesz* in Hungary (governing continuously since 2010) and the *Law and Justice Party* (PiS) in Poland (governing with an outright majority since 2015) are the most conspicuous countries in this regard, but there is a wider trend.[6] Till some years ago it was widely agreed that established democracies in Western Europe were immune to the trend of declining democratic quality. Notwithstanding the increasing participation of populist parties in government, there was little evidence that these parties were effective in challenging democratic rights and freedoms.[7] There are some signs that this is changing and that established liberal democracies are also vulnerable to

5 See: A Lührmann and SL Lindberg, 'Keeping the Democratic Façade: Contemporary Autocratization as a Game of Deception' (2018) The Varieties of Democracy Institute Working Paper Series 2018 https://www.v-dem.net/media/filer_public/9c/6f/9c6fe0b9-7f78-4aac-8775-c1cccbd43df2/v-dem_working_paper_2018_75.pdf accessed 11 September 2019.
Although Jan Werner-Mueller suggests that 'illiberal' democracy is a contradiction in terms, he also concedes that the Hungarian regime that has been established by Orbán is a 'defected democracy', acknowledging that elements of democracy are still to some extent intact in Hungary. See: J-W Müller, What Is Populism? (University of Pennsylvania Press 2016).

6 M Minkenberg, *The Radical Right in Eastern Europe: Democracy under Siege?* (Palgrave MacMillan US, 2017); J Rupnik, 'Surging Illiberalism in the East' [2016] 27(4) *Journal of Democracy* 77.

7 T Akkerman, Populist parties in power and their impact on liberal democracies. in RC Heinisch and C Holtz-Bacha and O Mazzoleni (eds), Political Populism: A Handbook (Nomos 2017); T Akkerman and SL de Lange, 'Radical Right Parties in Office: Incumbency records and the Electoral Costs of Governing' [2012] 47(4) *Government & Opposition* 574; D Albertazzi and S Mueller, 'Populism and Liberal Democracy: Populists in Government in Austria, Italy, Poland and Switzerland' [2013] 48(3) *Government & Opposition* 343.

deconsolidation. Although Western European countries still rank as the most democratic in the world and most countries are considered full democracies,[8] populist parties are gaining ground.[9] The previous Italian government of the two populist parties *Lega* and *M5S* stands out in this respect. Former interior Minister Matteo Salvini of the right-wing populist party *Lega* loudly and clearly supports the evictions of immigrants and refugees and members of the minority Roma community from camps despite a stop order issued by the European Court of Human Rights. This was the main reason for the Economist Intelligence Unit to downgrade Italy in ranking on the democracy index in 2018[10] In other countries in Western Europe the quality of democracy is changing more subtly. Freedom House notes that populist leaders in Western Europe have increasingly demonized asylum seekers. Accordingly, some countries that are considered full democracies have suffered partial score declines for the protection of the rights of migrants and refugees, including the rights to due process, to freedom from discrimination and to seek asylum.[11] These recent reports of Freedom House or The Economist Intelligence Unit suggest that populist parties have a negative impact on liberal aspects of the established democracies in Western Europe. Populism is a label, however, that covers parties among the political spectrum from the far left to the far right and some in between. It is far from clear to what extent they all are deconsolidating fundamental liberal rights or are sharing an outright 'illiberal' agenda.

4 What is Populism?

Populism is the great danger of our times according to world leaders in the West. Obama, on his last trip to Europe as president, warned against populist movements on the Left and the Right in Europe. Pope Francis said that "populism is evil and ends badly as the

8 Full democracies are according to the Economist Intelligence Unit (EIU) nations where civil liberties and basic political freedoms are respected and reinforced. These nations have a valid system of governmental checks and balances, an independent judiciary whose decisions are enforced, governments that function adequately, and diverse and independent media.

9 L Rensmann and SL de Lange and S Couperus, 'Editorial to the Issue on Populism and the Remaking of (Il) Liberal Democracy in Europe' [2017] 5(4) *Politics and Governance* 106.

10 See: France 24, 'Far-right policies see Italy's democracy ranking plummet' *France24* (Rome, 9 January 2019) https://www.france24.com/en/20190109-far-right-policies-see-italys-democracy-ranking-plummet accessed 11 September 2019.

11 Freedom House, 'Democracy in Retreat: Freedom in The World 2019' (*Freedom House)* https://freedomhouse.org/report/freedom-world/freedom-world-2019 accessed 11 September 2019.

past century showed," in an interview with a German newspaper. Juncker, the head of the European Commission said in his annual State of the Union address in 2016 that the EU was facing a "galloping populism" and that "we need to be aware of that and protect ourselves against it".[12] Academic scholars also tend to see it as an ideology that inspires political parties or politicians to make undemocratic claims. Various scholars claim that populism is inherently in tension with core tenets of liberal democracy.[13] However, the term 'populism' is loosely used by politicians and pundits and ranges from left-wing politicians and parties such as Hugo Chavez, Jeremy Corbyn, Bernie Sanders, Syriza, and Podemos to right-wing politicians like Donald Trump, Marine Le Pen, and Geert Wilders amongst others. The Guardian devoted a series of articles to populism based on academic research in 2018. The opening headline claimed that one in four Europeans vote populist.[14] The claim was alarming, because it was assumed that the rise of populist parties poses a challenge to liberal democracies in Europe. The parties labeled as populist varied from far-left parties like La France Insoumise, Die Linke, and the Socialist Party to far -right parties like Rassemblement National (formerly Front National), Partij voor de Vrijheid, Alternative fur Deutschland and others. There is still little evidence, however, for the assumption that all these parties share a populist agenda that challenges liberal democracy.

Clear definitions and operationalizations are always important, but even more so in this case, because populism is a broad concept that is also used politically as a denigrating label. The definition that will be used in this article is an elementary definition that is widely used to identify parties and politicians. This definition holds that populists divide societies in two opposing groups, the 'good people' and the 'bad elites'.[15] Parties or politicians tend to be labeled populist based on their expressed distrust of vested politics. They target vested parties and politicians as 'bad elites' because they allegedly do not listen to the common people, hand each other well-paying jobs or are corrupt.

12 J Mason, 'Obama, on last trip to Europe, warns against nationalism, populism' *Reuters* (15 November 2016) https://www.reuters.com/article/us-greece-obama-trump-idUSKBN13A23I?il=0 accessed 11 September 2019; SIR, 'Pope Francis: to Die Zeit, "populism is evil and ends badly"' *SIR* (9 March 2017) https://agensir.it/quotidiano/2017/3/9/pope-francis-to-die-zeit-populism-is-evil-and-ends-badly accessed 11 September 2019; European Commission, 'State of the Union 2016: Towards a Better Europe – A Europe that protects, empowers and defends' (2016) http://europa.eu/rapid/press-release_SPEECH-16-3043_nl.htm accessed 11 September 2019.

13 C Mudde, *Populist Radical Right Parties in Europe* (Cambridge University Press 2007); J-W Müller, What Is Populism? (University of Pennsylvania Press 2016); N Urbinati, Populism and the Principle of Majority. in C Rovira Kaltwasser and others (eds), *The Oxford Handbook of Populism* (Oxford University Press 2017).

14 P Lewis and others, 'Revealed: One in Four Europeans Vote Populist' *The Guardian* (20 November 2018) https://www.theguardian.com/world/ng-interactive/2018/nov/20/revealed-one-in-four-europeans-vote-populist accessed 11 September 2019.

15 KA Hawkins & C Rovira Kaltwasser, 'The Ideational Approach to Populism' [2017] 52(4) *Latin American Research Review* 513; C Mudde and C Rovira Kaltwasser (eds), *Populism in Europe and the Americas: Threat or Corrective for Democracy?* (Cambridge University Press 2012); M Rooduijn, 'The Nucleus of Populism: In Search of the Lowest Common Denominator' [2014] 49(4) *Government & Opposition* 573.

Apart from political elites, populists also criticize economic elites like 'greedy bankers' that grow rich at the cost of hardworking people or cultural elites that are too cosmopolitan to understand the culture of 'ordinary' people. This rhetoric can be found in the manifestoes, speeches and press material of a variety of parties and is most prevalent among parties at the flanks of the political spectrum.[16] It should be noted that a reference to the people in a positive sense is not typical only for populists, but is also a common claim of vested parties.[17] Typical for populists is that they not only claim to represent the people, but also criticize elites. To object to political elites being deaf to the needs of common people or to economic elites being greedy is not anti-democratic, however. This definition is neutral with respect to the democratic views of populists. In sum, parties are considered populist when they tend to view society as being divided by a conflict between 'bad' elites and the 'good' people.

5 Left and Right Populism

Left and right populist parties in Western Europe share criticism of political elites and dissatisfaction with vested political parties. Although they also tend to share a hostile attitude to globalization and the EU, their ideologies and policies only marginally overlap. Left and right populists conceive the people and elites in different ways. Left-wing populist parties define *the people* primarily in economic terms, referring mostly to the divide between elites and the people in terms of economic inequality. They mainly seek to protect the people from exploitation by capitalist elites. In contrast, right-wing populist parties define *the people* on a cultural base and seek to protect the people against cosmopolitan elites and ethnic or cultural minorities that are perceived as dangerous others[18] The notion of the people differs fundamentally because it is coloured by the core ideologies of left and right populists. At the core of right-wing populist programs is a xenophobic nationalism while the programs of left populist parties are based on a socialist or social-democratic ideology. Both these ideologies could potentially challenge liberal tenets of democracy. Xenophobic nationalism can be exclusivist with regard to ethnic, religious or cultural minorities. A radical left socio-economic ideal of equality can be exclusivist regarding groups that are considered to be 'class-enemies'.

16 M Rooduijn and T Akkerman, 'Flank attacks: Populism and left-right radicalism in Western Europe' [2017] 23(3) *Party Politics* 193.

17 M Saward, 'The Representative Claim' [2006] 5(3) *Contemporary Political Theory* 297.

18 L March, *Radical Left parties in Europe* (Routledge 2012); Y Meny and Y Surel, *Populism in Western democracy* (Oxford University Press 2002); C Mudde and C Rovira Kaltwasser, 'Exclusionary vs. Inclusionary Populism: Comparing Contemporary Europe and Latin America' [2013] 48(2) *Government & Opposition* 147; M Rooduijn and T Akkerman, 'Flank attacks: Populism and left-right radicalism in Western Europe' [2017] 23(3) *Party Politics* 193.

However, studies that compare these two types of populist parties indicate that left-wing populist parties in Western Europe nowadays tend to embrace an inclusive view of the people, while right-wing populists tend to have an exclusive view of the people. Ivaldi et al conclude that radical right populists like National Front or Lega Nord advance an exclusionist ethnocultural view of the people. Both parties portray immigration as a 'threat to national identity' and refer to the menace of 'islamization'. Such a cultural and exclusionist view is absent from radical left-wing populist parties. Podemos in Spain has a left-libertarian universalistic profile advocating minority rights.[19] Similar conclusions are drawn by March in a case-study of radical left and right populist parties in the United Kingdom. March shows that the populist left-wing Scottish Socialist Party and the allied Respect coalition raised awareness about the Muslim population in the United Kingdom and initiated a pro-Muslim discourse.[20] Moreover, this contrast between right and left populists does not only hold for the parties but also for their voters. As surveys show, voters of left-wing populist parties are in contrast to those of right-wing populist parties, not inclined to exclusivist attitudes of the people.[21]

These empirical comparisons of the ways in which left and right populist parties conceive of the people indicates that they probably will have diverging agendas when it comes to the rights of minorities. It is to be expected, therefore, that the liberal protection of minorities is potentially less safe in the hands of right-wing populists than those of left-wing populists. The value that populists attach to checks and balances, however, is still mainly a black box. Although it is sometimes assumed that populist parties generally see no need to check executive power as they represent the will of the people, there is scarce research regarding these aspects of liberal democracy.[22] There are incidental examples of left-wing populist parties that have demanded to shift power away from parliament and courts to the ruling executive, such as Fico's Smer in Slovakia.[23] It is far from clear, therefore, to what extent the agendas of left and right populists diverge in this respect.

6 Research Design

For a comparison of left-wing and right-wing populist parties a selection has been made of pairs of left and right populist parties that co-exist in one country. Specific policy

19 G Ivaldi and ME Lanzone and D Woods, 'Varieties of Populism across a Left-Right Spectrum: The Case of the Front National, the Northern League, Podemos and Five Star Movement' [2017] 23(4) *Swiss Political Science Review* 354.

20 L March, 'Left and right populism compared: The British case' [2017] 19(2) *The British Journal of Politics and International Relations* 282.

21 A Akkerman and C Mudde and A Zaslove, 'How Populist Are the People? Measuring Populist Attitudes in Voters' [2014] 47(9) *Comparative Political Studies* 1324.

22 An exception is: RA Huber and CH Schimpf, 'On the Distinct Effects of Left-Wing and Right-Wing Populism on Democratic Quality' [2017] 5(4) *Politics and Governance* 146.

23 ibid.

proposals of parties can be best compared when they share a national context. The selection consists of parties that have been relatively well-established and fairly new parties. The Dutch left-wing Socialistische Partij (SP) and right-wing Partij voor de Vrijheid (PVV), the French left-wing La France Insoumise (LFI) and the right-wing Rassemblement National (formerly Front National) (RN), and the German left-wing Die Linke (DL) and the right-wing Alternative fur Deutschland (AfD) are all widely acknowledged as populist parties.[24]

Taking a qualitative but systematic approach, the manifestoes of the parties used in the most recent nationwide election campaign of 2017 will be analysed.[25] To provide more contextual information, they will be supplemented by published statements of party leaders or spokespersons.

The two main dimensions of liberal democracy – individual and minority rights on the one hand and checks and balances on the other – will be central to the analysis. For each of these dimensions, a list of questions has been developed in order to guarantee a systematic analysis (see Appendix 1). To assess the agendas with regard to the principle of individual and minority rights, questions regarding equality before the law, fundamental rights, and access of citizens to justice have been included. With regard to the principle of checks and balances, questions with respect to the independence of the judiciary and the balance between legislative and executive power have been included.

With respect to individual and minority rights, only the classical liberal rights will be included. Statements or policy proposals about social rights such as the right to education, housing or labour will be ignored. With respect to the principle of equality before the law, only formal equality will be assessed. Endorsements or rejections of 'positive discrimination', for instance, will be left aside. Proposals that touch upon conflicting fundamental rights, such as freedom of speech or freedom of religion on the one hand and protection against discrimination on the other hand, will also be excluded in order to mai ntain an elementary assessment of agendas regarding liberal rights.

6.1 The agendas compared: Explicit and implicit views of liberal democracies

The right-wing populist parties do not challenge or endorse liberal democracy explicitly. None of the parties considered in this contribution, for instance, endorses the regime change that Victor Orbán has initiated in Hungary. That is not to say that Orbán is not admired by the leaders of these parties. Geert Wilders, the leader of the Dutch right-wing Party for Freedom (Partij voor de Vrijheid, PVV) called Orbán a hero who deserves the

24 L March, *Radical Left parties in Europe* (Routledge 2012); M Rooduijn, 'A Populist Zeitgeist? The Impact of Populism on Parties, Media and the Public in Western Europe' (PhD thesis, University of Amsterdam 2013).

25 The PVV has published an extremely short manifesto in 2017. In addition the manifesto of 2012 has been used as well.

Nobel prize, because he dared to close the borders for 'Islamic fortune-seekers'.[26] Marine le Pen, the leader of the French Rassemblement National (RN) compared the France of Macron negatively to the Hungary of Orbán, the latter being a lot more democratic in her view. She made this comparison when she criticized the raids by the Paris public prosecutor's office on the headquarters of the left-populist France Insoumise and the private residences of its high-ranking members, including that of its leader Jean-Luc Melenchon.[27] Christian Luth, the press spokesman of the German right-wing populist party Alternative fur Deutschland (AfD), recommended Orbán for the highest price that Germany has for European leaders, the Charlemagne Prize, which is given for "distinguished service on behalf of European unification".[28]

The left-wing populist parties neither question nor defend liberal democracy explicitly. These parties tend to be inspired by populist leaders in Latin-America rather than strongmen like Orbán. Jean-Luc Melenchon, leader of France Insoumise, praised Hugo Chavez and defended his successor Maduro unconditionally without mentioning the autocratic power and repression of the regime.[29] Heike Hansel, spokesperson in parliament for Die Linke, also supported Maduro unconditionally against the coup of opposition leader Guaido in January 2019, but there is some internal discussion in the party about the extent to which the Venezuelan regime still represents worthy socialism.[30] The Dutch Socialist Party has most clearly distanced itself from the repression under Maduro, when upholding its opposition to intervention in the Venezuelan conflict.[31] In sum, although the left parties share a supportive attitude for left-wing populist regimes in Latin America, they differ in the extent to which they denunciate repression or authoritarian features of these regimes.

6.2 *Equality before the law and individual and minority rights*

Equality before the law and the protection of individual and minority rights as general principles are not or marginally endorsed in the manifestoes of the right-wing populist

---

26 'Tweet Geert Wilders' (*PVV*, 12 September 2018) https://www.pvv.nl/36-fj-related/geert-wilders/9827-tweet-geert-wilders-21.html accessed 11 September 2019.

27 LCI, 'Marine Le Pen sur LCI: "La Hongrie d'Orban est beaucoup plus démocratique que la France de Macron"' *LCI* (17 October 2018) https://www.lci.fr/politique/marine-le-pen-sur-lci-la-hongrie-d-orban-est-beaucoup-plus-democratique-que-la-france-de-macron-2101717.html accessed 11 September 2019.

28 C Lüth, 'Unser Kandidat für den Karlspreis heißt: Viktor Orbán' (*AfD Kompakt*, 14 September 2017) https://afdkompakt.de/2017/09/14/karlspreis-fuer-viktor-orban accessed 11 September 2019.

29 JL Mélenchon, 'France & Venezuela' (*Twitter*, 4 February 2019) https://twitter.com/JLMelenchon/status/1092349856398618626 accessed 11 September 2019.

30 M Niewendick, 'Maduros Venezuela – für manche Linke noch aufrechter Sozialismus' *Welt* (24 February 2019) https://www.welt.de/politik/deutschland/article189319811/Linke-Parteitag-Solidaritaetsaktion-mit-Venezuelas-Praesident-Maduro.html accessed 11 September 2019.

31 S Karabulut, 'Een coup blijft een coup, geweld is geweld' *Het Parool* (8 February 2019) https://www.parool.nl/opinie/-een-coup-blijft-een-coup-geweld-is-geweld~a4622826 accessed 11 September 2019.

parties. The ways in which the parties uphold these principles when making policy proposals regarding Islam or immigration diverge substantially. There is a contrast between Rassemblement National on the one hand and the Party for Freedom and Alternative fur Deutschland on the other hand. The latter two parties define the people as belonging to a Christian and Humanist nation, while RN under Marine Le Pen has been most inclined to define the nation as a secular republic.[32] While all three the parties aim to defend the nation against immigration and Islamic fundamentalism, they do so in diverging ways. AfD and PVV regard Islam as fundamentally incompatible with the German or Dutch nation. Islam is an extremist or 'fascist' ideology, according to the PVV, and therefore, constitutionally protected rights do not hold for Islam. RN under Marine le Pen upholds the idea of impartiality and freedom of religion, while the other two parties maintain that these principles should be overridden in the case of Islam. Marine Le Pen has embraced the ideology of 'laïcité', implying strict neutrality of the state with respect to religion. In contrast to the special status that other right-wing populist leaders such as PVV leader Geert Wilders reserve for Islam, Marine Le Pen maintains that Islam may be dangerous, but it should be treated like other religions. The comparison she made in 2010 between Muslim prayers in the streets of French cities and the time of the German occupation some years ago caused a lot of uproar and is reminiscent of the aggressive language of right-wing populist leader Geert Wilders who regards Islam as an occupying power.[33] Yet, Le Pen invokes the principle of neutrality, extending the principle to extreme limits by arguing that 'laïcité' does not allow for public manifestations of religion. In the campaign of 2017, she has called for banning the headscarf along with the Jewish kippa and large crosses in all public settings.[34] Moreover, while the 2017 program of the RN is far less preoccupied with immigration and Islam than those of PVV and AfD, the policy proposals regarding these issues are relatively spare, moderate and formulated in line with the principle of

32 HG Betz, 'The New Front National: Still a Master Case?' (2013) European Science Foundation Working Paper 30 http://www.recode.info/wp-content/uploads/2014/01/Final-RECODE-30-Hans-Georg-Betz_Final_fin.pdf last accessed 12 September 2019; G Ivaldi, 'A new course for the French radical right? The Front National and 'de-demonisation' in T Akkerman and SL de Lange and M Rooduijn (eds), *Radical Right-Wing Populist Parties in Western Europe: Into the Mainstream?* (Routledge 2016). Notwithstanding this contract between the 'secular' approach of RN and the 'civilizational' approach of PVV and AfD, Marine Le Pen sometimes emphasizes the importance of Christianity/Catholicism. See: R Brubaker, 'Between nationalism and civilizationism: the European populist moment in comparative perspective' (2017) 40 Ethnic and Racial Studies 1191; E Green, 'The Specter of Catholic Identity in Secular France' *The Atlantic* (6 May 2017) https://www.theatlantic.com/international/archive/2017/05/christian-identity-france/525558 accessed 12 September 2019.

33 Le Monde, 'Marine Le Pen compare les "prières de rue" des musulmans à une "occupation"' *Le Monde* (13 December 2012) https://www.lemonde.fr/politique/article/2010/12/11/marine-le-pen-compare-les-prieres-de-rue-des-musulmans-a-une-occupation_1452359_823448.html accessed 12 September.

34 L'Express, 'Marine Le Pen veut interdire voile et kippa dans la rue: "La laïcité n'est pas la négation du fait religieux" pour Boutin' *L'Express* (21 September 2012) http://www.lexpress.fr/actualite/politique/marine-le pen-veut-interdire-le-voile-et-la-kippa-dans-la-rue_1164264.html accessed 12 September 2019.

impartiality. AfD and PVV, in contrast, target Islam exclusively. Promoting a ban on new mosques (AfD) or all mosques (PVV), minarets and the muezzin call (AfD), headscarves in public functions, the burka and niqab (PVV and AfD), the Quran (PVV), Islamic schools (PVV) and funding from abroad for mosques (PVV and AfD). RN does not call for a ban on (building) mosques but opposes public financing for religious institutions generally. RN also defends the freedom of choice regarding schools.

When it comes to security and the fight against Islamic terrorism, the three parties have more in common.[35] All three the parties propose to strip Jihadists with double passports of their nationality. AfD promises to take nationality away even when this would lead to persons becoming stateless. These proposals are discriminating as far as they apply only to persons with double nationality, and they are in conflict with fundamental rights when implying that persons will become stateless.[36]

While RN recognizes Islam as a religion, the other two parties hold that Islam is a 'totalitarian ideology'. Geert Wilders has identified Islam as a 'fascist' ideology and AfD deputy leader Beatrix von Storch held that Islam is a political ideology that is not compatible with the constitution.[37] In the German context the identification of Islam as incompatible with the constitution implies a legitimate exception from constitutionally protected freedoms. The German Federal Constitutional Court implemented the idea of a 'militant democracy' in 1956 to protect the constitution against 'verfassungswidrige' organizations or parties. In contrast, Marine Le Pen argued in an interview with a Moroccan news magazine, that Islam was generally compatible with *laïcité*; it was sharia, which she considered to be fundamentally incompatible with the republic.[38] In contrast to the call of Geert Wilders to stop immigration from non-western or from Islamic countries, Marine Le Pen argued that the problem was not that there were too many North Africans in France, but too many immigrants.[39] Overall, it can be concluded that the agendas of the three right-wing populist parties diverge with regard to the liberal principle of formal equality and individual and minority rights, with RN being careful to defend the nation against immigration and Islam in a liberal way while the other two parties discard liberal principles in favour of a 'militant' defence of democracy.

---

35 D Stockemer and M Barisione, 'The 'new' discourse of the Front National under Marine Le Pen: A slight change with a big impact' [2017] 32(2) *European Journal of Communication* 100.

36 WJ Veraart, *De rechtsstaat, een quick scan: De partijprogramma's voor de verkiezingen 2017 rechtsstatelijk?* (Report by 'de Commissie Rechtsstatelijkheid in Verkiezingsprogramma's', Nederlandse Orde van Advocaten 2017).

37 P Carrel, 'Islam not compatible with German constitution, says AfD party' Reuters (Berlin, 17 April 2016) https://www.reuters.com/article/us-germany-afd-islam/islam-not-compatible-with-german-constitution-says-afd-party-idUSKCN0XE0T0 accessed 12 September 2019.

38 Interview with Marine Le Pen, *Le courier de l'Atlas*, no. 55, January 2012, p. 25. (as cited in HG Betz, 'The New Front National: Still a Master Case?' (2013) European Science Foundation Working Paper 30, 10).

39 Interview with Marine Le Pen, *Le courier de l'Atlas*, page 24. (as cited in HG Betz, 'The New Front National: Still a Master Case?' [2013] *European Science Foundation Working Paper 30* 12).

The agendas of left-wing populist parties straight-out oppose those of right-wing populists. The left-wing populist parties explicitly and emphatically endorse equality before the law and individual and minority rights. All three parties emphasize that they are committed to equal rights for all citizens, and that they fight against discrimination. Their view of the people differs in this regard from that of the right-wing populists. They have a pluralist view of the people as consisting of various kinds of groups and minorities that all should be treated on an equal footing. Die Linke promises, for instance, equal rights for men and women, for sexual and gender related lifestyles, for all minorities. DL also reaffirms the right to asylum and its respect for the freedom of religion. France Insoumise holds that it is important to extend equal rights to all domains of society, that all forms of racism should be rejected, that patriarchy should be abolished and that the right to asylum should be reasserted. The Socialist Party also explicitly underlines that all Dutch people have equal rights, and discrimination and racism is to be rejected. More concretely, the party proposes to extend Article 1 of the Constitution, that upholds equality before the law and prohibits discrimination on several foundations, to include sexual preference, age and disability.

The left-wing parties have felt more pressure to compete electorally with right-wing populists since the 'refugee crisis' of 2015/16 and this has incited internal discussions. The Dutch left-wing populist Socialist Party, for instance, lost voters to the right-wing Party for Freedom in 2017 and this has incited some internal debate in the party about immigration.[40] In the German left-wing populist party Die Linke a debate about the party's positions regarding immigration and asylum came up under pressure of the increasing electoral success of the right-wing populist AfD in 2017. As a result of internal tensions, the leader of Die Linke, Sahra Wagenknecht, announced in March 2019 that she would step down. Although internal discussions about immigration, the right of free movement and open borders have become more prominent in all the three parties recently, the right to asylum is not contested.[41]

The left-wing populist parties also clearly diverge from the right-wing parties in their emphasis on equal access to justice. Die Linke emphasizes that there should be financial

40 P Van den Dool, 'Migratieparagraaf leidt op SP-partijraad tot fel debat' *NRC* (23 February 2019) https://www.nrc.nl/nieuws/2019/02/23/migratieparagraaf-leidt-op-sp-partijraad-tot-fel-debat-a3655174 accessed 12 September 2019.

41 Leading member of Die Linke, Sahra Wagenknecht told the Linke party conference in June 2018 that she was in favour of asylum but against open borders; she also wanted tighter controls for economic migrants trying to enter Germany's labour market. The comments drew ire from many in her party, and criticism that she was latching on to the anti-immigration ideology of the AfD. See: J Schneider, 'Sahra Wagenknecht, die Buhfrau' *Süddeutsche Zeitung* (Leipzig, 10 June 2018) https://www.sueddeutsche.de/politik/linkspartei-sahra-wagenknecht-die-buhfrau-1.4009728 accessed 12 September 2019; A similar discussion has been taking place in France Insoumise when a prominent member signed the 'Manifest pour l'accueil des migrants' while other leading members refused to sign. See: M Bompard, 'A propos manifeste pour l'accueil des migrants' (*Manuel Bompard Député européen)* http://www.manuelbompard.fr/a-propos-manifeste-laccueil-migrants/ accessed 12 September 2019.

assistance for those who cannot afford the costs of a lawsuit. Money should never decide who gains protection of the law, according to Die Linke. France Insoumise wants to halt the impoverishment of the judiciary. The SP also is in favour of more money for the judiciary and effective legal aid. The right-wing parties do not address this issue.

In sum, left-wing and right-wing populists differ fundamentally about minority rights and equality before the law. The militant approach of AfD and PVV differs most from the explicitly inclusive and pluralist notion of the nation of the left-wing populist parties, because it implies a rejection of liberal principles in order to defend democracy against Islam. RN also has an agenda that differs from those of the left populist parties, as the party rejects open borders squarely in order to defend the values of the republic. Yet, in contrast to PVV and AfD, RN upholds the liberal principle of equality before the law, even though the freedom of religion is being restricted by stretching the idea of laïcité.

6.3 Checks and balances

Left-wing and right-wing populists may differ with respect to minority rights and equality, but it can be argued that they are more similar when it comes to checks and balances. The left and right parties share a criticism of established political elites, pessimism about the functioning of vested parties and advocacy for the use of referenda as a way to exercise control over political elites and return power to the 'people'.[42]

Left-wing populists as well as right-wing populists promote direct forms of democracy. All parties promise to introduce referendums and/or popular initiatives in the spirit of the Swiss model. This is an important feature they have in common. The left-wing populist parties also tend to emphasize the importance of democracy in local communities and social and economic institutions. Die Linke and the SP in particular emphasize that it is essential to democratize companies in order to enhance the power of employees. Yet, the crucial question is as to whether direct forms of democracy will weaken the legislative and judicial constraints on the executive. This is not easy to assess as the parties do not address this issue. What the introduction of extension of direct forms of democracy might imply for the role of parliament, for instance, or for the protection of minorities against majorities, are issues that are not elaborated upon. Right-wing populist parties tend to promote smaller parliaments, but it is not clear if this is driven by populist opposition to a 'elitist' institution or by a wish to make parliament more effective and stronger. The AfD, for instance, aims at shrinking the number of parliamentary representatives in the Bundestag and to reduce the civil service, but it should be underlined that a smaller parliament is a broadly sustained wish among

42 J Olsen, 'The Left Party and the AfD: Populist Competitors in Eastern Germany' [2018] 36(1) *German Politics and Society* 70; RA Huber and CH Schimpf, 'On the Distinct Effects of Left-Wing and Right-Wing Populism on Democratic Quality' [2017] 5(4) *Politics and Governance* 146.

German parties. The Bundestag has gradually exceeded its standard number of representatives due to some provisions in the electoral law, and the issue of bringing numbers back again has been on the agenda for some time. RN also wants to 'abaisser le nombre de deputes et senateurs', but this is not an exceptional position either. President Macron made the same promise to reduce the number of deputies and senators during the presidential campaign of 2017, and has confirmed this promise when elected. In the Netherlands, the PVV is neither the only party to propose a reduction of the number of parliamentary representatives.[43] The mainstream right-wing party VVD also wanted a smaller parliament in the past, fitting in with the neo-liberal belief of the party in a small state, but the VVD is not in favour of referendums.[44] The PVV also proposes to lower the salaries of all political functions including parliamentarians, and to abolish 'ample' financial arrangements of parliamentarians. In this respect there is some overlap with the Dutch left-wing populist party. The SP does not aim to reduce the number of parliamentarians, but the party promises a reduction of 'ample' financial arrangements.

It is striking, though, that the left-wing populist parties refrain from proposals reducing the number of parliamentarians. Die Linke, SP and FI do not address the issue. FI proposes instead to change the relation between executive and parliament in favour of the latter. The presidential system in France with its strong executive power incites FI to propose the abolishment of 'the presidential monarchy' and to move power from the president to parliament. The FI is exceptional among the populist parties in wishing to enhance the legislative check on executive power in France, but the left parties generally are less critical of a large parliament than the right-wing parties. In sum, the populist parties generally believe without qualifications in the need to give more power to the people through direct forms of democracy without reflecting on the question how this might affect the legislative checks on the executive.

With respect to the judicial constraints on executive power, the right-wing populist parties do not tend to propose fundamental reforms. The AfD is exceptional among the right-wing populists with its proposals to fortify the separation of powers and to depoliticize the judiciary. Die Linke shares this proposal. DL also argued that the separation of powers should be enhanced by reducing the influence of the Minister of Justice in appointing judges in Germany. RN does not devote any attention to this issue in its election manifest, apart from the proposal to abolish the *Ecole nationale de la magistrature*. In public statements, however, RN leader Marie Le Pen has often complained about partiality of the judiciary; for instance:

43 This is not mentioned in the very short manifest in 2017, but in earlier manifestoes the party also pleaded for a smaller Lower House and a removal of the Senate.

44 VDD, 'Het cabinet wil de Tweede Kamer verkleinen' (*VDD*, 13 July 2012) https://www.facebook.com/VVD/posts/het-kabinet-wil-de-tweede-kamer-verkleinen-van-150-naar-100-leden-de-eerste-kame/458056957546124 accessed 12 September 2019. The VVD wanted to implement a reduction of parliament when the party governed with support of the PVV from 2010-2012.

> L'État de droit est le contraire du gouvernement des juges [...]. Les magistrats sont là pour appliquer la loi, pas pour l'inventer, pas pour contrecarrer la volonté du peuple, pas pour se substituer au législateur.[45]

FI wants to enhance the influence of parliament and judges in appointing the highest judicial body, the *Conseil superieur de la magistrature*. The PVV is the most outspoken in its distrust of the judiciary. The party proposes to make top positions in the judiciary electable. It is not clear in what way such elections should be taken place. The PVV even leaves open whether these top functionaries should be elected directly, by parliament or otherwise. PVV leader Geert Wilders has more than once argued that judges are not impartial. He stated, for instance, that the court that indicted him in December 2016 for inciting discrimination was 'fake' and consisted of PVV- hating judges.[46]

There appears to be some overlap between the right-wing and left-wing populist parties as they all tend to question the impartiality of the judiciary. The solutions diverge from none (RN) to reducing the influence of the Minister of Justice (AfD, DL) to making top functions electable (PVV). In sum, the populist parties generally tend to question the political independence of the judiciary, but there is no clear pattern to their proposals for reform.

7 Conclusion

The right-wing and left-wing populist parties that have been central to this article do not promote 'illiberal' democracy or question liberal democracy explicitly. However, that does not imply that they endorse liberal democracy in all respects. Liberal democracy rests upon two pillars; the protection of individual and minority rights on the one hand and legislative and judicial constraints on the other hand. The agendas of populist parties do not fundamentally diverge when the constraints on executive power are at stake. All populist parties promote direct forms of democracy. None of the parties qualifies these proposals. It is therefore unclear what these reforms imply for the checks on executive power or for the protection of minority rights. The agendas of left-wing and right-wing populist parties diverge substantially, however, when it comes to individual and minority rights. The left-wing populist parties explicitly and emphatically endorse equality before the law and individual and minority rights for all kind of groups, emphatically reject discrimination and uphold fundamental rights like freedom of religion or the right to asylum. In endorsing a pluralist view of the people consisting of various groups that

45 A Boudet, 'Que propose Marine Le Pen pour réformer le système judiciare qu'elle accuse de complot?' *Huffington Post* (28 February 2017) https://www.huffingtonpost.fr/2017/02/28/que-propose-marine-le-pen-pour-reformer-le-systeme-judiciaire-qu_a_21845341 accessed 12 September 2019.

46 G Wilders, 'PVV-hatende rechters' (*Twitter*, 9 December 2016) https://twitter.com/geertwilderspvv/status/807172752658563072 accessed 12 September 2019.

should be treated equally, the agendas of the left populist parties straight out oppose the agendas of right-wing populist parties. Yet, the right-wing populist parties differ as well in the ways in which they respect the liberal principle of equality before the law. While RN upholds the principle of equality before the law for immigrants and Islam, AfD and PVV reject this liberal principle in favour of a militant approach.

Populism in Times of Social Media

Hoai-Thu Nguyen[*]

1 Introduction

There have been many claims in the last decade that liberal democracy is endangered, alternatively by the rise of populism or the rise of social media, depending on the focus of the debate. A stable democracy requires a well-functioning public sphere, in which information can be shared freely with a view to forming public opinion. The rise of social media platforms has had an incisive impact on this process. On the one hand, facilitated access to information on the internet and social media can promote citizens' participation in democratic processes. On the other hand, voters can, through the manipulation and individual targeting of information, be influenced in a much more unregulated manner than was possible before, both by political and by commercial actors. The rise of social media platforms[1] in combination with the increasing use of big data analyses in modern election campaigns,[2] has allowed for political campaigning to become increasingly cost-effective, personalized, and targeted towards individual voters. Because social media platforms have a filtering effect,[3] political parties can, through behavioral targeting techniques,[4] ensure that only messages which conform to voters' political beliefs are advertised on their social media platforms to the exclusion of other information.[5] In the same vein, users can influence the content to which they are exposed by limiting their contacts to like-minded individuals, leading to a situation in which their own political views are perpetually reinforced on their newsfeeds.[6]

---

* Assistant Professor, Faculty of Law, Maastricht University.

1 For an overview over social media platforms, see: K Anderson, 'Getting acquainted with social networks and apps: combating fake news on social media' [2018] 35(3) *Library Hi Tech News* 1.

2 Rubenstein summarizes 'big data' as "the 'three v's' – volume (the amount of data being created), variety (the range of data types and sources), and velocity (the speed at which data is generated and must be analyzed)". See: I Rubinstein, 'Voter Privacy in the Age of Big Data' [2014] *Wisconsin Law Review* 864.

3 P Lee and others, 'Social Media and Political Partisanship – A Subaltern Public Sphere's Role in Democracy' [2018] 35(7) *Telematics and Informatics* 1950.

4 Dobber and others. called this phenomenon 'political behavioral targeting (PBT)'. See: T Dobber and others, 'Two Crates of Beer and 40 Pizzas: The Adoption of Innovative Political Behavioural Targeting Techniques', (2017) 6(1) *Internet Policy Review* 3.

5 Committee of Experts on Media Pluralism and Transparency of Media Ownership, Study on the Use of Internet in Electoral Campaigns: The Rules of the Game: the Internet, Social Media and Election Communication (MSI-MED (2016)10rev4) 14-15.

6 P Lee and others, 'Social Media and Political Partisanship – A Subaltern Public Sphere's Role in Democracy' [2018] 35(7) *Telematics and Informatics* 1950.

At the same time, the rise of populist parties can pose a threat to liberal democracy where they come with illiberal agendas trying to undermine core liberal democratic components such as minority rights, pluralism and the rule of law. If we employ a definition of populism that is put forward by Jan-Werner Müller, as this volume does, the crucial characteristic of populist parties is that they claim to speak for the people who are not truly represented by the political elites in power.[7] Müller's definition of populism is that it is inherently anti-elite, and against both the political establishment and traditional media alike. On the basis of this definition, it comes as no surprise that various studies have found a strong link between populist actors and their use of social media.[8]

This chapter seeks to describe the relationship between populism and social media and analyse the impact that the concurrent rise of both have on the state of liberal democracy. The first part will set a brief theoretical framework by taking the Habermasian public sphere as a starting point and describe the role of both traditional media and social media there within. The second part will focus on the relationship between populism and social media and explain why the specifics characteristics of social media as a political communication platform can be in particular be appealing to populists. The third part will then analyse the consequences of the relationship between populism and social media for the state of liberal democracy, before the fourth and last part offers some suggestions for solutions to mitigate the risks thereof.

2 Traditional media, social media and the public sphere

The idea that a stable democracy requires a well-functioning public sphere, which in turn is strongly linked to the existence of mass media, is most strongly connected with the work of Habermas. In his early work Habermas described the public sphere as the societal realm in which public opinions are formed through the provision of information by mass media such as television, radio and newspapers, which in turn have an influence on those receiving the information.[9] Only in a polity in which information is accessible to the public can the latter exercise proper democratic control,[10] thus making a functioning public sphere a precondition for a robust system of liberal democracy. The public sphere, first transformed by the rise of mass media, has continuously changed over the

7 J-W Müller, *What is Populism?* (University of Pennsylvania Press 2016).

8 See e.g.: P Gerbaudo, 'Social media and populism: an elective affinity?' [2018] 40(5) *Media, Culture & Society* 745; N Ernst and others 'Extreme parties and populism: an analysis of Facebook and Twitter across six countries' [2017] 20 *Information, Communication & Society* 1347.

9 J Habermas, *Strukturwandel der Öffentlichkeit* (Luchterhand 1962).

10 J. Habermas and S Lennox and F Lennox, 'The Public Sphere: An Encyclopedia Article' [1974] *New German Critique* 49.

last decades, not lastly through the digitalization of the media world.[11] The public sphere finds it formal institutional features in the existence of "media organizations and regulatory frameworks that include questions of ownership, financing, control, procedures for licensing, rules for access" as well as "the legal frameworks defining the freedoms of and constraints on communication (e.g. libel and privacy issues)".[12] The media in this context serves to inform and educate the public by putting information into context and providing a place for societal debates, thereby influencing the formation of public opinion.[13] At the same time, it is argued that too many media forms can be a hindrance to this goal. The idea is that the more media alternatives exist in a political system the more fragmented and prone to disinformation or populist messages the system becomes. In contrast, the universal recognition of a limited number of news media, which are considered to have a high reputation and quality, can have a unifying effect on the audience.[14]

The rise of social media platforms as a new form of media has arguably transformed the public sphere by slowly but significantly changing the way we communicate not only in private but also in public debates.[15] While it is true that both traditional media, i.e. press and broadcast, and new digital media serve as a means of transmitting political information, "online technologies serve communication processes that are no longer one-directional".[16] Instead, in particular social media platforms have transformed the way in which we communicate in the public sphere from a 'one-to-many' structure between traditional media and the wider public to a 'many-to-many' structure in which essentially every citizen can distribute information to a wider audience through social media platforms.[17] Through their algorithmic architecture, social media platforms choose which information is being transmitted, which information is prioritized, and which information is silenced. This in turn means that they can also enable voices to be heard, for example, that might normally be excluded from the public debate because they are not represented in traditional mass media. This can include both citizens and political outsiders that, for one reason other another, are not part of the public debate in mainstream media, which can have a sort of gatekeeping effect in this regard. Social

---

11 See e.g.: A Bruns and T Highfield, Is Habermas on Twitter? Social Media and the Public Sphere. in A Bruns and others (eds), *The Routledge Companion to Social Media and Politics* (Routledge 2015).

12 P Dahlgren, Public Spheres, Societal Shifts and Media Modulations. in Gripsrud and L Weibull, *Media, Markets and Public Spheres: European Media at the Crossroads* (Intellect Books 2010).

13 BP Lange, Media and Elections: Some Reflections and Recommendations. in BP Lange and D Ward (eds), *The Media and Elections: A Handbook and Comparative Study* (Lawrence Erlbaum Associates 2004) 208.

14 E Humprecht and F Esser and P Van Aelst, 'Resilience to Online Disinformation: A Framework for Cross-National Comparative Research' [2020] *The International Journal of Press/Politics* 8.

15 T Wischmeyer, 'Making social media an instrument of democracy' [2018] 25(2) *European Law Journal* 173.

16 B Thomass, Deficits and Potentials in of the Public Sphere. in J Trappel and others (eds), *Media in Europe Today* (Intellect 2011) 123.

17 J Tucker and others, 'From Liberation to Turmoil: Social Media And Democracy' [2017] 28(4) *Journal of Democracy* 48-49.

media thus makes it possible for citizens to find like-minded people as well as to find politicians and political parties which they would like to support.[18] This could, for example, also be witnessed during protest movements such as the Arab Spring, the Gezi Protests in Turkey or the Stuttgart 21 protests in Germany.[19]

Generally speaking, in a liberal democracy, citizens rely on the media to provide them with information, based on which they take decisions, both political and otherwise. There is an expectation that "the news media supplies its publics with specific information, which serves to orientate users in a complex and otherwise unmanageable society."[20] Similarly, politicians may rely on the media to put information into context before they take policy decisions.[21] As a matter of fact, in the public sphere in which traditional media – understood as mass media platforms of press, television and radio – still dominated, a certain interdependence, if not symbiotic relationship, between politicians and journalists could be observed.[22] While politicians relied on journalists to have their policies and messages transmitted to the wider public, journalists relied on politicians for their stories and information.[23] In that sense, either side needed the other one to fulfil their respective roles.[24] Such interdependence has been increasingly diffused by the rise of social media platforms, communication through which now no longer necessitates journalists as an intermediary between politicians and citizens, even though two different consequences can be drawn from this. On the one hand, social media can constitute an alternative to traditional media through which politicians directly reach their target audience, thereby entirely replacing the latter as a means of transmitting information in the public sphere. On the other hand, it can also function as a steppingstone for partisan messages, which, once posted and shared on social media platforms, are subsequently picked up and broadcast by traditional media outlets.[25] This could, for example, be observed during the Trump presidency in the US where his

18 This contribution will not be concerned with the potential of social media to bring together collective interests and to promote citizens' participation in democratic processes by, for example, allowing for the organization of political protests online.

19 A Haller and K Holt, 'Paradoxical populism: how PEGIDA relates to mainstream and alternative media' [2019] 22(12) *Information, Communication & Society* 1667.

20 F Zimmermann and M Kohring, 'Mistrust, Disinforming News, and Vote Choice: A Panel Survey on the Origins and Consequences of Believing Disinformation in the 2017 German Parliamentary Election' [2020] *Political Communication* 4.

21 BP Lange, Media and Elections: Some Reflections and Recommendations. in BP Lange and D Ward (eds), *The Media and Elections: A Handbook and Comparative Study* (Lawrence Erlbaum Associates 2004) 208.

22 C Fisher and D Marshall and K McCallum, 'Bypassing the press gallery: from Howard to Hanson' [2018] 167(1) *Media International Australia* 58.

23 Fisher, Marshall and McCallum also note that this 'symbiotic' relationship was not without conflicts as journalists were at the same time expected to hold those into power to account, which could be in tension with their dependence on politicians. See: ibid.

24 C Fisher and D Marshall and K McCallum, 'Bypassing the press gallery: from Howard to Hanson' [2018] 167(1) *Media International Australia* 58.

25 See R Schroeder, 'Digital Media and the Entrenchment of Right-Wing Populist Agendas' [2019] 5(4) *Social Media + Society* 1.

tweets often made it into both national and international mainstream news after being shared on Twitter.

3 The appeal of social media for populists

This edited volume uses the definition of populism by Jan-Werner Müller, which focuses on the rise of populism where an appeal is made to the people whose views are not represented by the political elites in power, including mainstream media. Secondly, Müller argues that populists prefer emotions over rational arguments in the political debate, thereby often simplifying complex political issues.[26] Social media is conducive to both of these elements and arguably constitutes an ideal meeting point for populists and their targeted audience. As mentioned above, the rise of social media has deeply changed the way we communicate, moving from a 'one-to-many' structure to a 'many-to-many' structure, in which not only a much wider audience can be reached by essentially anyone. The exchange of (political) information can nowadays also be done virtually without any delays,[27] as well as across borders and internationally.[28] This in turn on the one had significantly reduces the time for discussion on political issues;[29] on the other hand it also opens up political debates to a much wider array of views that might before not have been represented in (national) mainstream media. Research has shown that mainstream media, as the gatekeeper between politicians and citizens, fulfilled this role more often to the benefit of established political parties and to the disadvantage of political outsiders. Esser et al. thus found that populist parties received less coverage in traditional media than other parties where their electoral strength and standing in poll was low; it was only after a certain level of success that their coverage by the media became more intense and nuanced.[30] Therefore it does not seem too far off to assume that the recourse to social media is particularly appealing to populists. Gerbaudo writes in this regard (albeit not without some qualifications to the notion that social media serve the interests of the people who are otherwise not represented in mainstream media)[31]:

26 J-W Müller, *What is Populism?* (University of Pennsylvania Press 2016).

27 J Tucker and others, 'From Liberation to Turmoil: Social Media And Democracy' [2017] 28(4) *Journal of Democracy* 48-49.

28 B Thomass, Deficits and Potentials in of the Public Sphere. in J Trappel and others (eds), *Media in Europe Today* (Intellect 2011) 123.

29 T Wischmeyer, 'Making social media an instrument of democracy' [2018] 25(2) *European Law Journal* 173.

30 F Esser and A Stepinska and DN Hopmann, Populism and the Media: Cross-National Findings and Perspectives. in T Aalberg and others (eds), *Populist Political Communication in Europe* (Routledge 2016).

31 Most notably, he (rightfully) claims that social media platforms are first and foremost corporate platforms, controlled by companies such as Google and Facebook, which have as their main objective not the ordinary people's interests but monetary profits. See P Gerbaudo, 'Social media and populism: an elective affinity?' [2018] 40(5) *Media, Culture & Society* 749.

> If social media has come to provide a suitable channel for populist appeals, it is first and foremost because of the way in which it has come to be understood as a platform for the voice of the people in opposition to the mainstream news media, accused of being in cahoots with the financial and political establishment. This narrative harks back to the discourse of 'Web 2.0' which emerged after the dot.com bubble burst in 2001 and conceived of the 'social web' as a space in which ordinary people and 'amateurs' could express themselves directly, by-passing broadcasters and journalists and all other 'unnecessary mediators'.[32]

The argument that social media is "a platform for the voice of the people in opposition to the mainstream news media" is a common one. Thus, Haller and Holt find that "[s] uspiciousness against mainstream media as well as the preference for online and social media are both characteristic of many contemporary populist, far-right and anti-system movements", which commonly argue that "hegemonic mainstream media conceal or distort information that does not fit a 'politically correct' agenda".[33] Populists claiming to represent the demands of the people require "direct, unmediated access to the people's grievances",[34] made possible through social media, which provide populists with a direct connection to the people.[35] Ernst et al. identify in their work four factors in particular, which make social media highly attractive for populists: direct access to their audience without media interference, close connection to the people, infinite opportunities for personalization, as well as the possibility to target specific groups.[36] In the following, these four factors will be considered together in pairs of two: (1) unmediated access and close connection to the people and (2) personalization and targeting of specific groups in filter bubbles.

3.1 Unmediated access and close connection to the people

Social media platforms offer politicians the possibility to directly engage and communicate with citizens by bypassing journalistic interventions.[37] Politicians can thus directly transmit messages to voters without having journalists filtering, editing or

32 P Gerbaudo, 'Social media and populism: an elective affinity?' [2018] 40(5) *Media, Culture & Society* 749.

33 A Haller and K Holt, 'Paradoxical populism: how PEGIDA relates to mainstream and alternative media' [2019] 22(12) *Information, Communication & Society* 1665.

34 H Kriesi, 'The Populist Challenge' [2014] 37(2) *West European Politics* 363.

35 S Engesser and others, 'Populism and social media: how politicians spread a fragmented ideology' [2017] 20 (8) *Information, Communication & Society* 1113.

36 N Ernst and others 'Extreme parties and populism: an analysis of Facebook and Twitter across six countries' [2017] 20(9) *Information, Communication & Society* 1357.

37 Ernst and others, 'Populists Prefer Social Media Over Talk Shows: An Analysis of Populist Messages and Stylistic Elements Across Six Countries' [2019] 5(1) *Social Media + Society* 5.

framing the content as would be common in press, television or radio, all the while neither requiring special technical knowledge nor unlimited financial means to do so.[38] Such a bypassing of traditional media is of course the more appealing the more a political party or political actor feels that they are being gatekept by the mainstream news outlets. The less coverage a party thus receives in traditional media, the more beneficial a direct access to the wider public as offered by social media platforms will be. It was mentioned in the previous section that research has shown that populist parties seem to receive less coverage in traditional media than other parties for as long as they are considered to be political outsiders; the level of coverage only changed once they have reached a certain level of success.[39] As a result, the use of social media as a means of communication makes it possible for populists, in particular those with a high number of followers on social media, to gather political support without having to rely on the benevolence of traditional media to reach their voters.

The use of social media by populists makes sense, in particular, when considering that populists claim to represent the interests of the people against the domination of a political and media elite in power. It would be somewhat paradox therefore for them to use exactly those media institutions whose legitimacy they are calling into question in their campaigns to launch their campaigns if other possibilities exist. After all, such an anti-elite claim against both the political establishment and the mainstream media is somewhat more believable if the ones making such claims do not rely on exactly the institutions that they are criticizing to do so.[40] Thus, when in the past populists became mostly visible through the coverage in tabloid media, social media platforms make it much easier for them nowadays to place blame on political opponents such as the elite in power.[41] Basically, populists claiming to represent the demands of the people also require "direct, unmediated access to the people's grievances".[42] To put it in the words of Krämer:

> [S]taging a boycott of the mainstream media or emphasizing the necessity and ability to circumvent them is a symbolic matter for populists. They often cannot completely dispense with the mass media as a platform and source of information, which leads to a number of paradoxes, such as the populist communication paradox identified by Holt and Haller (2016): populists

38 K Jacobs and N Spierings, 'A populist paradise? Examining populists' Twitter adoption and use' [2019] 22 (12) *Information, Communication & Society* 1683-1684.

39 F Esser and A Stepinska and DN Hopmann, Populism and the Media: Cross-National Findings and Perspectives. in T Aalberg and others (eds), Populist Political Communication in Europe (Routledge 2016).

40 A Jungherr and R Schroeder and S Stier, 'Digital Media and the Surge of Political Outsiders: Explaining the Success of Political Challengers in the United States, Germany, and China' [2019] 5(3) Social Media + Society 2.

41 G Bobba, 'Social media populism: features and 'likeability' of Lega Nord communication on Facebook' [2019] 18(1) European Politcal Science 12.

42 H Kriesi, 'The Populist Challenge' [2014] 37(2) West European Politics 363.

> denounce the 'lying press' while using the media as a source when the coverage fits the populist worldview. However, populists often strive to demonstrate that they, not the established media, represent the people's interests and consequently need a platform to convey this very message and their further claims. It is on this platform that they can criticize the media for being unfair and unbalanced and thus put them under pressure to cover them more intensively and favorably.[43]

In addition to bypassing the gatekeepers in traditional media that might be reluctant to print or broadcast populist messages in their coverage, populists can also bypass the risk of having their messages edited or altered where they are printed or broadcast in newspapers, television or radio. In mainstream media, journalists can – and do – edit information by deleting or adding certain aspects as well as put it into context based on their own negative or positive evaluation of the content.[44] Populists can avoid such edits by directly communicating with the public on social media. This way they also no longer need to adapt their language, or political viewpoints, to the requirements of journalists in mainstream media in order to be able to transmit their messages.[45] This means that they can also, for example, employ more offensive and emotional language than would otherwise be edited before publication by traditional media outlets.[46] As a matter of fact, the use of particularly offensive language might even be beneficial on social media as provocative messages on social media can go viral within minutes, potentially even spilling over into traditional media without any further edits.[47] Or, alternatively, populists can also employ very simple, if not oversimplifying, language on social media, without having to risk that it will be subsequently edited by journalists, to reach their audience in order to demonstrate their close connection to the 'common people'. This is often directly contrasted with the elitist and complex language of the elite in power. This is particularly the case for Twitter, a platform designed for short and straightforward communication.[48] In line with this, Ernst et al. for example found in their research that new challenger parties (such as Swiss SVP, German AfD, Italian Lega Nord, or UKIP)

43 B Krämer, 'Populist online practices: the function of the Internet in right-wing populism' [2017] 20(9) *Information, Communication & Society* 1303.

44 K Jacobs and N Spierings, 'A populist paradise? Examining populists' Twitter adoption and use' [2019] 22 (12) *Information, Communication & Society* 1684.

45 A Jungherr and R Schroeder and S Stier, 'Digital Media and the Surge of Political Outsiders: Explaining the Success of Political Challengers in the United States, Germany, and China' [2019] 5(3) *Social Media + Society* 4.

46 S Engesser and others, 'Populism and social media: how politicians spread a fragmented ideology' [2017] 20 (8) *Information, Communication & Society* 1123.

47 K Jacobs and N Spierings, 'A populist paradise? Examining populists' Twitter adoption and use' [2019] 22 (12) *Information, Communication & Society* 1683-1684.

48 K Jacobs and N Spierings, 'A populist paradise? Examining populists' Twitter adoption and use' [2019] 22 (12) *Information, Communication & Society* 1685.

well as political parties at the end of the political spectrum (such as German Linke or British Green party), albeit to a lesser extent, were more likely to employ populistic communication than mainstream parties.[49]

In consequence, the possibilities to reach voters through social media immensely facilitates the potential of populists to become a relevant political actor in the political system and to shape political opinion even beyond their initial success without having to rely on traditional media.[50] Engesser et al. conclude in this respect that "social media are particularly well-suited to meet the communicative preferences of populist actors and that they provide them with a convenient instrument to spread their messages".[51] As a result, established political and media institutions have increasingly less control over the political discourse, which, before social media, they were able to structure significantly by being indispensable for any political actor seeking to obtain power.[52] The political discourse has thus "lost the guard rails which have kept political competitors from the extremes where they would normally remain ostracized and without access to resources."[53]

3.2 Personalization and filter bubbles

In addition to the direct, unmediated access to the wider public that social media offers to populist and non-populist politicians alike, it also enables a high degree of personalization and easy targeting of specific groups. Thus, the use of 'big data' in modern election campaigns allows for microtargeting practices, in which campaigns are personalized and geared towards the individual preferences and political affiliations of each voter. Moreover, because social media platforms have a filtering effect,[54] political parties can, through behavioral targeting techniques,[55] ensure that only messages which conform to voters' political beliefs are advertised on their social media platforms to the

49 Ernst and others, 'Populists Prefer Social Media Over Talk Shows: An Analysis of Populist Messages and Stylistic Elements Across Six Countries' [2019] 5(1) *Social Media + Society* 11.

50 A Jungherr and R Schroeder and S Stier, 'Digital Media and the Surge of Political Outsiders: Explaining the Success of Political Challengers in the United States, Germany, and China' [2019] 5(3) *Social Media + Society* 2.

51 S Engesser and others, 'Populism and social media: how politicians spread a fragmented ideology' [2017] 20 (8) *Information, Communication & Society* 1123.

52 A Jungherr and R Schroeder and S Stier, 'Digital Media and the Surge of Political Outsiders: Explaining the Success of Political Challengers in the United States, Germany, and China' [2019] 5(3) *Social Media + Society* 4.

53 A Jungherr and R Schroeder and S Stier, 'Digital Media and the Surge of Political Outsiders: Explaining the Success of Political Challengers in the United States, Germany, and China' [2019] 5(3) *Social Media + Society* 9.

54 P Lee and others, 'Social Media and Political Partisanship – A Subaltern Public Sphere's Role in Democracy' [2018] 35(7) *Telematics and Informatics* 1950.

55 T Dobber and others, 'Two Crates of Beer and 40 Pizzas: The Adoption of Innovative Political Behavioural Targeting Techniques', (2017) 6(1) *Internet Policy Review* 3.

exclusion of other information.[56] The reinforcement of such messages in the users' newsfeed is often referred to as a so-called 'filter bubble', which can emerge when users on a platform (choose to) communicate exclusively with like-minded users to the exclusion of other users.[57]

Filter bubbles can arise both through the intention of the users involved (self-selected personalisation) and through the way social media platforms prioritize content in their newsfeed (pre-selected personalisation).[58] While self-selected personalisation relates to the platform users' deliberate choices regarding what kind of information they would like to see and engage with – and what kind of information they are avoiding, such as information which would challenge their political opinion –, pre-selected personalisation concerns the way in which social media platforms choose to personalise the content displayed in the users' newsfeeds through algorithmic decisions without the users' explicit knowledge or consent about the latter.[59] The danger of such personalization of content is that it reinforces existing attitudes and standpoints by fortifying and only exposing users to positions that are compatible with their own views. In particular where this concerns controversial topics social media filter bubbles can make users feel that their views or beliefs are acceptable even if they are not approved by society at large.[60] At the same time, being exposed to the same or similar views on social media can also have an effect on what users believe to be valid messages. Research has shown that the more often a statement is repeated the more a person will believe in the truthfulness of that statement.[61] This means that repeated exposure to content on social media which correspond to users' belief systems might not only result in them believing that their views, which are rejected in the wider public, are acceptable; it might also lead to a consolidation of such beliefs by increasing the perceived validity of the content.

Such filter bubbles can constitute an advantage for populism as they allow for "disgruntled individuals embracing ideas regarded as improper by liberals [to] find each other and form online crowds", which in turn can be crucial for the rise of anti-establishment candidates in political systems.[62] They thus can have a mobilizing effect by bringing together people that share the same political views, even where there was no

56 Committee of Experts on Media Pluralism and Transparency of Media Ownership, Study on the Use of Internet in Electoral Campaigns: The Rules of the Game: the Internet, Social Media and Election Communication (MSI-MED (2016)10rev4).

57 A Bruns, 'Filter Bubble' [2019] 8(4) *Internet Policy Review* 4.

58 FJ Zuiderveen Borgesius and others, 'Should we worry about filter bubbles?' [2016] 5(1) *Internet Policy Review* 3.

59 FJ Zuiderveen Borgesius and others, 'Should we worry about filter bubbles?' [2016] 5(1) *Internet Policy Review* 3.

60 P Lee and others, 'Social Media and Political Partisanship – A Subaltern Public Sphere's Role in Democracy' [2018] 35(7) *Telematics and Informatics* 1951.

61 L Hasher and D Goldstein, 'Frequency and the Conference of Referential Validity' [1977] 16(1) *Journal of Verbal Learning and Verbal Behaviour* 107.

62 P Gerbaudo, 'Social media and populism: an elective affinity?' [2018] 40(5) *Media, Culture & Society* 745.

prior links between them.[63] Because social media platforms offer a place for like-minded people to come together, to influence each other and to validate each other's viewpoints in a very selective manner, they can ultimately end up socializing themselves *into* a populist worldview.[64] This becomes even more exacerbated where the consequence drawn from this by users would be the avoidance of mainstream media altogether.[65] These filter bubbles, in which users' own political views are perpetually reinforced are conducive to populism by creating the impression that messages from 'the people', which are otherwise excluded by the mainstream media, are in this way allowed to be spread and heard.[66] This can create a vicious circle, in which the claim that mainstream media cannot be trusted because they exclude views that do not conform to their own political beliefs can drive more users onto social media platforms, where they will in turn will be exposed to more populist messages.[67] In addition, the relationship between political parties, citizens and social movements become much more intertwined and their distinction becomes much more fluid on social media than in a media environment where traditional media have a clear gatekeeping function,[68] thus creating a feeling of closeness between the politicians and citizens.[69] Social media also makes it possible to spread populist messages much simpler and faster. As mentioned above, the sharing of (political) information can nowadays be done basically instantly on platforms such as Twitter or Facebook, as well as across borders and internationally. In particular Twitter's retweet function can create a snowball effect,[70] with messages capable of going viral within matters of minutes.

---

63 P Gerbaudo, 'Social media and populism: an elective affinity?' [2018] 40(5) *Media, Culture & Society* 748-749.

64 B Krämer, 'Populist online practices: the function of the Internet in right-wing populism' [2017] 20(9) *Information, Communication & Society* 1302.

65 B Krämer, 'Populist online practices: the function of the Internet in right-wing populism' [2017] 20(9) *Information, Communication & Society* 1302.

66 K Jacobs and N Spierings, 'A populist paradise? Examining populists' Twitter adoption and use' [2019] 22 (12) *Information, Communication & Society* 1686.

67 E Humprecht and F Esser and P Van Aelst, 'Resilience to Online Disinformation: A Framework for Cross-National Comparative Research' [2020] *The International Journal of Press/Politics* 17.

68 S Stier and others, 'When populists become popular: comparing Facebook use by the right-wing movement Pegida and German political parties' [2017] 20 *Information, Communication & Society* 1368-1369.

69 Interestingly though, Jacobs and Spierings found in their research that populists are, in fact, on average less likely to interact with other users than other politicians, while at the same time being more selective about who they befriend on Twitter. See: K Jacobs and N Spierings, 'A populist paradise? Examining populists' Twitter adoption and use' [2019] 22(12) *Information, Communication & Society* 1692-1693.

70 K Jacobs and N Spierings, 'A populist paradise? Examining populists' Twitter adoption and use' [2019] 22 (12) *Information, Communication & Society* 1686.

4 Implications for liberal democracy

Starting from the idea that a stable democracy requires a well-functioning public sphere, in which public opinions are formed through the provision of information by mass media, it is indisputable that the rise of social media has deeply altered the latter. At the same time, the prevalence of social media is also closely connected to the rise of contemporary populism. This is not to say that populism could not exist or rise into power without social media as there is plenty of evidence to the contrary in history; but rather that there exists a close link between social media and populism, even if it is not a causal one. Thus, Ernst et al. showed in their research that populist communication strategies on social media are furthermore more often used by opposition parties than government parties.[71] This in turn fits with the claim that social media are an opportune way for populists to attack the elite in power while claiming to represent the interests of the people without having to resort to the mainstream media elite to do so. Social media thus enables the amplification and proliferation of populism and allows it penetrate domains of the public sphere which before might have been inaccessible to it.[72]

The rise of populism, whether in connection with social media or not, has consequences for the state of liberal democracy. Substantively, it is an inherently illiberal concept, displaying disregard for essential components of liberal democracies such as minority rights, pluralism and the rule of law.[73] Procedurally, as Young argues in her contribution to this edited volume, populism has negative consequences for political discussions because it homogenises the will of the people and replaces deliberation and reason with rhetoric and emotion.[74] In a very similar fashion, also social media as a new platform of political communication is not necessarily geared towards the harmonization between and the reconciliation of different viewpoints, which is indispensable in a well-functioning democracy. In the fast pace of the internet, there is little time to engage in deep reflection and discussion with opposing political opinions. Instead, messages on social media rather tend to augment and fortify specific positions and agendas,[75] perhaps not lastly because moderate, balanced statements are less likely to go viral on platforms such as Twitter or Facebook than sensationalist and emotionalised content. In this regard, algorithmic decision-making on social media

71 N Ernst and others 'Extreme parties and populism: an analysis of Facebook and Twitter across six countries' [2017] 20(9) *Information, Communication & Society*.

72 What is interesting to note here is that social media does not only constitute a tool for populist to rise into power; it also is a tool for populists, once in power, to silence political opponents and/or those with an opposing political viewpoint. This is in particular the case in illiberal democracies where social media and online platforms can be used to employ online harassment, propaganda, distraction and denial-of-service to quiet critics as well as distort the information space. See J Tucker and others, 'From Liberation to Turmoil: Social Media And Democracy' [2017] 28(4) *Journal of Democracy* 47.

73 See e.g.: C Mudde, 'Europe's Populist Surge: A Long Time in the Making' [2016] 95(6) *Foreign Affairs* 25.

74 A Young, 'Populism and the United Kingdom' in this edited volume.

75 T Wischmeyer, 'Making social media an instrument of democracy' [2018] 25(2) *European Law Journal* 173.

platforms seems to reward in particular provocative statements. In other words: "With the rise of social media, the balanced press statement is replaced by the provocative tweet."[76] The danger of an unbalanced and unmoderated political discussion is further exacerbated by the existence of filter bubbles. The lack of exposure to opposing political views on social media caused thereby has led to concerns that the public sphere may be endangered as discussions on common problems and solutions in a polity become more difficult.[77]

As a consequence of these developments, large parts of the political debate now escape the remit of journalistic filters and standards and are no longer guided and moderated, and perhaps even bridled, by television, radio or newspaper editors. In the same fashion, also political parties are increasingly losing their status as the forum in which salient political issues are brought together in order to form a coherent political platform, which can be translated into electoral manifesto and policy decisions. As a result, both established political institutions and traditional media are increasingly losing control over the public discourse, which, before social media, they were able to structure significantly by yielding a certain amount of control over the type of information shared and distributed in the public sphere. This is coupled with the rise of not only populism but also phenomena of disinformation and so-called 'fake news'. Again, as with social media and populism, disinformation and populism do not have a causal relationship but nonetheless can be interlinked. They both concern "the spread of partisan information that supports one particular party's attitudinal stance while discrediting information from the other party", while employing a moral divide between 'we' and 'them',[78] though it would be misleading to conflate the two concepts. Rather, fake news can constitute one of the tools available to populists to target their audience. Both concepts have in common, however, that they have an impact on the quality of political debate and thus the state of liberal democracy. In this context, Mudde speaks of a populist *Zeitgeist* that has taken hold in Europe and which dominates and controls the agenda of the public debate with anti-elite rhetoric and frequent references to 'the people', even by mainstream parties.[79]

The rise of populism and social media, coupled with how they interact with one another, has thus profound implications for the public sphere and for liberal democracy. Mainstream mass media in the form of television, radio and press find themselves increasingly in competition with alternative media platforms including, but not limited to, social media. As mentioned previously in this chapter, the existence of mass media is a prerequisite for a public sphere in which information is to be exchanged

---

76 ibid.

77 See e.g.: C Sunstein, #Republic – Divided Democracy in the Age of Social Media (Princeton University Press 2018).

78 E Humprecht and F Esser and P Van Aelst, 'Resilience to Online Disinformation: A Framework for Cross-National Comparative Research' [2020] *The International Journal of Press/Politics* 7.

79 C Mudde, 'Europe's Populist Surge: A Long Time in the Making' [2016] 95(6) *Foreign Affairs* 29.

with the purpose of contributing to the formation of public opinion. The fragmentation of the media landscape in contemporary times as well as the way social media operates when it comes to information sharing – unmediated, in filter bubbles, at high speed, with a tendency to prioritize sensationalist content that have the potential of going viral over more measured messages – have made this process arguably more difficult. While it is true that social media provides direct access to the wider public, both to populist and mainstream party alike, it has been also argued in this chapter that the way social media platforms function is more conducive to the anti-elitist and emotionalist modus operandi of populist parties than it is to mainstream parties. The question thus poses itself whether, and how, the interference into the public sphere by populists on social media could be mitigated by new regulations. This will be discussed in the next section, in which some suggestions will be made as to how to mitigate the impact of these developments on liberal democracy.

5 Suggestions for solutions

Liberal democracy presupposes a functioning public sphere, which in turn requires a well-functioning media landscape through which information can be shared freely with a view to forming public opinion. The latter has arguably been rendered more difficult through the rise of social media and populism and, in particular, their interaction with one another in contemporary times. The main causes for the endangerment of liberal democracy through the use of social media by populists that were identified in this chapter were (1) the possibility of unmediated access to the people and (2) the possibilities for personalization and targeting of specific groups in filter bubbles. This section will consider both issues in turn, with a view of suggesting possible solutions on how to mitigate their impact on liberal democracy. In essence, traditional media regulations have as their objective the establishment of a framework in which a diversity of opinions becomes possible, all the while ensuring the freedom of the press and freedom of speech to the widest extent possible without having the exercise of those freedoms causing any damages.[80] This should also be kept in mind when discussing regulatory proposals for social media platforms.

Firstly, unmediated access of populists to the people on social media arguably poses a risk to liberal democracy to the extent that it takes away the capability of journalists in traditional media – meaning television, radio and press – to structure the political discourse by filtering information and by putting that information into a larger context. Criticisms aside that some media institutions might fulfil this task more objectively than others, traditional mass media are subject to journalistic and ethical standards that simply

80 A Koltay, *New Media and Freedom of Expression: Rethinking the Constitutional Foundations of the Public Sphere* (Hart Publishing 2019) 223.

do not apply to social media platforms. Information and content posted onto social media platforms such as Twitter and Facebook do not only go unchecked; they can also go viral in a matter of minutes without any prior verification. This, for one, increases the risk of false, or at least partially false, information to be shared. Secondly, it also allows for the augmentation and fortification of specific positions without any accompanying moderating comments. If we want thus to ensure that also on social media the variety in opinions in the political debate is fully reflected in order to guarantee right of citizens to be informed in a comprehensive manner, one solution could be to ensure that information on social media is checked for both accuracy and balance, with the possibility of removing content that is deemed to be false. The German Network Enforcement Act (NetzDG), which came into effect on 1 January 2018, for example, constitutes one attempt to combat hate speech on the internet by requiring social media platforms to set up a complaint mechanism and to delete obviously illegal content (e.g. breach of public order, incitement to hatred, insult or defamation) within 24 hours of receiving the complaint where possible. It has since been widely criticised for being both ineffective and a restriction on fundamental rights, most notably the freedom of speech.[81] Other jurisdictions have attempted to regulate the problem of online disinformation in different ways: there is, for example, the EU code of conduct on hate speech, the French co-regulation approach with social media platforms or the UK online harms paper.[82] The inherent problem that all of these attempts face is, however, the same as for the German NetzDG: there seems to a fundamental conflict between the need regulate content on social media as a means to ensure an open and balanced public discourse and the need to protect the right to free speech in a democracy. Moreover, the question is in how far such an approach would be suitable for the problem of populist messages on social networks in as far as such messages do not constitute hate speech or other illegal content. For such cases, I would propose a different focus when thinking about solutions which concentrates not on social media platforms but rather on the people themselves in the form of information literacy.

If we can neither rely on journalists to filter information and to put that information into a larger (political) context for us nor can expect social media platforms to do so in lieu of traditional media, then such a task necessarily falls to each individual citizen themselves. Studies have shown, however, that a growing number of people are no longer simply uninformed, but in fact disinformed, meaning that they form their

81 See for a discussion of the German NetzDG Law e.g.: M Hong, Hate Speech im Internet – Grundrechtliche Rahmenbedingungen ihrer Regulierung. in M Albers and I Katsivelas, *Recht & Netz* (Nomos 2018); H Tworek and P Leerssen 'An Analysis of Germany's NetzDG Law' (2019) Working Paper of the Transatlantic High Level Working Group on Content Moderation Online and Freedom of Expression; W Schulz, 'Regulating Intermediaries to Protect Privacy Online – the Case of the German NetzDG' (2018) HIIG Discussion Paper Series.

82 See for an overview of attempts to regulate online platforms: M Vermeulen, 'Online Content: To Regulate or Not to Regulate – Is that the Question?' (2019) APC Issue Paper 2.

preferences based on inaccurate factual beliefs.[83] Kuklinski et al. already argued in 2000 that this development is not to be underestimated as "[i]t is one thing not to know and be aware of one's ignorance. It is quite another to be dead certain about factual beliefs that are far off the mark".[84] The crucial difference is that people who are uninformed about facts are more susceptible to a change in preference as a response to cues they receive from the political argument; for them "the way that competitive political elites frame an issue determines which set of reasons for or against comes to mind and thus what [they] decide".[85] This is, however, not necessarily the case for *misinformed* people, who are much more unlikely to change their beliefs and preferences.[86] The consequence of this distinction for any policy recommendations regarding the impact of the interplay between populism and social media on liberal democracy is that measures looking to increase citizens' information literacy must focus in particular on their ability to recognize and critically question false, amplified or populist information on the internet.

Secondly, the possibilities offered by social media to populists to personalise their messages and target specific groups, whose views are reinforced through filter bubbles, pose a risk to liberal democracy in that they make an open discussion on common problems and solutions in a polity significantly more difficult. It also increases the danger of misinformation by facilitating both specifically targeted political campaigns by populists and a lack of exposure to different political views for its users. This is a two-fold problem, the causes of which should also be treated separately: one is the possibility of microtargeting – i.e. the practice of displaying individually targeted political advertisements to users based on data collected about them –, the other one is that the effects of such microtargeting techniques can be further exacerbated by filter bubbles and the lack of exposure to other viewpoints there within.

The issue of political microtargeting has been widely analysed in scholarship already, with many of the discussions focussing on data protection, in particular under the EU General Data Protection Regulation (GDPR) which entered into force in May 2018.[87] And while I agree that stricter regulations on the collection and processing of data is indispensable for the prevention of microtargeting practices, for the purpose of this

83 E Humprecht and F Esser and P Van Aelst, 'Resilience to Online Disinformation: A Framework for Cross-National Comparative Research' [2020] *The International Journal of Press/Politics* 2.

84 JH Kuklinski and others, 'Misinformation and the Currency of Democratic Citizenship' [2000] 62(3) *The Journal of Politics* 809.

85 JH Kuklinski and others, 'Misinformation and the Currency of Democratic Citizenship' [2000] 62(3) *The Journal of Politics* 810.

86 JH Kuklinski and others, 'Misinformation and the Currency of Democratic Citizenship' [2000] 62(3) *The Journal of Politics* 810.

87 See e.g.: T Dobber and RF Fahy and FJ Zuiderveen Borgesius, 'The regulation of online political micro-targeting in Europe' [2019] 8(4) *Internet Policy Review* 2; O Papakyriakopoulos and others, 'Social media and microtargeting: Political data processing and the consequences for Germany' [2018] 5(1) *Big Data & Society* 1; M McDonagh, Freedom of processing personal data for the purpose of electoral activities after the GDPR. in N Witzleb and M Paterson and J Richardson (eds), *Big Data, Political Campaigning and the Law* (Routledge 2019).

chapter I would like to focus on a different approach. If the objective is to ensure a pluralistic information landscape on social media, in which the people can access and exchange information in a comprehensive manner with a view to forming public opinion, the question is perhaps not necessarily how to target political microtargeting but rather how to ensure that microtargeted advertisement are not the *only* political advertisements to which citizens are exposed on social media. The most obvious answer to this question would be a limitation of both self-selected personalisation and pre-selected personalisation on social media platforms. While the former is inherently more difficult to regulate – after all, it is not for policymakers to decide with whom citizens can be friends with on Facebook or who they should follow on Twitter – transparency requirements with regard to the latter can be a suitable approach to the problem. As was explained in a previous section, pre-selected personalisation concerns the way in which social media platforms choose to personalise the content displayed in the users' newsfeeds through algorithmic decisions, often without the users' explicit knowledge or consent about the latter. By requiring social media platforms to make transparent to users why certain content appears on their newsfeed as well as to provide users easy access to information that is no appearing on their immediate newsfeed based on algorithmic decisions, the effects of the personalisation of information could be mitigated. At the same time, this would require users to not only be interested in such information but also to be able to put such information into context, which in turn relates back to my previous argument that the best way to ensure a functioning public sphere with a balanced public discourse might perhaps be measures to (significantly) improve the information literacy of the people.

At this point it might also be necessary to point out that the suggestions for solutions made here are mostly, if not exclusively, related to the question of how to ensure a balanced and comprehensive public debate on social media, which functions inherently different than traditional mass media. They do not, in first instance, serve to protect liberal democracies against populism. In this edited volume many different authors have analysed the effectiveness, or ineffectiveness, of national constitutional safeguards against populism in their own countries. These safeguards, in the form of, for example, judicial independence, electoral laws, procedures for constitutional amendments, are, and should remain, the primary means of protecting liberal democracies against the rise of populism. A well-regulated social media landscape can contribute to the improvement of the quality of political debate; it will not, however, prevent populists from rising into power where the constitutional safeguards are not sufficiently effective and stable to do so. In the same manner, unregulated social media platforms might assist populists in spreading their message, but it will nonetheless be difficult, if not impossible, for populists to undermine liberal democracy where constitutional safeguards protecting the latter are sufficiently strong in the first place.

6 Conclusion

The objective of this chapter was to describe the relationship between populism and social media and to make some suggestions on how to mitigate their impact on the state of liberal democracy. I argued in this chapter that with populism and social media, we are facing two very distinct concepts that both, independently from each other, can pose a threat to liberal democracy. At the same time, they are also closely connected to one another in that the nature of social media platforms as a means of political communication is particularly beneficial for and conducive to populism. However, *because* they are two very different phenomena, it is very difficult to propose solutions that would tackle both issues simultaneously. Instead, I argue that liberal democracy cannot be protected against populism through the regulation of social media; rather the focus of any such efforts should be and remain on the institutional and constitutional safeguards of liberal democracies that are discussed in the different country chapters of this edited volume. This is not to say that we should not focus on social media at all in this regard. Quite to the contrary: on the one hand, a well-regulated social media landscape can contribute to the slowing down of the rise of populism (even though not prevent it); on the other hand, and more importantly, it can facilitate the continued existence of an open and balanced public sphere, which in turn is indispensable for a functioning liberal democracy.

Referendums and Democratic Constitutionalism: Is There a Way for Reconciliation?

*İlker Gökhan Şen**

1 Introduction

The expedience of the use of referendums in democracies is a controversial issue. One of the arguments typically brought forward against the referendum is that it may damage liberal democracy by creating a tyranny of the majority. Unwise and hasty political leaders may use this device to evade the parliamentary and/or civil-society deliberation process and take bad decisions that may, at the same time, overlook or violate the preferences or the rights of political minorities.[1] Besides, the "all-or-nothing" or "yes-or-no" nature of the decision making in many referendums creates a risk of social polarization and may damage pluralism and democratic quality. Thus, it is no surprise to see that populist and authoritarian political actors like the referendum. Indeed, referendums have not been scarcely used as a tool for political legitimization in authoritarian regimes.

* İlker Gökhan Şen holds a doctorate in law from the University of Zurich. The author wishes to thank Blickwechsel:
Contemporary Turkey Studies (https://www.blickwechsel-tuerkei.de/en/index.php) for their support. This chapter draws on research conducted during his fellowship at: https://www.socialresearch-turkey.org/projects.

1 M Laurence, The Democratic Criticism of Referendums the Majority and True Will of the People. in L Morel and M Qvortrup (eds), *Routledge Handbook to Referendums and Direct Democracy* (Routledge 2018) 149; I Budge, *The New Challenge of Direct Democracy* (Polity Press 1996) 60-83; T E Cronin, *Direct Democracry: The Politics of Initiative Referendum and Recall* (Harvard University Press 1999) 90-99; D Butler and A Ranney, Theory. in D Butler and A Ranney (eds), *Referendums Around the World: The Growing Use of Direct Democracy* (Macmillan 1994) 19.

One may recall here the votes held during all kinds of authoritarian and totalitarian regimes, such as Nazi-Germany, Fascist Italy, Soviet Union and post-Soviet states, to name but a few.[2]

The guiding question for this chapter is whether there is a way to save referendums from populist manipulation. For this purpose, Part I will provide a brief introductory note on the relationship between populism and referendums. In fact, legal doctrine and practice have always discerned "good practices" from bad ones – or, put differently – democratic referendums from non-democratic ones. Keeping this in mind, Part II will offer a definition of the concept of "authoritarian referendum" and a historical account of authoritarian referendums, particularly in France under Napoleon(s) and in Hitler's Germany. Finally, Part III will discuss, *a contrario* the authoritarian referendums, that there are emerging standards of democratic (good) referendums in comparative constitutional law and international documents; and a synthesis of these standards may be taken as a guideline in the path of securing a pluralist and democratic system of referendum.

2 Populism and Referendums

"Populism" is an ambivalent term having diverse connotations and meanings in different contexts and for different authors. A definition attempt for the purpose of this chapter for populism may be as follows: Populism is a "label",[3] a pejorative generic term for any kind of political conduct, discourse or method to attain one's goal by manipulating the masses and distorting the very essence (the people's will), either formally or substantially, of democratic processes.

The main contours and content of this definition may be sensed in Müller's definition of populism who sees the concept as an empirical political phenomenon rather than a

2 In general, see: A T Jennsen and O Listhaug, Voters' Decisions in the Nordic EU Referendums. in M Mendelsohn and A Parking (eds), *Referendum Democracy: Citizens, Elites and Deliberation in Referendum Campaigns* (Palgrave 2001) 20-23; for Germany, see M Urban, The Self-Staging of a Plebiscitary Dictatorship: The NS-Regime Between "Uniformed Reichstag", Referendum and Reichsparteitag. in Ralph Jessen and H Richter (eds), *Voting for Hitler and Stalin Elections Under 20th Century Dictatorships* (Campus 2011) 42; for Italy, P Corner, Plebiscites in Fascist Italy: National Unity and the Importance of the Appearance of Unity. in R Jessen and H Richter (eds), *Voting for Hitler and Stalin Elections Under 20th Century Dictatorships* (Campus 2011) 178-179; E Fimiani, Elections, Plebiscitary Elections, and Plebiscites in Fascist Italy and Nazi-Germany: Comparative Perspectives. in R Jessen and H Richter (eds), *Voting for Hitler and Stalin Elections Under 20th Century Dictatorships* (Campus 2011) 244; for Soviet Union, S Merl, Elections in the Soviet Union, 1937-1989: A View into a Paternalistic World from Below. in R Jessen and H Richter (eds), *Voting for Hitler and Stalin Elections Under 20th Century Dictatorships* (Campus 2011) 285-289; for post-Soviet states, D Ó Beacháin, Faking It: Neo-Soviet Electoral Politics in Central Asia. in R Jessen and H Richter (eds), *Voting for Hitler and Stalin Elections Under 20th Century Dictatorships* (Campus 2011) 218-220.

3 C Mudde and C R Kaltwasser, *Populism: A Very Short Introduction* (Oxford University Press 2017) 2.

"codified doctrine".[4] In a similar way of Müller's definition, populism has three chief elements: "the people, the elite, and the general will."[5] The populist political leaders have their own perception of authentic and genuine people, consisting only of those who support their policies. Anti-elitism (anti-establishment) is another core concept that goes along with the discourse of fighting for the rights and interests of these underrepresented "underdogs". Populists condescend to any kind of anti-majoritarian institutions of democracy (and which are crucial – for example Constitutional Courts – for the protection of minority rights) as being elitist, and thus, as the enemy of the people. "In addition to being anti-elitist, populists are always *anti-pluralist*. Populists claim that they, and they alone, represent the people."[6]

So, populist political actors not only arrogate themselves the exclusive right to identify and decide who constitute the people, but they also disregard any sort of deliberative democratic processes in the decision of what is good for the society. Furthermore, "the emphasis on a singular common good that is clearly comprehensible to common sense and capable of being articulated as a singularly correct policy that can be collectively willed at least partly explains why populism is so often associated with the idea of an oversimplification of policy challenges."[7] Referendums may come in handy for populists in their oversimplification of the political decision process. Indeed, when not properly (or democratically) held, referendums appear to damage the liberal democracies by their crude majoritarian nature and their demoting the complex political questions to a take-it-or-leave-it offer.[8]

This leads us to consider the "dark side" that all sorts of populisms may have. The anti-pluralist and exclusionist conceptions of "people" and "general will" of populism are prone to create an authoritarian way of political conduct – if not a full-fledged authoritarian political regime. Even if these two terms may not be taken at face value as two synonyms, authoritarianism and populism, in most cases, overlap in their methods

---

4 J-W Müller, *What is Populism?* (University of Pennsylvania Press 2016) 10. Please also note that this chapter excludes the perception of populism as understood in 19th century US politics. The populist movement in the US in the 1890s had proposed and guaranteed the reception of popular initiatives (referendums on laws proposed by the people) and referendums (votes on laws enacted by the legislature) in the constitutional systems of several states. (M Qvortrup, The History of Referendums and Direct Democracy. in L Morel and M Qvortrup (eds), *Routledge Handbook to Referendums and Direct Democracy* (Routledge 2018) 18); in the same vein, Sciarini coins a dichotomy of a *populist* (*unmediated*) vs. a *plebiscitary* version of referendums. According to this classification, the former refers to citizen initiatives as found in some US states, "which are submitted to the voters without intervention of the state government and parliament". In the "plebiscitary version" of direct democracy, the initiation of referendums falls within the competence of the executive, (P Sciarini, Voting behavior in direct democratic votes. in L Morel and M Qvotrup (eds), *Routledge Handbook to Referendums and Direct Democracy* (Routledge 2018) 290).

5 C Mudde and C R Kaltwasser, *Populism: A Very Short Introduction* (Oxford University Press 2017) 9.

6 J-W Müller, *What is Populism?* (University of Pennsylvania Press 2016) 20.

7 J-W Müller, *What is Populism?* (University of Pennsylvania Press 2016) 26.

8 See on the binary nature of referendums: P Taillon, The Democratic Potential of Referendums Intrinsic And Extrinsic Limitations L Morel and M Qvotrup (eds), *Routledge Handbook to Referendums and Direct Democracy* (Routledge 2018) 174.

and goals. Mudde and Kaltwasser, remind how populist political discourse and method come closer to Carl Schmitt's theory on the "people" and political will-formation. As the founding-father-theorist of the Nazi Regime, Schmitt believed that the homogeneity of the people was crucial for the creation of a democratic order and the general will should be based on the unity of the people. Likewise, the oversimplified and absolute nature of the "general will" of populism tends to legitimize authoritarian policies and illiberal attacks on the perceived enemies and threats against the so-called unified people.[9] As explained in more detail below, Schmitt's theory paved the way for the Nazi takeover of the democratic order, and the referendums played a considerable role in this regard. Indeed the withdrawal from the league of nations – and thus the first step of relinquishing the pacifist international politics of Post-WWI Weimar Republic – was realized by a referendum held in 1933. One year later in 1934, another referendum took place for merging of the offices of the President and the Chancellor and conferring all relevant executive powers to Hitler.[10] This referendum, it may be argued, "confirm(ed) Hitler as dictator".[11] In 1936, the Nazi regime remilitarized the Rhineland, a decision which contravened the disarmament clauses of the Treaty of Versailles. This decision too was approved in a referendum in the same year. Finally, annexation of Austria was the subject of the referendum held in 1938.[12]

Therefore, it is safe to assume that the populist use of referendums tends to display the same features as the referendums held in authoritarian settings. For a typical populist leader, a referendum is "not about initiating open-ended processes of democratic will-formation among citizens. Populists simply wish to be confirmed in what they have already determined the will of the real people to be. Populism is not a path to more participation in politics."[13]

So, is there a way to avoid the populist manipulation of referendums? Giving a plain answer or offering a one-size-fits for all panacea to this question would be too pretentious. On the other hand, we may describe and analyze the referendums held by populist/authoritarian political actors and derive lessons from them. To this end, the following section will coin the term and explain the concept of "authoritarian referendum" from a historical perspective.

9 C Mudde and C R Kaltwasser, *Populism: A Very Short Introduction* (Oxford University Press 2017) 18.

10 M Urban, The Self-Staging of a Plebiscitary Dictatorship: The NS-Regime Between "Uniformed Reichstag, Referendum and Reichsparteitag. in Ralph Jessen and H Richter (eds), *Voting for Hitler and Stalin Elections Under 20th Century Dictatorships* (Campus 2011) 42; M Suksi, *Bringing in the People* (Kluwer 1993) 100.

11 M E Newton, *The Path to Tyranny: A History of Free Society's Descent Into Tyranny* (Eleftheria Publishing 2010) 201.

12 M E Newton, *The Path to Tyranny: A History of Free Society's Descent Into Tyranny* (Eleftheria Publishing 2010) 201; M Urban, The Self-Staging of a Plebiscitary Dictatorship: The NS-Regime Between "Uniformed Reichstag, Referendum and Reichsparteitag. in Ralph Jessen and H Richter (eds), *Voting for Hitler and Stalin Elections Under 20th Century Dictatorships* (Campus 2011) 42; M Suksi, *Bringing in the People* (Kluwer 1993) 101.

13 J-W Müller, *What is Populism?* (University of Pennsylvania Press 2016) 102.

3 The Concept of Authoritarian Referendum

3.1 *What is "authoritarian referendum"?*

The discerning feature of authoritarian referendums is that people do not deliberate or discuss political decisions, but only respond to the proposals given by their leaders, with the answers "yes" or "no". Such referendums cannot be described as people's free choice, since the referendum process (and particularly propaganda) is flawed with oppression and manipulation. Another common feature of the authoritarian referendums is the ballot question, which usually serves as an acclamatory vote of confidence for the dictators, or at best, for uncompromising political leaders.[14]

In fact, the concept is not new, and has occurred since the initial stages of the practice of referendums in the modern state. Such referendums appear as "formally or de facto, a vote of confidence about the accession or permanence in power of a person."[15] The literature, however, tends to use the term "*plebiscite*" for the referendums used by authoritarian political actors. This term dates back to the Roman era, meaning a decree (*scitum*) voted and approved by the plebs – the social strata composed of common people.[16] Yet the term "*plebiscite*" is quite ambivalent, since many authors and sources attribute different meanings to it. These may be divided into three groups. In the first group, the term "*plebiscite*" is used for the authoritarian referendums or the referendums held by populist leaders. In Uleri's words, "Plebiscite could...denote any kind of popular vote...where there is no real possibility to compete in a free and fair way."[17] Zoller defined the plebiscite as a degenerate type of referendum.[18] In a similar train of thought, Gözler asks four questions to discern the "*plebiscite*" from a (genuinely democratic) "referendum": 1. What is voted on: "a name" of a political leader or "a text" of a piece of legislation or constitutional amendment? 2. Is there any kind of oppression? 3. Is there a free and fair environment for debate? 4. Are the masses entranced?[19] Qvortrup, Morris and Kobori discern two sort of plebiscites "legitimizing referendums" (legitimizing plebiscites) and "repressive referendums". The term

14 M Qvortrup, *Referendums and Ethnic Conflict* (University of Pennsylvania Press 2014) 99-101.

15 L Morel, Referendum. in M Rosenfeld and A Sajo (eds), *The Oxford Handbook of Comparative Constitutional Law* (Oxford University Press 2012) 502.

16 A Berger, *Encyclopedic Dictionary of Roman Law* (Law Exchange 2004) 63; R K Barnhart (eds), *The Barnhart Concise Dictionary of Etymology* (Harpercollins 1995) 576; A Ernout Alfred and A Meille, *Dictionnaire étymologique de la langue latine* (Klincksieck 1967) 514; L Morel, Referendum. in M Rosenfeld and A Sajo (eds), *The Oxford Handbook of Comparative Constitutional Law* (Oxford University Press 2012) 502.

17 P V Uleri, Italy: referendums and initiatives from the origin to the crisis of a democratic regime. in M Gallagher and P V Uleri (eds), *The Referendum Experience in Europe* (Macmillan Press Ltd 1996) 4.

18 E Zoller, *Droit Constiutionnel* (PUF 1999) 365.

19 K Gözler, 'Referandum mu Plebisit mi?' (Online) (Accessed 29 November 2019) http://www.anayasa.gen.tr/plebisit.pdf, 7-14.

"legitimizing referendums" denotes the votes held by authoritarian regimes, as "a crude means of acquiring legitimacy". The term "repressive referendums", on the other hand, is used for the votes held in a "more totalitarian system" as a "sophisticated means of repression".[20]

For some authors, "*plebiscite*" is used for the referendums initiated by the governments on an *ad hoc* basis (lacking a prior legal base), which may, mostly because of the preceding political events and the ballot question, turn into a vote of confidence. According to this conception, such referendums are not necessarily undemocratic but the personalization of what is voted in the ballot is still an issue. This leads us to conclude that the term "plebiscite" may always have "a slightly negative connotation".[21]

Indeed, the majority of the literature use the term to denote the abuse of the voting processes and/or manipulating the democratic tenets in the referendums. In certain cases, such an abuse seems to appear as the most flagrant such as the votes held during the Napoleonic France, Nazi Germany or Mussolini in Italy. These historical experiences were marked with the lack of even the minimum requirement of a democratic vote: mass intimidation of the voters, lack of a democratic campaign and infringement of secrecy of the vote. In other cases, however, the votes and campaign take place in a relatively democratic and free atmosphere, but still, the promoter of the referendum (a political leader, mostly the head of the executive) tries to manipulate the whole process by using his/her political popularity and turning the referendum into a vote of confidence to himself/herself and his/her political activities. Dezso's account is useful here, which distinguishes between democratic and undemocratic "*plebiscites*". While the referendums that were initiated by Napoleon in France, Hitler in Germany and Mussolini in Italy belong to the former, the referendums that took place in France during the Presidency of De Gaulle belong to the latter.[22]

A second group includes the authors that use the term *plebiscite* as an equivalent or synonym of referendum without any implication of difference.[23] Thirdly, the term *plebiscite* is used in a completely different context, denoting the referendums held according to international law, to decide on the border disputes or international status of certain territories.[24]

20 M Qvortrup Matt and C Morris and M Kobori, Australasia. in M Qvortrup (ed), *Referendums Around the World* (Palgrave Macmillan 2008) 240-242.

21 M Suksi, *Bringing in the People* (Kluwer 1993) 11.

22 M Dezso, Plebiscites and Referendums. in A Auer and M Bützer (eds), *Direct Democracy: The Eastern and Central European Experience* (Ashgate 2001) 265.

23 V Bogdanor, Referendums and Separatism: II. in A Ranney (ed), *The Referendum Device* (American Enterprise Institute for Public Policy Research 1981) 143.

24 Y Beigbeder, *International monitoring of plebiscites, referenda and national elections: self-determination and transition to democracy* (Brill Nijhoff 1994); S Wambaugh, *Plebiscites Since the World War: With a Collection of Official Documents* (Carnegie Endowment for International Peace 1933).

In the face of ambiguity and polysemy of the term *plebiscite*,[25] it is preferable to use a more descriptive and unequivocal term to denote the referendums that deviate from or contravene good and democratic practices. Therefore, for the purpose of this essay and for further possible research, the term "authoritarian referendum" appears to be more useful.

3.2 A short history of authoritarian referendums

Initial examples of authoritarian referendums may be found during Napoleonic France in the beginning of the 19th Century. Four referendums took place during this period in 1800, 1802, 1804 and 1815.[26] The first two referendums paved the way for Napoleon's life-long rule of France. The first referendum introduced the consulate (a strong executive) and the second one allowed Napoleon to be consul for life. With the help of the third referendum in 1804, Napoleon ultimately seized uncontrolled political power as emperor, thus establishing the Empire. Napoleon's nephew, Louis Napoleon also followed his path by submitting his post-*coup d'état* constitution to the vote. With the same referendum, he was also elected president for 10 years. Finally, the referendum of 1852 established the second Empire and elected Louis Napoleon as an emperor.[27]

The common view about these referendums is that they were farcical votes that legitimized the post-*coup d'état* authoritarian policies of Napoleon(s) and were far from being genuine democratic choice of the people. Commenting on the referendums held in 1800 and onwards, Crook assumes that the effect of these referendums "on the exercise of political power was minimal."[28] Also, the voting procedure itself contravened the secrecy of the vote, where the voters were invited to sign the registers in the official buildings. All the referendums resulted in almost hundred percent turnout and approval rate, a dubious and absurd demonstration of national unity. Indeed, in the absence of a genuine and impartial control of the referendum process, the Napoleon regime could unduly inflate the turnout and voting figures to its advantage. These figures should not be "taken at face value"; in reality they were as low as 50%.[29] This Napoleonic use of referendum is the main reason of widespread skepticism of French doctrine and political thought regarding

25 A X Trechesel and F Esposito, Why Plebiscite? A Critique of a Nebulous Concept. in A Auer and M Bützer (eds) *Direct Democracy: The Eastern and Central European Experience* (Ashgate 2001) 272-274.

26 M Crook, The Uses of Democracy. Elections and Plebiscites in Napoleonic France. in M F Cross and D Williams (eds), *The French Experience from Republic to Monarchy, 1792-1824* (Palgrave 2000). Only the first three are of importance and relevant to this section.

27 V Bogdanor, Referendums and Separatism: II. in A Ranney (ed), *The Referendum Device* (American Enterprise Institute for Public Policy Research 1981) 49.

28 M Crook, The Uses of Democracy. Elections and Plebiscites in Napoleonic France. in M F Cross and D Williams (eds), *The French Experience from Republic to Monarchy, 1792-1824* (Palgrave 2000) 58.

29 M Crook, The Uses of Democracy. Elections and Plebiscites in Napoleonic France. in M F Cross and D Williams (eds), *The French Experience from Republic to Monarchy, 1792-1824* (Palgrave 2000) 60.

the referendum device.[30] Moreover, "[t]his use of democracy provided a forerunner for those 'elections without choice' that have characterized authoritarian regimes of both Right and Left in more recent times."[31]

One significant user of such referendums was Hitler. As explained above, referendums in Nazi Germany helped to introduce and strengthen the main components of the National Socialist rule in Germany. Withdrawal from the League of Nations and quitting the disarmament process in 1933, merging the posts of president and prime minister under Hitler giving him dictatorial powers, and the annexation of Austria in 1938 were all realized through referendums. One may rightfully assert that, "[t]hese referendums are not "people's vetoes" in the traditional sense of constitutional referendums."[32]

The Nazi regime adopted the "Law on Popular Vote" (*Gesetz über Volksabstimmung*) on 14 July 1933, soon after taking control of political power in Germany. This law claimed to strengthen the direct democracy component of the Weimar constitution, which had already included the referendum. Yet, the abolition of the quorum rule and prohibition of formation of new political parties in the same day as this law, were strong indications for Hitler's use of referendum as a surrogate to parliamentary debates, to legitimize his new authoritarian regime.[33]

The procedures and political environment, in which these referendums were held, were characterized by intimidation and fear including several violations of voting rights, curbing the freedom, equality and secrecy of the vote:

> For example, the "right to vote" was declared a "duty to vote", which is the reason why potential non-voters were visited at home by a *Schleppdienst* and taken to the polling station. And, as at National Socialist fundraising campaigns, small badges were given to those who had already voted, which made identifying those who had not yet done so easier. Furthermore, opponents of the regime could never be sure that the confidentiality of the ballot would be observed, since in some areas ballot papers were marked so that voters could be identified later. Also, in many places, an attempt was made to normalize the practice of not using the polling booth to vote in, the

30 P Ardant, *Institutions Politiques & Droit Constitutionnel* (L.G.D.J. 2005) 148; F Hamon, *Le référendum: étude comparative* (LGDJ 1995) 57; H Roussilon, 'Contre le référendum' [1996] 77 *Pouvoirs* 184-190.

31 M Crook, The Uses of Democracy. Elections and Plebiscites in Napoleonic France. in M F Cross and D Williams (eds), *The French Experience from Republic to Monarchy, 1792-1824* (Palgrave 2000) 60.

32 M Qvortrup, *Referendums and Ethnic Conflict* (University of Pennsylvania Press 2014) 97.

33 M Urban, The Self-Staging of a Plebiscitary Dictatorship: The NS-Regime Between "Uniformed Reichstag, Referendum and Reichsparteitag. in Ralph Jessen and H Richter (eds), *Voting for Hitler and Stalin Elections Under 20th Century Dictatorships* (Campus 2011) 41.

consequence of which was that anyone who insisted on using the polling booth to preserve their anonymity attracted suspicion.[34]

More recent authoritarian uses of referendums can be observed in the Post-Soviet Central Asian States. Soon after the dissolution of the USSR, the presidents of Turkmenistan, Uzbekistan and Kazakhstan resorted to referendums as a way to avoid the regular elections that would put their continued grip on political power at risk. Referendums took place that asked the voters whether they wanted the incumbent president to continue his rule or whether they endorsed his policies. The fact that there was no alternative or opponent in the referendums, as opposed to the elections, was the main reason for holding such referendums. Therefore, it saved the incumbent president from the risk of losing political popularity, if not his charismatic authority. As D Ó Beacháin noted, these referendums served to create and disseminate the view among the public that "the president has, *deus ex machina*, come as a founding father, to guide the nation through the first generation of independent statehood."[35]

This brief historical account shows that authoritarian referendums tend to occur when an authoritarian leader wants to legitimize his rule or his policies. It is used as a way of mass mobilization of the people and, under the guise of national or political unity, as a way of their devotion and obedience to the political leader. Also, such votes take place, by means of the leader's strategic and manipulative timing in initiating the vote, as an "attempt to confer democratic legitimacy, or at least the appearance of it, on a person or party."[36]

4 Standards of Democratic Referendums

This section argues that there are emerging standards for democratic referendums on international level and among democratic states. There may be three interrelated components for the standards of a democratic referendum: 1. International standards 2. Lessons from past practices 3. Common features in comparative constitutional law of democratic states that regulate and practice referendums.

International standards are mainly derived from international treaties. Article 25 of the International Covenant on Civil and Political Rights lays down the basic principles

34 M Urban, The Self-Staging of a Plebiscitary Dictatorship: The NS-Regime Between "Uniformed Reichstag, Referendum and Reichsparteitag. in Ralph Jessen and H Richter (eds), *Voting for Hitler and Stalin Elections Under 20th Century Dictatorships* (Campus 2011) 41.

35 D Ó Beacháin, Faking It: Neo-Soviet Electoral Politics in Central Asia. in R Jessen and H Richter (eds), *Voting for Hitler and Stalin Elections Under 20th Century Dictatorships* (Campus 2011) 218. Also, see: S White and R J Hill, Russia, the Former Soviet Union and Eastern Europe. in M Qvortrup (ed), *Referendums Around the World* (Palgrave Macmillan) 124-134.

36 J W Patzelt, Elections in Modern Dictatorships: Some Analytical Considerations. in R Jessen and H Richter (eds), *Voting for Hitler and Stalin Elections Under 20th Century Dictatorships* (Campus 2011) 135.

regarding elections and referendums, which are freedom, secrecy, equality, and universality. On the European level, an important regulation may be found in the Article 3 of the First Protocol to the European Convention on Human Rights (A3-P1), requiring the contracting states to hold: "free elections at reasonable intervals by secret ballot, under conditions which will ensure the free expression of the opinion of the people in the choice of the legislature." However, extending the scope of this regulation to referendums by interpretation is quite problematic, since the article expressly limits itself to the election of the legislature only. Moreover, the case-law of the European Court of Human Rights (ECtHR) is also consistent in its denial of its competence to rule on referendums through a broad interpretation of A3-P1.[37]

There is one legitimate question here of course: if A3-P1 guarantees the free election of the legislature, would it not *a fortiori* apply to referendums, whose outcomes are likely to affect the constitutional status or existence of the legislature themselves? The ECtHR answers this question in the negative, as may be seen in its most recent decision concerning the independence referendum held in Scotland. In *Moohan and Gillon v. the United Kingdom,* the ECtHR made it clear that it would continue to deny any sort of competence to decide on referendums, notwithstanding the fundamental importance of the ballot question. In fact, the ECtHR admitted that; "at first glance it might appear anomalous for such a referendum to fall outside the sphere of protection provided by Article 3 of Protocol No. 1, while elections concerning the choice of the legislature fall within it." Yet for the Court, exclusion of the referendum from the ambit of the A3-P1 is "consistent with…the wording of the Article – which is more narrowly drafted than Article 25 ICCPR".[38] In short, in terms of the A3-P1, there is no valid legal argument to claim an international obligation for ECHR countries, regarding the legal framework and practice of referendums.

This will lead us to consider the moral obligations that may be observed in the soft-law (non-binding) legal instruments in international law. Despite their non-binding nature, the effect of soft law instruments should not be underestimated, since they take most of their content from the practices of democratic states. "The Code of Good Practice on Referendums", published by the Venice Commission, is the seminal document in this respect and reflects certain widely endorsed principles in the practices of democratic states. An earlier document, yet more specific, is the Guidelines on Constitutional

37 European Court of Human Rights, *Guide on Article 3 of Protocol No. 1 to the European Convention on Human Rights*, 31 August 2017. Relevant case law of the European Court of Human Rights: *Nurminen v Finland* App no 27881/95 (26 February 1997); *Castelli and Others v Italy*, App nos 35790/97 and 38438/97 (Decision of 14 September 1998) 102; *Hilbe v Liechtenstein* ECHR 1999VI App no 31981/96; *Z v Latvia*, App no 14755/03 (26 January 2006); *Niedzwiedz v Poland*, App no 1345/06 (11 March 2008); *McLean and Cole v the United Kingdom*, App nos. 12626/13 and 2522/12 (11 June 2013).

38 ECtHR, *Moohan and Gillon v. the United Kingdom(dec)* Applications nos. 22962/15 and 23345/15, para 41.

Referendums.[39] Similarly, "Referendums in Europe an Analysis of the Legal Rules in European States" by the Venice Commission is another useful document in this regard.[40] A more recent document by the Venice Commission is the "Compilation of Venice Commission Opinions and Reports Concerning Referendums".[41]

The remainder of this section will describe the main contours of democratic referendums as may be sketched from these international sources, as well as, laws and practices of democratic states.

4.1 *Initiation*

As mentioned above, authoritarian referendums take place when an authoritarian leader wishes to legitimize his rule and policies, and as history shows, the main component is the leader's unrestrained control of the whole process. Needless to say, the key notion here is the power to start the referendum, and thus, set and control the relevant political agenda.

For the purpose of this section, referendums may be classified as either "decision promoting" or "decision controlling".[42] The distinction lies in whether the initiator of the referendum and the author of its subject matter (i.e. the legislation/political decision) is the same.[43] I argue at this point that the referendum device should serve as a veto power for the political minorities, rather than as a forum for popular acclamation of decisions taken by political leaders, and for this, democratic constitutions should prefer decision controlling referendums. Therefore, conferring the right to start a referendum to political minorities as a tool to contest the decisions of the majority is preferable.

The same assertions may also be valid for popular initiatives, where a portion of voters propose a piece of legislation and then submit it to referendum. As 'grassrooty' as it seems, the decision-promoting nature of this device gives an uneven opportunity for

---

39 Venice Commission, Guidelines for Constitutional Referendums at National Level: Adopted by the Venice Commission at its 47th Plenary Meeting (Venice, 6-7 July 2001) CDL-INF(2001)010-e.

40 European Commission for Democracy Through Law (Venice Commission) *Code of Good Practice on Referendums* Study No 371/2006, 20 January 2009 CDL-AD(2007)008rev-cor; European Commission for Democracy Through Law (Venice Commission). *An Analysis of the Legal Rules in European States* Study No 287/2004, Council of Europe, Strasbourg, 2 November 2005, CDL-AD (2005)034.

41 European Commission for Democracy Through Law (Venice Commission) *Compilation of Venice Commission Opinions and Reports Concerning Referendums*, 10 March 2017 CDL-PI(2017)001. This document is a "a compilation of extracts taken from opinions and reports/studies adopted by the Venice Commission on issues concerning referendums, (which aims to) to give an overview of the doctrine of the Venice Commission in this field. This compilation is intended to serve as a source of references for drafters of constitutions and of legislation relating to referendums, researchers." (ibid 3).

42 P V Uleri, Italy: referendums and initiatives from the origin to the crisis of a democratic regime. in M Gallagher and P V Uleri (eds), *The Referendum Experience in Europe* (Macmillan Press Ltd 1996) 10-12; M Setala, *Referendums and Democratic Government: Normative Theory and the Analysis of Institutions* (Palgrave Macmillian 1999) 74.

43 L Morel, Referendum. in M Rosenfeld and A Sajo (eds), *The Oxford Handbook of Comparative Constitutional Law* (Oxford University Press 2012) 509.

populist leaders and their followers, whose mobilizing abilities (or better to say "instincts") around certain divisive issues of immigration and state sovereignty, outweigh the political motivation of any other political groups in a society. In Switzerland, for example, where the popular initiative is an important component of the constitutional system, the Swiss People's Party (SVP), a populist radical far right party, has been a very active user of this.[44] As Mazzoleni observed, "without the opportunities offered by Swiss direct democracy, it would be virtually impossible for the SVP to consolidate its radicalization over time."[45] Indeed, political extremism, xenophobia and bigotry found their most fertile grounds in the arena of popular initiatives in Switzerland.

As regards the referendum competence of the head of the executive, as of 2004, a survey on comparative constitutional law shows that none of the consolidated democracies confers the exclusive right to the heads of the executive, to start a referendum.[46] Particularly, Turkey is the only country in Europe, whose constitution confers the President the exclusive competence to initiate a referendum.[47] By "exclusive competence", I mean both the exclusive competence in the procedure of initiating a specific referendum and the absence of other types of referendums in the Constitution to counter balance the president's referendum power. So, in Turkey, the president does not need the counter-signature of the ministers, nor does he need to collaborate, in any other way, with any other political actor in using his competence to initiate a referendum. Also, the Constitution does not include any other sort of referendum (such as a popular veto) to counter-balance the referendum power held by the president.

For up-to-date comparative information, one may refer to the Freedom House ratings. According to the Freedom House ratings of 2018, 88 countries are rated as free, among 195 countries of the World.[48] And a survey of the constitutions of these free

---

44 C Mudde, *Populist Radical Right Parties in Europe* (Cambridge University Press 2007) 152.

45 O Mazzoleni, Staying away from the mainstream: The case of the Swiss People's Party. in T Akkerman and S L de Lange and M Roodujn (eds), *Radical Right-Wing Populist Parties in Western Europe into the Mainstream?* (Routledge 2016) 202.

46 P Lauvaux, *Les grandes démocraties contemporaines* (Presses Universitaires de France 2004) 105.

47 B Kaufmannn and R Büchi and N Braun, *Guide to Direct Democracy in Switzerland and Beyond* (Rub Graf-Lehmann 2007) 236; to compare with the legal provisions for referendums in Western Europe: M Laurence, The Democratic Criticism of Referendums the Majority and True Will of the People. in L Morel and M Qvortrup (eds), *Routledge Handbook to Referendums and Direct Democracy* (Routledge 2018) 21-31. According to Özbudun, the President's competence to submit constitutional amendments to referendum is "in line with the Constitution's general philosophy of strengthening the Presidency as an "impartial arbiter." (E Özbudun, *The Constitutional System of Turkey: 1876 to the Present* (Palgrave Macmillan 2011) 130).

48 https://freedomhouse.org/report/freedom-world-2018-table-country-scores accessed 25 November 2019.

countries reveals that only the Chilean constitution confers the President the exclusive power to initiate an optional referendum on constitutional amendments, if the President disagrees with the 2/3 of the Chilean Congress.[49] Interestingly, this provision is a remnant of the Pinochet constitution of 1980, which had been prepared and approved in conditions almost identical to the 1982 Constitution of Turkey. Indeed, in both Chile and Turkey the constitution was made under the strict control of the army, which had overthrown the civil government by a military *coup d'etat* (Chile in 1973; and Turkey in 1980) Also the both the Pinochet Constitution and Turkish Constitution was approved in a referendum held under the military regimes. The referendum in Chile was held in 1980, whereas the referendum for the approval of the Turkish constitution took place in 1982. One may be tempted to infer that this provision inspired the constitution making process of 1982 in Turkey, which was under the strict control of the leaders of the military regime of the time.[50]

Comparative political studies show that in all cases when the head of the executive has the power to start a referendum, it has produced counter-parliamentary and anti-consensual results. The main problem lies in the fact that initiating a referendum is a legislative power, and conferring such a power to the head of the executive may risk disturbing the checks and balances system by giving the head of the executive a strengthened veto or law-making power.[51]

The danger of the referendum device (with a decision promoting function) to liberal democracy becomes imminent if it appears as an exclusive constitutional privilege of the executive. The only role of the people in such referendums, is to legitimize the decisions of the authoritarian (or at best high-handed) political leaders, and to do so only at the end of the process. In other words, if we discern three consecutive steps of decision-taking – that is: proposal, deliberation, and approval – the people's role is demoted to saying "Yes" or "No" in the final step. In such referendums, since they almost always take place in authoritarian settings, there is also no free discussion environment that could allow articulation of different views. "The easiest measures for dictatorial regimes..." are the

49 Please note that according to Art. 72 of the Constitution of Korea, "The President may submit important policies relating to diplomacy, national defense, unification and other matters relating to the national destiny to a national referendum if he deems it necessary." However, there is a mandatory referendum in a separate provision that regulates the constitutional amendment (Art. 130). See: http://aceproject.org/epic-en/CDCountry?country=KR accessed 17 November 2019.

50 For The military coup of 1980 and ensuing constitution making process until 1982 in Turkey see: Özbudun 15-17; for Chile see: D Nohlen, Chile. in D Nohlen (ed), *Elections in the Americas A Data Handbook VOLUME II South America* (Oxford 2005) 254.

51 M S Shugart and J M Carey, *Presidents and Assemblies: Constitutional Design and Electoral Dynamics* (Cambridge University 1992) 59-152. Also in a similar context, Lijphart (A Lijphart, *Patterns of Democracy: Government Forms and Performance in Thirty-Six Countries* (Yale University Press 1999) 148) says: Governments "only hold referendums when they expect to win"'. For Walker, (M C Walker, *Strategic Use of Referendums: Power, Legitimacy, and Democracy* (Palgrave Macmillan 2003)): "Executives can better position themselves than legislatures along a policy spectrum to win when introducing referendums".

referendums "initiated by the government or by the head of state. These allow for purposeful mass mobilization of the population and give the impression at least of national or political unity."[52]

This may be better understood by comparing the theory and practices of Carl Schmitt's "Führer Democracy" and referendums in Hitler's Germany on the one hand, and Dicey's conception of "people's veto" on the other hand. For Schmitt,[53] "authority comes from above [and] confidence comes from below". He considered the referendums as an alternative way of policy making against the tedious and futile parliamentary processes of debate. Yet lacking completely the democratic element, Schmitt's referendum conception was rather a ritual of publicly praising the Führer (and his decisions), than a genuine and free choice of the people: "the people acclaims a leader [führer], a master with whom the people is identical and 'the people says, in other words, amen' to his proposal". Also, the rubberstamp function of the people's vote on the decisions already taken by the leader was quite evident in his assertions of the people's role in such referendums: "the people…cannot advise, deliberate or discuss. They cannot govern or administer. They furthermore cannot set norms but can only sanction norms by consenting to a draft of norms laid before them. Above all they cannot pose a question but can only answer with a yes and no to a question put before them". These views of Schmitt have served as a direct inspiration for Hitler's referendums in the process of establishing and legitimizing Nazi Germany.[54]

By way of contrast, Dicey's conception of "people's veto" focused on the check-and-balance function of the referendums. Dicey was most concerned that Parliament could make "a fundamental change passing into Law which the mass of the nation (did) not desire". Therefore, he saw a "people's veto" in the referendum, which could prevent parliament from enforcing "any important Act which does not command the sanction of the electors."[55] In short, Dicey clearly preferred the decision controlling referendums.

However, it is important to note that, in practice, referendums in the UK have been used *ad hoc* by political parties to overcome internal conflicts and/or to wash their hands of hard and divisive constitutional questions such as the Devolution and EU

---

52 J W Patzelt, Elections in Modern Dictatorships: Some Analytical Considerations. in R Jessen and H Richter (eds), *Voting for Hitler and Stalin Elections Under 20th Century Dictatorships* (Campus 2011) 135.

53 Unless mentioned otherwise, all quotations and verbatim from Carl Schmitt are derived from: M Qvortrup, *Referendums and Ethnic Conflict* (University of Pennsylvania Press 2014) 7-102.

54 M Qvortrup, Types of Referendums, Provisions and Practice at the National Level Worldwide. in L Morel and M Qvortrup (eds), *Routledge Handbook to Referendums and Direct Democracy* (Routledge 2018) 11.

55 A V Dicey, *Introduction to the Study of the Law of the Constitution* (8th Edition). Available from http://www.constitution.org/cmt/avd/law_con.htm accessed 10 November 2012. In fact, as Qvortrup noted, Dicey supported the referendum from a conservative's point of view: "Concerned about the Liberal government's intention to introduce Home Rule for Ireland without having campaigned for this in a general election, Dicey wanted to introduce a check on the elected government at a time when the House of Lords had lost its position as a veto-player." (M Qvortrup, Types of Referendums, Provisions and Practice at the National Level Worldwide. in L Morel and M Qvortrup (eds), *Routledge Handbook to Referendums and Direct Democracy* (Routledge 2018) 6).

membership; rather than based on a Diceyan normative principle of constitutional entrenchment.[56] As could be dramatically observed during the Brexit referendum, this feature is one of the soft spots of the British referendum regime vis-à-vis populists. When the political leaders escape from deciding on these constitutional issues, the gap is filled by populist discourse. Not only are referendums held on a case-by-case basis, the relevant subject matter, ballot question, campaign process and quorum are decided shortly before by an act of Parliament and a parliamentary majority.

This feature of referendum practice in the UK may lead some to argue that in British practice, the initiator of the referendum and the author of the relevant legislation is the same agent – i.e. the parliamentary majority; and in line with the principle of parliamentary sovereignty, the parliament is the final decision organ concerning the initiation and the result of these referendums. So, if this view is taken at face value, the British use of referendums comes closer to the Schmittian conception than to Diceyan one, at least in the sense that the author of a decision and the initiator of referendum for it is the same. (i.e. decision promoting referendum). Yet, this argument may be easily refuted by a relatively new, but increasingly dominant view in the British doctrine, asserting that the referendum has become a part of the British unwritten constitution as a constitutional convention. Bogdanor argues that "the referendum has become in part an instrument of entrenchment since it prevents the power of Parliament from being transferred without the approval of the people."[57] There are two implications of this: 1. parliament cannot overrule the results of a referendum by evoking its non-binding character and 2. parliament cannot escape a referendum when deciding on important constitutional issues such as Northern Ireland, the devolved status of territories, EU membership and the ECHR.

After all, the case of the UK is unique due to the particularity of the uncodified nature of its constitution.[58] By looking at the rest of the democratic world having codified constitutions, we may unequivocally demonstrate that exclusive competence of the head of the executive or government[59] to start a referendum is virtually non-existent.

56 See on this: S Tierney, 'We the Peoples': Constituent Power and Constitutionalism in Plurinational States in The Paradox of Constitutionalism. in M Loughlin and N Walker (eds), *Constituent Power and Constituent Form* (Oxford University Press 2007) 198.

57 V Bogdanor, Conclusion. in V Bogdanor (ed), *The British Constitution in the Twentieth Century* (Oxford University Press 2003) 697.

58 G Martinico, 'Preserving Constitutional Democracy from Populism - The Case of Secession Referendums' [2019] 39(2) *National Journal of Constitutional Law* 152.

59 Either in the form of the president or as the parliamentary majority in the parliamentary systems.

4.2 Campaign

In most cases, referendum campaigns include two different components, that is, voter education and propaganda. Voter education is all about giving necessary information to the voters about the legal nature of the text subject to referendum, so that they can understand the ramifications of their preference for either "Yes" or "No". Propaganda, on the other hand, involves persuasion of the voters to vote for, or against, the proposal in the referendum. This double aspect of referendum campaigns is the fundamental difference from the campaigns of parliamentary or presidential elections where the candidates are identified through their party affiliations.[60]

In referendums, on the contrary, voters do not have any cognitive cues or shortcuts to understand the issue in question.[61] Thus, there are two challenges for a referendum administration in terms of the referendum campaign: 1) ensuring an effective and accurate voter education, and 2) securing a democratic atmosphere for fair and equal representation of the opposing views.

In a democratic system of referendums, explanatory notes, both printed and online, are indispensable elements of voter education. Such notes should include: the plain text of the proposed amendment, its concise and compact explanation and the possible change on constitutional system, and a list of the main arguments of pros and cons in an objective manner. They may be found in the practices of American States and Switzerland, where the referendums constitute a central element of policy making.[62]

The objectivity of these notes may be secured either through supervision by an impartial body (mostly the judiciary), or through direct involvement of such a body in the preparation. For example, in Latvia, Portugal and Poland, national electoral commissions are obliged to provide impartial information to the voters. Also in France, the Constitutional Council oversees the impartiality and accuracy of information conveyed during referendum campaigns.[63]

---

60 F Hamon, *Le référendum: étude comparative* (LGDJ 1995) 34-37.

61 A T Jennsen and O Listhaug, Voters' Decisions in the Nordic EU Referendums. in M Mendelsohn and A Parking (eds), *Referendum Democracy: Citizens, Elites and Deliberation in Referendum Campaigns* (Palgrave 2001) 174.

62 For the American states, T E Cronin, *Direct Democracy: The Politics of Initiative Referendum and Recall* (Harvard University Press 1999) 238; particularly in California and Oregon, the government or an impartial electoral authority is entitled to provide neutral information to the voters, to be found in pamphlets or brochures (International Institute for Democracy and Electoral Assistance (2008) 157); for Switzerland see the official website of Swiss Government, particularly https://www.bk.admin.ch/bk/fr/home/documentation/Abstimmungsbuechlein_Design.html accessed 15 September 2018.

63 European Commission for Democracy Through Law (Venice Commission) *Referendums in Europe – An Analysis of the Legal Rules in European States* Study No 287/2004, Council of Europe, Strasbourg, 2 November 2005, CDL-AD (2005)034, para 86-87.

4.3 *Judicial review*

Effective judicial review is a fundamental condition for a credible and democratic referendum. "The appeal body in referendum matters should be either an electoral commission or a court. In any case, final appeal to a court must be possible."[64] As opposed to elections, judicial review of referendums involves material aspects in addition to formal aspects.

The formal issues (or formal validity) may also be divided into matters related to the administration of the vote (electoral procedure) and other procedural aspects specific to referendums, such as the initiation of the referendum, the clarity of the ballot question and the single subject rule. Material aspects include the legal nature of the text put to the vote, in particular its conformity with higher law, such as the constitution or international obligations. Additionally, in more general terms, the question of review of referendums both in formal and material aspects, concerns the judicial review of the constitutionality of laws.[65] Thus, we may consider judicial review of referendums as an element of the broader topic of judicial review of constitutionality; and, as in every consolidated constitutional democracy, referendums should be reviewed by the highest court in the legal system, equivalent to a constitutional court.

For this reason, and as comparative studies on referendums show, judicial review of referendums is generally conducted by constitutional courts or their counterparts in different legal systems. "The study of comparative law (of democratic systems) reveals a clear tendency of attributing the control of the referendum process to the constitutional courts."[66]

Examples are abundant and cover a range of countries from more to less frequent users of referendums. In American States (such as California, Oregon, Washington, Colorado and Arizona), state supreme courts are competent to fulfill judicial review both on material and formal disputes, and they are very vigilant regarding their mission. Roughly, half of the laws approved in referendums are invalidated by the state supreme courts. In Italy, the administration of the vote is reviewed by *Ufficio centrale per*

64 European Commission for Democracy Through Law (Venice Commission). *Code of Good Practice on Referendums* Study No 371/2006, 20 January 2009, CDL-AD(2007)008rev-cor, 10.

65 L Morel, Referendum. in M Rosenfeld and A Sajo (eds), The Oxford Handbook of Comparative Constitutional Law (Oxford University Press 2012) 522; *cf.* Venice Commission: "Judicial review in the field of referendum applies first a priori and addresses the decision to submit a matter to referendum. It may also take place during the procedure, and address procedure itself or the voting rights and, after the vote, the validity of results. Finally, a posteriori control of the text adopted by referendum is conceivable." European Commission for Democracy Through Law (Venice Commission). *Referendums in Europe – An Analysis of the Legal Rules in European States* Study No 287/2004, Council of Europe, Strasbourg, 2 November 2005, CDL-AD (2005)034, para 146.

66 M Fatin-Rouge Stefanini, *Le controle du référendum par la justice constitutionnelle* (Economica 2004) 145; *but cf.* European Commission for Democracy Through Law (Venice Commission) *Referendums in Europe – An Analysis of the Legal Rules in European States* Study No 287/2004, Council of Europe, Strasbourg, 2 November 2005, CDL-AD (2005)034, para 150.

il referendum, which is a department of the high administrative court. On the other hand, the Constitutional Court of Italy reviews the clarity and the unity of ballot question, as well as material issues such as the conformity of the referendum question to international obligations.[67]

According to the French Constitution, "The Constitutional Council shall ensure the proper conduct of referendum proceedings and shall proclaim the results of the referendum." (Article 60). As to the material dimension, Article 61 says: The legislative proposals "mentioned in article 11 before they are submitted to referendum [...] shall be referred to the Constitutional Council, which shall rule on their conformity with the Constitution". It is interesting to note that Article 61 provides for *a priori* control of constitutionality only for the parliamentary bills, leaving the governmental bills unregulated. However, in practice, this is unlikely to create a difference, since the Constitutional Council, in its *Hauchemaille*[68] decision, had already found itself competent to review certain pre-referendum actions, including the decision of the President to start a referendum. A similar provision may be found in the Constitution of Romania (Constitution of Romania, Article 144/g). In Austria, the Constitutional Court is entitled to decide on any objections to the results of referendum and the public initiatives (Constitution of Austria, Article 141/3). In the same way, the Croatian Constitutional Court oversees the constitutional and legal compliance of national referendums with the Constitution (Constitution of Croatia, Article 128). The validity of constitutional amendment referendums in Poland is declared by the Supreme Court (Constitution of Poland, Article 125/4 and 235/6).

4.4 The ballot question

The formation of the ballot question is another issue specific to referendums. The main difference between referendums and elections in the proper sense is that the voters vote for a political decision in the former, whereas they vote for political parties or political leaders in the latter. In a referendum, the voters face a question they are supposed to answer with "Yes" or "No". The problem related to such a question may entail two issues. First, the wording of the question should be clearly understandable to the voters. This may be termed as the "clarity of the question". According to the Venice Commission:

67 L Morel, Referendum. in M Rosenfeld and A Sajo (eds), *The Oxford Handbook of Comparative Constitutional Law* (Oxford University Press 2012) 522.

68 Décision n° 2000-21 REF du 25 juillet 2000. Available from: http://www.conseil-constitutionnel.fr/conseil-constitutionnel/francais/les-decisions/acces-par-date/decisions-depuis-1959/2000/2000-21-ref/decision-n-2000-21-ref-du-25-juillet-2000.105924.html accessed 15 August 2013.

> The clarity of the question is a crucial aspect of voters' freedom to form an opinion. The question must not be misleading; it must not suggest an answer, particularly by mentioning the presumed consequences of approving or rejecting the proposal; voters must be able to answer the questions asked solely by yes, no or a blank vote; and it must not ask an open question necessitating a more detailed answer.[69]

"Secondly, the voters should not be forced to vote for more than one option, which are disparately included in a single question. This is the rule of unity of content (or "single subject rule" as called in the United States)".[70] "...[There] must be an intrinsic connection between the various parts of each question put to the vote, in order to guarantee the free suffrage of the voter, who must not be called to accept or refuse as a whole provision without an intrinsic link."[71]

Both the clarity of the question and the single subject rule are very important for referendums, particularly for those whose subject matter is of constitutional importance. In such cases, the main assumption, according to political observers, is that the phraseology of the ballot question may have an important effect on the outcome of the vote. More particularly, the political leaders who are active during the process of the referendum might shape the wording of the question to be somewhat ambiguous/polyvalent or even incomprehensible; in order to manipulate voters.[72]

The problem of the clarity of the question is a complex one and requires a case-by-case approach. One common theme is that the clarity of the question is a necessary pillar in ascertaining the democratic will of the people, but there is no one-size-fits-all legal solution to secure this clarity. As one seminal example, we may be reminded of the secession reference of the Supreme Court of Canada. The Supreme Court, while giving its reference decision on the secession process of Quebec from Canada, opined that "[t]he referendum result, if it is to be taken as an expression of the democratic will, must be free of ambiguity both in terms of the question asked and in terms of the support it achieves... However, it will be for political actors to determine what constitutes 'a clear majority on a clear question' in the circumstances under which a future referendum vote may be taken".[73]

Another issue to be tackled under this section arises where referendums have a short and clear wording but have complex and interrelated issues in their background and in their legal ramifications. As Rocher and Lecours put it:

---

69 European Commission for Democracy Through Law. (Venice Commission). *Code of Good Practice on Referendums* Study No 371/2006, 20 January 2009 CDL-AD(2007)008rev-cor 17.

70 I G Şen, Sovereignty Referendums in International and Constitutional Law (Springer 2015) 256.

71 European Commission for Democracy Through Law. (Venice Commission). *Code of Good Practice on Referendums* Study No 371/2006, 20 January 2009. CDL-AD(2007)008rev-cor 17.

72 Rocher and Lecours, (2018) 227.

73 Reference re Secession of Quebec, [1998] 2 SCR 217.

> Intuitively, one could easily agree, on the surface, that a good question should be (1) simple, (2) short, (3) intelligible, and (4) neutral. However, a question that meets these four criteria may not guarantee a lack of ambiguity. For example, a voter asked to vote on a straightforward question on independence could question the meaning of that term. The terms of the secession may have been discussed in a government document, which would help to give particular meaning to the notion of independence.[74]

Indeed, referendums whose ballot questions are of constitutional importance, such as secession of a territory from a sovereign state,[75] or withdrawal from an international organization (*Brexit* 2016) are quite problematic. These referendums have short and clear questions in the wording; yet, the same is not true for their legal results. Indeed, it is easy to assume that the question "*Should the United Kingdom remain a member of the European Union or leave the European Union?*" failed to provide true and complete information about many important questions regarding the future relations between the UK and the EU, such as the withdrawal procedure and timing, the future status of the free movement of persons, services and goods and/or any other sort of post-withdrawal problems between the UK and the EU. Overall, the question in the Brexit referendum was fairly silent about complex and mass ramifications of Brexit, in both international law and UK constitutional law. Here, the problem is not about the ballot question per se; but rather about the subject matter of the referendum. Referendums on the subject matter of independence, adhesion to a supra-national community, or withdrawal from such a community could be called "sovereignty referendums"[76]; and all sovereignty referendums, by their legal nature, are about a political community's move from one legal/constitutional order to another. Therefore, such referendums may have several legal results which are interrelated. For this reason, the above-mentioned assumptions about the clarity of the question and the single subject rule might meet their limits in the structure and legal nature of the subject matters of such sovereignty referendums.

---

74 F Rocher and A Lecours, The correct expression of popular will: does the wording of a referendum question matter? in L Morel and M Qvortrup (eds), *Routledge Handbook to Referendums and Direct Democracy* (2018) 228.

75 As was the case in the two Quebec referendums held in 1980 and 1995 and in the referendum of Scotland in 2014. These referendums are commonly called "independence referendums". See I G Şen, *Sovereignty Referendums in International and Constitutional Law* (Springer 2015) 66.

76 I G Şen, *Sovereignty Referendums in International and Constitutional Law* (Springer 2015) 10.

To overcome this conundrum, these referendums could be designed to have the effect of initiating a procedure only, enabling and obliging state authorities to start a procedure or to prepare a draft of the document that will put the subject matter in legal effect; this document could subsequently be put to a second referendum to ensure the legitimacy of the final decision.[77]

4.5 Qualified majority (quorum)

There may be two sorts of qualified majority of the voters in a referendum. First is the "quorum of participation" (minimum turnout), which requires a certain portion of the registered voters to participate in the referendum. Second is the "quorum of approval" which denotes the "Yes" votes given by a qualified percentage of the voters (such as 55%, 60 % and so on), rather than by a simple majority.[78] Also, it is possible to apply either one or both of these quorums in a referendum.

The main question here is whether it is legitimate and/or desirable to stipulate a qualified majority as a condition for approval in a referendum. This question involves a conciliation of two counter-arguments; both of which are fairly convincing. According to the first, the quorum may impair the democratic stability – since it enables a minority of the voters to block a decision which is supported by the majority, and the abstainers will be deemed to have voted "No". According to the second argument, on the contrary, when there is no quorum, the abstainers will be assimilated with the "Yes"-voters. Therefore, the ephemeral majorities may make fundamental changes to the constitution and this goes against the pluralistic view of constitutionalism, which sees the genuine social contract in the most possible inclusion of different viewpoints in the constitution-making (or changing) process. "This difficulty with the quorum results in the fact that it is not a universal value imposed on states for the democratic soundness of referendums. If a qualified majority of approval is to be considered, a fair balance between the concerns for securing the maximum consent and practicability should be observed."[79]

---

77 Such a referendum framework may be deemed as legitimate by an analogy to the procedure of total revision of the constitution according to the Swiss Constitution. According to the article 140/2 (in conjunction with the article 193/2) of the Swiss Constitution, a preliminary vote/vote of principle(votation préalable/vote de principe) must be held; if the proposal for a total revision of the constitution comes from a popular initiative, or there is a disagreement between the Councils of the Swiss parliament; in order to decide whether a total revision of the constitution should be carried out. (A Auer and G Malinverni and M Hottelier, *Droit constitutionnel suisse. Vol. I*: L'Etat (Stämpfli 2000) 188).

78 European Commission for Democracy Through Law (Venice Commission) *Referendums in Europe – An Analysis of the Legal Rules in European States* Study No 287/2004, Council of Europe, Strasbourg, 2 November 2005, CDL-AD (2005)034, para 110.

79 I G Şen, *Sovereignty Referendums in International and Constitutional Law* (Springer 2015) 232-236.

Here are some democratic countries whose constitutions require a quorum in referendums, either in the form of turnout or approval: In Bulgaria, Croatia, Italy and Malta, Lithuania at least a majority of the total registered voters should participate in the referendum. In Latvia, there should be a turnout of half of the voters who participated in the last election of Parliament and in Azerbaijan, it is 25% of the registered voters. In Poland and Portugal, if the turnout percentage does not reach the threshold of 50%, the referendum is considered as non-binding. In Lithuania, the amendment of the 1st Article of the Constitution concerning the nature of the State as an independent democratic republic must secure a vote of 75% of the electorate (Constitution of Lithuania, Art. 148.1) In *Denmark*, a constitutional amendment must be approved by 40% of registered voters in addition to a majority of the votes cast (Constitution of Denmark, Article 88). In referendums on bills of statutory level, the text put to the vote is deemed rejected if the majority of voters taking part in the referendum and at least 30% of the registered voters vote against the bill (Constitution of Denmark, Article 42 (5)).[80]

These data may be taken as examples for the advising of the requirement of quorum in the referendums. Moreover, one tends to endorse the quorum requirement when the referendums are about constitutional amendments. For example, commenting on the independence referendum in Montenegro (2006) the Venice Commission said: "regarding international practice, a minimum turnout of 50 % of the registered voters seems appropriate for a referendum on the change of state status."[81] This assertion may be easily endorsed for other constitutional changes, particularly changes on the democratic nature of a constitution, which may be considered in terms of the (internal) "sovereignty" component of a state.[82] Moreover, from a point of constitutional law, since rigid constitutions require an enhanced majority in the parliament for their amendment, a requirement for a similar enhanced majority during the referendum in amendment process may be considered legitimate.

5 CONCLUSION

As mentioned above, populism and authoritarianism are two different concepts; yet they display many common features in their methods and forms. Bearing in mind the perils of

80 European Commission for Democracy Through Law (Venice Commission) *Referendums in Europe – An Analysis of the Legal Rules in European States* Study No 287/2004, Council of Europe, Strasbourg, 2 November 2005, CDL-AD (2005)034, para 112-113.

81 European Commission for Democracy Through Law. (Venice Commission) *Opinion on the Compatibility of the Existing Legislation in Montenegro Concerning the Organization of Referendums With Applicable International Standards.* Opinion No 343/2005, Council of Europe, Strasbourg, 19 December 2005, para 26.

82 I refer to the concept of "statehood" and right to self-determination in international law at this point. According to Article I of the Montevideo Convention on the Rights and duties of States, the State as a person of international law should possess the following qualifications: (1) a permanent population; (2) a defined territory; (3) an effective government (sovereignty).

oversimplification of the complex problem of contemporary challenges to democratic constitutionalism, one may assume that the distortion (or manipulation, or degeneration) of normative tenets such as "popular will" and "consent of the governed" is the pivotal element in both contemporary populist and authoritarian politics. So, if we recall the fact that the "authoritarian referendum" is a degenerate form of democratic processes, it may be quite easy to conclude that the populist political actors will try to make the most of it. However, this is an intuitive conclusion and one may rightfully challenge this by referring to the aggregate description and analysis of the referendum experience around the world: "Much as there has been talk about populism and a move away from constitutional government, the use of referendums has not generally been part of this trend.".[83]

Even if this assumption may be statistically true, the historical and contemporary experiences seen from a qualitative point of view, still raise a red flag whenever a populist leader uses the referendum. "Populist policies are often connected in a package referendum leading to a stronger executive.... so most of these referendums are presidential plebiscites, where the head of the executive controls the electorate and expect certain results."[84] Therefore, without the necessary constitutional guards for a democratic referendum, there is always the danger of sliding to authoritarianism in a populist political setting and/or at the hands of a populist political leader.

So, what may be these constitutional guards? Having described historical experiences of authoritarian referendums and the regulation of referendums in comparative constitutional law of democratic states; we may come to a conclusion for the necessary components of a constitutional framework for a democratic referendum regime.

Most notably, the initiator of the referendum and the author of its subject matter – either in the form of a piece of legislation, or a constitutional amendment, or a policy orientation – should not be identical. Maybe the most common reason of the populist/ authoritarian manipulation of the referendums is its decision-promoting nature. The referendum should be a veto tool for political minorities against legislation or policy change. More importantly, drafters of the constitutions should be prudent when conferring the right to start a referendum on the head of the executive, and exclusive competence in that respect should be avoided at all cost. If the referendum becomes a minority veto tool, even if a political party has the necessary majority that may secure the passing of a piece of legislation or a policy change in the parliament, their promoter will have to compromise with all levels of society, particularly with the main opposition party, to avoid the referendum.

---

83 M Qvortrup, Two Hundred Years of Referendums. in M Qvortrup (ed), *Referendums Around the World* (Palgrave Macmillan 2018) 271, commenting on the referendums held in democratic countries between 1900-2010.

84 N Kersting, Africa. in M Qvortrup (ed), *Referendums Around the World* (Palgrave Macmillan 2018 220-221) commenting on the African referendum practice from the 1960's up until today.

Another important lesson to be drawn from authoritarian and/or populist use of referendums concerns judicial review. In this context, constitutions should expressly authorize constitutional courts (or equivalent highest judicial organs) to oversee the procedural aspects of voting, as well as other referendum-specific issues, including the clarity of the ballot question and the unity of content. Also, in this context, constitutions should require the ballot questions to be free of ambiguity and to conform to the rule of unity of content.

Also, there is the issue of a fair referendum campaign, and this cannot be secured by using general electoral regulations, which fall far short of the specific requirements for referendums. The legal framework of campaigning must meet the specific needs of the referendums. In this vein, firstly, there should be an impartial, non-governmental body responsible for voter education. Secondly, the legal framework for propaganda should allow all political organizations to organize themselves into two opposing camps of "Yes" and "No", as in the case of the model of umbrella organizations.

Finally, for a more inclusive way of decision taking, and rather more convincingly for the questions of constitutional importance, a qualified majority may help overcome the stark majoritarian nature of the referendum device.

Part II: Country Reports

Austria – Protecting the Liberal Constitution

*Maria Bertel**

1 Introduction

Populist trends in politics are not a new topic for Austria. In fact, the current Freedom Party (FPÖ) which was founded in 1956 as "Verband der Unabhängigen" can be considered a populist party.[1] Their participation in the last government (2017-2019)[2] at the national level, led to discussions on how to deal with populist parties once again.[3]

It is against this background that I will lay down the constitutional safeguards for liberal constitutionalism in Austria. The core question of the chapter is to discover how robust the constitution is against illiberal tendencies. In order to do so, I will first focus on some basic definitions (section 2.1), history (section 2.2) and the constitutional and legal situation (sections 2.3, 2.4). Based on this, I will discuss the robustness of the Constitution (3). I will then show some practical experiences, a case study (section 4) and more recent trends (section 5), that will illustrate that the dangers for the liberal core of the Austrian Constitution are changing. I will close the chapter with an outlook (section 6).

---

* Dr. Maria Bertel is the Elise-Richter-Fellow (Austrian Science Fund) at the University of Innsbruck, Department of Public Law, State and Administrative Theory.
The research for this contribution was financed by Central European University Foundation, Budapest (CEUBPF). The theses explained herein represent the ideas of the author and do not necessarily reflect the opinion of CEUBPF.

1 See e.g. A Pelinka, 'Die FPÖ im internationalen Vergleich. Zwischen Rechtspopulismus, Deutschnationalismus und Österreich-Patriotismus' [2002] 1(1) *conflict & communication online* 12 *et seq*; H Bergsdorf, 'Rhetorik des Populismus am Beispiel rechtsextremer und rechtspopulistischer Parteien wie der „Republikaner", der FPÖ und des „Front National"' [2000] 31(3) *Zeitschrift für Parlamentsfragen* 620 *et seq*.

2 See e.g. Die Zeit, 15th December 2017, 'ÖVP und FPÖ einigen sich auf Regierungsbildung' Die Zeit (15 December 2017) https://www.zeit.de/politik/ausland/2017-12/oesterreich-oevp-fpoe-regierung-koalition accessed 2 January 2020.

3 F-S Gady, 'Has Austria Found the Answer to Right-Wing Populism?' *Foreign Affairs* (11 September 2018) https://www.foreignaffairs.com/articles/austria/2018-09-11/has-austria-found-answer-right-wing-populism accessed 2 January 2020.

2 Constitutional Safeguards for Liberal Constitutionalism in Austria

2.1 *Definitions*

The chapter is linked to buzzwords such as populism, democratic backsliding, and illiberalism. Since these terms are vague, it is useful to provide them with more specific definitions within the legal and constitutional implications of populist movements and parties in Austria. In this regard, I am relying on the findings of Nadia Urbinati and Jan-Werner Müller. According to Urbinati:

> A populist movement that succeeds in leading the government of a democratic society tend to move toward institutional forms and a political reorganization of the state that change, and even shatter constitutional democracy, like centralization of power, weakening of checks and balances, disregard of political oppositions, and the transformation of election in a plebiscite of the leader.[4]

From a constitutionalist perspective, the danger of populism lies in the possible reorganization of the state, which can consist of lowering the standards regarding the rule of law and democratic backsliding.[5] Following such a definition, "populism is […] illiberal".[6] As already mentioned above, the core question of the chapter is to what extent the Austrian Constitution is suited to prevent such an illiberal reorganization.

2.2 *Short history*

In order to examine the level of protection of the liberal content of a constitution in a particular country, we first have to find out whether it is a liberal constitution. This question specifically arises because the Austrian Constitution is comparatively old and has survived historically illiberal times, such as the period of so-called Austrofascism[7] and the Nazi occupation of Austria.[8] In order to answer this question, I will first try to show

4 N Urbinati, 'The Populist Phenomenon' (2013) 51 (3) *Raisons politiques* 137.

5 See H Aziz and T Ginsburg, 'How to Lose a Constitutional Democracy' (2018) 65 UCLA *Law Review* 78 *et seq.*

6 J-W Mueller, 'Getting a Grip on Populism' (23rd September 2011) https://www.dissentmagazine.org/blog/getting-a-grip-on-populism accessed 2 January 2020.

7 J Thorpe, 'Austrofascism: Revisiting the 'Authoritarian State' 40 Years On' [2010] 45(2) *Journal of Contemporary History* 315.

8 T Öhlinger and H Eberhard, *Verfassungsrecht* (12th edn, 2019) 46; T Kirk, 'Austrian fascisms, 'Austrofascism' and the working class' in Tim Kirk (ed), *Nazism and the working class in Austria: Industrial unrest and political dissent in the "national community"* (Cambridge University Press 1996).

the liberal content of the Austrian Constitution against the background of history. In my understanding, a liberal constitution is a constitution that seeks to safeguard the liberty of individuals. The liberal content of a constitution, therefore, focusses on human rights and the rule of law.[9]

The Austrian Constitution was inspired by the Constitutions preceding it, especially the so-called December Constitution of 1867.[10] It consisted of five basic laws (*Staatsgrundgesetze*) and can be considered a typical constitution of a constitutional monarchy.[11] The December Constitution in its entirety was in force until the end of the monarchy, and most importantly, parts of it contained individual guarantees of rights that are in force until the present day. Yet, the (present) Austrian Constitution differs from it and its predecessors, especially with regard to at least some of its contents, e.g. the republican form of state and electoral laws.

In the aftermath of the collapse of the monarchy and as a nation defeated in World War I,[12] the Austrian political system changed radically, and a new constitution was developed.

On the 1st of October 1920 the Austrian Federal Constitution, which cannot be thought without mentioning the name of Hans Kelsen, was enacted.[13] Chancellor Karl Renner had asked Kelsen to provide him with a draft constitution, which was then discussed (first within the parties and then in parliament)[14] and, as mentioned, enacted in 1920. This makes Austria's Constitution one of the oldest in Europe.[15]

The constitution-making process was very difficult, due to the different ideological orientation of the parties involved. It does therefore not come as a surprise that in 1920 the parties could not agree on all the topics pending.[16] The Constitutional Document of 1920 did not contain a bill of rights.[17] Yet, from its beginning, the Constitution foresaw

9 On liberalism, see: G Gaus and SD Courtland and D Schmidtz, 'Liberalism' (The Stanford Encyclopedia of Philosophy, Spring 2018) https://plato.stanford.edu/archives/spr2018/entries/liberalism accessed 2 January 2020.

10 W Berka, *Verfassungsrecht: Grundzüge des österreichischen Verfassungsrechts für das juristische Studium* (7th edn, Verlag Österreich 2018) 406.

11 ibid 8-9.

12 For an overview on the consequences of WW I, see: 'Diese Folgen hatte der Erste Weltkrieg' *Süddeutsche Zeitung* (5 November 2018) https://www.sueddeutsche.de/politik/geschichte-diese-folgen-hatte-der-erste-weltkrieg-1.4198466 accessed 2 January 2020.

13 W Berka, *Verfassungsrecht: Grundzüge des österreichischen Verfassungsrechts für das juristische Studium* (7th edn, Verlag Österreich 2018) 9; see also: H Schambeck, Betrachtungen über die wehrhafte Demokratie - ein Beitrag zum Verständnis der Parteienstaatlichkeit in Österreich und Deutschland. in H Schambeck and A Janko (eds), *Beiträge zum Verfassungs- und Europarecht* (Verlag Österreich 2014) 133.

14 W Goldinger, Die Erste Republik. in Institut für Österreichkunde (ed), *Die Entwicklung der Verfassung Österreichs* (Verlag Hirt 1963) 115.

15 For a comparison with other constitutions, see the constitutions available at: E Zachary and J Melton and T Ginsburg, 'Constitute Project' (Constitute) https://constituteproject.org accessed 2nd January 2020.

16 W Goldinger, Die Erste Republik. in Institut für Österreichkunde (ed), *Die Entwicklung der Verfassung Österreichs* (Verlag Hirt 1963) 115.

17 ibid.

the procedural steps to be taken in order to challenge infringements of constitutionally guaranteed rights (Article 144 Austrian Constitution).[18]

Instead of a new bill of rights, the old provisions in that regard, namely those of the December Constitution, were upheld.[19] According to the literature, there was not much discussion about human rights, neither by the public nor in the academy.[20] The fact that a bill of rights was not part of the core document of the Austrian Constitution is an interesting characteristic, especially when it comes to its liberal content. Whereas concepts like the legality principle or the separation of powers were part of its central document (*Bundes-Verfassungsgesetz*, B-VG), since it was first enacted the same central document has never contained a bill of rights. However, one has to admit that since the Austrian Constitution consists of different sources,[21] the old *Staatsgrundgesetz über die allgemeinen Rechte der Staatsbürger vom 21. Dezember 1867* is formally part of the Constitution and Austria, therefore, was not a country without human rights.

Consensus on a genuine bill of rights was never achieved and attempts to reform the Constitution in this regard always failed.[22] Instead, years later, Austria made the ECHR an integral part of its Constitution.[23] This also later had important consequences for the Constitutional Court's jurisprudence: It moved from a rather strict judicial self-restraint towards a more dynamic jurisprudence, not only respecting the ECHR's jurisprudence but also actively incorporating the methodological approach of the Strasbourg Court.[24]

The Constitution of 1920 was originally designed as an "extreme form of a parliamentary government",[25] which manifested itself in an assembly government (*Konventsregierung*).[26] This was changed in 1929 with a constitutional reform[27] that moved the system towards a presidential system.[28] Yet a system we could call a fully presidential system was not realized; it again was a compromise.[29] Instead of the election of the president through the 'federal assembly' (*Bundesversammlung*), the

18 H Kelsen and G Froehlich and A Merkl, *Die Bundesverfassung vom 1. Oktober 1920* (Verlag Österreich 2003) 278.

19 W Berka, *Verfassungsrecht: Grundzüge des österreichischen Verfassungsrechts für das juristische Studium* (7th edn, Verlag Österreich 2018) 9-11.

20 F Ermacora, 'Die Grundrechte in der Verfassungsfrage 1919/20', *Die Österreichische Verfassung von 1918 bis 1938* (Verl. f. Geschichte u. Politik 1980) 53.

21 T Öhlinger and H Eberhard, *Verfassungsrecht* (12th edn, 2019) 26.

22 ibid 302.

23 Austria had joined the ECHR already in 1958 (BGBl 210/1985); its constitutional character was clarified by an authentic interpretation of the National Council in 1964 (BVG vom 4.3.1964, BGBl 59/1964).

24 T Öhlinger and H Eberhard, *Verfassungsrecht* (12th edn, 2019) 300.

25 ibid 156.

26 ibid.

27 For an overview on the reform, see: W Goldinger, Die Erste Republik. in Institut für Österreichkunde (ed), *Die Entwicklung der Verfassung Österreichs* (Verlag Hirt 1963) 116.

28 The reform also meant a shift between the republican and the democratic principle according to B Kneihs, 'Die „demokratische Republik": Zu den Befugnissen des Bundespräsidenten' [2017] 25(2) Journal für Rechtspolitik 75.

29 T Öhlinger and H Eberhard, *Verfassungsrecht* (12th edn, 2019) 156.

president is since then elected by the people (Article 60 of the Austrian Federal Constitution; hereinafter, AFC). Moreover, it is the president who appoints the chancellor and the members of the government according to the proposal of the chancellor (Article 70 paragraph 1 AFC). Also, the president has the possibility to dissolve the government (Article 70 paragraph 1 AFC). The remainder of the parliamentary system is the dependence of the government on the confidence of the national assembly (Article 74 AFC). Moreover, the president is bound to proposals of the government or a minister whenever he wants to act and the countersignature of the chancellor or a minister is foreseen for his/her acts (Article 67 AFC).[30] According to Öhlinger and Eberhard, we can, therefore, talk of a "parliamentary system of government with a presidential touch".[31]

Article 60 paragraph 4 AFC of 1920 excluded members of ruling houses or former ruling houses from standing as a president. This expressed the fear of the election of a member of the Habsburg family as president and the potential return to a monarchy as a consequence.[32] It manifests the picture of strong republican sentiment.

Hand in hand with the republican principle goes the democratic principle, as was already laid down by Kelsen, Froehlich, and Merkl in their commentary on the Austrian Constitution dating back to the 1920s.[33] In accord with this, Article 7 of the Austrian Constitution, the equality principle, has to be mentioned. Whereas nowadays a rich jurisprudence of the Constitutional Court has expanded its scope of application significantly and made it one of the most influential fundamental rights,[34] its origin lies in the democratic spirit of the Constitution, as already earlier pointed out. Kelsen, Froehlich and Merkl considered it important that "the politically important principle of equality before the law, in which the democratic achievements are particularly expressed" was emphasized.[35]

With regard to illiberalism, these basic decisions of the Constitution are interesting, as they express a strong idea of equality (not only a rejection of the monarchy but also the annulment of the aristocracy) and moreover, link the republican and the democratic principle.

Austria's Constitution does not include an incorporation requirement.[36] Amendments to the Constitution can be part of the Austrian Federal Constitution, they can be separate Constitutional Laws, or they can be part of an ordinary law. In the latter

30 ibid 221.

31 ibid 156.

32 H Kelsen and G Froehlich and A Merkl, *Die Bundesverfassung vom 1. Oktober 1920* (Verlag Österreich 2003) 152.

33 ibid 64.

34 T Öhlinger and H Eberhard, *Verfassungsrecht* (12th edn, 2019) 338.

35 H Kelsen and G Froehlich and A Merkl, *Die Bundesverfassung vom 1. Oktober 1920* (Verlag Österreich 2003) 74.

36 W Berka, *Verfassungsrecht: Grundzüge des österreichischen Verfassungsrechts für das juristische Studium* (7th edn, Verlag Österreich 2018) 22.

case, the constitutional provision has to be named as such (*Verfassungsbestimmung*), and the constitutional requirements for the enactment of constitutional law have to be followed.[37] This makes the Austrian Constitution a rather 'scattered' Constitution, i.e. constituted of different documents and texts.

2.3 Constitutional and legal safeguards of democratic constitutionalism and the rule of law

2.3.1 Constitutional amendment/procedural safeguards

The Austrian Constitution provides for a special procedure for the amendment of the Constitution. Article 44 paragraph 1 AFC stipulates that amendments to the Constitution require the presence of at least half of the members of the National Council and a two-thirds majority to pass.[38] These requirements change in case of specific amendments linked to the federal structure of Austria. When law-making or administrative or judiciary competences of the *Länder* are to be changed, those changes require a special procedure in the Federal Chamber (*Bundesrat*), the second chamber of the Austrian parliament; at least half of the members of the Federal Chamber have to be present and the amendment needs approval of two-third of the members present, Article 44 paragraph 2 AFC.

The Austrian Constitution distinguishes between the so-called partial amendment (*Teiländerung*) and the comprehensive amendment (*Gesamtänderung*).[39] The difference between the two concepts is a qualitative one. A change that has a substantial impact[40] on a so-called fundamental principle requires a special procedure. Not only at least half of the members of the National Council have to be present but two-thirds have to approve the amendment. In addition, a referendum has to take place and the people have to approve the amendment (Article 44 paragraph 3).[41] For partial changes of the Constitution, a referendum can take place, when one third of the members of the National Council or the Federal Chamber require one (Article 44 paragraph 3 AFC). It

37 T Öhlinger and H Eberhard, *Verfassungsrecht* (12th edn, 2019) 25 *et seq*. See also the rich literature, e.g.: A Somek, *Rationalität und Diskriminierung: Zur Bindung der Gesetzgebung an das Gleichheitsrecht* (Springer 2001); M Pöschl, *Gleichheit vor dem Gesetz* (1st edn, Verlag Österreich 2008); M Holoubek, Artikel 7 Abs 1 Sätze 1 und 2. in K Korinek and others (eds), *Österreichisches Bundesverfassungsrecht: Kommentar* (Verlag Österreich 2018).

38 W Berka, *Verfassungsrecht: Grundzüge des österreichischen Verfassungsrechts für das juristische Studium* (7th edn, Verlag Österreich 2018) 23.

39 A Janko, *Gesamtänderung der Bundesverfassung* (Verlag Österreich 2004); E Wiederin, Gesamtänderung, Totalrevision und Verfassunggebung. in M Akyürek and others (eds), *Staat und Recht in europäischer Perspektive: Festschrift Heinz Schäffer* (Manz 2006).

40 A Gamper, *Regeln der Verfassungsinterpretation* (Forschungen aus Staat und Recht, vol 169, Springer 2012) 234.

41 W Berka, *Verfassungsrecht: Grundzüge des österreichischen Verfassungsrechts für das juristische Studium* (7th edn, Verlag Österreich 2018) 34.

is the Constitutional Court which is ultimately deciding on the question of whether a change is a comprehensive amendment or a partial amendment.[42] Different than e.g. in the German Constitution,[43] there is no eternity clause.[44] The Austrian Constitution can, therefore, be classified as a rather flexible[45] constitution.[46]

2.3.2 Material safeguards: The fundamental principles

The question of which principles of the Austrian Constitution can be considered fundamental principles can only be answered with an interpretation of the constitutional system.[47] In practice, this also requires a look at the Constitutional Court's jurisprudence. The Constitution itself points only at the existence of special procedures in case of a comprehensive change of the Constitution but does not specify which principles are specially protected.[48]

Doctrine recognizes between four and six fundamental principles. The democratic, the republican, the federal and the rule of law principles are not disputed.[49] Some add the liberal principle and the principle of the separation of powers.[50]

Compared to 'ordinary' constitutional law, the fundamental principles are privileged. They have supremacy over ordinary constitutional law. Again, this can be deduced from Article 44 paragraph 3 AFC and the special procedural requirements for comprehensive changes of the Constitution. The hierarchic supremacy of the fundamental principles also translates into the Constitutional jurisprudence. The Constitutional Court examines ordinary constitutional law with regard to its compliance with the fundamental principles of the Constitution and can eventually repeal ordinary constitutional law, when fundamental constitutional law contradicts ordinary constitutional law.[51]

In contrast with e.g. the German Constitution,[52] the Austrian constitution does not contain a so-called eternity clause,[53] and therefore does not preclude any constitutional

---

42 See, VfSlg 10.932/1986 and T Öhlinger and H Eberhard, *Verfassungsrecht* (12th edn, 2019) 67 *et seq.*

43 UK Preuss, 'The Implications of "Eternity Clauses": The German Experience' [2011] 44(3) *Israel Law Review* 429.

44 For a discussion of whether there is constitutional law, that cannot be changed see: M Vašek, *Unabänderliches Verfassungsrecht und Revisionsschranken in der österreichischen Bundesverfassung: Dargestellt am demokratischen, republikanischen und bundesstaatlichen Prinzip* (vol 4, Verlag Österreich 2013).

45 A Weber, *Europäische Verfassungsvergleichung: Ein Studienbuch* (Beck 2010) 45.

46 W Berka, *Verfassungsrecht: Grundzüge des österreichischen Verfassungsrechts für das juristische Studium* (7th edn, Verlag Österreich 2018) 35.

47 ibid.

48 ibid.

49 ibid.

50 ibid 36.

51 A Gamper, *Regeln der Verfassungsinterpretation* (Forschungen aus Staat und Recht, vol 169, Springer 2012) 234.

52 Art. 79 para 3 (German) Basic Law (Grundgesetz).

53 For the history of the German eternity clause see: OE Kempen, 'Historische und aktuelle Bedeutung der „Ewigkeitsklausel" des Art. 79 Abs. 3 GG' [1990] 21(2) *Zeitschrift für Parlamentsfragen* 354.

provision from being changed. Yet, fundamental changes that overturn a fundamental principle are rare. As laid down above, additional to the parliamentary requirements, they make a referendum necessary.

Only twice was a national referendum held in Austria. One related to a law that prohibited a nuclear power plant. In that case, the referendum was solicited by a third of the members of the National Council. Hence, this case did not fall into the category of a fundamental change of the Constitutional order.[54] The second case was the accession of Austria to the EU.[55] The legislature had chosen to enact a constitutional law, the Federal Constitutional Act on the Accession of Austria to the European Union,[56] which authorized the signature of the state treaty on the accession of Austria to the EU.[57] This law was put to referendum.[58] In the referendum, the law on the accession of Austria to the EU was accepted and this worked as the 'opening clause' to the further changes that the accession brought.[59]

The actual frequency of changes to the Constitution depends on the majorities in parliament. In the past strong and stable majorities in the National Congress guaranteed the government almost unlimited possibilities of amending the Constitution.[60] Beginning a few years ago, majorities have not been as predictable as in the past, and this can lead to a standstill on the constitutional level.[61] Yet, this has a positive side, as it prevents the constitutionalization of norms which are usually not considered part of a constitution.[62] Moreover, it prevents changes of the Constitution lowering values or standards. However, once a two-third majority in the National Congress is obtained, relevant changes of the Constitution can take place.

(Representative) democracy as a fundamental principle

With regard to democratic backsliding, it seems especially interesting to think about when the threshold required for a *Gesamtänderung* (comprehensive amendment), i.e. when changes to the democratic configuration of the Austrian Constitution are undertaken, could be reached. It is important to realize that the configuration of the

---

54 E Wagner, Atomkraft an den Grenzen des Rechts? in E Wagner and W Bergthaler (eds), *Interdisziplinäre Rechtswissenschaft - Schutzansprüche und Schutzaufgaben im Recht: Festschrift für Ferdinand Kerschner zum 60. Geburtstag* (Verlag Österreich 2013) 565.

55 W Hummer and W Obwexer (eds), *10 Jahre EU-Mitgliedschaft Österreichs: Bilanz und Ausblick* (Springer 2006) 584.

56 BGBl 744/1994.

57 BGBl 45/1995.

58 W Berka, *Verfassungsrecht: Grundzüge des österreichischen Verfassungsrechts für das juristische Studium* (7th edn, Verlag Österreich 2018) 93.

59 ibid 14.

60 ibid 24, 44, 69.

61 ibid 69.

62 See, e.g.: norms regarding the administrative procedure in § 38 para 1, 2 and 4 Abfallwirtschaftsgesetz 2002 or the so-called „care regress“ (Pflegeregress) in § 330a General Social Security Act (Allgemeines Sozialversicherungsgesetz)

Austrian democracy, as laid down in the Constitution, matters. Austria is, as the Constitutional Court laid down in the past, a 'representative' democracy:

> It is the prevailing doctrine to understand the democratic fundamental principle as a representative-democratic fundamental principle with the exception of the direct-democratic elements expressly provided for by the constitutional legislature.[63]

This could e.g. be the case, if binding forms of direct democracy were introduced into the Austrian Constitution. The limits of direct democracy were laid down by the Constitutional Court a few years ago.[64] The *Land* of Vorarlberg wanted to introduce a special kind of referendum.[65] The Constitutional Court considered this unconstitutional:

> The provision under consideration provides that [...] a legislative initiative supported by a majority of voters even against the will [of the majority] of the state parliament 'becomes the law', it thus makes it possible to produce a law even against the [majority] will of Parliament. Such 'popular legislation', however, is not compatible with the basic idea of representative democracy as provided by the Austrian Constitution [...].[66]

Interestingly, there is a link to federalism here. There are several cases where the Court recognized representative democracy as a fundamental principle involving the federal state level in one or the other way.[67] However, these cases cannot be linked to democratic backsliding in the sense of the lowering of democratic standards, as the circumstances of all the cases were not linked to attempts to circumvent or weaken democracy. Not every change of the fundamental principle of democracy means democratic backsliding. A change could also bring an improvement to democracy.

Limits for political activities based on the democratic principle derive from Article 79 paragraph 2 numeral 1 lit a AFC[68] and the prohibition of Nazi activities[69] according to

63 "Es entspricht der herrschenden Lehre, das demokratische Baugesetz als repräsentativ-demokratisches Grundprinzip mit ausnahmehaft vom Verfassungsgesetzgeber ausdrücklich vorgesehenen direkt-demokratischen Elementen zu verstehen" (VfSlg 13.500/1993).

64 A Gamper, 'Direkte Demokratie und bundesstaatliches Homogenitätsprinzip' (2003) 24 Österreichische Juristen-Zeitung 441; T Kreiter, *Grundfragen und Perspektiven des Volksabstimmungsautomatismus: Eine Analyse der Volksgesetzgebung zwischen Politik und Recht* (Verlag Österreich 2017) 50.

65 VfSlg 16.241/2001.

66 VfSlg 16.241/2001 (authors translation).

67 VfSlg 13.500/1993, 15.302/1998, 16.241/2001.

68 See also Art. 9a para 1 AFC.

69 For other provisions prohibiting such activities, see: M Vašek, *Unabänderliches Verfassungsrecht und Revisionsschranken in der österreichischen Bundesverfassung: Dargestellt am demokratischen, republikanischen und bundesstaatlichen Prinzip* (vol 4, Verlag Österreich 2013) 85.

the so-called *Verbotsgesetz*, the National Socialism Prohibition Act 1947.[70] Whereas Article 79 paragraph 2 numeral 1 lit a AFC is linked to the role of the Austrian army regarding dangers from outside,[71] the Prohibition Act is directed at activities inside the republic.[72] The role of the Constitutional Court in applying the Prohibition Act can be described as protective towards democracy.[73] In 1985, for example, it stated, that the Prohibition Act has to be taken into account with regard to any governmental action.[74] Therefore, the Prohibition Act also plays a role whenever a norm is interpreted.[75]

The republican principle

Although the republican principle is one of the fundamental principles of the Constitution it has been invoked very rarely. The mentioned laws on the abolishment of nobility and the Habsburg provisions of the Constitution can be seen as expression of the republican principle.[76] The republican principle entails a negation of the monarchy and a secular understanding of the republic.[77] Linked to the republican principle is the configuration of the republic as a *res publica*. This means that civil society is the foundation of the state and public officials are responsible to the people.[78]

70 Verbotsgesetz 1947, StGBl. 13/1945 as amendend.

71 M Vašek, *Unabänderliches Verfassungsrecht und Revisionsschranken in der österreichischen Bundesverfassung: Dargestellt am demokratischen, republikanischen und bundesstaatlichen Prinzip* (vol 4, Verlag Österreich 2013) 70.

72 ibid 71.

73 B Bailer, 'Das NS-Verbotsgesetz - ein Instrument zur Bekämpfung von Neonazismus und Holocaustleugnung' [2015] *juridikum* 202 *et seq*; M Vašek, *Unabänderliches Verfassungsrecht und Revisionsschranken in der österreichischen Bundesverfassung: Dargestellt am demokratischen, republikanischen und bundesstaatlichen Prinzip* (vol 4, Verlag Österreich 2013) 78.

74 VfSlg 10705/1985.

75 See, for a recent practical question: E Matti and A Wagner, 'Von Leaks und Lücken: Mandatsverlust in der ÖH?' [2017] 4 *juridikum* 472. On the Prohibition Act and freedom of expression in general, see C Bezemek, *Freie Meinungsäußerung: Strukturfragen des Schutzgegenstandes im Rechtsvergleich zwischen dem Ersten Zusatz zur US Verfassung und Artikel 10 der Europäischen Menschenrechtskonvention* (Forschungen aus Staat und Recht, Verlag Österreich 2015) 147 *et seq*.

76 T Öhlinger and H Eberhard, *Verfassungsrecht* (12th edn, 2019) 56.

77 ibid 56.

78 W Berka, *Verfassungsrecht: Grundzüge des österreichischen Verfassungsrechts für das juristische Studium* (7th edn, Verlag Österreich 2018) 47.

The principle of the federal state

The principle of the federal state[79] has had more echoes in the constitutional jurisprudence.[80] For the constitutional court, the elements of the federal state are the distribution of competences between the federal level (*Bund*) and the states (*Länder*) and the possibility of the states to participate in the legislation on the federal level.[81] In that regard, the principle of the federal state can be seen as a form of the distribution of powers, as horizontal form of the separation of powers. In that aspect it is supporting liberal democracy.

The principle of rule of law (Rechtsstaatliches Prinzip)

The history of the rule of law principle is older than the Constitution of 1920 and dates back to 1867.[82] At the core of the rule of law principle lies Article 18 AFC, which ties the executive state power to the law (formal rule of law principle).[83] This approach ties the rule of law principle to the idea of democracy and republic, since the rule of law is not only understood as limiting state power. Rather, the democratic law constitutes the basis for any state action.[84]

Apart from the formal rule of law, the existence of institutions for the legal protection of the individual are also covered by the rule of law principle.[85] The principle of the rule of law is one that nowadays strongly protects the individual[86] and is therefore one of the

79 For the history of federalism in Austria see the contributions in: MP Schennach (ed), *Rechtshistorische Aspekte des österreichischen Föderalismus: Beiträge zur Tagung an der Universität Innsbruck am 28. und 29. November 2013: Sammelband* (Verlag Österreich 2015) and for the younger history: E Wiederin, Einheitsstaat oder Bundesstaat? Diskurse und Entscheidungen 1945. in MP Schennach (ed), *Rechtshistorische Aspekte des österreichischen Föderalismus: Beiträge zur Tagung an der Universität Innsbruck am 28. und 29. November 2013: Sammelband* (Verlag Österreich 2015); P Bußjäger, Zwischen Entmachtung und Vetomacht: Die Entwicklung des österreichischen Föderalismus seit 1945 mit besonderem Blick auf Landtage und Landeshauptleute. in MP Schennach (ed), *Rechtshistorische Aspekte des österreichischen Föderalismus: Beiträge zur Tagung an der Universität Innsbruck am 28. und 29. November 2013: Sammelband* (Verlag Österreich 2015).

80 This is especially linked to the distribution of competences, where the Constitutional Court developed its own method of interpreting the Constitution, the so-called "petrification theory" (*Versteinerungstheorie*), see: T Öhlinger and H Eberhard, *Verfassungsrecht* (12th edn, 2019) 135; and in the recent jurisprudence: VfSlg 20206/2017.

81 ibid 58 with reference to Constitutional Court 2455/1952.

82 T Öhlinger, Der Rechtsstaat. Geschichte, Gegenwart, Gefährdung. in S Schmid (ed), *Auf dem Weg zum hypermodernen Rechtsstaat?: Tagung der Österreichischen Assistentinnnen und Assistenten Öffentliches Recht. Band I, Obergurgl 2010* (Jan Sramek Verlag 2011).

83 T Öhlinger and H Eberhard, *Verfassungsrecht* (12th edn, 2019) 59.

84 T Öhlinger, Der Rechtsstaat. Geschichte, Gegenwart, Gefährdung. in S Schmid (ed), *Auf dem Weg zum hypermodernen Rechtsstaat?: Tagung der Österreichischen Assistentinnnen und Assistenten Öffentliches Recht. Band I, Obergurgl 2010* (Jan Sramek Verlag 2011) 3.

85 T Öhlinger and H Eberhard, *Verfassungsrecht* (12th edn, 2019) 60.

86 W Berka, *Verfassungsrecht: Grundzüge des österreichischen Verfassungsrechts für das juristische Studium* (7th edn, Verlag Österreich 2018) 53.

pillars of Austrian liberal democracy. This is also reflected in the rich jurisprudence of the Constitutional Court.[87] As early as in 1955, the Constitutional Court laid e.g. down that:

> [t]he meaning of the principle of the rule of law culminates in the fact that all acts of state organs must be founded in law and [...] ultimately in the constitution.[88]

Moreover, the principle foresees a "minimum degree of effectiveness" of legal protection.[89] Apart from that, the principle sets other standards protecting the liberal Constitution, such as access to legal norms and their comprehensibility.[90] With the accession to the ECHR, human rights started to play a bigger role within the framework of the rule of law principle. This reflects a more general trend of a shift from the administrative state towards a judicial state.[91]

Nowadays, the Court is regularly applying the rule of law principle leading to a complex body of case law.[92]

The principle of division of powers and the liberal principle

Although the Austrian constitution does not explicitly refer to the principle of the division of powers, the norms of the Constitution, seen holistically, do contain a principle of division of powers.[93] The liberal principle can be deduced from the fundamental rights enshrined in the constitution, but is mostly seen as part of the rule of law.[94] The fundamental rights separate the state from society.[95] Hence both the principle of division of powers and the fundamental rights can be seen as supporting the liberal content of the Austrian Constitution.

87 ibid 55; and, with more details: T Öhlinger, Der Rechtsstaat. Geschichte, Gegenwart, Gefährdung. in S Schmid (ed), *Auf dem Weg zum hypermodernen Rechtsstaat?: Tagung der Österreichischen Assistentinnnen und Assistenten Öffentliches Recht. Band I, Obergurgl 2010* (Jan Sramek Verlag 2011).

88 Already early VfSlg 2929/1955 and W Berka, *Verfassungsrecht: Grundzüge des österreichischen Verfassungsrechts für das juristische Studium* (7th edn, Verlag Österreich 2018) 55 *et seq.*

89 See, e.g. VfSlg 20.239/2018.

90 Already early VfSlg 3130/1956.

91 T Öhlinger, Der Rechtsstaat. Geschichte, Gegenwart, Gefährdung. in S Schmid (ed), *Auf dem Weg zum hypermodernen Rechtsstaat?: Tagung der Österreichischen Assistentinnnen und Assistenten Öffentliches Recht. Band I, Obergurgl 2010* (Jan Sramek Verlag 2011) 7 *et seq.*

92 M Hiesel, 'Entwicklungen der Rechtsstaatsjudikatur des Verfassungsgerichtshofs' [2016] 28(5) *Österreichische Juristen-Zeitung* 212.

93 W Berka, *Verfassungsrecht: Grundzüge des österreichischen Verfassungsrechts für das juristische Studium* (7th edn, Verlag Österreich 2018) 60.

94 With references to the Constitutional Court ibid 59.

95 T Öhlinger and H Eberhard, *Verfassungsrecht* (12th edn, 2019) 60.

The Role of the Fundamental Principles

As laid down above, the fundamental principles taken together protect the liberal democratic core of the Constitution, and if we are investigating the strength of liberal democratic constitutionalism in Austria, they can be seen as a strong rampart. The fundamental principles of the Austrian constitution are not only the core values of the Constitution and are as such protected by a special form of amendment,[96] they are sometimes even referred to as the 'very' constitution.[97]

2.3.3 The Constitutional Court and its role for the protection of constitutionalism

As in some other liberal democracies, the Constitutional Court is crucial when it comes to the protection of the liberal core of the constitution. The basic configuration of the Court is laid down in Article 147 of the Constitution.[98] More detailed provisions on the Constitutional Court judges are laid down in the (ordinary) law on the Procedure of the Constitutional Court (*Verfassungsgerichtshofgesetz* 1953 – VfGG). The constitutional prerequisites for judges are therefore rather vague, but this is not surprising, as e.g. the German Basic Law is even less detailed when it comes to the judges of the Federal Constitutional Court of Germany (Article 94 Basic Law).[99]

The Austrian Constitutional Court consists of twelve judges, a vice-president and the president of the Court. Moreover, the Court has six substitute members (Article 147 paragraph 1). The appointment of judges is laid down in Article 147 paragraph 2 AFC, which reads as follows:

> The President, the Vice-President, six further members and three substitute members shall be appointed by the Federal President on the recommendation of the Federal Government; these members and substitute members shall be drawn from the circle of judges, administrative officials and professors of a law subject at a university. The remaining six members and three substitute members shall be appointed by the Federal President on the basis of proposals submitted by the National Council for three members and two

96 See above.

97 W Berka, *Verfassungsrecht: Grundzüge des österreichischen Verfassungsrechts für das juristische Studium* (7th edn, Verlag Österreich 2018) 35.

98 See in comparison to other judges: A Gamper, 'Verfassungsrechtliche Voraussetzungen des öffentlich-rechtlichen Richteramts in Österreich und Europa' in KJ Giese and G Holzinger and C Jabloner (eds), *Verwaltung im demokratischen Rechtsstaat: Festschrift für Harald Stolzlechner zum 65. Geburtstag* (Verlag Österreich 2013) 144.

99 A Gläß, 'Das Bundesverfassungsgericht als ‚Hüter der Verfassung" – Zur Rolle und Bedeutung von Verfassungsgerichten in Krisenzeiten in Ph Donath et al (eds), *Verfassungen – ihre Rolle im Wandel der Zeit* (Nomos Verlag 2019) 263 *et seq.*

> substitute members and by the Federal Council for three members and one substitute member.[100]

Therefore, the appointment of judges mainly depends on the power relations in Congress. Dependent on the vacant positions during a legislature, Court packing is possible.

Article 147 paragraph 2 AFC also secures a federal element in the appointment procedure, as "[t]hree members and two substitute members must have their permanent residence outside the Federal Capital Vienna."

Being a judge of the Constitutional Court is not a full-time job; judges usually keep their primary occupation, such as lawyer in a law firm or University professor.[101] An exemption exists for civil servants:

> Administrative civil servants on official status who are appointed as members or substitute members shall be decommissioned and their remuneration shall cease. This does not apply to administrative officials appointed as substitute members who have been exempted from all activities subject to instructions for the duration of this exemption.[102]

Article 147 paragraph 3 states the prerequisites for an appointment as a judge of the Constitutional Court. Potential candidates have to "have completed law studies or law and political science studies and shall have ten years' professional experience in law".[103] Being a member 'of the Federal Government, of a *Land* government, of a general representative body or of the European Parliament' precludes a person from being appointed. Whereas for members of the federal or a *Land* government it suffices to resign:

> for members of a general representative body or of the European Parliament who have been elected for a specific legislative or period of office, the incompatibility shall continue until the end of the legislative or period of office even in the case of early waiver of the mandate.[104]

This rather loose approach towards former members of government was criticized when the former minister of justice was appointed in February 2018. It led to discussions whether a 'cooling-off' phase for former members of government was necessary, since

100 T Öhlinger and H Eberhard, *Verfassungsrecht* (12th edn, 2019) 474.
101 ibid.
102 Art. 147 para 2 AFC.
103 Art. 147 para 3 AFC.
104 ibid.

former members of government might be biased, because e.g. they proposed a law they should decide upon.[105] A cooling off phase of five years only exists for the office of president or vice-president of the Constitutional Court (Article 147 paragraph 5). Whereas being a party member does not inhibit persons from being appointed, being an employee or an official of a political party does constitute an obstacle for the appointment (Article 147 paragraph 3).

Generally, the Austrian institutional model not only allows the judges of the Constitutional Court to continue their professional activities, but actively supports other professional activities, as it is construed as a Court which sits in sessions and is in that sense non-permanent.[106] The system seems to work quite well, as judges declare themselves incapable of sitting on the bench whenever they see their impartiality or the appearance of impartiality not guaranteed.[107] In such cases, a substitute member takes over for that specific case.[108]

Once appointed, the judges of the Constitutional Court usually serve until they reach the age of 70; the age limit set by Article 147 paragraph 6 AFC. Their term ends by 31 December of the year in which the member or alternate member turns 70. Strategies entailing the reduction of the retirement age for judges in order to get rid of a certain judge, would therefore make a constitutional amendment necessary.[109] The Constitution is silent on the question of how to remove a Constitutional Court judge once appointed. According to the ordinary law on the Constitutional Court, however, the decision to remove a constitutional court judge from his office lies with the Constitutional Court (§ 10 VfGG).

2.3.4 The guardians of the Constitution

It is obvious that the Constitutional Court is the direct guardian of the Constitution. Yet, the Constitutional Court cannot act *ex officio* in most of the cases. Therefore, the question who is able to initiate the proceedings of the Constitutional Court regarding an alleged unconstitutional norm does matter.

---

105 'Ex-Minister Brandstetter als Verfassungsrichter oft befangen' *Der Standard (online)* (Vienna, 21 September 2018) https://derstandard.at/2000087836337/Ex-Minister-Brandstetter-als-Verfassungsrichter-oft-befangen accessed 2 January 2020; 'Wahl-Anfechtung: FPÖ und Verfassungsrichter Schnizer schließen Vergleich' *Die Presse (online)* (27 November 2017) https://diepresse.com/home/innenpolitik/5328251/WahlAnfechtung_FPOe-und-Verfassungsrichter-Schnizer-schliessen accessed 2 January 2020; C Böhmer, 'Causa Rami: Neos fordern Berufsverbot für Verfassungsrichter' *Kurier (online)* (28 January 2019) https://kurier.at/politik/inland/causa-rami-neos-fordern-berufsverbot-fuer-verfassungsrichter/400389983 accessed 2 January 2020; 'Verfassungsrichter: Experte Mayer für strengere Kriterien' *Die Presse (online)* (21 February 2018) https://diepresse.com/home/innenpolitik/5375614/Verfassungsrichter_Experte-Mayer-fuer-strengere-Kriterien accessed 2 January 2020.

106 T Öhlinger and H Eberhard, *Verfassungsrecht* (12th edn, 2019) 474.

107 § 12 VfGG.

108 § 6 para 2 VfGG.

109 See the case of *Baka v Hungary* Applic. no. 20261/12 (ECtHR, 23 June 2016).

Access to the Constitutional Court varies according to its competencies. The Austrian Constitutional Court is not only competent for the protection of human rights ("constitutionally guaranteed rights" according to Article 144 AFC). It moreover exercises the concrete and abstract control of norms. This entails ordinary laws, administrative regulations, agreements between *Land* governments and/or the Federal government (Article 138a AFC) and state treaties. Additionally, the Constitutional Court is called upon to settle conflicts arising between different state actors (Article 138 AFC). Apart from some other competences (such as its competence to decide on pecuniary claims or on conflicts arising from the Rules of Procedure of the National Council (Article 138b AFC)), the court also functions as the electoral court (Article 141 AFC).[110]

An Austrian peculiarity is the concept of 'constitutionally guaranteed rights'. They encompass not only the rights laid down in the main document of the Constitution (the AFC), but also those laid down in other constitutional laws[111] or constitutional provisions in ordinary laws.[112] Moreover, the *Staatsgrundgesetz über die allgemeinen Rechte der Staatsbürger*,[113] and the Law on the Protection of Domestic Authority,[114] have to be mentioned. Yet, the most important document for human rights protection is the ECHR, which forms part of the Austrian Constitution.[115]

The history of the human rights adjudication of the Constitutional Court is characterized by progress in the sense of a development towards a more protective approach. This is mainly due to the fact that the ECHR forms part of the Austrian Constitution. If the court was hesitant in the beginning to follow the ECHR's jurisprudence (judicial self-restraint), it can be considered as open to the ECHR's jurisprudence since the late 1960s.[116]

When it comes to the EU Fundamental Rights Charter (FRC),[117] the Court has taken a very active role. In a landmark judgment of March 2012 (VfSlg 19.632/2012), it stated

---

110 For a complete list of the competencies, see W Berka, *Verfassungsrecht: Grundzüge des österreichischen Verfassungsrechts für das juristische Studium* (7th edn, Verlag Österreich 2018) 347.

111 E.g. Bundesverfassungsgesetz vom 29. November 1988 über den Schutz der persönlichen Freiheit.

112 E.g. Bundesgesetz zum Schutz natürlicher Personen bei der Verarbeitung personenbezogener Daten (Datenschutzgesetz – DSG), BGBl I Nr 165/1999, as amended BGBl I Nr 24/2018).

113 RGBl Nr 142/1867. For more details, see: PM Judson, The Lost Heroes of Austria´s Fundamental Laws. in F Merli and M Pöschl and E Wiederin (eds), *150 Jahre Staatsgrundgesetz über die allgemeinen Rechte der Staatsbürger* (Manz 2018) 1; A Gamper, '150 Jahre Staatsgrundgesetz - Befund und Ausblick zum Grundrechtsschutz in Österreich' in Gerhard Baumgartner (ed), *Öffentliches Recht: Jahrbuch 2018* (1st edn, NWV Verlag 2018).

114 Gesetz vom 27. October 1862, zum Schutze des Hausrechtes, RGBl Nr 88/1862.

115 BGBl Nr 210/1958.

116 T Öhlinger and H Eberhard, *Verfassungsrecht* (12th edn, 2019) 300.

117 For the implications of the FRC on the national legal orders in general, see: K Pabel, 'Zusammenwirken mitgliedstaatlicher und unionaler Grundrechte' in S Griller and A Kahl and B Kneihs (eds), *20 Jahre EU-Mitgliedschaft Österreichs: Auswirkungen des Unionsrechts auf die nationale Rechtsordnung aus rechtswissenschaftlicher, politikwissenschaftlicher und wirtschaftswissenschaftlicher Sicht* (Verlag Österreich 2016) 229.

that the FRC is also a standard of review before the Court if certain conditions are satisfied.[118] Up until now probably the most interesting cases are asylum cases linked to Article 47 FRC,[119] as these cases are not yet covered by Article 6 ECHR.[120]

The people as 'guardians of the Constitution'

People can act as guardians of the Constitution when they access the Constitutional Court. For individuals in the area of public law, access to the Constitutional Court is granted when they have a decision from an administrative court and they claim a violation of a so-called constitutionally guaranteed right or the application of an illegal or unconstitutional norm (Article 144 B-VG). Moreover, an individual can file a complaint in cases where norms can be applied to them directly without having the possibility of complaint in order to obtain a decision of an administrative court (Article 139 and Art 140 B-VG).

Individuals in civil law cases cannot lodge an appeal against decisions of ordinary courts. Ordinary courts, however, have to call the Constitutional Court whenever they have concerns regarding the constitutionality of norms they apply when deciding (see Article 89 AFC).[121] When a court does not do so, up until 2015 no legal remedy was foreseen for such cases. In 2015 this legislative gap was filled with the introduction of access to the Constitutional Court in such cases (*Parteiantrag auf Normenkontrolle*).[122] This does not entail a competence of the Constitutional Court to revise the decision but aims at a possibility of control of the underlying norm.

Although the Austrian Constitution does not recognize an *actio popularis* regarding presumed unconstitutional laws, possibilities of access are relatively generous: Whenever an individual is touched upon their legal sphere by an unconstitutional action, it has the

118 AT Müller, An Austrian "Ménage à Trois". The Convention, the Charter and the Constitution. in KS Ziegler and E Wicks and L Hodson (eds), *The UK and European human rights: A strained relationship?* (Hart Publishing 2015) 304; for the implications on the national human rights protection, see: A Wimmer, Die Normenkontrollkompetenzen der 166 österreichischen Grundrechtsgerichte. in A Kahl and N Raschauer and S Storr (eds), *Grundsatzfragen der europäischen Grundrechtecharta* (Verlag Österreich 2013) 87.

119 E.g. Constitutional Court 26.11.2018, E4221/2017; 9.10.2018, E2449/2018; 24.9.2018, E3106/2018.

120 VfSlg 19.632/2012.

121 The Court has developed a quite strict jurisprudence in terms of by which cases it examines the unconstitutionality of a norm that underlies the decision of a civil court, see with more details: M Oswald, 'Die Abgrenzung des Anfechtungsumfanges bei der konkreten Normenkontrolle' [2016] 138 (7) *Juristische Blätter* 413.

122 H Eberhard, Der Parteiantrag auf Normenkontrolle - Zwischenbilanz und Perspektiven. in Ludwig Adamovich and others (eds), *Festschrift für Gerhart Holzinger* (Verlag Österreich 2017); M Jestaedt, Die (Möglichkeit einer) Gesetzesbeschwerde an den Verfassungsgerichtshof. in M Holoubek (ed), *Die Verwaltungsgerichtsbarkeit erster Instanz* (Linde 2013); L Khakzadeh-Leiler, 'Der Parteiantrag auf Normenkontrolle' [2015] 74(12) Österreichische Juristen-Zeitung 543; B Kneihs, Die Gesetzesbeschwerde zwischen Entscheidungsbeschwerde und Individualantrag. in Gerhard Baumgartner (ed), *Öffentliches Recht: Jahrbuch 2014* (1st edn, NWV Verlag 2014).

possibility of access to the Court (provided that some criteria are fulfilled, such as that there is no other remedy available).[123]

In the context of constitutional backsliding this means that the possibilities for citizens to bring cases to the Constitutional Court are quite ample. What matters in this regard is the question of costs. In order to file a complaint with the Constitutional Court, applicants have to be represented by a lawyer and pay a fee according to § 17a VfGG (currently: 240 Euro). Financial assistance for the proceedings can be provided according to § 35 VfGG and §§ 63 ff. ZPO. Therefore, access to the Constitutional Court can be described as comparatively low-threshold.

Apart from the administrative court decisions against which individuals can appeal, individuals can also appeal to the Constitutional Court when they feel violated in their legal sphere through an administrative regulation or an ordinary law (Articles 139, 140 AFC). The Constitutional Courts jurisprudence is much stricter in these cases. Different criteria have been developed in order to restrict access to the Court.[124]

Although one can question whether it should be citizens protecting the liberal constitution, citizens do play a major role in safeguarding the constitutionality of the law and eventually also the Constitution.

2.4 *The electoral system as realization of the democratic principle*

Only the main features of the Austrian electoral system are laid down in the Constitution. Article 26 AFC regulates the elections to the National Council (*Nationalrat*), the first chamber of parliament. The Elections have to be organized according to the fundamental principles for voting: equal, direct, personal, free and secret suffrage of men and women who have reached the age of 16 on the day of the election. The second chamber, the *Bundesrat*, is not directly elected. The members of the *Bundesrat* are elected by the *Land* parliaments (Article 35 AFC).

The electoral system is a proportional system. The constitutional bases for the electoral system are further elaborated in ordinary laws.[125] The elections to the representative bodies in the *Länder* fall into the competence of the respective *Land* legislator. Yet, the *Länder* are bound by the Constitution: The electoral rules in the *Länder* can only be more generous than the basic rules laid down in the Federal Constitution. Therefore, e.g., it would be possible for a *Land* to deviate from the rule that citizens are entitled to vote once they are 16, but the Land could only further lower the voting age. The other way around, raising the voting age, would not be possible.

123 W Berka, *Verfassungsrecht: Grundzüge des österreichischen Verfassungsrechts für das juristische Studium* (7th edn, Verlag Österreich 2018) 372.

124 T Öhlinger and H Eberhard, *Verfassungsrecht* (12th edn, 2019) 493.

125 Nationalrats-Wahlordnung, BGBl 471/1992 last amended BGBl I 32/2018.

Compared to its neighbouring countries, Austria is not at all an exception. Germany as well as Switzerland lack detailed electoral rules on the Constitutional level.[126]

When it comes to the voting districts, the Austrian Constitution is quite specific, because they are laid down in the Constitution. Article 26 paragraph 2 AFC lays down the following:

> The territory of the Federal Republic shall be divided into constituencies whose boundaries shall not cross regional borders; these constituencies shall be subdivided into regional constituencies. The number of deputies shall be distributed among the eligible voters in the constituencies (electoral bodies) in proportion to the number of citizens who, according to the results of the last census, had their principal residence in the respective constituency, increased by the number of citizens who, although not having their principal residence in the territory of the Federal Republic on the day of the census, were registered in the electoral register in a municipality in the respective constituency; in the same way, the number of deputies assigned to a constituency shall be distributed among the regional constituencies. The electoral regulations for the National Council must provide for a final determination procedure in the entire federal territory, through which both a balance of the electoral parties allocated to the election candidates in the constituencies and a distribution of the mandates not yet allocated are carried out according to the principles of proportional representation. It is not permissible to divide the electorate into other constituencies.

This is a somewhat technical provision but makes it difficult to fundamentally change constituencies, i.e. with the aim of gerrymandering.[127]

The background for it lies with the historical situation in 1920. The drafters of the constitution wanted to make sure that the equality of the voting system was upheld; unequal distribution of mandates to the electoral constituencies should be prevented.[128] The safeguard was the constitutionalization of the electoral law[129] in this case: Changing the provision became more complicated. Apart from equality, the purpose of the

126 See, with more details, M Bertel, Konstitutionalisierung des Wahlrechts als Beitrag zur Stabilisierung der Demokratie? in Ph Donath and others (eds), *Verfassungen – ihre Rolle im Wandel der Zeit* (Nomos Verlag 2019) 251 *et seq*.

127 In Austria gerrymandering is not a big issue. For the situation in the US, see: EJ Engstrom, *Partisan gerrymandering and the construction of American democracy* (The University of Michigan Press 2013).

128 H Kelsen and G Froehlich and A Merkl, *Die Bundesverfassung vom 1. Oktober 1920* (Verlag Österreich 2003) 94.

129 See (for the US): R Pildes, 'The Supreme Court 2003 Term' [2004] 118(29) *Harvard Law Review* 28.

provision was to safeguard the federal principle of the constitution. As constituencies had to be drafted within the limits of the regions, the political unity of the regions was preserved.[130]

It is obvious that the Austrian Constitution relies on parties. Although referring to parties several times, the Austrian Constitution is silent on what the term is understood to mean.[131] The term 'party' can be understood in two different ways in the Austrian context. Party means political party, but also an electoral party. The two are different concepts. Whereas the political party is defined, according to § 1 Abs 2 PartG, as:

> A permanently organized association which, through joint activity, aims to exert a comprehensive influence on the formation of state will, in particular through participation in elections to general representative bodies and the European Parliament, and whose statutes are deposited with the Federal Ministry of the Interior.

The electoral party is the list that participates in a specific electoral process.[132]

The formation of parties is relatively easy in Austria. Section (§) 1 of the Law on Parties is a constitutional provision and lays down the role of parties in Austria. According to § 1, "[t]he existence and diversity of political parties are essential components of the democratic order of the Republic of Austria."[133] Forming a party is not restricted, as long as constitutional limits are respected.[134] This concerns in particular the so-called *Verbotsgesetz*, a law dating back to 1947 that aims at preventing National-Socialist re-activation.

Recent reforms[135] with relation to the parties are linked to party finances.[136] Those reforms were due for a long time but got more pressing when the coalition of the Peoples party and the Freedom party broke down because of a political scandal. A video, shot in Ibiza, showed vice-chancellor Strache, who (amongst others) explained to a decoy who

---

130 H Kelsen and G Froehlich and A Merkl, *Die Bundesverfassung vom 1. Oktober 1920* (Verlag Österreich 2003) 95.

131 H Schambeck, Betrachtungen über die wehrhafte Demokratie - ein Beitrag zum Verständnis der Parteienstaatlichkeit in Österreich und Deutschland. in H Schambeck and A Janko (eds), *Beiträge zum Verfassungs- und Europarecht* (Verlag Österreich 2014) 124.

132 T Öhlinger and H Eberhard, *Verfassungsrecht* (12th edn, 2019) 163.

133 Author's translation.

134 When it comes to democracy within parties, the Austrian Law on Parties is rather generous, compared e.g. to Germany, see: M Stelzer, Innerparteiliche Demokratie. in M Akyürek and others (eds), *Staat und Recht in europäischer Perspektive: Festschrift Heinz Schäffer* (Manz 2006) 792.

135 Yet, the ideas for a reform of the electoral system reflect the complex state of the Austrian electoral rules, see: P Grohma and M Lidauer and A Rabitsch, 'Vorschläge für eine Reform des österreichischen Wahlrechts' [2018] 26(1) Journal für Rechtspolitik 13.

136 BGBl 55/2019.

was secretly filming him, how to take over the media and how to circumvent the existing rules on party financing.[137]

3 EXPERIENCES – A SICK OR A ROBUST CONSTITUTION?

3.1 *Overall assessment: A robust Constitution*

Overall (and this is proved by various international rankings), the Austrian democratic system can be described as robust.[138] This is certainly due to the prudent drafting of the Austrian Constitution, which, due to the time it was drafted, focussed on procedural safeguards and checks and balances as described above. The biggest crisis of the Constitution probably took place in 1933, when the three presidents of the National Council (*Nationalrat*) stepped back and for a short time a vacuum was created.

3.2 *Stability through dialogue?*

Austrian liberal democracy can be described as stable. Two factors are decisive for the stability of the Austrian liberal democracy after World War II. On the one hand during a long period the so-called *Sozialpartnerschaft* (social partnership), which can be best described as a form of corporatism,[139] worked perfectly.[140] On the other hand, but linked to the social partnership, Austria was – with some exceptions – long characterized by a balance between the two main parties: The Social Democratic Party (*Sozialdemokratische Partei Österreichs,* SPÖ) and the Austrian People's Party (now: *Die neue Volkspartei*, ÖVP). Both parties mostly governed together in the so-called *Große Koalition* (big coalition).[141] This led to a certain stability, which lasted until the late

137 F Obermaier, 'Das Beben in Österreich' *Süddeutsche Zeitung (online)* (19 May 2019) https://www.sueddeutsche.de/politik/ibiza-video-das-beben-in-oesterreich-1.4453042 accessed 2 January 2020.

138 See, e.g.: Freedom House, 'Freedom in the World 2018: Austria profile' (Freedom House, 2018) https://freedomhouse.org/report/freedom-world/2018/austria accessed 2 January 2020; A Pelinka and R Winter-Ebmer and R Zohlnhöfer, 'Austria Report: Sustainable Government Indicators 2018' [2018] 24 http://www.sgi-network.org/2016/Austria/Quality_of_Democracy accessed 2nd January 2020; The World Justice Project, 'WJP Rule of Law Index 2019' (The World Justice Project, 2019) 40 https://worldjusticeproject.org/our-work/research-and-data/wjp-rule-law-index-2019 accessed 2 January 2020.

139 E Tálos (ed), *Sozialpartnerschaft: Kontinuität und Wandel eines Modells* (Verlag für Gesellschaftskritik 1993); For a critical discussion with regard to democracy, see: E Tálos, '»Zwangskammerstaat«? Zur Demokratiequalität der Sozialpartnerschaft' (März 1996) Institute für Advanced Studies, Vienna, Political Science Series No. 29.

140 Lately, the "Sozialpartnerschaft" is more and more questioned, see: A Wöckinger, 'Adieu Sozialpartnerschaft?' [2017] 2017(4) *juridikum* 421.

141 O Lehner, *Österreichische Verfassungs- und Verwaltungsgeschichte: Mit Grundzügen der Wirtschafts- und Sozialgeschichte* (4th edn, Trauner 2007) 390.

1990s. With the rise of other parties, such as the Freedom Party (*Freiheitliche Partei Österreichs*, FPÖ), but also the Green party (*Die Grünen*) and the Neos (*Das Neue Österreich und Liberales Forum*), the time of the two big players seems to be over. The party landscape became more fluid and voters more flexible in their voting decisions. In this sense, Austria does seem to fit the bigger pattern throughout Europe.[142]

In the following, I will first present a case study (section 4) on the so-called Ortstafelstreit, which kept Austrian politics busy during several decades and culminated in the refusal of former Land president Jörg Haider to recognize and follow a decision of the Constitutional Court. Second, I will show the challenges the liberal core of the Constitution is facing nowadays (section 5). Those challenges arise e.g. in the field of law making, where a certain professionalization has taken place in the last years and are reflected in the increased importance of parliamentary inquiry committees.

4 Case study – *Ortstafelstreit*[143]

The following case study illustrates the practical problems constitutional rules and Constitutional Court rulings envisage, when politicians are reluctant to comply with them and are thus testing liberal democracy.

4.1 The facts

The so-called *Ortstafelstreit* kept Austria, and more specifically, the *Land* Carinthia busy up until 2011.[144] In 2011 an amendment to the *Volksgruppengesetz*[145] that solved the conflict was finally enacted. At the centre of the conflict was the question which villages and towns in Carinthia needed bilingual signs at their entrance. At the core of the conflict over the bilingual signs lay the question how Austria wanted to deal with minority rights as foreseen in the treaty of Vienna.[146] The roots of the conflict date back to 1955: The

142 See, e.g. the rise of new parties: TA Kremer, 'A New Political Paradigm – The Rise of Smaller Parties' [2016] 105(4) *The Round Table* 423.

143 A detailed analysis is provided by Jürgen Pirker, see: J Pirker, *Kärntner Ortstafelstreit: Der Rechtskonflikt als Identitätskonflikt* (vol 16, Nomos 2010).

144 For the law on minorities in general see: J Marko, System des österreichischen Volksgruppenrechts und Minderheitenschutzes. in G Heißl (ed), *Handbuch Menschenrechte: Allgemeine Grundlagen - Grundrechte in Österreich - Entwicklungen - Rechtsschutz* (facultas.wuv 2009).

145 BGBl I 46/2011.

146 E Schwelb, 'The Austrian State Treaty and Human Rights' [1956] 5(2) *The International and Comparative Law Quarterly* 268.

treaty of Vienna foresaw that ethnic Slovenians and Croatians have the right to bilingual signs in areas where Austrians and ethnic Slovenians and Croatians live. However, the treaty did not further specify the conditions.[147]

Beginning in the 1970s, the Kreisky government decided to put up bilingual signs in places where more than 20% of the population spoke Slovenian (or Croatian).[148] The efforts of putting up bilingual signs were accompanied by protests and the demolition of the signs by German-speaking people.[149] In July 1976 the Federal Act on the legal status of the ethnic groups in Austria was enacted.[150] It contains detailed provisions on the topographic names in Article 12. The wording of § 12 was the following:

> Topographical names
> § (1) In the areas of the territorial units designated in accordance with § 2 para. 1 subpara. 2, names and inscriptions of a topographical nature affixed by territorial authorities or other public corporations and institutions shall be written in German and in the language of relevant ethnic groups. This obligation shall not apply to the designation of localities outside the area of such parts of the territory.
> (2) The ordinance pursuant to § 2 para. 1 subpara. 2 shall also specify the localities which are eligible for bilingual designation as well as the topographical designations in the language of the relevant ethnic groups, which shall be applied in addition to the German-language designation. In this respect, the local practice and the results of scientific research shall be taken into account.
> (3) Topographical designations existing only in the language of an ethnic group shall be used unchanged by local authorities.

Whereas the fact that topographic names had to be bilingual in some territories was laid down in the Ethnic Groups Act, it was left open as to which specific territories this was mandatory. This question was delegated to a regulation that had to be taken by the

147 D Kolonovits, 'Volksgruppenrecht im Jahr 2007 - Oder: Die weiterhin ungelöste Ortstafelfrage und die aktuelle Rechtsprechung des VfGH' in Georg Lienbacher and Gerhart Wielinger (eds), *Öffentliches Recht. Jahrbuch 2008* (Neuer Wissenschaftlicer Verlag 2008) 192; 'Chronologie: Der Ortstafel-Streit seit 1955' *Die Presse (online)* (26 April 2011) https://diepresse.com/home/politik/innenpolitik/647029/Chronologie_Der-OrtstafelStreit-seit-1955 accessed 2January 2020.

148 'Chronologie: Der Ortstafel-Streit seit 1955' *Die Presse (online)* (26 April 2011) https://diepresse.com/home/politik/innenpolitik/647029/Chronologie_Der-OrtstafelStreit-seit-1955 accessed 2 January 2020.

149 ibid; J Maier, Die Kärntner Ortstafelregelung 2011 – Ein Ergebnis des erfolgreichen Regierens auf mehreren Ebenen. in P Bußjäger and C Gsodam (eds), *Tourismus und Multi-Level-Governance im Alpenraum* (new academic press 2017) 274.

150 J Maier, Die Kärntner Ortstafelregelung 2011 – Ein Ergebnis des erfolgreichen Regierens auf mehreren Ebenen. in P Bußjäger and C Gsodam (eds), *Tourismus und Multi-Level-Governance im Alpenraum* (new academic press 2017) 275; BGBl 396/1976.

territorial authorities. The Ethnic Groups Act foresaw however, that one-fourth of the population was considered the threshold that triggered the need for bilingual town signs.[151]

In May 1977 the so-called *Verordnung der Bundesregierung vom 31. Mai 1977 über die Bestimmung von Gebietsteilen, in denen topographische Bezeichnungen in deutscher und slowenischer Sprache anzubringen sind* (the 'regulation on topography') was enacted. It foresaw that bilingual town signs had to be put up.[152] A second regulation specified the names of these places in the Slovenian language (*Festsetzung der slowenischen Bezeichnungen für Ortschaften*).[153]

In 1988 the Constitutional Court issued its first decision regarding the Ethnics Group Act:[154] As far as the Ethnics Group Act (or any of the regulations mentioned) repeated Article 7 § 3 first sentence of the Treaty of Vienna, it did not take away the direct applicability of the provision of the Treaty of Vienna. The fact, that § 13 Ethnics Group Act excluded the use of the Croatian minority language in areas with a Croatian or mixed population, as long as no regulation had been issued, was seen as a contradicting Article 7 § 3 first sentence of the Treaty of Vienna. Therefore, the Court declared parts of § 13 Ethnics Group Act unconstitutional.[155]

In 2000, the first German-Croatian town sign was put up in the federal state of Burgenland. In Carinthia, the Slovenian part of the population called for changes of the Ethnics Group Act.[156] In 2001 the Constitutional Court declared parts of the Ethnics Group Act unconstitutional, because it considered the 25% threshold too high.[157] Moreover, parts of the Regulation on the Topography were struck down. The court considered a 10% threshold as legitimate and gave the legislature a year to redesign the Ethnics Group Act.

The Constitutional Court's decision resulted in critique[158] and verbal attacks by the president of the *Land*, Jörg Haider against the president of the Constitutional Court, Ludwig Adamovich.[159] Jörg Haider announced that he would not follow the

151 BGBl 307/1977.

152 BGBl 1977/306.

153 BGBl 1977/308.

154 VfSlg 11585/1987.

155 VfSlg 115585/1987.

156 'Chronologie: Der Ortstafel-Streit seit 1955' *Die Presse (online)* (26 April 2011) https://diepresse.com/home/politik/innenpolitik/647029/Chronologie_Der-OrtstafelStreit-seit-1955 accessed 2 January 2020.

157 VfSlg 16.403/2001; J Maier, Die Kärntner Ortstafelregelung 2011 – Ein Ergebnis des erfolgreichen Regierens auf mehreren Ebenen. in P Bußjäger and C Gsodam (eds), *Tourismus und Multi-Level-Governance im Alpenraum* (new academic press 2017) 276.

158 D Kolonovits, Volksgruppenrecht im Jahr 2007 - Oder: Die weiterhin ungelöste Ortstafelfrage und die aktuelle Rechtsprechung des VfGH in Georg Lienbacher and Gerhart Wielinger (eds), *Öffentliches Recht. Jahrbuch 2008* (Neuer Wissenschaftlicer Verlag 2008) 194.

159 M Hiesel, Politik und Effektivität gerichtlichen Rechtsschutzes. in A Bammer and others (eds), *Rechtsschutz gestern - heute - morgen: Festgabe zum 80. Geburtstag von Rudolf Machacek und Franz Matscher* (NWV Neuer Wissenschaftlicher Verlag 2008) 209.

Constitutional Court's decision.[160] He called for a popular consultation and collected the necessary signatures.[161] Yet, the popular consultation was not allowed by the *Land* electoral authority.[162] Instead, Haider sent out letters to selected towns in Southern Carinthia. Those letters consisted of three questions and resulted in a majority rejecting more bilingual town signs (although Haider had preferred and recommended another solution).[163] In the following, a commission was set up, but its proposal, to put up 147 bilingual town-signs was rejected by the Slovenians.[164] Another proposal presented by a historian proposed 158 bilingual town-signs.[165]

In May 2005, bilingual signs were put up, but less than two years later Haider removed at least some of them.[166] In December 2006, another judgement of the Constitutional Court was issued. The background was that instead of bilingual town signs, a monolingual town sign had been installed and a – smaller – additional sign in Slovenian had been put up.[167] The Constitutional Court laid down that it was a

> [...] legal requirement to indicate both the German and the Slovenian 'name of the place' on the sign 'Ortstafel' or 'Ortsende' [...]. The indication of the name of a place [...] however on additional signs [...] is excluded [...].[168]

160 Redaktion, 'Haider vs. Adamovich' *Der Standard (online)* (7 January 2002) https://www.derstandard.at/story/825741/haider-vs-adamovich accessed 2 January 2020.

161 D Kolonovits, Volksgruppenrecht im Jahr 2007 - Oder: Die weiterhin ungelöste Ortstafelfrage und die aktuelle Rechtsprechung des VfGH in Georg Lienbacher and Gerhart Wielinger (eds), *Öffentliches Recht. Jahrbuch 2008* (Neuer Wissenschaftlicer Verlag 2008) 194; Redaktion, 'Ortstafeln: Haider hat Unterschriften für Volksbefragung' *Der Standard (online)* (11 April 2006) https://derstandard.at/2410144/Ortstafeln-Haider-hat-Unterschriften-fuer-Volksbefragung accessed 2 January 2020.

162 D Kolonovits, Volksgruppenrecht im Jahr 2007 - Oder: Die weiterhin ungelöste Ortstafelfrage und die aktuelle Rechtsprechung des VfGH in Georg Lienbacher and Gerhart Wielinger (eds), *Öffentliches Recht. Jahrbuch 2008* (Neuer Wissenschaftlicer Verlag 2008) 194; Redaktion, 'Haiders Ortstafel-Befragung: Mehrheit gegen weitere zweisprachige Tafeln' *Der Standard (online)* (Klagenfurt, 29 June 2006) https://www.derstandard.at/story/2495190/haiders-ortstafel-befragung-mehrheit-gegen-weitere-zweisprachige-tafeln accessed 2 January 2020.

163 Redaktion, 'Haiders Ortstafel-Befragung: Mehrheit gegen weitere zweisprachige Tafeln' *Der Standard (online)* (Klagenfurt, 29 June 2006) https://www.derstandard.at/story/2495190/haiders-ortstafel-befragung-mehrheit-gegen-weitere-zweisprachige-tafeln accessed 2 January 2020.

164 'Chronologie: Der Ortstafel-Streit seit 1955' *Die Presse (online)* (26 April 2011) https://diepresse.com/home/politik/innenpolitik/647029/Chronologie_Der-OrtstafelStreit-seit-1955 accessed 2 January 2020.

165 ibid.

166 ibid.

167 D Kolonovits, Volksgruppenrecht im Jahr 2007 - Oder: Die weiterhin ungelöste Ortstafelfrage und die aktuelle Rechtsprechung des VfGH in Georg Lienbacher and Gerhart Wielinger (eds), *Öffentliches Recht. Jahrbuch 2008* (Neuer Wissenschaftlicer Verlag 2008) 201.

168 VfSlg 18044-18318/2006.

But again, instead of putting up bilingual town signs, Haider moved the original monolingual town sign,[169] which was later declared illegal. Additionally, the Court decided, that the use of different sizes regarding the name in German and Slovenian language did not comply with the law.[170] Finally, in June 2006 a political solution with an amendment of the Constitution was envisaged but failed again. After several additional decisions of the Constitutional Court a final solution was found in 2012:[171] a threshold of 17.5% of Slovenians triggers bilingual town signs. As a consequence, 164 bilingual town signs were put up.[172]

4.2 *The significance of the Ortstafelstreit*

The town sign conflict shows the clash between politics and the Constitutional Court. It was not only the heritage of an unsolved conflict – namely the question of a minority (in that case the Slovenians). It also shows how fragile such compromises are. As the numerous events of the crisis show, the whole process can be almost characterized as a game of cat-and-mouse between the different players and especially the Constitutional Court and the reaction of the then *Land* president. The result was an unconstitutional situation for quite some time.[173] The dispute was characterized by the use of populist tactics, such as a specific rhetoric and legal means (e.g. the consultation) by Jörg Haider.[174]

The conflict especially raised the issue of how to enforce decisions of the Constitutional Court. The Austrian president would have been responsible to enforce the decisions (Article 146 para 2 Austrian Constitution). The procedure would have to be initiated by the Constitutional Court and would then entail the president to act, in the extreme with the help of the Austrian army.[175] Yet, the problem of the case was that the

169 J Maier, Die Kärntner Ortstafelregelung 2011 – Ein Ergebnis des erfolgreichen Regierens auf mehreren Ebenen. in P Bußjäger and C Gsodam (eds), *Tourismus und Multi-Level-Governance im Alpenraum* (new academic press 2017) 279.

170 VfSlg 19128/2010.

171 J Maier, Die Kärntner Ortstafelregelung 2011 – Ein Ergebnis des erfolgreichen Regierens auf mehreren Ebenen. in P Bußjäger and C Gsodam (eds), *Tourismus und Multi-Level-Governance im Alpenraum* (new academic press 2017) 280.

172 'Chronologie: Der Ortstafel-Streit seit 1955' *Die Presse (online)* (26 April 2011) https://diepresse.com/home/politik/innenpolitik/647029/Chronologie_Der-OrtstafelStreit-seit-1955 accessed 2 January 2020).

173 M Hiesel, Politik und Effektivität gerichtlichen Rechtsschutzes. in A Bammer and others (eds), *Rechtsschutz gestern - heute - morgen: Festgabe zum 80. Geburtstag von Rudolf Machacek und Franz Matscher* (NWV Neuer Wissenschaftlicher Verlag 2008) 210.

174 On Jörg Haider's rhetoric in general: C Zöchling, 'Zum zehnten Todestag: Haiders langer Schatten' *profil (online)* (9 October 2018) https://www.profil.at/oesterreich/todestag-haiders-schatten-10399699 accessed 2 January 2020

175 T Öhlinger and H Eberhard, *Verfassungsrecht* (12th edn, 2019) 522.

Constitutional Court struck down a regulation. As the duty to enact a new regulation was not part of the decision, but result of an ordinary law, enforcement would have been impossible.[176]

Although minority protection is constitutionally entrenched with the treaty of Vienna, the conflict shows the importance of infraconstitutional norms in applying a constitution and in rendering constitutional provisions effective. It is telling that the conflict was finally resolved with the constitutionalization of the relevant provisions, as the amendment of the Ethnic Group Act consisted partly of constitutional provisions.[177] One of the aims of the constitutionalization of norms is their 'immunization'.[178] Immunization means that since a specific content is then part of the Constitution, it cannot be examined by the Constitutional Court, unless, as noted above, the Court could examine the provision with regard to compliance with one of the fundamental principles of the Austrian Constitution.

5 NEW CHALLENGES

Whereas the Ortstafelstreit reflects the dangers of populist politicians not wanting to follow the Constitutional Court's decisions, new challenges for liberalism are arising. The future will show whether they represent a general trend or whether they are limited to the last government, consisting of a coalition between the ÖVP and the FPÖ, led by Chancellor Kurz and Vice-Chancellor Strache.

The first important area is information management in politics. The former minister of the interior Herbert Kickl proposed to restrict the media's access to information on government activities. This proposed restriction to the freedom of the press led to a backlash. The proposal led to strong reactions in the media and then Chancellor Kurz emphasized the importance of the freedom of the press.[179] The ÖVP-FPÖ government moreover did not introduce freedom of information but kept the principle of secrecy (Amtsgeheimnis). Yet, former governments had failed to do so as well.[180]

---

176 H Mayer, Durchsetzung (Exekution) verfassungsgerichtlicher Erkenntnisse. in M Holoubek and M Lang (eds), *Das verfassungsgerichtliche Verfahren in Steuersachen* (Linde 2010) 209.

177 BGBl I 46/2011.

178 J Pirker, Stabilität und Nachhaltigkeit durch (Verfassungs-)Recht?, *Sicherung von Stabilität und Nachhaltigkeit durch Recht: Tagung der Österreichischen Assistentinnen und Assistenten Öffentliches Recht, Band 5, Wien 2014* (Sramek 2015) 166.

179 'Sebastian Kurz wendet sich gegen Ausgrenzung bestimmter Medien', *Zeit online* (25 September 2018) https://www.zeit.de/politik/ausland/2018-09/oesterreich-ausgrenzung-medien-sebastian-kurz-bundeskanzler-kritik-fpoe accessed 2 January 2020.

180 See M Bertel, 'Informationsfreiheit statt Amtsgeheimnis? Art. 22a B-VG neu auf dem Prüfstand' [2014] 22 (4) *Journal für Rechtspolitik* 203 *et seq.*

The second crucial point worth mentioning is lawmaking. Whereas the professionalization of law-making through impact assessments[181] and expertise[182] has to be seen as a positive, over-professionalization may lead to non-transparent processes of legislating. When information is provided mainly by lobbyists and when certain stakeholders get too powerful, parliament is reduced to a symbolic lawmaker.[183] There was, e.g. wide consensus in Austria that a bill aiming at the development of Austria as a business location, was not only against EU law[184] but also unconstitutional.[185] In its initial form, it would have privileged economic interests over e.g. environmental concerns, when the procedure for obtaining certain permissions linked to the building of new industrial plants would have exceeded a certain amount of time.[186] The bill was adopted, but some concerns remain.[187] The fact that the EU Commission began to become involved in 2019 after the amended bill was enacted shows that not all doubts have been resolved.[188]

The third crucial point is the increase of parliamentary inquiry committees. Since 2015, the installation of an inquiry committee in parliament is a minority right.[189] This means that opposition parties do not need the votes of the parties in government anymore. We can expect, therefore, that the opposition will install more inquiry commissions in the future. Since parliamentary inquiry committees are a tool of (political) control of the parliament over government, this is a positive development. The last inquiry committee, for example, investigated a raid of the Austrian police forces (they are responsible to the minister of interior, then Herbert Kickl) that had taken place in the Federal Office for the Protection of the Constitution and Counter-Terrorism (*Bundesamt für Verfassungsschutz und Terrorismusbekämpfung*, BVT). The raid had raised suspicion about the politically motivated influence of the government on the BVT. Whereas before 2015, the installation of an inquiry committee would have been (politically) impossible because the government parties would most probably not agree to it, the example of the BVT inquiry committee shows that this reform has

181 Art. 51 para 8 Austrian Constitution and https://www.oeffentlicherdienst.gv.at/wirkungsorientierte_verwaltung/folgenabschaetzung/rechtsgrundlagen/rechtsgrundlagen.html accessed 2 January 2020.

182 See on this topic, C Jabloner, Privatisierung der Rechtsetzung. in WiR – Studiengesellschaft für Wirtschaft und Recht (eds), Privatisierung der Rechtssetzung (Linde 2010) 17 *et seq.*

183 ibid 17 *et seq.*

184 See European Commission, Infringement No 20192224, Formal notice Art. 258 TFEU and https://ec.europa.eu/commission/presscorner/detail/EN/INF_19_5950 accessed 2 January 2020.

185 Law on infrastructure projects in the 'special public interest', BGBl I 110/2018.

186 See 67/ME, XXVI. GP, available at https://www.parlament.gv.at/PAKT/VHG/XXVI/ME/ME_00067/fname_702573.pdf accessed 2 January 2020.

187 See, e.g., the critic of environmental organizations, https://www.umweltdachverband.at/inhalt/umweltdachverband-zum-standortentwicklungsgesetz-neu-geplanter-uebertragungsmechanismus-ist-verfassungswidrig?ref= accessed 2 January 2020.

188 See European Commission, Infringement No 20192224, Formal notice Art. 258 TFEU and https://ec.europa.eu/commission/presscorner/detail/EN/INF_19_5950 accessed 2 January 2020.

189 BGBl I 101/2014.

strengthened the liberal constitution. The challenge within the creation of inquiry committees can be seen in the fact that there is the need for opposition parties to be actively engaging in monitoring government and bring to life the relevant provisions.

6 Conclusion

As shown, the Austrian Constitution can be described as robust. Not only the history after World War II but also the recent events following the so-called Ibiza scandal have demonstrated that the Constitution still provides solutions to political crises. The Ibiza video uncovered the fact that some FPÖ politicians were openly thinking about acts that could be classified as corruption and endangering the liberal constitution (e.g. influencing the media),[190] yet, none of these ideas were realized. The consequence of the publication of the Ibiza video was the failure of the government coalition between the ÖVP and the FPÖ. Then, for the first time since 1945, a motion of confidence in parliament was successful and led to the dismissal of the government. From June 2019, an interim government consisting of experts was in charge of government operations.[191] Elections in October 2019 returned governance to a democratically legitimized government. This was not only due to the Austrian Constitution, which has shown its durability and robustness once again. Whereas the Constitution assigns an important role to the President in cases like this, then-President Alexander Van der Bellen also demonstrated sensitivity in the transition. The protection of the liberal Constitution is therefore not only an important aim of the Constitution but translates into political practice.

What the future will be like, will not only depend on the Austrian Constitution. Much will depend on further developments in the EU and Europe. Yet, even though the Austrian Constitution is quite old, the conditions it provides for a stable future remain strong.

190 For the Ibiza videos, see I Mijnssen, 'Strache ausgeschlossen – ein Überblick über #Ibizagate und seine Folgen', *Neue Zürcher Zeitung* (13 December 2019) https://www.nzz.ch/international/strache-tritt-ab-und-was-wir-ueber-ibiza-wissen-ld.1482831 accessed 2 January 2020.

191 H Jankowski, '"Mach' ma schon": Eine "typisch österreichische" Angelobung', *Die Presse* (3rd June 2019) https://www.diepresse.com/5638363/mach-ma-schon-eine-typisch-osterreichische-angelobung# accessed 2 January 2020.

East-Central Europe – Populist Constitutionalism

*Paul Blokker**

1 Introduction

Populism is a much-debated phenomenon in contemporary democracies. In the European context, particular concern has been raised (not least by EU institutions) with regard to countries in the Eastern part of the continent. While the populist phenomenon is present in the political arena of almost any European country, it is fair to ask whether there is specific dimension to populism in those countries that have embarked on democratization trajectories only in the last three decades. On one hand, then, it is evident that liberal democracies are affected by populist tendencies in general, on the other, the question emerges as to how populism might be a distinctive force in the post-communist countries in East-Central Europe.[1]

This chapter starts from the supposition that there is something distinctive to East-Central European populism. The distinctive dimension regards the specific transformation trajectories in these countries since 1989. A key dimension to populism in this region is a form of backlash against what can be understood as the 'legal revolutions' and/or 'rights revolutions' of the 1990s.[2] The backlash expresses itself in

* Department of Sociology and Business Law, University of Bologna/Institute of Sociological Studies, Charles University, Prague. E-mail: paulus.blokker@unibo.it. The author acknowledges a standard research grant from the Czech Science Foundation (GACR) (18-25924S) for the project "Transnational Populism and European Democracy' (TRAPpED) (2018-2020).

1 The chapter uses the geographical identification of East-Central Europe, following Johann Arnason in identifying a distinctive historical region, distinct from both a Germanic *Mitteleuropa* and Russian-controlled Eastern Europe proper, see: JP Arnason, 'Introduction: Demarcating East Central Europe' [2005] 8(4) *European Journal of Social Theory* 387.

2 Jiří Přibáň, for instance, spoke of the 'fiction of legal revolutions', see: J Přibáň, *Dissidents of Law* (Ashgate 2002) 89, and together with Wojciech Sadurksi of a 'self-limiting and legalistic revolution' (see: J Přibáň and W Sadurski, The Role of Political Rights in the Democratization of Central and Eastern Europe. in W Sadurski (ed), *Political Rights under Stress in 21st Century Europe* (Oxford University Press 2006)196-238, 299), while Andrew Arato related to the '"gentle" and "legal" revolutionaries' (see: A Arato, 'Dilemmas Arising from the Power to Create Constitutions in Eastern Europe' [1993] 14(3-4) Cardozo Law Review 661) and the former Chief Judge of the Hungarian Constitutional Court László Sólyom related to the 'revolution under the rule of law' (see: L Sólyom, 'The role of constitutional courts in the transition to democracy: with special reference to Hungary' [2003] 18(1) *International Sociology* 133).

some cases as a veritable *counter-revolution by law* or *counter-constitutionalism.*[3] At the same time, this chapter will acknowledge the fact that populism manifests itself differently in countries in the region, and a key focus will be on the two most prominent cases of populism-in-government, that is, Poland and Hungary, while also the cases of Czechia, Romania, and Slovakia will be discussed.

It is argued here that a crucial part of understanding current manifestations of populism in the region needs to be related to how (and how profoundly) constitutional democracy was institutionalized in the years after 1989. What is particularly relevant is the widespread adoption of a *legal-constitutional design*, and the choices in that design as well as in the actual set-up of legal and constitutional institutions. In a variety of ways, the current constitutional politics of the populists are going strongly against the tide of 30 years of building constitutional democracy according to the legal-constitutional blue-print. The populist counterforces take, however different guises in distinctive domestic contexts, while in all cases they form part of a durable contestation to the legal-constitutional model, criticizing a political and too invasive role of judicial institutions, a hindering of majoritarian politics, and an undue favouring of distinctive (liberal, and in some cases, post-communist) political forces.

The chapter will first discuss the institutionalization of a legal-constitutional institutional set-up throughout the region in the wake of 1989. Second, the populist challenges to liberal and legal constitutionalism in five countries in the region – the Czech Republic, Hungary, Poland, Romania, and Slovakia – will be explored.

2 Constitution-making in East-Central Europe

Populism has been a significant political phenomenon in most parts of East-Central Europe since the early 1990s.[4] What is more recent is its electoral weight, in particular in the cases of Hungary and Poland, and its central (rather than marginal) position in domestic politics. Populism has been part and parcel of the transformation processes, in the struggle over the nature of transformation and the distinctive political form to be institutionalized. Whereas the dominant model to be implemented was supported by domestic liberal forces and strongly endorsed by international institutions (the European Union (EU), the Council of Europe), this model has always been contested by a variety of – including nationalist and extremist – political forces. The novelty of

3 KL Scheppele, The Social Lives of Constitutions. in P Blokker and C Thornhill (eds), *Sociological Constitutionalism* (Cambridge University Press 2017); A Sledzinska-Simon, 'The Polish Revolution: 2015-2017' (*Blog of the International Journal of Constitutional Law*, 25 July 2017) www.iconnectblog.com/2017/07/the-polish-revolution-2015-2017 accessed 29 October 2019.

4 P Blokker, 'Populist Nationalism, Anti-Europeanism, Post-nationalism, and the East-West Distinction' [2005] 6(2) *German Law Journal* 371.

recent years is that the liberal predominance is increasingly marginalized in favour of alternative, populist projects.

The 'backlash' to the liberal democratic-constitutional model also means that the consensus on what I will call below a 'legal-constitutional' form of constitutionalism has waned, and that the latter is now openly contested. This also means that what around 1989 seemed natural and convincing in terms of constitutional choices has become much more problematic in the light of events since 2010. Perhaps it might even be argued that in some cases the legal-constitutional model has been less 'natural' and more contested even at the start of the democratic transformation.[5]

In 1989, the *Zeitgeist* entailed, not least due to active promotion by international actors, a strong emphasis on a *legal-constitutional*[6] or *new constitutional* approach[7] to the building of democracy. Indeed, many observers at the time claimed that post-communist constitution-making was about implementing well-tested designs, while any creative local input was mostly greeted with suspicion. From the perspective of the globally predominant understanding of constitutionalism, the emphasis on legalism, legal continuity, and the rule of law was rather related to a radical, binary view of legalism, that is, as an antidote to the 'ideological'[8] or 'contradictory'[9] socialist legality of the communist regimes. After 1989, the 'return' to constitutionalism and the rule of law or, at the very least, the rejection of the communist instrumentalization of the law for political purposes, reconnected with this trend of 'new' constitutionalism. The internationally endorsed role of new constitutionalism – in East-Central Europe fortified through the institutions of the EU and the Council of Europe – was that of securing the transition to robust constitutional democratic orders.[10]

The legal-constitutional template – in its Kelsenian emphasis on independent apex courts[11] (à la the German Constitutional Court), significant forms of judicial review, extensive and entrenched rights catalogues, and a strong or even absolute separation

5 As, for instance, in the Polish case, see: E Kowalewska, 'Competing visions of Constitutionalism in Post-Socialist Poland' ("New constitutionalism? New forms of democracy and rule of law beyond liberalism" conference, International Institute for the Sociology of Law, Oñati, Spain, July 2018); W Sadurski, *Poland's Constitutional Breakdown* (Oxford University Press 2019); for the Hungarian case, see: G Halmai, 'Silence of transitional constitutions: The "invisible constitution" concept of the Hungarian Constitutional Court' [2018] 16(3) *International Journal of Constitutional Law* 969.

6 A Sajó and R Uitz, *The Constitution of Freedom: An Introduction to Legal Constitutionalism* (Oxford University Press 2017).

7 T Győrfi, *Against the New Constitutionalism* (Edward Elgar 2016).

8 SA Arjomand, 'Law, Political Reconstruction and Constitutional Politics' [2003] 18(1) *International Sociology* 7.

9 J Přibáň and W Sadurski, The Role of Political Rights in the Democratization of Central and Eastern Europe. in W Sadurski (ed), *Political Rights under Stress in 21st Century Europe* (Oxford University Press 2006).

10 B Bugarič, 'A crisis of constitutional democracy in post-Communist Europe: "Lands in-between" democracy and authoritarianism' [2015] 13(1) *International Journal of Constitutional Law* 219.

11 A Stone Sweet, Constitutional courts. in M Rosenfeld and A Sajó (eds), *The Oxford Handbook of Comparative Constitutional Law* (Oxford University Press 2012).

between parliamentary politics and the constitutional order – was largely without historical precedent in the constitutional cultures in the region. Despite its alien, imported nature in most of the post-communist societies, this emphasis on written constitutions with an entrenched 'catalogue of rights', and a 'system of constitutional justice to defend those rights'[12] is not surprising. Many perceived legalism, legal continuity, and the rule of law as robust *antidotes* to the socialist legality of the communist regimes. The post-1989 'return' to constitutionalism and the rule of law constituted a strong rejection of the communist instrumentalization of the law for political purpose, and legal constitutionalism was to secure the transition to robust constitutional democratic orders.

Below I will briefly discuss the diffusion of legal constitutionalism in East-Central Europe, in particular with regard to separate and strong constitutional courts and the nature of constitutional norms as higher law. This will serve as a backcloth to the 'backlash' by a variety of populist forces in the region against the predominant institutional and constitutional model endorsed in particular throughout the first 20 years of transformation in the region.

2.1 Constitutional Courts

A key dimension in the post-1989 transformations has been the creation of constitutional courts. All countries in the region adopted a more or less similar, Kelsenian model of concentrated or centralized review, in which one singular institution has the responsibility and independent status to 'authoritatively scrutinise laws in terms of their constitutionality'.[13] Many countries looked to Western Europe for inspiration, not least Germany. This does not mean, however, that the constitutional systems developed in the same manner[14] or that constitutional adjudication is homogeneous throughout the region.[15] Despite significant similarities, the development of constitutional courts has differed importantly throughout the region (as we will see below). In the institutionalization of constitutional courts, important differences could be observed during, and even before, the years of transformation.

In the Czech Republic and Slovakia, for instance, separate constitutional courts ultimately emerged in the wake of a brief period of a federal constitutional court of Czechoslovakia (which existed until 1992). Czechoslovakia had experienced a brief and

12 A Stone Sweet, Constitutions and Judicial Power. in D Caramani (ed), *Comparative Politics* (Oxford University Press 2007) 219.

13 W Sadurski, *Rights Before Courts: A Study of Constitutional Courts in Postcommunist States of Central and Eastern Europe* (Springer 2008) 5.

14 P Blokker, *Multiple Democracies in Europe: Political Culture in New Member States* (Routledge 2010).

15 K Pócza (ed), *Constitutional Politics and the Judiciary: Decision-making in Central and Eastern Europe* (Routledge 2018).

modest moment of a Kelsenian type of constitutional judiciary in the interwar period, while in 1968, a constitutional act of the communist regime indicated the establishment of a federal court (which was, however, never implemented.[16] The Czech case is archetypal for the region's general experience in that the 1992 Constitution was 'adopted as a response to the totalitarian past of Czechoslovakia', while the drafters associated the Constitution with the 'revolutionary fervour of the 1989 Velvet Revolution and attempted to annihilate the Communist heritage'.[17] The Czech Constitution created a strong Constitutional Court which became the Constitution's 'most powerful protector'.[18]

The Slovak Court was set up after the 'velvet divorce' of the Czech Republic and Slovakia and became operative in March 1993. The Slovak Court follows a general pattern – as identified by Wojciech Sadurksi – in terms of powers of 'concentrated' or 'centralised' constitutional review by an independent and specialized institution.[19] As also argued by Broest and others:

> Currently prevailing trends indicate that the protection of constitutionality should be invested in permanent and special court authorities, which have the indispensable system of guarantees of their independence and impartiality [...] Just as other countries of Central and Eastern Europe, the Slovak Republic has also accepted this prevalent trend, and in its Constitution of 1992 it created a permanent specialized authority of constitutional protection.[20]

The Court's jurisprudence was, however, frequently ignored by national-populist governments in the 1990s.[21] In 2001, the Slovak Constitutional Court became more powerful due to initiated in the light of EU accession. According to Broestl and others, the 2001 amendments added up to the "strengthening of the position and legal powers of the Constitutional Court".[22] The strengthening and autonomization of the Constitutional Court's powers included the increase of number of judges and the extension of their terms.

---

16 K Šipulová, The Czech Constitutional Court: Far away from political influence. in K Pócza (ed), *Constitutional Politics and the Judiciary* (Routledge 2019) 1384.

17 Z Kühn, The Czech Republic: From a Euro-Friendly Approach of the Constitutional Court to Proclaiming a Court of Justice Judgment Ultra Vires. in A Albi (ed.), *National Constitutions in European and Global Governance: Democracy, Rights, the Rule of Law* (Springer 2018) 796.

18 ibid 796.

19 W Sadurski, *Rights Before Courts: A Study of Constitutional Courts in Postcommunist States of Central and Eastern Europe* (Springer 2008).

20 A Broestl and others, *Constitutional Court of the Slovak Republic (Organization, Process, Doctrine)* (Constitutional Court of the Slovak Republic 2001) 13.

21 C Boulanger, 'Constitutionalism in East Central Europe? The Case of Slovakia under Meciar' [1999] 33(1) *East European Quarterly* 30.

22 A Broestl and others, *Constitutional Court of the Slovak Republic (Organization, Process, Doctrine)* (Constitutional Court of the Slovak Republic 2001) 169.

In Poland, some initial steps towards legal constitutionalism emerged before 1989, as a Constitutional Tribunal was set up already on 26 March, 1982 (while becoming operative only in 1985,[23] in an attempt to enhance legitimacy of the communist regime. According to Sadurski, the "establishment of the court could be seen more as part of a disingenous 'charm offensive' by General Jaruzelski than [as] a genuine wish to bring in democratic changes".[24] Soon after 1989, however, the Tribunal became an "active partner and controller of the legislature and executive through filling in the blanks of the constitutional text".[25] It took however until the new Polish Constitution of 1997 for a legal-constitutionalist situation to become institutionalized, i.e. the Tribunal was made the final arbiter of constitutional interpretation (while in Romania, as indicated below, it was only with amendments in 2003 that the Constitutional Court gained a final say in matters of constitutionality).

The Hungarian Constitutional Court was established in 1989 by means of the Act on the Constitutional Court (Act XXXII). The court was both endorsed by the anti-communist opposition that wanted an independent institution and by the governing communist party that wanted to institutionalize its influence beyond the imminent elections.[26] The Constitutional Court played a major role in the democratic transition in that it was the main actor in promoting legal continuity as the creation of the rule of law by means of the rule of law. In terms of its prerogatives, it has been argued that the Hungarian Court is the strongest of its kind in a global perspective (at least with regard to the 1990s). As Scheppele has argued, "[f]or close to a decade, the Hungarian Constitutional Court has been perhaps the most powerful court of its kind in the world".[27] Under the 1989 constitution, it "has an exceptionally wide jurisdiction even in international comparison since it initially had to oversee the activity also of the [...] Parliament".[28] Two dimensions of the early Hungarian court stood out: its activism and its recourse to a so-called 'invisible constitution'.[29] Its activism related to its active part in

---

23 W Sadurski, *Poland's Constitutional Breakdown* (Oxford University Press 2019).

24 ibid.

25 ibid.

26 G Halmai, The Hungarian Approach to Constitutional Review: The End of Activism? The First Decade of the Hungarian Constitutional Court. in W Sadurski (ed), *Democratic Legitimacy and Constitutional Courts in Post-Communist Europe in a Comparative Perspective* (Springer 2003) 191.

27 KL Scheppele, 'The New Hungarian Constitutional Court' [1999] 8(4) *East European Constitutional Review* 81.

28 G Halmai, The Hungarian Approach to Constitutional Review: The End of Activism? The First Decade of the Hungarian Constitutional Court. in W Sadurski (ed), *Democratic Legitimacy and Constitutional Courts in Post-Communist Europe in a Comparative Perspective* (Springer 2003) 192.

29 G Halmai, 'Silence of transitional constitutions: The "invisible constitution" concept of the Hungarian Constitutional Court' [2018] 16(3) *International Journal of Constitutional Law* 969.

shaping the institutions and form of constitutional democracy throughout the 1990s (as for instance in its famous decision on the death penalty).[30] The idea of the invisible constitution meant that the court perceived its role also in terms of filling out gaps in the existing constitution (which was based on the work-in-progress of the amended communist constitution), by taking recourse its own ideas of constitutionalism, apparently grounded in a wider, European constitutional tradition. The president of the Court, Solyom argued later that:

> [b]y receiving international and eminently European standards, the constitutional court became the representative in Hungary of an important ideological trend, which was non-nationalist and which emphasized the return to Europe, and the same time an equality with older democracies.[31]

Important changes with regard to the status of the Hungarian Constitutional Court have taken place since 2010, when the centre-right *Fidesz*-government started a veritable constitutional counter-revolution (see below). Some of the implications of the *Fidesz* constitutional programme include a drastic curtailment of the independence of the Hungarian constitutional court as well as of its powers of constitutional review, including a curtailment of powers to review financial legislation. The Constitutional Court's functionality has been importantly reduced because of a radical restriction in terms of the actors that are able to initiate constitutional review. Other amendments involved changes in the nomination of judges, the extension of the judges' mandate as well as the number of judges, and the nomination of the chief judge.

In Romania, the idea of a Constitutional Court constituted one of the most important conflicts in the debate on the new Constitution in the early 1990s. As argued by Renate Weber, "[m]any were either reticent or sceptical about the Constitutional Court by the time of its establishment".[32] During the constitutional debates in 1991, it was, for instance, feared that the Constitutional Court would become a 'fourth power' within

30 The court has been criticized for its activism and its judges labelled 'activist human rights fundamentalists' or 'parliamentary legal allies', see: G Halmai, The Hungarian Approach to Constitutional Review: The End of Activism? The First Decade of the Hungarian Constitutional Court. in W Sadurski (ed), *Democratic Legitimacy and Constitutional Courts in Post-Communist Europe in a Comparative Perspective* (Springer 2003) 196.

31 L Solyom, 'The Role of Constitutional Courts in the Transition to Democracy: With Special Reference to Hungary'[2003] 18(1) *International Sociology* 152.

32 R Weber, Constitutionalism as a Vehicle for Democratic Consolidation in Romania. in R Elgie and J Zielonka (eds), *Democratic Consolidation in Eastern Europe Volume 2: Constitutions and Constitution-Building: A Comparative Perspective* (Oxford University Press, 2001) 215; R Weber, The Romanian Constitutional Court: In Search of its Own Identity. in W Sadurski (ed), *Constitutional Justice, East and West. Democratic Legitimacy and Constitutional Courts in Post-Communist Europe in A Comparative Perspective* (Kluwer International 2002).

the architecture of the Romanian state.[33] Others argued, in contrast, that constitutional control was not only a "sinecure for lawyers, but an irrepressible necessity and [something] unanimously acknowledged".[34] To add to the complexity, in Romania there was something of a tradition of judicial review by the High Court of Cassation and Justice, while the new Constitutional Court seemed to clash with the role of the already existing Supreme Court. Ultimately then, and as argued by Ion Muraru, president of the Romanian Constitutional Court in the 1990s, "[i]n our country, in the debates in the Constituent Assembly, it was hard to convince even the lawyers that we needed a distinct authority of this sort".[35]

It is not surprising in the light of its contested nature that the Romanian Constitutional Court played a rather secondary role in the Romanian democratization process, at least until the early 2000s. Some observers argue that it held a marginal and largely irrelevant position during the 1990s, in which the Court issued only one decision of public impact, related to the legitimization of a third consecutive presidential mandate of Ion Iliescu.[36] As observed above, until the amendment of 2003, the Romanian court was the only court in the region (with the Polish Constitutional Tribunal until 1997) that was not considered the final arbiter in constitutional matters. Indeed, article 145 of the 1991 constitution allowed a two-third majority in parliament to override its rulings.[37] In addition, as argued by Sadurski, the Romanian court was less strong than some of its counterparts in the region, because prior to the 2003 revision it could not arbiter conflict between public institutions. Up until 2003, it could then be argued that the Romanian case did not constitute a form of legal constitutionalism all the way, but allowed for a form of legislative supremacy. The parliament formally held a final say in constitutional matters, which in reality, it however never successfully used.

Throughout the 1990s there appears to have been little parliamentary acceptance of Constitutional Court rulings as mandatory, also due to the Court's apparent openness to

33 *Geneza Constituției României. Lucrările Adunării Constituante,* (Bucharest, Regia Autonomă Monitorul Oficial, 1998) 876.

34 *Geneza Constituției României. Lucrările Adunării Constituante,* (Bucharest, Regia Autonomă Monitorul Oficial, 1998) 854.

35 A Mungiu-Pippidi, 'Interview with President of the Romanian Constitutional Court, Ion Muraru' [1997] *East European Constitutional Review* 79; Valea mentions other critical positions that were articulated during the constitutional debate, including an outright rejection of the idea of a constitutional court as a 'superpower', and 'alien body', and an 'extra-parliamentary body' 'situated above the parliament' (DC Valea, 'The Constitutional Court – an innovation in the Romanian constitutional system' [2010] 1 *Curentul Juridic* 58; *Geneza Constitutiei* (n 34) 856-864).

36 Decision 1/1996. See: B Iancu, Constitutionalism in Perpetual Transition: The Case of Romania. in B Iancu (ed), *The Law/Politics Distinction in Contemporary Law Adjudication* (Eleven Publishing 2009) 187.

37 The original article 145 stated: "In cases of unconstitutionality, of the in accordance with Article 144 Constitutional subparagraphs a) and b), the law or Court standing orders shall be returned for reconsideration. If the law is passed again in the same formulation by a majority of at least two thirds of the members of each Chamber, the objection of unconstitutionality shall be removed, and promulgation thereof shall be binding".

political interference.[38] Weber argues that 'silence and ignorance' characterized the first decade of the court's operation.[39] As another observer puts it more staunchly:

> [f]or a very long time after the adoption of the 1991 Constitution, neither public debates nor political disputes were framed in the language and logic of constitutionality or constitutionalism. The local 'Guardian of the Constitution' was relegated to a marginal, almost irrelevant position.[40]

In this, the 2003 revision has contributed to a fairly drastic change in status, visibility and activity of the Court since the early 2000s. What is more, the Court has made various decisions with significant political clout and conflictive potential. The Court became increasingly the object of referrals, while also 'many public and political debates have suddenly started to be carried out within constitutional parameters'.[41] In particular in the second half of the 2000s, the Court has attempted to mediate in cases of high-level political conflict (predominantly between the President and the government) and constitutional crisis.

2.2 Higher law

An additional key feature of legal constitutionalism – that of the constitution as the apex of the legal system and as subject to (in some cases incisive) judicial review – has been a prominent characteristic of all post-1989 constitutions. Legal constitutionalism understands the constitution as a law that is situated 'above' ordinary laws and is rendered difficult to change by political means. This relatively strong separation between a higher law, guarded by judicial institutions, and parliamentary politics has proven a key point of contention for majoritarian populists. The level of entrenchment of the constitution, however, differs importantly between constitutions in the region. As indicated, entrenchment relates importantly to judicial review in that constitutional court decisions are more difficult to override the more entrenched a constitution is. As Sadurski has argued:

38 C Gilia, 'Comments on Decision no. 727 of 9th July 2012 of the Constitutional Court of Romania' [2012] 8 (3) *Juridica. Acta Universitatis Danubius* 71.

39 R Weber, Constitutionalism as a Vehicle for Democratic Consolidation in Romania. in R Elgie and J Zielonka (eds), *Democratic Consolidation in Eastern Europe Volume 2: Constitutions and Constitution-Building: A Comparative Perspective* (Oxford University Press, 2001) 284.

40 B Iancu, 'Post-Accession Constitutionalism With a Human Face: Judicial Reform and Lustration in Romania' [2010] 6 *European Constitutional Law Review* 28.

41 ibid.

> [t]he degree of 'finality' of decisions of constitutional courts may then be measured by the degree of entrenchment of the constitution: the easier it is to amend the constitution, the less final are the court's decisions. On the one side of spectrum, there will be cases of an 'absolute' entrenchment: when the constitution itself precludes a possibility of amending certain provisions [...] On the other side of the spectrum, there will be constitutions that are weakly entrenched, that is, those that envisage a reasonably easy amendment process'.[42]

Hence, in order to avoid undue political meddling with, and abuse of, the law by 'suspicious' political forces (not least the former communists), the constitutional law was situated 'above' ordinary laws and rendered difficult to change by political means.[43] Judicial review was adopted everywhere in the region, so that constitutional courts would hold the final right to interpret constitutional principles, while their decisions were made increasingly impossible to override by political means. The higher law status has constitutionally been enshrined in the form of limitations of revision ranging from simple supermajorities (as in the case of Hungary a two-third parliamentary majority), to complex provisions regarding initiators of revision, parliamentary approval, and ratification by means of a popular referendum (such as in the case of Romania).

An equally important, and related, feature was the entrenchment of a set of essential individual rights. Rights became a widely endorsed element of the ECE constitutions, stimulated by accession to the Council of Europe, and later on in the transition, the EU Charter of Fundamental Rights. The communist constitutions had included ample catalogues of rights, without, however, granting these rights the status of individual entitlements. Rather, individual rights were benefits granted by the state to citizens who were supposed to fulfil a range of duties, and were anyway interpreted arbitrarily and always within the context of the socialist ideal.[44] A main aim in all post-1989 constitutions was to entrench rights so as to protect these from political interference and arbitrariness.

Generally, the post-1989 transformations have seen the promotion of a democratic-constitutional model that displays features of a certain distrust towards political elites and politics in general. Contestation of such a distinctive approach to liberal democracy has been, however, a constant factor in the transformations, also as there is hardly any tradition of constitutional courts in the region and the idea of an independent apex court was entirely alien to most domestic constitutional cultures. In the early transition

---

42 W Sadurski, *Rights Before Courts: A Study of Constitutional Courts in Postcommunist States of Central and Eastern Europe* (Springer 2008) 80-81.

43 W Sadurski, *Poland's Constitutional Breakdown* (Oxford University Press 2019).

44 J Kurczewksi and B Sullivan, 'The Bill of Rights and the Emerging Democracies' [2002] 65(2) *Law and Contemporary Problems* 254-5.

period, the idea of a constitutional court was hence fiercely contested in quite a few ECE countries. In Poland, for instance, the constitutional court was perceived by some as a superfluous – or worse – type of institution, a view not least articulated by Jarosław Kaczyński, who in 2006 considered the Tribunal a 'fundamental mistake'. Throughout the region, contestation over the independence and composition of the court as well as its perceived activism – or interference in political matters – have remained an important issue of contention.

This contested nature of the *legal-constitutional design* is particularly evident in the most conspicuous cases of backsliding in the region, even if not only there. Currently, we witness a strong political reaction against the legal-constitutionalist model, and the assault on constitutional courts by majority governments, particularly evident in the cases of both Hungary (since 2010) and Poland (since 2015), while in Romania a significant struggle – between political forces and the President – over a model based on judicial independence and the rule of law – has become ever more explicit since early 2017.

3 POPULISM AND CONSTITUTIONALISM IN THE ECE

Populist forces now so prominent in the ECE region – in particular in Hungary and Poland taken a conservative-nationalist guise,[45] but equally present elsewhere[46] – ideologically question the legal-constitutional model, as endorsed during the transformation process by liberal political forces in their own societies as well as by supranational institutions such as the European Union and the Council of Europe (in particular the Venice Commission). Various populist forces are reacting to the liberal post-communist project of the 1990s, frequently portrayed as a project endorsed by an alliance between local liberals and former communists, on the one hand, and international liberal institutions, on the other. Populists criticize the legalistic, technocratic approach to constitutionalism in the transformation process, which they now counter with a strong insistence on the primacy of majoritarian politics and sovereigntism. Populism in a conservative guise (most prominently so in Hungary and Poland) includes the rejection of liberal values and the rule of law and endorses the sovereign right to self-government. A prominent ingredient of many populist political programs is *counter-constitutional reform* or even complete overhaul of the constitutional order, in the name of an alleged refoundation of national sovereign

45 P Blokker, 'Populist Counter-Constitutionalism, Conservatism, and Legal Fundamentalism' [2019] 15(3) *European Constitutional Law Review* 519; KL Scheppele, 'The opportunism of populists and the defense of constitutional liberalism' [2019] 20(3) *German Law Journal* 314.

46 B Trencsényi and others, *A History of Modern Political Thought in East Central Europe: Volume II: Negotiating Modernity in the 'Short Twentieth Century' and Beyond, Part I: 1918-1968* (Oxford University Press 2018) chapter 6.

power. The populist projects frequently feature a 'legal-skeptical' position towards liberal understandings of constitutionalism and the law, while at the same time putting the law upfront in the construction of alternative constitutional orders.[47]

There is a distinctive normative and 'ideological' thrust to the discourse and policies of populist governments, most conspicuously so in the cases of the Fidesz and PiS governments (populist government of Law and Justice), but in different guises noticeable elsewhere in the region too. The roots of many of the populist projects in East-Central Europe lie in anti-liberalism and conservatism, a distinctive set of ideas which antedates 1989, and which could be found in designated parts of the opposition to communism.[48] Liberalism is singled out as the main enemy and is displayed as 'evil and threatening'.[49] For Polish conservatives, for instance, liberalism – in its promotion of modernity, Western civilization grounded in moral decline, consumerist thinking and a negatively understood pluralism and multiculturalism – is undermining culture, religion, and national identity.[50] In Hungary, a similar conservative mindset is upfront in public debate as well as in politics. In the words of Frank Furedi, the "political outlook of Fidesz is best described as a synthesis of conservative nationalism and Christian democracy".[51]

While the most forceful populist projects are following a conservative approach, not all manifestations of populism in the region do so to the same extent. As I will indicate below, in the Czech Republic, for instance, the populism of the government of Andrej Babiš has been characterized as a pragmatic 'technopopulism',[52] while in Romania and Slovakia populist governments do invoke ethnonationalist and religious symbols, but so far have not engaged in full-blown counter constitutional projects. What is more, a kind of 'populism from below' has emerged in both cases in what Alina Mungiu-Pippidi has labelled 'anti-corruption populism'. Below, I will discuss the five countries mentioned in terms of the nature of the populist challenge and the nature and substance of ongoing political change.

47 P Blokker, 'Populism as a constitutional project' [2019] 17(2) *International Journal of Constitutional Law* 536.

48 E Dąbrowska, New conservatism in Poland: The discourse coalition around Law and Justice. in K Bluhm and M Varga (eds), *New Conservatives in Russia and East Central Europe* (Routledge 2018).

49 A Wolff-Powęska, 'Trommler der Revolution Jungkonservative und Polens Rechte' [2018] 3(5) *Osteuropa* 59.

50 ibid.

51 F Furedi, *Populism and the European Culture Wars: The Conflict of Values Between Hungary and the EU* (Routledge 2017) 5.

52 V Havlík, 'Technocratic Populism and Political Illiberalism in Central Europe' [2019] *Problems of Post-Communism* 1.

3.1 Czech Republic

In the case of the Czech Republic, it has often been argued that it is less prone to populist forces, in that it did not experience any 'hybrid regime' in the 1990s (as in Slovakia under Vladimír Mečiar at the the time), nor saw the emergence of strong populist forces in the 2000s, as in Poland and Hungary.[53] Moreover, it is frequently argued that the 'Czech Republic has a stronger system of checks and balances that is an impediment to any quick slide toward illiberal democracy'.[54] In the view of Katarina Sipulova, the Czech Constitutional Court is the "most isolated from various external political factors within the region".[55] Also in the view of Zdenek Kuhn, the Czech "Constitution created a strong Constitutional Court [...] which soon became its most powerful protector".[56] As a strong and relatively independent apex court it has so far been able to withstand pressure from populist forces.

Nevertheless, it may be argued that also in the case of the Czech Republic, important challenges of a populist nature can be identified.[57] As Jiri Priban has argued, the Czech system is challenged by a dual threat of excessive instrumentalism and/or realism:

> taking politics as merely a tool for trade (whether legal or criminal) and the conviction that politics is nothing more than the recycling among the powerful, while the powerless citizens can only look on.[58]

A distinctive populist threat has become particularly clear from 2011 onwards, when a new political movement (and later party) came unto the Czech scene: ANO or 'Action of Dissatisfied Citizens', headed by the current Prime Minister Andrej Babiš. ANO has been defined as a case of a 'populist-technocratic anti-party'.[59] In this, ANO is prominently different from the manifestations of conservative populism as in the Hungarian Fidesz and Polish PiS (see below). ANO's technopopulism does not so much promote Czech ethno-nationalism as it promotes a myth of Czech efficiency, resilience, and tradition of

---

53 ibid.

54 J Pehe, 'Czech Democracy Under Pressure' [2018] 29(3) *Journal of Democracy* 72.

55 K Šipulová, The Czech Constitutional Court: Far away from political influence. in K Pócza (ed), *Constitutional Politics and the Judiciary* (Routledge 2019) 1891.

56 Z Kühn, The Czech Republic: From a Euro-Friendly Approach of the Constitutional Court to Proclaiming a Court of Justice Judgment Ultra Vires. in A Albi (ed.), *National Constitutions in European and Global Governance: Democracy, Rights, the Rule of Law* (Springer 2018).

57 See: J Baroš and P Dufek and D Kosař, 'Separation of Powers in Democratic Theory: Understanding Populism and Rise of the Unelected. The Case of Central Europe', draft, on file with author.

58 J Přibáň, *The Defence of Constitutionalism: The Czech Question in Post-national Europe* (Karolinum Press 2017) 116.

59 V Havlík, 'Technocratic Populism and Political Illiberalism in Central Europe' [2019] *Problems of Post-Communism* 6.

craftmanship.[60] At the same time, however, it can be argued that Babiš and his ANO 'electoral party' form a similar threat to liberal constitutionalism, in that its anti-political and anti-establishment ideas point to not dissimilar forms of reform of the constitutional democratic system. The comprehensive distrust towards traditional political parties translates into a distrust towards parliamentary institutions, deliberation, and checks and balances. Babiš hence endorses 'simpler' and 'faster decision-making'.[61] He criticizes the slowness of the existing institutions and hence 'pointless and ultimately unnecessary discussions'. Indeed, the 'ideal situation' for Babiš would be the "existence of one-party majority governments with very few restraints on the implementation of cabinet policies".[62] Babiš' 'managerial narrative' stresses the executive over legislative powers, endorses less parliamentary control over the executive, and criticizes the Senate (an institution with important constitutional prerogatives. Hence, in Babiš' *What I Dream About When I Happen to Be Sleeping*, he fantasizes about the abolishment of the Senate, and the shift of its powers towards the President:

> Of course, the Senate has some powers, too, for instance how to prevent anarchy [*bezvladi*], or violent constitutional changes. So these powers should be delegated to the president when is elected directly. The most important changes, the constitutional changes or international treaties, should be decided in referenda by everyone.[63]

The populist challenge in the Czech Republic is enhanced by the fact that President Milos Zeman, currently in his second mandate (and close to Babiš), has proven to be a more explicitly national-populist threat to the liberal-democratic system. In 2013, as referred to by Jiri Přibáň, Zeman attempted to "do away with the parliamentarian regime and all its constitutional conventions, which he went so far as to proclaim "idiotic", and impose a semi-presidentialist regime".[64] It was only in the last minute that parliament prevented Zeman from doing so.

60 ibid 7.

61 ibid 11.

62 ibid.

63 Babiš, cited in: V Havlík, 'Technocratic Populism and Political Illiberalism in Central Europe' [2019] *Problems of Post-Communism* 12.

64 J Přibáň, *The Defence of Constitutionalism: The Czech Question in Post-national Europe* (Karolinum Press 2017) 118.

3.2 Hungary

The Hungarian case has been widely seen and discussed as the most serious, problematic, and far-progressed manifestation of populism in the region. Concerns regarding constitutional democracy started in particular with the new Hungarian constitution, drafted and adopted in the period 2010-11. The new constitution indicates a shift away from the Hungarian attachment to a secular state, grounded in liberal, European traditions, as was evident in the constitutionalization process since 1989, and has led to the institutionalization of a new constitutional order that has its foundations in sovereigntist, conservative, and religious traditions.

In the early transition years, the Hungarian trajectory was based on the opposite rationale of the current populist, counter constitutional project: an elite narrative that strongly emphasized liberal, representative democracy, the rule of law, European constitutionalism, and technocratic governance.[65] Importantly, Hungary was long considered a front-runner in the East-Central European region, with the most successful record in adopting legal constitutionalist institutions, including an enormously strong Constitutional Court, an elite endorsement of a Europeanist constitutional culture, and powerful forms of rights protection. Indeed, throughout the 1990s, Hungarian democracy was often portrayed as an archetypal case of adherence to a human-rights-based legal constitutionalism.

The disembedded, elitist nature of the legal-constitutionalist-cum-rule-of-law state and the lack of a widespread support for the liberal-constitutional framework facilitated strong counter-reactions. As argued by András Bozóki, from the Round Table talks of 1989 onwards, the project of constitutional democracy was one driven by technocratic elites, who promoted a programme of "Westernization, free speech, freedom of the press, human rights, checks and balances, rule of law with strong guardian institutions like the constitutional court and the ombudsman". As Bozóki continues, "[i]t was a very sophisticated set of institutions – but without the spirit of democracy' and the 'participatory aspect of democracy was missing".[66] Various observers have noted the lack of a robust, positive consensus on a constitutional framework in the early 1990s. When the – anyhow limited – elitist liberal consensus started waning in the second part of the 1990s, a counter-reaction could emerge, mobilized by a transformed Fidesz party, which manipulated nationalist and populist sentiments amongst the losers of the transformation. Fidesz mobilized parts of the population that had been identifying liberalism and the rule of law increasingly with a Western import, foreign interests, and upper-class ideas.

---

65 G Halmai, 'Silence of transitional constitutions: The "invisible constitution" concept of the Hungarian Constitutional Court' [2018] 16(3) *International Journal of Constitutional Law.*

66 Interview with András Bozóki, see: J Ferrer, 'Hungary's U-Turn' (*John Ferrer,* 25 April 2014) http://www.johnfeffer.com/hungarys-u-turn accessed on 19 November 2019.

The culmination of illiberalism and populism came with Fidesz winning an absolute majority in the 2010 elections, which allowed it to start its constitutional counter-project. This project involves clear dimensions of what I have labelled elsewhere 'legal resentment'.[67] Scheppele already referred to such a sentiment in the early 2000s under the name of the 'counterconstitutionalism'.[68] The thrust of much of the counter-constitutional process has been against the democratic-constitutional order that has emerged since 1989.

The conservative thrust in the Fidesz project can be related to 'communitarian' as well as 'illiberal' views of constitutionalism.[69] What identifies such forms of constitutionalism is the perception of a 'common enemy' in liberal constitutionalism, and a critique of both the 'meta-liberal value of normative individualism' and its understanding of the 'neutral state'.

Fidesz's counterconstitutional project has by now (anno 2019) drastically changed the post-1989 political system. In 2010, Fidesz took immediately action against the Constitutional Court's jurisdiction, by talking away the Court's power over fiscal matters, making it largely impossible for the Court to rule on the constitutionality of budgets or taxes.[70] More drastically, with the Fourth Amendment of the new Hungarian Fundamental Law in 2013, review powers of the Court were restricted to procedural matters only, while the earlier case law of the Court of the 1990-2011 period was annulled. The new constitution in general shows strong tensions with checks and balances and the rule of law, as well as shows strong contrasts with fundamental rights guarantees (in particular after the Fourth Amendment in March 2013[71]). The Fundamental Law has been amended 7 times since its adoption (anno 2019), and a system of 'limited constitutional review', a strong break with the post-1989

67 P Blokker, 'Populist Counter-Constitutionalism, Conservatism, and Legal Fundamentalism' [2019] 15(3) *European Constitutional Law Review.*

68 KL Scheppele, 'Counter-constitutions: Narrating the Nation in Post- Soviet Hungary' (paper given at George Washington University, 2004).

69 L Thio, Constitutionalism in illiberal polities. in M Rosenfeld and A Sajó (eds), *The Oxford Handbook of Comparative Constitutional Law* (Oxford University Press 2012).

70 M Bánkuti and G Halmai and KL Scheppele, 'Hungary's Illiberal Turn: Disabling the Constitution' in P Krasztev and J van Til (eds), *The Hungarian Patient: Social Opposition to an Illiberal Democracy* (Central European University Press 2015) 38-9.

71 As argued by Human Rights Watch in its review of the Hungarian situation, in particular after the Fourth Amendment, the new constitution of the Fidesz government is problematic 'in ways that weaken legal checks on its authority, interfere with media freedom, and otherwise undermine human rights protection in the country', see: Human Rights Watch, 'Wrong Direction on Rights: Assessing the Impact of Hungary's New Constitution and Law' (Human Rights Watch report, 2013) http://www.hrw.org/sites/default/files/reports/hungary0513_ForUpload.pdf accessed 8 November 2019, 3; See also the Opinion of the European Commission for Democracy Through Law (Venice Commission): Council of Europe, 'Opinion on the New Constitution of Hungary, Adopted by the Venice Commission at its 87th Plenary Session (Venice, 17-18 June 2011)' (Council of Europe, 2011) http://www.venice.coe.int/webforms/documents/CDL-AD(2011)016-E.aspx accessed 8 November 2019.

Constitution implemented, while various rights – including the right to vote and freedom of expression – have been curtailed.[72]

The Hungarian counterconstitutional project also contains a significant nationalist and religious dimension. As Gabor Halmai claims, the Hungarian Fundamental Law of 2011:

> shows the role of religion in national legitimation through characterizing the nation referred to as the subject of the constitution not only as the community of ethnic Hungarians, but also as a Christian community, narrowing even the range of people who can recognize themselves belonging to it.[73]

In particular the Fundamental Law's preamble is littered with religious references, including a reference to the Hungarian Roman Catholic tradition. But equally the actual text of the Fundamental Law reflects clear religious dimensions, for instance in its definition of community and preferred family model, and its provision of the protection of the unborn child.[74] The Hungarian populist project is not merely about symbolic and legitimating ornament, but has clear implications for society.[75] One of these implications was embodied in one of the (afore-mentioned) Cardinal Laws, which radically changed the status of legally recognized churches, leading to the deregistration of some 200 previously recognized (non-Christian) churches and greatly reducing the freedom of establishing new churches in Hungary.[76]

The Hungarian developments and its moving towards illiberal democracy and even authoritarianism have strongly affected its status as an EU Member State as well as its more general relation to European constitutional and human rights regimes.[77] On various occasions, Hungary has clashed with EU law and the Charter.

---

72 N Chronowski and others, Hungary: Constitutional (R)evolution or Regression? in A Albi and S Bardutzky (eds), *National Constitutions in European and Global Governance: Democracy, Rights, the Rule of Law: National Reports* (Asser Press 2019).

73 G Halmai, 'Religion and Constitutionalism' (2015) MTA Law Working Paper 2015/5, 75 https://jog.tk.mta.hu/uploads/files/mtalwp/2015_05_%20Halmai.pdf accessed 30 October 2019.

74 ibid.

75 In the latest, seventh amendment of the Fundamental Law, the populist and sovereigntist dimension appears to be particularly upfront. It inter alia aims at the 'protection of Hungary's self-identity' and promotes the idea that Hungary's 'Christian culture is the duty of all state organizations', see G Halmai, 'Fidesz and Faith: Ethno-Nationalism in Hungary' (European University Institute, 29 June 2018) https://blogs.eui.eu/constitutionalism-politics-working-group/fidesz-faith-ethno-nationalism-hungary accessed 2 November 2019.

76 G Halmai, 'Religion and Constitutionalism' (2015) MTA Law Working Paper 2015/5, 75 https://jog.tk.mta.hu/uploads/files/mtalwp/2015_05_%20Halmai.pdf accessed 30 October 2019 76.

77 N Chronowski and others, Hungary: Constitutional (R)evolution or Regression? in A Albi and S Bardutzky (eds), *National Constitutions in European and Global Governance: Democracy, Rights, the Rule of Law: National Reports* (Asser Press 2019).

3.3 Poland

In important ways following in the footsteps of Hungary, in Poland the conservative, populist forces have been equally reacting directly to the legal-constitutional project of the 1990s. The conversative critique on the liberal-democratic model has been an intrinsic part of the post-1989 transformation process. For Polish conservatives, liberalism, in its promotion of modernity, Western civilization – grounded in moral decline, consumerist thinking and a negatively understood pluralism and multiculturalism –, is undermining Polish culture, religion, and national identity.[78] Poland, just as Hungary, was widely considered a front-runner in the process of democratization, not least do to prominent manifestations of dissidence before 1989, and Poland was considered a consolidated liberal democracy early on, but the contested nature of the liberal-democratic system remained a prominent factor.[79] The new post-1989 constitution was adopted only in 1997 and was heavily contested by conservative forces at the time, who did not participate in its formulation and had put forward an alternative constitutional text. Bruce Ackerman has recently argued that the late adoption of the Polish Constitution and its limited societal support form main factors in explaining the current populist backlash.[80] Many of the arguments made by the current populist government of Law and Justice (PiS) were already part of the highly polarized discussions in the 1990s, between post-communists and left-liberals on the one hand, and the centre-right conservatives, gathered in Solidarity Electoral Action (AWS) (in 2001, PiS formed out of parts of this conservative political grouping), on the other. For instance, Krzaklewski, leader of AWS, strongly argued against the draft constitution as violating the convictions of larger part of society.[81]

In Poland, a constitutional crisis started with the electoral victory of PiS at the end of October 2015, and its subsequent confrontation with five Tribunal judges appointed by the out-going Civic Platform (PO) government in early October. PiS made the Constitutional Tribunal its first main institutional target, and started its confrontation with the Tribunal by contesting five Tribunal judges appointed by the out-going centre-right Civic Platform (PO) government. PiS justified its actions by invoking the need for extensive judicial reform and the development of a different type of constitutionalism. It disregarded a prominent constitutional convention (the oath of the newly appointed judges to be taken by the President), re-amended the Act on the Constitutional Tribunal, denying the legal status of the judges appointed by PO and rapidly appointed its own judges. The PiS-controlled Sejm, the Polish lower house, subsequently approved

78 A Wolff-Powęska, 'Trommler der Revolution Jungkonservative und Polens Rechte' [2018] 3(5) *Osteuropa*.

79 P Blokker, *Multiple Democracies in Europe: Political Culture in New Member States* (Routledge 2010).

80 B Ackerman, *Revolutionary Constitutions: Charismatic Leadership and the Rule of Law* (Harvard University Press 2019).

81 See: R Brier, 'The Roots of the "Fourth Republic" Solidarity's Cultural Legacy to Polish Politics' [2009] 23(1) *East European Politics and Societies* 65.

amendments of the Act, which changed the necessary quorum for decisions from 9 to 13 judges, out of a total of 15, effectively paralysing the court. On top of this, later rulings by the Tribunal, which found the changes unconstitutional, were delayed in publication or failed to be officially published at all. The taking over of the Tribunal was complete once, after a year, PiS gained a majority of judges on the Tribunal and the presidency was taken up by Julia Przyłębska (installed by means of a newly invented position of 'acting president', replacing the outgoing president Andrzej Rzepliński).[82]

In contrast to Fidesz in Hungary, PiS did not gain an extensive majority so as to be able to change the constitution, and has proceeded with reforms (frequently of an unconstitutional nature) that have turned the Constitutional Tribunal into a 'government enabler' (rather than an independent guardian of the Constitution), led to the adoption of various illiberal laws (e.g. reducing the freedom of assembly), and in recent times have focused on an extensive reform of the judicial system. After the capture of the Constitutional Tribunal, the PiS government extended reform to the Supreme Court and the National Council of the Judiciary (KRS). PiS assumed control over the KRS by terminating the terms of existing members and giving parliament the right to appoint a majority of the replacements.[83] In December 2017, PiS adopted a new law which added two new chambers to the Supreme Court, while changing the rules of appointment of Supreme Court judges, forcing all justices of over the age of 65 to retire, unless their terms are extended with presidential approval.[84] In general, PiS changed appointment rules so that it is the parliamentary majority that is now in charge of the appointment of members of both the KRS and the Supreme Court, while the President has gained extensive powers in appointing the president of the Court as well as regarding its internal functioning.

3.4 Romania

The Romanian case has often been cited as a third major concern in the EU, next to Hungary and Poland, in terms of democratic backsliding and populist politics undermining the rule of law.[85] Indeed, parallels have been drawn between the Hungarian and Romanian situations, partially unjustly so (as yet, a full-blown counter-

---

82 W Sadurski, 'How Democracy Dies (in Poland): A Case Study of Anti-Constitutional Populist Backsliding' (2018) Sydney Law School Research Paper 18/01, 22-23 https://papers.ssrn.com/sol3/papers.cfm?abstract_id=3103491 accessed 2 November 2019.

83 C Davies, 'Hostile Takeover: How Law and Justice Captured Poland's Courts' (Nations in Transit brief, Freedom House 2018) 5 https://freedomhouse.org/sites/default/files/poland%20brief%20final.pdf accessed 8 November 2019.

84 ibid; This part of the reform has been challenged by the European Court of Justice and PiS has reversed the retirement of judges.

85 B Iancu, 'Quod licet Jovi non licet bovi?: The Venice Commission as Norm Entrepreneur' [2019] 11(1) *Hague Journal on the Rule of Law* 201.

constitutional project is absent in the Romanian case, as is a related conservative-populist constitutional narrative). The Romanian case does warrant, however, specific attention.

It needs to be acknowledged that the Romanian transformation in the 1990s, in a way not dissimilar to the Slovakian case discussed below, was dominated by national-populist forces. The post-communist National Salvation Front (NSF) promoted a particular vision of an 'original democracy', based on the idea of a national consensus and a single-party system. The post-communist NSF defended above all a vision of the national unitary state, which was informed by a 'discourse of limited change'[86] and built on traditions of Romanian particularism as well as the national communism of the second half of the communist period. This nationalist discourse served in a strategic sense to defeat the voices of more radical change that emerged from the side of the Hungarian minority (which had played an important role in the anti-communist protests of the late 1980s) as well as from that of the democratic opposition in formation, both of which endorsed a Western-oriented, civic and rights-based discourse.[87]

From the mid-1990s onwards, the Romanian democratic transformation has, however, moved much closer towards a liberal democratic system based on the rule of law,[88] but at the same time, key aspects of the reforms regarding the independence of judicial institutions as well as the institution of the president have remained a significant object of political contention. In recent years, a major stand-off has developed between political forces that strongly endorse the EU's agenda of judicial independence and anti-corruption and those forces that contest such a position and endorse majority rule and the reduction of formal-legal constraints on government.[89] A deep, structural conflict has become visible in a number of constitutional conflicts and struggles over judicial reform, and is particularly outspoken since a (first) presidential crisis in 2007, a second such crisis in the summer of 2012,[90] and a third, renewed conflict over judicial reform and anti-corruption policy in 2017-19.

From one perspective, the Romanian constitutional turmoil is surprising, in that, from the early 2000s onwards, Romanian constitutional democracy seemed to consolidate a stable democratic system based on the rule of law, and what in general could be called a form of legal constitutionalism. But what becomes clear from recent developments is that the rule of law-driven and constitutional reforms of 2003 have amplified political and constitutional conflict, and in the wake of the 2007 EU accession have seen the emergence

86 P Blokker, 'Modernity and its varieties: a historical sociological analysis of the Romanian modern experience' (PhD thesis, European University Institute 2004).

87 ibid.

88 In a way surprisingly so, see: A Mungiu-Pippidi, 'Romania's Italian-style anticorruption populism' [2018] 29 (3) *Journal of Democracy* 104.

89 ibid.

90 The 2012 crisis triggered an (unsuccessful) attempt by the then government of Victor Ponta to revise the Constitution in 2013-14, not least in order to deal with the question of relations between president, parliament, and government.

(or return) of less virtuous forms of democratic politics and a more outspoken critique of EU interference in national matters. Ongoing conflict is related, at least in part, to an instrumental approach to constitutionalism and a form of 'legal resentment' or a skeptical view of some of the political forces (in particular the Social Democratic Party) regarding rigid, legalist constitutions and strong constitutional courts, as well as, in a related way, external interference into domestic constitutional politics.

As mentioned earlier, the second decade of post-1989 constitutionalization saw an increase in importance of the rule of law and rights as well as of the roles of the judiciary and the Constitutional Court. Paradoxically though, in the same period, constitutional conflicts became more frequent. The first moment of crisis emerged in 2007, when a direct confrontation between the president Traian Băsescu and the incumbent Liberal government led to the start of an impeachment procedure of the president, which in constitutional terms needs to be confirmed by a referendum. The popular referendum, held in the summer of 2007, reconfirmed however popular support for Băsescu, who stayed on as president. One of the salient constitutional dimensions to this crisis (apart from the head-on confrontation between political institutions) relates to the fact that according to the Romanian Constitution, impeachment can only follow from the identification of 'grave acts infringing upon Constitutional provisions' by the president (Article 95(1)). In an advisory opinion, the Constitutional Court ruled that relevant acts by the president could not be qualified as 'grave', and also that the final responsibility lied with the parliament (Advisory Decision 1, April 2007). Much of the crisis in 2007 had to do with 'presidential activism' and inter-party struggles, in relation to attempts to expand political power by various political actors.

The constitutional crisis of 2007 was repeated during the summer of 2012, when a renewed attempt to impeach president Băsescu was undertaken by the government of Victor Ponta, a social-democratic government.[91] The Ponta government did not merely repeat the impeachment procedure claiming the unconstitutionality of Băsescu's actions, but engaged in actions that themselves went into a clearly unconstitutional direction[92] by dismissing the speakers of both chambers of parliament (who were replaced by allies), as well as the Ombudsman, by restricting the powers of the Constitutional Court and threatening its judges with impeachment, and by issuing a decree (as well as a draft law) on the Law on Referendum in order to drastically increase the probability of a successful impeachment referendum. A further step taken was putting the control over

91 See: KL Scheppele, 'Romania Unravels the Rule of Law' *The New York Times* (5 July 2012) https://krugman.blogs.nytimes.com/2012/07/05/guest-post-romania-unravels-the-rule-of-law accessed 8 November 2019.

92 The Romanian constitutional scholar Ioan Stanomir has argued that the 'Romanian constitution has become an insignificant and irrelevant element' in Romanian politics, while commenting on the Ponta governments' actions, see https://evz.ro/ioan-stanomir-constitutia-romaniei-a-devenit-un-element-insignificant-991426.html accessed on 17 January, 2020.

the publication of the official gazette in the government's hands, thereby having effective sway over the public promulgation of laws (and therefore their implementation).[93]

The dramatic nature of the constitutional assault by the Ponta government became clear from the reaction of the Constitutional Court, which sent two very unusual complaint letters – in July and August 2012 – to the Council of Europe's Venice Commission as well as to European officials to ask for help against "virulent attacks" on its independence by the government. The Constitutional Court clearly also showed some strength in resisting the attacks, by, first of all, issuing a negative decision on the amendment of the law on public referenda (against the government's intent to implement a simple majority), and second, in its decision on the invalidity of the referendum held on the impeachment of Băsescu. This referendum, held on 29 July, failed to reach the quorum of 50% of the electorate, as upheld by the Constitutional Court in its earlier ruling. Therefore, the Constitutional Court ruled that the referendum was void, which meant that Băsescu was re-installed. Ponta ultimately accepted the Court's decision.

The Romanian constitutional crisis of 2012 can be interpreted as part of a wider struggle between political forces that are in favour or against strong anticorruption policies, a political divide that overlaps with pro-European, rule-of-law positions of the centre-right and majoritarian, populist positions on the centre-left.[94] The struggle between those forces that claim that existing judicial institutions are overpoliticized (in particular, the PSD (Social Democratic Party)) and those that defend existing judicial independence in the name of the rule of law has (currently most visibly represented by President Klaus Iohannis) have continued ever since. As argued by Bogdan Iancu, "[a] nticorruption discourses have become over the years a clear centre-right shibboleth", and,

93 The actions of the Ponta government were strongly criticized internationally, not least in a progress report on Romania of the European Commission, see: Commission, 'Annex Romania to the EU Anti-Corruption Report' COM(2014) 38 final; The latter called on the Romanian government to return to serious reform in the name of the rule of law, as recent events have "raised serious doubts about the commitment to the respect of the rule of law or the understanding of the meaning of the rule of law in a pluralist democratic system". The Commission's report triggered a response by a large number of Romanian intellectuals and representatives of civil society that replied with a Letter to the EU, in which they argue that the Commission ignores the fundamental legal principle of "audiatur et altera pars" and thereby underestimates the unconstitutional and undue political behavior of Băsescu. In addition, it fails to acknowledge the detrimental consequences of the crisis for Romanian parliament, which has turned into an "empty shell", see: Stelian Tănase, 'Scrisoare Către Uniunea Europeană, Bruxelles' (Desk Report, 23 July 2012) http://www.stelian-tanase.ro/la-zi/scrisoare-catre-uniunea-europeana-bruxelles accessed 8 November 2019); The response was restated in the European Parliament on 12 September by the MEP Renate Weber, who accused in particular the Commissioner Reding for an exaggerated reaction not based on the facts, and ignoring the illegitimacy of Băsescu, see: Act Media, 'Heated debates among MEP groups over the political situation in Romania' (Act Media, 13 September 2012) http://actmedia.eu/daily/heated-debates-among-mep-groups-over-the-political-situation-in-romania/42025 accessed 8 November 2019.

94 A Mungiu-Pippidi, 'Interview with President of the Romanian Constitutional Court, Ion Muraru' [1997] *East European Constitutional Review.*

in Romania, "anticorruption is fused to the hip with rule of law ideologies and latter-day anticommunism",[95] while the (post-communist) centre-left (PSD) has increasingly attempted to become the sole defender of traditional, Orthodox values and nationalist-conservative messages, even if not necessarily in an anti-EU manner.[96] Moreover, the PSD and its allies counter criticism of corruption with 'allegations of collusion between the heads of state, prosecutorial and judicial elites, and the secret services, which they call, ominously "the parallel state".[97]

The events since early 2017, when the governing PSD attempted to introduce a decree law that importantly 'relaxed' or diminished anti-corruption measures,[98] have seen a strong reaction in the form of popular protest[99] against the government and in the name of the anti-corruption agency DNA and the protection of an independent judiciary. In 2017, the PSD embarked on a judicial reform process that was allegedly to level the Romanian judicial institutions with EU standards (which would have inter alia touched upon the independence of courts and led to the relaxation of anticorruption rules[100]), but was, in contrast, perceived by both the opposition and the EU as a threat for the rule of law. Indeed, the European Commission has threatened with legal steps against the Romanian government. The matter subsided due to a popular referendum, initiated by President Iohannis, in which citizens were asked to express their agreement with the prohibition of amnesties and pardons for corruption offences as well as on the usage of emergency ordinances by the government. On 26 May 2019, a majority of Romanian citizens voted against the judicial reforms in the referendum. While the judicial reforms of the PSD government have been frequently labelled as populist, in their intent to enhance intervention by the political majority into the judicial process, the referendum initiated by the President has by some observers been depicted as a strategic usage of the referendum tool for mobilizational purposes, tapping into the strength of the civic protests of recent years. This protest is stimulated by the opposition against the PSD government, but at the same time, observers claim the

95 B Iancu, 'Quod licet Jovi non licet bovi?: The Venice Commission as Norm Entrepreneur' [2019] 11(1) *Hague Journal on the Rule of Law* 201.

96 Cf. A Momoc, 'Populism 2.0, digital democracy and the new "enemies of the people"' [2018] *Communication Today* 9(1) 74.

97 B Iancu, 'Quod licet Jovi non licet bovi?: The Venice Commission as Norm Entrepreneur' [2019] 11(1) *Hague Journal on the Rule of Law* 202.

98 R Ursu, In the Name of the Law. in A Adi and DG Lilleker (eds), *#rezist – Romania's 2017 anti-corruption protests: causes, development and implications* (Quadriga University of Applied Sciences 2017) 39.

99 The #Rezist movement, see: A Ştefănel, Some populist discursive aspects of the #Rezist movement. in A Adi and DG Lilleker (eds), *#rezist – Romania's 2017 anti-corruption protests: causes, development and implications* (Quadriga University of Applied Sciences 2017).

100 L Pech and V Perju and S Platon, 'How to Address Rule of Law Backsliding in Romania: The case for an infringement action based on Article 325 TFEU' (Verfassungblog, 29 May 2019) https://verfassungsblog.de/how-to-adress-rule-of-law-backsliding-in-romania accessed 10 November 2019.

opposition instrumentalizes the rule of law and a pro-EU position as well as a mobilized public for electoral gain.[101]

3.5 *Slovakia*

Slovakia has been often represented as a country of political stability and relatively untainted by illiberal populism in recent years, at least when compared to other Visegrad countries. The country appeared to show a solid attachment to liberal-democratic norms.[102] The relation between populism and Slovak democracy is, however, more complex. This becomes clear from both its overall transformation trajectory (and in particular the manifestations of populist-nationalist governments in the 1990s) and the dramatic events in recent years.

Even if Slovakia's democratization trajectory is widely regarded as one involving a 'successful democratic transition',[103] a structurally polarized political landscape – between forces that promote liberal-democratic values and institutions and those that endorse illiberal and authoritarian ones – needs to be acknowledged. In the 1990s, the latter forces already played an important role when two governments under Vladimír Mečiar indicated a clear populist-nationalist direction of Slovak politics, in which constitutional structures were ignored. The Mečiar government, as a kind of early precursor of current nationalist-populist governments in ECE, had an authoritarian leaning and disrespected the decisions of the Constitutional Court and the legislature at the time used an intolerant form of majoritarianism towards the opposition as well as minorities, disrespecting the latter's constitutional rights.[104] The Mečiar government further tried (unsuccessfully) to curb the powers of the Constitutional Court.[105] The chairman of the governmental coalition partner the Slovak National Party (SNS) stated at the time that the Constitutional Court 'does not have the right to tell the parliament what to do, because the parliament is the highest authority in the land'.[106]

The gradual marginalization of Mečiar and his Movement for a Democratic Slovakia (HZDS) did not necessarily mean the disappearance of populist tendencies. Rather the opposite was the case, in that the predominance in Slovak politics of the centre-left

101 A Mungiu-Pippidi, 'Interview with President of the Romanian Constitutional Court, Ion Muraru' [1997] *East European Constitutional Review* 115; B Iancu, 'Quod licet Jovi non licet bovi?: The Venice Commission as Norm Entrepreneur' [2019] 11(1) *Hague Journal on the Rule of Law*; A Ştefănel, Some populist discursive aspects of the #Rezist movement. in A Adi and DG Lilleker (eds), *#rezist – Romania's 2017 anti-corruption protests: causes, development and implications* (Quadriga University of Applied Sciences 2017).

102 G Mesežnikov and O Gyárfášová, 'Explaining Eastern Europe: Slovakia's Conflicting Camps' [2018] 29(3) *Journal of Democracy* 78.

103 ibid 80.

104 C Boulanger, 'Constitutionalism in East Central Europe? The Case of Slovakia under Meciar' [1999] 33(1) *East European Quarterly*.

105 ibid 31.

106 ibid 31.

Direction-Social Democracy (SMER-SD) and its leader Robert Fico somehow meant the emergence of a successor to Mečiar's political approach. SMER-SD has been the most significant governing party from the mid-2000s onwards, and can be situated amongst those political parties (which also include an important part of the right-wing, and even radical-right, opposition) that prefer authoritarian, majoritarian-based politics and take recourse to the usage of national-populist forms of mobilization. The most important representative of the alternative political camp, of a liberal-democratic and pro-EU nature, was President Andrej Kiska, a role that is currently performed by President Zuzana Čaputová (since June 2019). The latter camp seems increasingly sustained by larger scale civic mobilization, which emerged most clearly in early 2018, after the murder of a Slovak journalist, who was investigating corruption, and his partner.

The continuous civic protests – organized not least by the newly found civic organization 'For a Decent Slovakia' – are not dissimilar to the anti-corruption protests in neighbouring Romania, in which equally the themes of corruption, the rule of law, and clientelism form key dimensions of the critique on the government and political parties. The main institutional dimensions of illiberalism in the Slovak democracy include forms of state capture, in which formal democratic institutions are marginalized and political institutions privatized, a selective justice system, in which judicial institutions are staffed with personnel loyal to the government and major politicians and groups linked to ruling political forces escape persecution, as well as a majoritarian style of government in which minority voices and opposition in general are marginalized.[107] As Kosař and others argue,[108] the former prime minister Róbert Fico and his Smer-SD party had managed to fill the Slovak Constitutional Court with loyal judges, immunizing the government from judicial review.[109] The fact that Fico lost the competition for the presidential position to Andrej Kiska in 2014 meant that he could not completely control the court and had to collaborate with Kiska. In October 2018, Fico attempted to eliminate the presidential powers in the selection of Constitutional Court judges, but in the end failed to do so.[110]

4 Conclusion

The argument in this chapter is that populism and populist constitutionalism in East-Central Europe needs to be understood in the context of the post-1989 transformation processes. Populism in the ECE region constitutes in significant ways a form of backlash

107 G Mesežnikov and O Gyárfášová, 'Explaining Eastern Europe: Slovakia's Conflicting Camps' [2018] 29(3) *Journal of Democracy* 80.

108 D Kosař and J Baroš and P Dufek, 'The Twin Challenge to Separation of Powers in Central Europe: Technocratic Governance and Populism' [2019] 15(3) *European Constitutional Law Review* 427.

109 ibid.

110 ibid.

against the 'legal revolutions' and/or 'rights revolutions' of the 1990s, and in some cases has taken the form of a counter-revolution by law or counter-constitutionalism. A crucial backcloth to populism and populist constitutionalism is related to the institutionalization of constitutional democracy in the years after 1989. The argument in the chapter is that the legal and political transformations in the ECE region have consisted in a widespread adoption of a legal-constitutional design and set-up of legal and constitutional institutions, endorsed by domestic liberal forces and international actors in the 1990s and the early 2000s. Contemporary populists are going strongly against the predominance of this liberal-constitutional model.

As argued, however, populism manifests itself differently throughout the region. In the two most prominent cases of populism-in-government, Poland and Hungary, populist parties are undertaking far-going attempts at institutionalizing an alternative populist-constitutional regime, based on conservatism, nationalism, religion, and illiberalism. In the case of the Czech Republic, the institutions of liberal, constitutional democracy have so far not been significantly alterated, but both the current ANO government and President Zeman articulate – even if in a rather fragmented way – political projects which appear to undermine liberal-democratic institutions. In the case of ANO, its project has been labelled 'techno-populism' and is based on a combination of extreme political majoritarianism with the idea of technocratic efficiency. What appears mostly absent in the Czech case is a strong emphasis on nationalism and sovereigntism. In the cases of Romania and Slovakia, the main cleavage relates to anti-corruption forces, which endorse the rule of law and a pro-EU attitude, societally sustained by large-scale and durable civic protests (which themselves show populist tendencies in a diffused critique on corrupt political parties, elites, and institutions) and majoritarian, populist forces, that invoke a prioritization of the will of the political majority to adopt legislation that attenuates strong rule of law considerations and rigid forms of separation of powers.

France – The Resilience of the Constitutional Order to Populism so far and Potential Threats to the Separation of Powers

Diane Fromage and Sébastien Platon***

1 Introduction

So far, no party that could be considered "populist" – in the sense of a specific form of identity politics that is critical of elites, anti-pluralist and has a moral claim of representation[1] – has managed to rise to power in France. However, there is no guarantee that this will never happen. 15 years after her father, Marine Le Pen, president of the extreme-right party *Front national* ((FN) "National Front",[2] renamed as *Rassemblement national* – "National Rally" – in 2018), managed to make it to the second round of the French Presidential election in 2017. The "glass ceiling"[3] that keeps the *Rassemblement National* away from power may therefore not hold forever. If this party were to come to power, would there be sufficient safeguards in the French legal order, and especially its constitution, to protect democracy and the rule of law? To address this "legal dystopia",[4] we suggest examining the Separation of powers and its guarantee in France, by asking two questions. First, as the law stands today, would it be

* Assistant Professor of European Law Maastricht University.
** Professor of Public Law, University of Bordeaux.
The authors would like to thank Charles Froger, Marion Lacaze and Florian Savonitto for their comments. The usual disclaimer applies.

1 J-W Müller, *What is populism?* (University of Pennsylvania Press, 2016) 2-3.

2 See on the historical evolution of the *Front national* and of right-wing populism in France and its main ideological claims: J Rydgen, 'France: The FRONT NATIONAL, Ethnonationalism and Populism', in D Albertazzi and D McDonnell (eds), *Twenty-First Century Populism The Spectre of Western European Democracy* (Palgrave Macmillan 2008) 166-180.

3 See on this concept: A Mondon, 'The Front National in the Twenty-First Century: From Pariah to Republican Democratic Contender? [2014] 22(3) *Modern & Contemporary France* 301; N Mayer, Le plafond de verre électoral entamé, mais pas brisé. in S Crépon and A Dézé and N Mayer (eds), *Les faux-semblants du Front national* (Presses de Sciences Po 2015) 297. For a mathematical analysis, see S Galam, 'Unavowed Abstention Can Overturn Poll Predictions' [2018] 6(24) *Frontiers in Physics.*

4 S Slama, L'étrange défaite des libertés. A droit constant, une dérive autoritaire est-elle possible? in K Abderemane and C Madelaine and G Kurt (eds), *La formation des régimes autoritaires: analyse comparée de récents développements européens*, to be published in Revue de Droit de l'Union Européenne.

possible for a ruling party to put the Judiciary under control (section 3)? Second, again as the law stands today, would it be possible for the Executive to side-line or even bypass the Parliament thereby effectively removing any checks and balances (section 4)? Answering these questions also demands that we examine the role played by the rules governing democratic processes in preventing any populist party from acceding to power in France so far (section 2).

2 The rules governing democratic processes as a factor explaining the failure of populist parties in their race to power (so far)

As stated in the introduction, so far no populist party has managed to come to power in France. There are three factors that may have contributed to this failure: the features of the French electoral system (section 2.1), the rules governing political campaigning and campaign financing (section 2.2) and those regarding political groups in Parliament (section 2.3).

2.1 Electoral system

According to the French Constitution (Fr. Constit.), the rules governing the French electoral system shall be defined in ordinary acts of parliament (Article 34) and political parties and groups are recognised in the Constitution (Article 4). The freedom to create a party is thereby established, and so is the freedom to carry out their activities freely. Parties must, however, respect the principles of national sovereignty and democracy, and '[they] shall contribute to the implementation of the principle set out in the second paragraph of Article 1 [Fr. Constit.]' (Art 4 §2), i.e. they are bound by the fact that 'France shall be an indivisible, secular, democratic and social Republic [which] ensure[s] the equality of all citizens before the law, without distinction of origin, race or religion [...and] respect[s] all beliefs.' (Art 1§ 1 Fr. Constit.). An ordinary act of parliament defines the rules applicable to political parties.[5]

Until the 2017 presidential elections, the French political system was largely bipolar: a block of right-wing parties opposed a block of left-wing parties and they were in power alternatively. This situation ended with the election of President Macron whose party, *En*

5 Loi no 88-227 du 11 mars 1988 relative à la transparence financière de la vie politique.

Marche! (since renamed: *La République en marche*), does not belong to any of the two blocks.

Another key factor in considering the electoral system and its impact on the rise of populist parties is the voting system applicable to parliamentary elections.[6] A two-round uninominal majority system has been in place for the elections to the National Assembly since 1958,[7] and it was only temporarily replaced by a system of proportional representation between 1985 and 1986. Unless one of the candidates obtains an absolute majority of the votes cast representing at least 25% of the registered voters, a second round must be organised. In that case, the candidate obtaining a relative majority of the votes cast is elected. Conditions are, however, set for a candidate to be allowed to participate in the second round: S(he) must have been a candidate during the first round, and (s)he must have obtained the votes of at least 12,5% of the voters legally registered.[8] This second condition has certainly contributed to limit the *FN*'s rise as elections with three candidates in the second round are particularly rare: in most cases, a right-wing candidate is competing with a left-wing candidate.[9] Some have noted in fact that, more than the type of voting system in place (i.e. uninominal or majority system), what matters is the fact that there is more than one round. The relative success of the extreme-right candidates in the elections to the European Parliament – which only have one round – seems to confirm this statement,[10] even if the fact that EP elections are based on a proportional system could play a role as well.

Possible reforms to include elements of proportionality have been discussed for a long time, and are in fact included in the proposal for a constitutional reform currently under discussion.[11] These reforms would imply that MPs are not elected individually in as many constituencies as there are seats, but that they are elected on the basis of lists and in proportion to the total number of votes obtained by each of these lists (a minimum threshold would presumably have to be inserted to avoid widespread fragmentation). If France were to implement such a reform, it would (finally?) apply rules similar to those in place in the majority of the European Union Member States (UK aside).[12] This change

6 Only the lower chamber, the National Assembly, is directly elected. Senators are elected by an electoral college. As shown by T Ehrhard however, views diverge in the role played by the electoral system in explaining the electoral results of the FN: it has been interpreted as both a safeguard and a factor contributing to its rise. T Eherhard, Le Front national face aux modes de scrutin: entre victoire sous conditions et influences sur le système partisan. in *Le Front national* (Pouvoirs 2016) 86.

7 Ordonnance du 13 octobre 1958 relative à l'élection des députes à l'assemblée nationale.

8 Art L162, para 3 Electoral Code. If, however, only one of the candidates to the first round fulfills this criterion, the candidate having obtained the highest percentage of votes is allowed to participate in the second round. Where none of the candidates to the first round fulfills this criterion, the two candidates having obtained the highest number of votes may participate in the second round.

9 J Gicquel and J-E Gicquel, *Droit constitutionnel et institutions politiques* (LGDJ 2018) 737.

10 T Eherhard, Le Front national face aux modes de scrutin: entre victoire sous conditions et influences sur le système partisan. in *Le Front national* (Pouvoirs 2016) 95.

11 Time of writing is October 2019.

12 E Grossman and N Sauger, Introduction aux systèmes politiques nationaux de l'UE [2007] *de Boeck* 72.

would also most probably inflate a sense of increased democracy since the votes for the candidate who does not obtain a relative majority would not simply be lost. It could also lead to an increase in the number of extreme-right MPs being elected. Part of the reluctance to introduce a proportional system indeed relates to the fact that the only time it was used in 1986 it led to a dramatic increase in the number of *FN* MPs:[13] no MP of that party had been elected in 1981, but 35 were in 1986 (out of 577). After the two-round uninominal majority system was reintroduced, the extreme-right party failed to obtain numerous seats again: It had 1 in 1988, 1 in 1993, 2 in 1997, 0 in 2002, 0 in 2007, 2 in 2012 and 8 in 2017.

Thus, changes could be expected if a proportional system were to be (re-)introduced.

2.2 *Political campaigning and campaign financing*

Another factor that can explain the *FN*'s relative low electoral results are the rules governing the financing of political parties, which are strictly defined by law.[14] The State sponsors political parties – the extent of this support depends, among other things, on the results obtained in the latest legislative elections. This rule tends to freeze the composition of the Parliament, to a certain extent, by providing more money to the parties who already fared well in previous elections. Companies and other private entities may not finance political parties, with the exception of individuals who may do so within certain limits. Furthermore, no foreign state or company may finance French political parties.[15]

The cost of political campaigns is also capped. Campaign financing has been an issue for the *FN* which was, for instance, seemingly not able to obtain any loan to finance the 2017 legislative campaign from neither a French nor a foreign bank and called upon citizens to lend the necessary funds.[16] This could indicate that the prohibition to receive funds from private companies combined with banks' reluctance to lend money to the extreme-right party sets it in a difficult financial position when it has to organise a political campaign thereby potentially limiting its success and expansion capacities. Additionally, the *FN*'s financing has been subject to judicial control, both at national and at European level. Russian loans were conceded to the *FN* in the past, and a

13 This notwithstanding the fact that the system was only 'semi-proportional' because the seats were divided on the basis of the results obtained in each *département* (province) and not on a regional or a national level. O Duhamel, Droit constitutionnel et institutions politiques [2011] *Seuil* 517.

14 ibid.

15 See on the financing of political parties in France, and its (social) consequences: J Cagé, Le prix de la démocratie [2018] *Fayard*.

16 Le Monde, 'Le Front national lance un «emprunt patriotique» pour les élections législatives' (*Le Monde*, 1 June 2017) https://www.lemonde.fr/elections-legislatives-2017/article/2017/06/01/le-front-national-lance-un-emprunt-patriotique-pour-les-elections-legislatives_5137030_5076653.html accessed 7 February 2020.

possible implication of the Russian State in this context was envisaged.[17] Though the *FN* has had serious financial difficulties, it is not the only party whose financing has been questioned. For instance, the legality of former President Sarkozy's campaigning costs was also subject to investigation.

2.3 *Political groups within Parliament*

When considering the *FN*'s role, it is also important to analyse the rules applicable to political groups within Parliament. Indeed, being in a position to form a political group guarantees those MPs (and thereby the parties they belong to) some additional prerogatives which set them in a (better) position to be influential within their assembly. In other words, '[t]he daily life of the assemblies is thought and organised around the [political] groups'.[18] In view of the limited number of extreme-right MPs that have been elected so far and of the resulting impossibility for them to form a group, this question is, for now, (still) hypothetical. However, the differences that result from the belonging to a political group, as opposed to being a non-ascribed MP or senator, deserve to be analysed.

Since the 2008 constitutional revision, political groups have been included in and attributed certain prerogatives by the Constitution. Its Article 51-1 defines, in general terms that '[t]he Rules of Procedure of each House shall determine the rights of the parliamentary groups set up within it. They shall recognize that opposition groups in the House concerned, as well as minority groups, have specific rights.' Article 48 furthermore establishes that 'One day of sitting per month shall be given to an agenda determined by each House upon the initiative of the opposition groups in the relevant House, as well as upon that of the minority groups.' (paragraph 4), whereas Article 50-1 acknowledges a parliamentary group's capacity to ask the Government to make a declaration on a given subject.

The minimum number of MPs and senators required to form a parliamentary group are 15 and 10 respectively (Article 19§1 of the Rules of procedure of the National Assembly (RoP NA) and Article 5§4 RoP of the Senate (RoP S)). The groups must make a declaration of political orientation. They receive certain rights besides those contained in the Constitution already mentioned: For instance, in the Senate they can set up an enquiry committee or a fact-finding mission (Article 6a§1 RoP S) whereas groups from the opposition in the National Assembly have longer speaking times in

---

17 Le Monde, 'La justice russe saisie sur le prêt bancaire consenti au Front national' (*Le Monde*, 4 January 2017) https://www.lemonde.fr/politique/article/2017/01/04/la-justice-russe-saisie-sur-le-pret-bancaire-consenti-au-front-national_5057637_823448.html accessed 7 February 2020.

18 P Avril and J Gicquel and JE Gicquel, Droit parlementaire [2014] *LGDJ* 113.

plenary (Article 49§7 RoP NA). Additionally, they are well-organised and have a secretariat for example. They also receive financial support from the two assemblies.

Rassemblement National MPs and senators have, so far, always been too few to form any political group alone. They are non-ascribed MPs and senators and have sometimes been constituted as a group with other non-ascribed in the Senate. Despite also receiving certain prerogatives, non-ascribed senators and MPs are in a less favourable situation than those who belong to a group for example because in the National Assembly, the seats in the permanent committees are first attributed proportionally to the different groups before non-ascribed MPs can choose among the remaining vacant seats (Article 37 RoP NA). Consequently, they cannot be expected to become members of the most important committees and thus remain 'second-class' MPs. These differences may have contributed in *Rassemblement National* MPs not playing an influential role so far.

Having examined some of the reasons that may have prevented a 'wave of populism' in France so far, the question can be asked as to whether the French constitutional and legal system has sufficient safeguards to ensure its continuity, were a populist party to come to power at some point in the future. We will consider the questions of the judiciary (42) and of Parliament (43) in turn in the remaining parts of this chapter.

3 Could the Judiciary in France be "captured"?

In analysing the safeguards available to protect the judiciary, we first examine the rules applicable to constitutional and supreme court judges (section 3.1), before turning to the procedural rules that govern the judicial system (section 3.2).

3.1 Selection, appointment, promotion and discipline procedure for French constitutional and supreme court judges

In France, there are two court systems, the 'ordinary' one which is neither administrative nor constitutional (section 3.1.1), and the administrative one (section 3.1.2); both are considered in turn here. This analysis will be followed by a study of the Constitutional Council (section 3.1.3).

3.1.1 Court of Cassation

The Court of Cassation is the Supreme Court of the French "ordinary" court system. Judges in the Court of Cassation are all "magistrates", a French status encompassing all the persons belonging to the ordinary judiciary body and including not only judges but also public prosecutors.

The independence of the Judicial "Authority"[19] is entrenched in Article 64 Fr. Constit. which makes the President of the Republic the "guarantor" of this independence. The other "guarantor" of this independence is the High Council for the Judiciary ("Conseil Supérieur de la Magistrature" – CSM), the existence, composition and functions of which are entrenched in Article 65 of the French Constitution.

The status of the magistrates is defined in an "Organic Act", a category of "Super-Acts of Parliament" defined in Article 46 Fr. Constit. that require special conditions to be met in order to be adopted. For example, the National Assembly can only have the last word over the Senate with an absolute majority of its members, and not only of votes cast, as is the case for ordinary Acts of Parliament. Also, organic Acts must be submitted for constitutional review before they are promulgated. According to this status, the majority of magistrates are appointed from the National School for the Judiciary, entry to which requires passing a national competitive exam.

Judges are independent. One of the guarantees of this independence is their irremovability, as they cannot be removed from their position, except for disciplinary reasons, without their consent, even for a promotion. The section of the CSM that has jurisdiction over judges is presided over by the Chief President of the Court of Cassation and comprises, in addition, five judges and one public prosecutor, one member of the Council of State appointed by it, one barrister appointed by the National Bar Council and six citizens, as well as six "qualified, prominent citizens who are not members of Parliament, the Judiciary or the administration", appointed by the President of the Republic (2), the President of the National Assembly (2) and the President of the Senate (2). Every appointment of a judge must be approved by this Section of the CSM, the opinion of which is binding. For the most important positions, the President of the Republic can only appoint the judges whose names have been put forward by this Section of the CSM. The CSM also serves as a disciplinary court for judges.

There are few weaknesses in this system and the guarantees it provides: three in particular are related to the CSM. First, the Constitution does not specify how the judges and public prosecutors who are members of the CSM are appointed. It is the 1994 Organic Act on the CSM that requires them to be elected by their peers.[20] Therefore, in theory, the principle of peer-election could be repealed by another Organic Act, except if the Constitutional Council were to decide that election by peers is necessary for the independence of the Judicial Authority enshrined in the Constitution. Second, it is worth noting that the magistrates who are elected by their peers do not have a majority in any section. It is true, however, that the "prominent citizens" appointed by other constitutional institutions do not have a majority either. Third, members are elected for a 4-year term. According to the 1994 Organic Act on the CSM, this term is "not immediately renewable". This means that it *is* renewable after one or more terms,

19 The Judiciary is not considered a Power in the French Constitution.

20 Loi organique no 94-100 du 5 février 1994 sur le Conseil supérieur de la magistrature.

which could affect the independence (or at least the appearance thereof) of "prominent citizens" appointed by other constitutional Institutions.

3.1.2 Council of State

One of the specificities of the French court system is the existence of a separate, autonomous Administrative Court System, having jurisdiction over administrative law matters.[21] Within that system, the legal situation of the members of its supreme court, the Council of State, is slightly but significantly different from the legal situation of the judges of lower administrative courts. Most notably, whereas a growing number of judges in lower administrative courts are appointed following a specific competitive exam, the members of the Council of State are mostly appointed after completing a curriculum at the National School of Administration ("Ecole Nationale d'Administration" – ENA).[22] The Government does not have a choice in that regard. Any person who successfully completes the curriculum in this prestigious school gets to choose between various high profile administrative positions, including those available at the Council of State, based solely on how high they rank compared to their fellows. This recruitment process is not entrenched in the Constitution, and new legislation could, in theory, change the way the members of the Council of State are recruited. This new procedure would however have to be compatible with the constitutional principle of independence of administrative courts. The independence of Council of State is indeed constitutionally guaranteed, even though it is not protected by any explicit constitutional provision. In 1980, the Constitutional Council found that the independence of administrative courts stemmed from an unwritten constitutional principle.[23] The independence of the members of the Council of State is also laid down in Article L131-2 of the Code of Administrative Justice (hereafter CJA for "Code de justice administrative) and several times in the (non-binding) Charter of ethics of the administrative courts.[24] However, certain (relative) weaknesses in the status of the members of the Council of State could, in theory, be used by a ruling party bent on subjugating the French Administrative Court System.

Unlike the ordinary court system, the CSM[25]-like Council for the Administrative Judiciary[26] only has jurisdiction over lower administrative courts and not over the Council of State. The Council of State essentially manages its own members when it

---

21 For a rather recent, and therefore up-to-date overview in English, see for example: H Flavier and Ch Froger, 'Administrative Justice in France. Between Singularity and Classicism' [2016] 3(2) BRICS Law Journal 80-111.

22 See below.

23 CC 80-119 DC, 22 July 1980, *Loi portant validation d'actes administratifs*.

24 See https://www.conseil-etat.fr/le-conseil-d-etat/organisation/deontologie-des-membres-de-la-juridiction-administrative.

25 See above.

26 Art L232-1 Code de justice administratif (CJA), Chapitre II Conseil Supérieur des Tribunaux Administratifs et des Cours Administratives d'Appel (CSTACAA).

comes to promotions and assignments. However, this power of self-management comes mainly from tradition and not from legal texts.[27]

For example, it is tradition that guarantees that the only criterion for promotion is seniority, for all ranks except for the top ones, i.e. Vice-President, Section Presidents, Chamber Presidents and deputy Presidents of the Litigation Section.[28] However, according to the texts, promotions are decided by the President of the Republic, after consulting an Advisory Committee,[29] and individual "merits" of a member could, in theory, influence promotion – which obviously would affect the independence of the members.

Similarly, Section Presidents are appointed by the President of the Republic, after having been proposed by the Vice-President deliberating with the Section Presidents and after consulting the Advisory Committee. It is customary for the President to systematically choose the name at the top of the three required proposals by the Vice-President, deliberating with the Section Presidents. But again, this comes from tradition, not law.

The President of the Council of State, confusingly called "Vice-President", is appointed by the President of the Republic from Section Presidents or State Councillors. This is where the executive branch enjoys the most discretion since there is no rule or even tradition that narrows down the options of the Head of State.

Furthermore, it is to be noted that the members of the Council of State with high ranking positions in the Council of State have neither a life tenure nor a fixed term. Legally, a President of the Republic can appoint new Presidents for the different Sections that comprise the Council, and even a new Vice-President, at any given moment.[30] This again can alter at least the appearance of independence of the Council of State.

All these (relative) weaknesses in the status of the members of the Council of State are combined with the existence of another appointment procedure, called the "external round", under which the President of the Republic can decide to appoint people directly to the Council of State, with absolute discretion. Whether this procedure can be used to alter the independence of the Council of State is debatable. On the one hand, this

27 See e.g. B Ribadeau Dumas, Les carrières dans et hors. in Le Seuil (eds), *Le Conseil d'Etat* (Pouvoirs 2007) 73. Whether a long-standing Republican tradition is harder or easier to break than written law is open to question, though probably more for political scientists or sociologists than for lawyers. The following developments owe much to: S Slama, L'étrange défaite des libertés. A droit constant, une dérive autoritaire est-elle possible? in K Abderemane and C Madelaine and G Kurt (eds), *La formation des régimes autoritaires: analyse comparée de récents développements européens*, to be published in Revue de Droit de l'Union Européenne.

28 See below for their appointment procedure.

29 Art L132-1 CJA.

30 S Slama, L'étrange défaite des libertés. A droit constant, une dérive autoritaire est-elle possible? in K Abderemane and C Madelaine and G Kurt (eds), *La formation des régimes autoritaires: analyse comparée de récents développements européens*, to be published in Revue de Droit de l'Union Européenne.

procedure could be used to appoint members who are loyal to the ruling party. On the other hand, it cannot be used to "pack" the Council of State since, at any given moment, there can never be a majority of members of different ranks appointed through this procedure. Additionally, conditions relative to age apply in some cases and the Vice-President must give his opinion prior to these special appointments being made, although there is no legal requirement for the President to abide by this opinion. Therefore, a President could legally go against the opinion of the Vice-President, even if it would (again) go against the tradition. It is true that any appointment to any administrative position (including to the Council of State) through the "external round" is subject to judicial review. This allows the administrative courts to assess whether the appointee has the minimal skills, experience and background necessary to work in their new position. This review is, however, limited to manifest error of assessment,[31] and therefore may be of limited use in order to avoid political appointments, provided that the appointee does not blatantly lack the minimum qualities to become a member of the Council of State.

More marginally (in terms of numbers), certain persons can be appointed at the Council of State for a limited time, as part of what is called "extraordinary service".

Finally, regarding disciplinary measures, the authority in charge depends on the gravity of the sanction. Minor disciplinary sanctions against the members of the Council of State are imposed by the Vice-President of the Council of State, whom, as we have seen, is appointed by the President, with discretion, from Section Presidents or State Councillors. More important disciplinary sanctions are pronounced by the "Appointing Authority" (the President of the Republic) but only upon a proposition of the Superior Commission of the Council of State. This Commission is chaired by the Vice-President and is composed of seven Section Presidents, eight members of the Council of State elected for three years by their peers (four State Councillors, three Masters of the Requests and an auditor) and three qualified personalities who do not exercise a parliamentary mandate and who are appointed, for a non-renewable period of three years, respectively, by the President of the Republic, the President of the National Assembly and the President of the Senate. When the Commission acts as a disciplinary authority, the Vice-President and the President of the Litigation Section do not sit. Unlike the CSM for magistrates, neither the existence of this Commission nor its role in the disciplinary procedure is constitutionally guaranteed but merely laid down in a legislative provision.[32] It could be argued that scrapping this Commission, or in any event giving more discretion to political authorities for disciplinary proceedings, would infringe the constitutional principle of independence of administrative courts, but there is no certainty. Furthermore, due to its composition, it is fair to assume that if a ruling party ever managed to "capture" the highest positions within the Council of State, it could also

31 CE, Ass., 16 December 1988, *Bleton*, 77713.

32 Art L132-1 and L136-4 CJA.

capture the Commission. Even if we consider the fact that the Vice-President and the President of the Litigation Section do not sit when the Commission acts as a disciplinary authority, the six other Section Presidents and the three "qualified personalities" still outnumber the eight members elected by their peers.

3.1.3 Constitutional Council

The Constitutional Council is the constitutional court of France. According to Article 56 Fr. Constit., "the Constitutional Council shall comprise nine members, each of whom shall hold office for a non-renewable term of nine years. One third of the members of the Constitutional Council shall be renewed every three years. Three of its members shall be appointed by the President of the Republic, three by the President of the National Assembly and three by the President of the Senate." In practice, each of these three authorities appoints one member every three years. Appointing authorities are therefore all political authorities, with a risk of a political appointment, aggravated by the lack of any condition that the appointees have any kind of legal background or experience as a legal academic or practitioner. As a matter of fact, many members of the Constitutional Council, past and present, did not have such a background. Since the 2008 constitutional revision, the Law Committees at the National Assembly and at the Senate can veto an appointment, after a hearing.[33] However, they can only veto *presidential* appointments, since the appointments made by the President of each house are only submitted for consultation to the relevant standing committee in that house. Furthermore, the required threshold (3/5 of the votes cast by the two committees) makes the use of this veto very unlikely. Furthermore, one should not rely on the courts to redress even a blatant abuse of appointment power, since the appointment of the members of the Constitutional Council is considered an "act of government" (French equivalent of the "act of State doctrine") and therefore cannot be subject to judicial review.[34]

In theory, depending on the circumstances, a given political party may appoint up to 9 members of the Constitutional Council. This hypothesis may seem to require either an unlikely alignment of the stars or some sort of electoral manipulation, since it would require the same party holding the Presidency of the Republic, the National Assembly (implying a majority) *and* the Senate (implying, again, a majority) for two consecutive terms. However, one should not forget that such an alignment of the stars actually already happened at the beginning of the 5th Republic, when the "Gaullists" controlled both the National Assembly and the Senate. It has also been suggested[35] that a President might

33 Art 56 French Constitution, first sub-paragraph, penultimate sentence.

34 CE, Ass., 9 April 1999, *Mme Ba*, no 195616.

35 S Slama, L'étrange défaite des libertés. A droit constant, une dérive autoritaire est-elle possible? in K Abderemane and C Madelaine and G Kurt (eds), *La formation des régimes autoritaires: analyse comparée de récents développements européens*, to be published in Revue de Droit de l'Union Européenne.

want to try to pack the Council with members loyal to him/her by, for example, strategically lowering the age limitation with immediate effect. This would require an amendment to the Organic Ordinance of November 7th, 1958 on the Constitutional Council,[36] which would require either a vote in Parliament or the use of Article 16 i.e. emergency powers. Given the recent case-law of the Court of Justice of the European Union,[37] such a move would however probably be an infringement to EU Law.

All in all, the probability that a ruling party may pack the Constitutional Council with loyal members appears rather limited, despite the real flaws in the appointment procedure of its members, but not null. Furthermore, even in the unlikely event that a ruling party manages to appoint a majority of loyal members to the Constitutional Council, one of the most controversial features of the Constitutional Council may then serve as a counterbalance. According to Article 56 of the French Constitution, in addition to the nine members described above, former Presidents of the Republic shall be *ex officio* life members of the Constitutional Council. As of today, there are 3 living former Presidents of the Republic, raising the overall number of members to 12 and therefore the majority to 7. In any event, the very presence of the former presidents guarantees that there cannot be a *full* packing of the Constitutional Council – depending, of course, on both the willingness to sit and the good health of the former inhabitants of the *Elysée* palace![38]

However, even if it would be difficult for a ruling party to "pack" the Constitutional Council, it would still be possible to influence its members. According to the 1958 "Organic ordinance" on the Constitutional Council, "during their term of office, the members of the Constitutional Council may not be appointed to any public office nor, if they are public officials, receive a promotion on merits."[39] However, there is no cooling-off period *after* their term. Furthermore, this provision, in practice, does not seem to apply to official honours. In several instances, members of the Constitutional Council were awarded various ranks within the prestigious Legion of Honour from the President of the Republic, while in office.[40] Therefore, even if it is unlikely that a ruling party may be able to *appoint* all the 9 non-*ex officio* members of the Constitutional Council, the President may be able to *influence* those already serving, for example by promising them honours (immediately) or prestigious public offices (after their term) in exchange either for compliance or leniency or, potentially, for an early departure – therefore allowing the appointing authority to replace the leaving member with a more loyal one. Without wishing to suggest any foul play, it is perhaps interesting that Nicole

36 Ordinances are acts of the government adopted either upon a delegation of power by Parliament or in cases especially provided by the Constitution.

37 Case C-619/18 *Commission v Poland* [2019] ECR I-1.

38 Since the first version of this text, one of them, Jacques Chirac, passed away.

39 Art 5 Ord. 58-1067 of the 7th November 1958 serving as Organic Act on the Constitutional Council, JORF, 9 November 1958 page 10129.

40 J Thomas, *L'indépendance du Conseil constitutionnel* (LGDJ 2010) 190.

Belloubet became Minister of Justice under Emmanuel Macron's presidency after having been a member of the Constitutional Council at a time when it had to adjudicate a case brought (successfully) by Emmanuel Macron's party concerning unequal access to air time on TV and radio.[41]

It is also noteworthy that, according to Article 56, sub-paragraph 3 Fr. Constit., the president of the Constitutional Council, who has a deciding vote in the event of a tie, is appointed by the President of the Republic. The President of the Republic does not even have to wait until the current president has left in order to appoint another one. In the past, François Mitterrand and Jacques Chirac both appointed a new president of the Council even though the current president had not at the time finished his term.

All these loopholes potentially allow for various forms of influence.

3.2 Procedural rules

The procedural rules that govern the French judicial system are also worth considering, especially the rules that 4regard access to constitutional justice (42.2.1) and those that govern the constitutional control of Treaties (42.2.2).

3.2.1 Access to constitutional justice

Up until 2010, private individuals did not have any access to constitutional justice in France. Article 61 of the French Constitution states that Acts of Parliament may be referred to the Constitutional Council before being promulgated by the President of the Republic, the Prime Minister, the President of the National Assembly, the President of the Senate or (since the 1974 constitutional amendment) sixty Members of the National Assembly or sixty Senators. This provision allows the opposition (if it has at least sixty MPs in one of the two Houses) to challenge an Act of Parliament, but only if the President does not promulgate it before they are able to do so. Since the Constitution does not set a minimum time before promulgation,[42] there could be a race for promulgation. There is also a possibility of violation of the Constitution by consensus,[43] if an Act of Parliament is adopted unanimously (or, at least, with an opposition of less than sixty MPs in each House).

41 CC 2017-651 QPC, 31 May 2017, *Association En marche! [Durée des émissions de la campagne électorale en vue des élections législatives]*.

42 There is only a maximum time at Art 10, first sub-paragraph, of the French Constitution: "The President of the Republic shall promulgate Acts of Parliament within fifteen days following the final passage of an Act and its transmission to the Government." According to Art 61, last sub-paragraph, of the French Constitution, referral to the Constitutional Council suspends the time allotted for promulgation.

43 This expression has been coined by B Mathieu, 'Le délit d'homophobie ou la violation de la loi par consensus' [2005] *AJDA* 113.

The 2008 constitutional amendment added Article 61-1 to the French Constitution, according to which "if, during proceedings in progress before a court of law, it is claimed that a legislative provision infringes the rights and freedoms guaranteed by the Constitution, the matter may be referred by the Council of State or by the Court of Cassation to the Constitutional Council which shall rule within a determined period." This new mechanism entered into force in 2010, under the name "priority question of constitutionality" («question prioritaire de constitutionnalité» – QPC).

However, it must be noted that, differently from procedures in Germany or Spain, individuals still do not have direct access to the Constitutional Council in France. Not only is it necessary to convince a court to refer a matter, but there is also a "filter" by the Supreme Court of each courts system (i.e. the Court of Cassation for the ordinary courts system, the Council of State for the administrative courts system). The matter must be referred to the Constitutional Council if a) the disputed provision is applicable to the litigation or the procedure, or constitutes the basis for the proceedings, b) it has not already been declared to be in conformity with the Constitution in a previous decision of the Constitutional Council, unless the circumstances have changed and c) the issue is not devoid of any seriousness. The Supreme Courts must also make sure that the matter is either new or serious. There is room for consideration here, and possibly even for abuse – especially considering that there is no appeal or remedy against a Supreme Court decision not to refer a matter to the Constitutional Council. We have discussed above the possibility of the Council of State being subjugated by a ruling party with members loyal to them, and we have found that this risk was small but not inexistent. If it were to happen, the ruling party would not only control the administrative justice, but also a significant portion of private citizens' access to constitutional justice – at least for cases falling within the jurisdiction of the administrative courts system.

3.2.2 Treaty-compliance review

We have envisaged above the possibility that the Constitutional Council could be subjugated by the ruling party. Just like the Council of State, we found that this risk was small, but not inexistent. However, if this were to happen, provided that the non-constitutional courts remain "uncaptured", it would still be possible for them to review Acts of Parliament without referring the matter to the Constitutional Council.

Article 55 Fr. Constit. establishes France as a monist system; This means that international treaties adopted by the French State become immediately and directly part of the French legal order. Accordingly, "treaties or agreements duly ratified or approved shall, upon publication, prevail over Acts of Parliament, subject, with respect to each agreement or treaty, to its application by the other party." Shortly after the Constitutional Council denied having jurisdiction to enforce this provision,[44] the Court

44 CC 74-54 DC, 15 January 1975, *Loi relative à l'interruption volontaire de la grossesse.*

of Cassation, in its *Jacques Vabre* ruling,[45] and (much) later the Council of State, in its *Nicolo* ruling,[46] both ruled that they had the power to set aside a provision of an Act of Parliament if this provision is incompatible with a Treaty provision, provided that said provision has direct effect.[47] Therefore, should private individuals fear that the Constitutional Council has lost its independence and that one of their rights recognised in an international Treaty to which France is party is threatened, they can decide to stop challenging the compatibility of Acts of Parliament with constitutional rights and ask instead the ordinary courts to review by themselves, without any need for a referral to the Constitutional Council, whether Acts of parliament are compatible with rights protected by international treaties, notably the European Convention on Human Rights (ECHR).

There is always, however, a risk that a populist government decides to denounce the ECHR, and all the other Human Rights treaties like the two 1966 UN International Covenants on Civil and Political Rights and on Economic, Social and Cultural Rights. After all, as recently as 2015, David Cameron declared that he was ready to withdraw from the ECHR.[48] In several instances, Marine Le Pen also said that she wished to remove France from the ECHR.[49] Less dramatically, there is also the possibility of suspending the full application of these treaties. In particular, according to Article 15(1) ECHR, "in time of war or other public emergency threatening the life of the nation any High Contracting Party may take measures derogating from its obligations under this Convention to the extent strictly required by the exigencies of the situation, provided that such measures are not inconsistent with its other obligations under international law." According to the reservation[50] that France made in respect of this paragraph, the circumstances specified in the various French regimes of crisis, notably Article 16 of the Constitution and the state of emergency "must be understood as complying with the purpose of Article 15 of the Convention". As regards Article 16 more specifically, the same reservation states that "for the interpretation and application of Article 16 of the Constitution of the Republic, the terms to the extent strictly required by the exigencies of the situation shall not restrict the power of the President of the Republic to take the measures required by the

45 Cass., ch. mixte, 24 May 1975, *Société des cafés Jacques Vabre*, Bull. ch. mixte, no 4.

46 CE Ass., 20 October 1989, *Nicolo*, no 108243.

47 CE Sect., 23 April 1997, *GISTI*, no 163043. See also, confirming the previous ruling and precising the conditions for direct effect: CE, Ass., 11 April 2012, *GISTI and FAPIL*, no 322326.

48 N Watt, 'David Cameron prepared to break with Europe on human rights' (The Guardian, 2 June 2015) https://www.theguardian.com/politics/2015/jun/02/david-cameron-prepared-to-break-with-europe-on-human-rights accessed 8 February 2020.

49 Le Point Politique, 'GPA: Marine Le Pen souhaite que la France quitte la CEDH' (Le Point Politique, 5 October 2014) https://www.lepoint.fr/politique/gpa-marine-le-pen-souhaite-que-la-france-quitte-la-cedh-05-10-2014-1869602_20.php accessed 8 February 2020; I Trippenbach, 'CEDH: Marine Le Pen veut sortir de la «camisole» des droits de l'homme' (L'Opinion, 18 January 2019) https://www.lopinion.fr/edition/politique/cedh-marine-pen-veut-sortir-camisole-droits-l-homme-174826 accessed 8 February 2020.

50 Reservation contained in the instrument of ratification, deposited on 3 May 1974.

circumstances." In other words, declaring a state of emergency or activating Article 16 of the French Constitution also allows the French Government to trigger Article 15 of the Convention and, therefore, to derogate from most of its obligations under the Convention.

3.3 *Interim conclusion*

Should a populist party come to power in France, it appears unlikely that it could immediately and easily jeopardise judicial independence. Yet, certain weaknesses could be used as shown in the preceding analysis. Besides, some flaws in terms of the procedures applicable could leave citizens' (human) rights unprotected. Perhaps these threats do not only regard the judiciary though, and the subsequent sub-parts turn to the executive.

4 Can the Executive bypass Parliament?

It should first be stated that the basic assumption of a populist party rising to power implies that both the President and the majority at the National Assembly are from the same party. Yet, France has seen several periods of "cohabitation", when the President and the majority at the National Assembly (and therefore the Government, accountable before the National Assembly) do not belong to the same party.[51] However, since 2002 and its reduction from seven to five years, the presidential term coincides with the legislature of the National Assembly and the presidential elections take place before the legislative elections. Since then, the legislative elections have always confirmed the outcome of the presidential elections and given the presidential party a majority in the National Assembly. This phenomenon has been sometimes described as a "parliamentary honeymoon",[52] making the legislative election a mere extension of the presidential election. If a populist candidate ever becomes president, he or she may also benefit from this "honeymoon". This will be our assumption here.

Of course, there would still be room for the opposition to be heard in Parliament, especially given the rights that the opposition was given by various constitutional amendments, notably in 1974 and 2008, as long as the Parliament exists and remains vested with its powers. However, one has to take into consideration the particularity of the French regime, and especially its emphasis on the executive in general and on the president in particular. The 1958 Constitution was designed as a reaction against the 4th Republic (1946-1958), which was characterised by an almighty and extremely divided

51 No confidence relationship exists between the Senate and the government.

52 É Dupoirier and N Sauger, 'Four Rounds in a Row: The Impact of Presidential Election Outcomes on Legislative Elections in France' [2010] 8(1) *French Politics* 21.

Parliament and a weak, unstable Government. By contrast, the 5th Republic is characterised by a shift of balance in favour of the executive branch, and more particularly the President, to whom the Constitution grants several powers that could be used by a populist government in order to side-line or even bypass the Parliament. This empowerment of the executive is visible in its capacities to adopt ordinances (43.1), to call for referendums (43.2) and to declare the existence of an imminent threat (43.3). A populist government could, furthermore, try to reform the Constitution to its advantage (43.4).

4.1 Article 38 ordinances

The simplest way to reduce parliamentary discussion to a minimum is by using Article 38 of the French Constitution. This Article provides that the Government may ask Parliament for authorization, over a limited period, to take by Ordinances measures on matters normally reserved to the Parliament. When requesting this authorisation, called "habilitation", the Government must state precisely the purpose of the measures it wants to take as well as the matter concerned. It does not have, however, to inform Parliament of the content of the orders it wants to make.[53] These Ordinances are issued "in the Council of Ministers", which means that they are signed by the President.[54] They must then be ratified, in explicit terms, by the Parliament. From then on, they have the same legal value as an Act of Parliament, and thus cannot be subject to judicial review before the administrative courts anymore but only to constitutional review. Even though the Parliament is involved *ex ante* and *ex post*, this form of delegated legislation is severely encroaching upon the separation of powers and dramatically limits the possibility of parliamentary discussion.

4.2 Referendums

If a populist President wants to completely bypass the Parliament, he or she can decide to make use of Article 11 of the French Constitution. According to this Article, the President of the Republic can submit for a referendum any Government Bill which deals with the organization of the public authorities, or with reforms relating to the economic, social or environmental policy of the Nation, and to the public services contributing thereto, or which provides for authorization to ratify a treaty which, although not contrary to the Constitution, would affect the way the institutions operate. The only conditions are that such a referendum must follow either a recommendation from the Government when

53 CC 99-421 DC, 16 December 1999, *Loi portant habilitation du Gouvernement à procéder, par ordonnances, à l'adoption de la partie législative de certains codes*, §12.

54 Art 13(1) of the French Constitution.

Parliament is in session or a joint motion of the two houses. Where the referendum is held on the recommendation of the Government, the latter shall make a statement before each house, which shall be followed by a debate, but the MPs do not get to vote on the matter, let alone veto the referendum.

The importance of this prerogative, and the danger it represents for constitutionalism, cannot be overstated. First, because the Constitutional Council considers that it has no jurisdiction to review Acts adopted by referendum, claiming that "it follows from the spirit of the Constitution, which made the Constitutional Council a regulating body for the activity of the public authorities, that the Acts that the Constitution intended to cover in its Article 61 are only the Acts voted by the Parliament and not those which, adopted by the people following a referendum, constitute the direct expression of national sovereignty".[55] Second, Article 11 has been used at least once to amend the Constitution, in 1962, in order to include in the Constitution that the President of the Republic is elected by direct universal suffrage.[56] The advantage (for the executive) of Article 11, compared to the normal revision provision, Article 89 – which also allows for constitutional amendment by referendum – is that Article 11, unlike Article 89, does not require the bill amending the Constitution to be passed by the two houses in identical terms before being submitted for a referendum.

Yet, despite the dangers of this procedure, the current government is planning to enlarge the scope of this provision by adding "reforms relating to social issues" (e.g. LGBT+ rights, gender issues, surrogacy, medically-assisted procreation, etc.) to the list of matters that can be submitted for referendum. Note that immigration, an important topic for populists, could easily fall into this category – which would be left to the executive to consider, since the Constitutional Council does not review Acts adopted by referendum.

4.3 *Article 16 of the French Constitution*

The Article 16 of the French Constitution stems from the very Schmittian conception of the Head of State that Charles de Gaulle expressed as early as 1946 (12 years before he was given the task of drafting a new Constitution for the French Republic), in a speech given in the medieval town of Bayeux, in Normandy: "His [the President], if it were to happen that the country was in peril, is the duty to be a guarantor of national independence and treaties concluded by France".[57] De Gaulle himself is the only French President who ever used Article 16, following the generals' putsch in Algiers

55 CC, 62-20 DC, 6 November 1962, *Loi relative à l'élection du Président de la République au suffrage universel direct, adoptée par le référendum du 28 octobre 1962.*

56 See section 4.4 below.

57 "à lui, s'il devait arriver que la patrie fût en péril, le devoir d'être garant de l'indépendance nationale et des traités conclus par la France".

during the spring of 1961. Although the putsch collapsed on the night of 25 to 26 April, Article 16 was however maintained in force until 29 September 1961.

According to Article 16, where "the institutions of the Republic, the independence of the Nation, the integrity of its territory or the fulfilment of its international commitments are under serious and immediate threat, and where the proper functioning of the constitutional public authorities is interrupted", the President of the Republic "shall take measures required by these circumstances", including measures on matters which are ordinarily reserved to the Parliament. There is no substantial limitation apart from the requirement that they "shall be designed to provide the constitutional public authorities as swiftly as possible, with the means to carry out their duties", which is extremely vague. The only procedural requirement is that the Constitutional Council shall be consulted with regard to such measures, but its opinion does not have to be published. Note also that there is a debate on whether the President can amend the Constitution on the basis of Article 16, or at least submit a constitutional amendment directly for a referendum, without involving the Parliament.[58]

Whether these measures may be subject to judicial review is rather unclear. What is clear is that, when these measures are taken on matters that are normally reserved to the Parliament, they cannot be appealed before the administrative courts, since they are not considered as administrative decisions but as statute law.[59]

It is furthermore doubtful that they can be subject to *ex ante* constitutional review, since this review normally takes place after an Act of Parliament has been passed and before it is promulgated by the President – a gap in time that does not exist for Article 16 measures.

However, these measures are arguably subject to two forms of *ex post* judicial review. First, it could be argued that they can be subject to *ex post* constitutional review (the priority question of constitutionality, or "QPC"[60]) since Article 61-1 only refers to "legislative[s] provision[s]" that "[infringe] the rights and freedoms guaranteed by the Constitution". It could be argued that the broad concept of "legislative provision" includes Article 16 measures taken within the scope of statute law. This, however, is not certain. A former Vice-President of the Council of State, for example, argued against this possibility.[61] Second, as we have discussed earlier, non-constitutional courts have the power to review whether Acts of Parliament are compatible with international treaties. The legal basis of this power is Article 55 of the Constitution, according to which "[t]reaties or agreements duly ratified or approved shall, upon publication, prevail over

58 See, considering that it is possible: M Voisset, *L'article 16 de la Constitution du 4 octobre 1958* (LGDJ 1969). For an opinion against this possibility, see J Lamarque, *La théorie de la nécessité et l'article 16 de la Constitution de 1958* (Librairie Générale de droit et de jurisprudence 1961) 558 and especially 617-618.

59 CE, Ass., 2 mars 1962, *Rubin de Servens* (see above).

60 See above.

61 R Denoix de Saint Marc, Foreword. in F Lamy and R Denoix de Saint Marc, État d'Urgence (Economica 2018) 7.

Acts of Parliament, subject, with respect to each agreement or treaty, to its application by the other party." The French word for "Acts of Parliament", "lois", is broad enough to be understood not organically (the Acts of the *Parliament*) but substantially (the measures taken within the ordinary scope of statute law). However, for lack of precedent, this is not certain. Furthermore, as discussed before, it has to be kept in mind that, whenever the President of the Republic activates Article 16, France can also, *de jure*, activate the derogation clause of the ECHR (Article 15), *as per* the wording of the reservation issued by France when it ratified the Convention in 1974.[62]

The substantial conditions for activating Article 16 are rather vague, leaving much discretion to the President. The procedural constraints are also very weak. Before activating Article 16, the President must formally consult the Prime Minister, the Presidents of the Houses of Parliament and the Constitutional Council. Pursuant to Article 53 of the Organic Ordinance of 7 November 1958, the opinion then sought from the Constitutional Council has to be "reasoned and published" and concerns whether the conditions required by Article 16 are met. However, the President is not bound by this opinion. The decision to activate Article 16, being considered an "act of Government" according to the case-law of the Council of State, cannot be subject to judicial review.[63] All in all, the President is the final arbiter of whether the conditions for triggering Article 16 are met.

Up until the 2008 constitutional revision, no authority apart from the President could end Article 16. Since this date, the Constitutional Council is involved, but with significant limitations. The first limitation is a time limitation. Only after thirty days (an eternity!) of the implementation of such emergency powers may the matter be referred to the Constitutional Council, so as to decide if the conditions required for the application of Article 16 still apply. In any event, the Constitutional Council shall carry out *ex officio* such an examination after sixty days of the exercise of emergency powers or at any moment thereafter. The second limitation is about the right to refer the matter to the Constitutional Council. Only the President of the National Assembly, the President of the Senate, sixty Members of the National Assembly or sixty Senators can refer the matter to the Constitutional Council after thirty days. These proceedings are, therefore, out of reach for individuals.

The Parliament is somehow protected by Article 16, in that the Parliament sits in session for the whole duration of Article 16, by derogation to ordinary session periods,[64] and the National Assembly cannot be dissolved whilst the emergency powers are in force.[65] However, the Parliament mostly has the role of a passive observer since it can neither stop the use of Article 16 nor overthrow the President. The only power it has

62 See above.

63 CE, Ass., 2 March 1962, *Rubin de Servens*, no 55049.

64 Art 16 French Constitution, 4th sub-paragraph.

65 Art 16 French Constitution, 5th sub-paragraph.

is to adopt a motion of no-confidence against the Government, but this does not directly impact the President.

4.4 *Constitutional revisions*

An additional scenario in which a populist government might seek to constrain parliamentary powers is that of constitutional revisions.[66] Article 89 Fr. Constit. defines the common procedure of constitutional revision[67] which is complemented by the procedure on referendums set out in Article 11 Fr. Constit. (section 4.2). Referendums may indeed be called on 'any Government Bill which deals with the organization of the public authorities' and therefore also be used to reform the Constitution. President de Gaulle used this procedure twice: A first time with success in 1962 when he managed to introduce the direct presidential elections[68] and a second time that ended in a failure when he tried to reform the Senate and initiate a process of regionalisation in 1969. This use of the possibility to call for a (constitutional) referendum was highly controversial though, and the Constitutional Council was called to check its constitutionality (which it, however, denied to do on the grounds of a lack of competence).[69] Some have claimed that the support expressed by the people in the form of their positive vote in fact cleared any remaining doubts as to the constitutionality of such a use of the referendum.[70] This notwithstanding, the debate went on during several decades.

As per Article 89 Fr. Constit., there exist two ordinary procedures to amend the Constitution that both start in the same way: the initiative pertains both to MPs and to the President who, however, proposes constitutional amendments on the recommendation of the Prime Minister. In this sense, this procedure differs from that applicable to ordinary acts which are proposed by the sole Prime Minister (Article 39 Fr. Constit.). After a proposal has been made by either the President or an MP, its text must be approved by both chambers in identical terms: as per Article 42 Fr. Constit., the first assembly that examines the draft may not vote on the text in plenary earlier than six weeks after it has received the draft text, and the second one may not do so before four weeks have elapsed. Once both chambers have agreed to the text (note also that no conciliation committee may be convened if they disagree), by default, it must be

66 Note, however, that no constitutional revision is possible when the presidency of the Republic is vacant (Art 7 French Constitution).

67 Another procedure of constitutional revisions had originally been included in Art 85 French Constitution. In reference to the relationship between France and its former colonies. It has since been abrogated.

68 Prior to 1962, the President had been elected indirectly by an electoral college composed of MPs, senators and provincial and local representatives.

69 CC, 62-20 DC, 6 November 1962, *Loi relative à l'élection du Président de la République au suffrage universel direct, adoptée par le référendum du 28 octobre 1962* and section 43.2 above.

70 J Gicquel and J-E Gicquel, *Droit constitutionnel et institutions politiques* (LGDJ 2018) 584.

submitted to popular vote by means of referendum. Yet, the President is free to submit it to both chambers sitting together in Congress instead where the government has started the amendment procedure. Then, a super majority of three fifth of the votes cast is required for the amendment to be approved. Considering that the President launches referendums or summons the Congress, it may decide to stop a revision procedure even if both chambers have agreed on a text, and summoned the Congress only three years after the two assemblies had agreed on a text in 1963.[71]

It is noteworthy that contrary to other European constitutions the French Constitution only sets very limited exceptions to constitutional amendments: They may not be started or concluded 'where the integrity of national territory is placed in jeopardy' and they also cannot affect the republican form of government. Besides, there exists no aggravated procedure for specific parts of the Constitution as it has been established in Spain (Article 168 Spanish Constititution). It should also be noted that the Constitutional Council has adopted a very deferential attitude vis-à-vis the executive which it considers to be fully sovereign and thus empowered to introduce new provisions even if they contradict previously established rules or principles of constitutional value. The Constitutional Council indeed declared that 'the constituent power [...] has power to repeal, amend and amplify constitutional provisions in such manner as it sees fit'.[72] It has also refused to check the constitutionality of revision proposals.[73]

The easiness with which the French Constitution may be amended may explain why revisions have been so numerous since its entry into force in 1958: no less than 24 revision procedures have been successful, 22 of which have intervened on the basis of Article 89 Fr. Constit.[74] A referendum was successfully used in only one occasion,[75] whereas the other 21 revisions were approved by the two assemblies in Congress.[76] It therefore appears that the Constitution of the 5th Republic differs from that of the 3rd and the 4th Republics which were hardly ever amended, and that amendments instead of changes of constitution have been favoured. Additionally, even if no revision has intervened since 2008 when no less than two revisions were performed,[77] the appetite for further revisions has not fainted. President Macron (2017-...) presented for instance a proposal in this sense in 2018.

71 J Gicquel and J-E Gicquel, *Droit constitutionnel et institutions politiques* (LGDJ 2018) 583.

72 Decision no 92-312 DC of September 2, 1992 Treaty on European Union (Maastricht II) para 34.

73 Decision no 2003-469 DC of March 3, 2003 Constitutional revision on the decentralised organisation of the Republic.

74 The other two revisions were made on the basis of Art 85 French Constitution (see no 66 above) and of Art 11 French Constitution (see section 4.2 above).

75 Constitutional Act 2000-964 of 2 October 2000 on the length of the presidential mandate.

76 A list of all constitutional amendments may be found on the Constitutional Council's website: https://www.conseil-constitutionnel.fr/la-constitution/les-revisions-constitutionnelles. The details of the vote casts may be found on the Senate's website: https://www.senat.fr/evenement/revision/revision_aboutie.html.

77 See on this revision: Special issue 'Révision de la Constitution' [2008] Revue française de droit constitutionnel.

It is against this background that the question needs to be asked as to whether there exist sufficient safeguards to guarantee constitutional integrity were a populist government to come to power. This analysis will only consider the ordinary procedure foreseen in Article 89 Fr. Constit. as the one possible by means of Article 11 Fr. Constit. has already been examined in section 42.2 above.

It appears first of all that the content of the Constitution could be widely amended in view of the interpretation made by the Constitutional Council's interpretation recalled above and since only its republican form may not be the object of a revision. Yet, the parliamentary approval that is required before a revision proposal can be submitted to either a popular vote or the Congress constitutes a first safeguard against the populist thirst for power. Secondly, the fact that a constitutional amendment proposal is made by the President on the Prime Minister's proposal implies that they must both agree and that therefore a difference in political allegiance, i.e. in case of *cohabitation* between a populist government and a democratic President, would prevent any constitutional reform being presented by the executive. This has, however, become unlikely to occur as shown above. A constitutional revision would only be possible if it also has the support of a majority of senators since it needs the support of 3/5, i.e. 555 out of 925 members of the Congress knowing that the National Assembly alone is composed of 577 MPs only. Therefore, reforming the Constitution to its advantage would not be an easy endeavour for a populist government, but if it had a super majority in parliament or if managed to hold a positive referendum, it would face no limitations in the changes it could make.

5 Conclusion

In this chapter, we have sought to provide (some) explanations as to why populist parties have not yet been successful in getting to power in France, and what changes such a success could have for the French constitutional legal order.

We have highlighted that the rules governing the electoral system – which relies on a two-round uninominal majority system – has played a crucial role in preventing parties like the *FN* from acceding to power. The dangers of a populist party leading a government in France thus appear to be limited as long as this system remains. Discussions regarding a reform of the electoral system have been recurrent, among other reasons because the system in place favours large parties and entails the loss of all votes from the minority. Considering the increasing difficulties in forming a long-lasting coalition government faced by numerous European States, the benefits that a change to a proportional system would bring can be questioned at this point.

With regard to the safeguards in place to preserve the balance of powers in France, although some risks exist in relation to the independence of the judiciary, the biggest dangers probably relate to the executive's powers. This is so both because the protection of human rights of individuals could be suspended, and also because the executive could use its power to by-pass parliament. Aware of this (arguably no-longer justified) predominance of the executive over parliament, President Sarkozy successfully pushed for a constitutional reform which led to the (relative) empowerment of Parliament in 2008. The constitutional reform that has been under discussion since 2017 does not necessarily appear to go in the same direction however. It would indeed reduce the number of MPs and Senators and, most importantly, it would limit the time available for debates in parliament. Furthermore, it would also on the one hand, imply that 15% of the MPs are elected based on a proportional system and that the independence of the judiciary is reinforced but, on the other hand, it would also not allow former Presidents to be members of the Constitutional Council anymore, thereby making it easier for a populist government to control the Constitutional Council. The debates on this reform have been on-going for two years, and its outcome is still uncertain. It should nevertheless be monitored, especially in terms of the changes it may bring for the functioning of the electoral system.

Greece – Populism and Constitutionalism

George Karavokyris[*]

1 Introduction

The debate on populism over Europe and overseas is not only of a conceptual nature, a long, sophisticated and controversial dialogue of scholars and academics about the definition of a "notorious slippery concept"[1] in various fields of knowledge, such as political science, constitutional law, discourse analysis and political sociology, but, above all, an empirical phenomenon, normatively and politically speaking, that has to be described and interpreted within the limits of our (liberal) democracy.[2] Thus, a national report on the subject shall be contextualized, so as to perceive the specifications of the legal, institutional and political incidents and to explore their connection to a certain and delimited concept of populism. In this framework, the recent financial crisis, which has severely struck and transformed the Greek State,[3] will constitute the background of this contribution on the rather ambiguous relation between populism, law and politics in the Greek case.

A precise and commonly acknowledged definition of populism remains always dubious from an epistemological point of view. Various and solid ideological and political preconceptions and prejudgments of the experts mediate the concept. For the radical left theory,[4] populism could be an effective response to the elitist liberal democracy, in the direction of the triumphal rebirth of the nominal and fictional (in liberalism) popular sovereignty.[5] Although the compatibility of this critical theory with the major normative pillars and standards of a liberal democracy is reasonably questioned, not to say absolutely rejected, by the liberal theory, its rhetoric force and

* Assistant Professor of Constitutional Law at the Aristotle University of Thessaloniki.

1 C Mudde, *Are Populists Friends of Foes of Constitutionalism?* (Policy Brief, The Foundation for Law, Justice and Society 2013) 2; C Mudde and C Rovira Kaltwasser, *Populism: A Very Short Introduction* (Oxford University Press 2017) 2.

2 N Urbinati, 'Political Theory of Populism' [2019] 22 *Annual Review of Political Science* 111 (forthcoming).

3 E Venizelos, 'State Transformation and the European Integration Project Lessons from the financial crisis and the Greek paradigm' (2016) CEPS Special Report 130/2016, https://www.ceps.eu/wp-content/uploads/2016/02/SR%20No%20130%20State%20Transformation%20and%20European%20Integration.pdf accessed 11 October 2019.

4 C Mouffe, 'The 'End of Politics' and the Challenge of Right-wing Populism' in F Panizza (ed), *Populism and the Mirror of Democracy* (Verso 2005) 50.

5 E Laclau, *On Populist Reason* (Verso 2005); E Laclau, Populism: What's in a Name? in F Panizza (ed), *Populism and the Mirror of Democracy* (Verso 2005) 32; C Mouffe, 'The 'End of Politics' and the Challenge of Right-wing Populism' in F Panizza (ed), *Populism and the Mirror of Democracy* (Verso 2005).

accent on popular sovereignty and the majority rule seem to capture the *hard core* of the populist theory and depict its use and proliferation in the political and constitutional ground. In other words, populism, for these theories, is an internal and indispensable feature of our democratic political and constitutional tradition, inherent to the legitimation of the rulers and to the mainstream political discourse. On the other hand, the notion of populism in American constitutional theory – eventually the only comprehensive constitutional theory of populism – has a rather positive connotation, suggesting the strengthening of the democratic features of the liberal democracy, the judicial restraint, the people's involvement in constitution-making and finally the primacy of the Congress and, in general, of the elected bodies in politics.[6] For political scientists Mudde and Kaltwasser, populism can address the right questions (about the letdowns and the world-wide elitism of liberal democracy), but cannot provide us with the right answers. In this balanced view, populism is:

> a thin-centered ideology that considers society to be ultimately separated into two homogenous and antagonistic camps, "the pure people" versus the "corrupt elite" and which argues that politics should be an expression of the volonté générale (general will) of the people.[7]

According to Müller, populism is a *shadow of the representative democracy*, a moralized manner to speak in the name of the people as a whole and to denounce the elites: a powerful rhetoric which can be deployed either and with the same efficiency by the left or the right.[8] Populism, in the mainstream political theory,[9] represents an actual threat to liberal democracy and legal constitutionalism, a malicious way of promoting the supremacy of constitutional and ordinary politics over the law.[10] Populist movements and parties radically interrogate the safeguards and the pillars of constitutional democracy, such as the *separation of powers*, the *representative political system* and the modern concept of the *rigid constitution*. Therefore, even though there is no such thing as

---

6 RD Parker, '"Here, the People Rule": A Constitutional Populist Manifesto' [1993] 27(3) *Valparaiso University Law Review* 531; A Kaidatzis, 'Populist Constitutionalism as a Critique on Liberal (or Legal) Constitutionalism' (2018), https://www.academia.edu/36909163 accessed 21 October 2019.

7 C Mudde and C Rovira Kaltwasser, *Populism: A Very Short Introduction* (Oxford University Press 2017) 5-6.

8 J-W Müller, *What is Populism?* (University of Pennsylvania Press 2016).

9 J-W Müller, *What is Populism?* (University of Pennsylvania Press 2016); S Rummens, Populism as a Threat to Liberal Democracy. in C Rovira Kaltwasser and others (eds), *The Oxford Handbook of Populism* (Oxford University Press 2017) 554; N Urbinati, Populism and the Principle of Majority. in C Rovira Kaltwasser and others (eds), *The Oxford Handbook of Populism* (Oxford University Press 2017) 571.

10 S Rummens, Populism as a Threat to Liberal Democracy. in C Rovira Kaltwasser and others (eds), *The Oxford Handbook of Populism* (Oxford University Press 2017); N Urbinati, Populism and the Principle of Majority. in C Rovira Kaltwasser and others (eds), *The Oxford Handbook of Populism* (Oxford University Press 2017).

a *continental* theory of 'constitutional populism', it is beyond doubt that political populism, as a 'constitutional project', bears its own and crucial normative effects on liberal democracy.[11]

In this contribution, populism in Greece will be reviewed through the lenses of the financial crisis. Certainly, the traces of the majoritarian concept of democracy can be identified throughout Greek constitutional history, as Greek politics were always characterized by polarization and majoritarianism. The political system of the schematically called 'Metapolitefsi' (1975-), the longest period of uninterrupted democracy and rule of law in the history of Greece, after the fall of the 1967-1974 military dictatorship, has dealt with a major crisis and has been substantively rearranged during the last 10 years. The impressive rise in power of the leftist party Syriza and its coalition with the extreme right-wing party of ANEL has provoked a wide and often extremely controversial debate about populism in Greek political and constitutional discourse and institutional policy.[12] The intensity and the extent of the economic crisis has enhanced the popularity of the anti-systemic and anti-hegemonic discourse, euro-skepticism and the anti-globalization movements. At the beginning of the crisis, the anti-austerity discourse has enriched the strategy of the (center) right party of New Democracy, while the party was in opposition between 2009 and 2012, and then has been escalated and aggravated (until 2015) by Syriza. The constant and aggressive reference to the governments applying the memoranda as the 'traitors' of the people and the 'servants' of the country's creditors has engaged the Greek political system into the vicious circle of a populist agenda.[13] At the same time, the financial crisis has given parliamentary birth (at 2012) to the neo-Nazi party of the Golden Dawn, which has embraced violence and advanced an extreme socio-nationalist, totalitarian and anti-European political discourse.[14]

---

11 P Blokker, 'Populism as a constitutional project' [2019] 17(2) *International Journal of Constitutional Law* 536; TS Pappas, *Populism and Liberal Democracy: A Comparative and Theoretical Analysis* (Oxford University Press 2019).

12 C Mudde, *SYRIZA: The Failure of the Populist Promise* (Palgrave Macmillan 2017).

13 IN Grigoriadis, *Democratic Transition and the Rise of Populist Majoritarianism: Constitutional Reform in Greece and Turkey* (Palgrave Macmillan 2018) 91.

14 Specifically, Golden Dawn can be defined "as an extreme variant of the far-right party family. The party claims ownership of nationalism and justifies all its policies on the basis of the nation; it espouses the use of violence and fascist ideals. The party's ideology goes beyond authoritarianism, understood as despotic rule, to the embrace of totalitarianism: the espousal of a system of total control by a party which sees itself not above the people but as the embodiment of the people The party rejects liberalism and socialism and endorses what it terms the 'third biggest ideology in history' – nationalism – combined with support for an all- powerful state premised on 'popular sovereignty'. It shares with other fascist movements both a fixation on societal degeneration and the proposed solution, which encompasses the necessity for national rebirth through a collective movement from below, understood as embodied by the Golden Dawn and its leader". See: D Halikiopoulou and K Nanou and S Vasilopoulou, 'Changing the policy agenda? The impact of the Golden Dawn on Greek party politics' (2016) Hellenic Observatory GreeSE paper series 103, http://www.lse.ac.uk/Hellenic-Observatory/Assets/Documents/Publications/GreeSE-Papers/GreeSE-No103.pdf accessed 21 October 2019.

Nevertheless, despite the populist pattern of Syriza, which, for some authors, can also qualify as a European inclusionary version of populism,[15] because it defends the vast 'majority' of the (pure) 'people' against the (corrupted and responsible for the economic crisis) 'elites', the social inclusion of the low-income classes and the 'cultural' minorities,[16] the Constitution has proven its (impressive) resilience. The Rule of Law guarantees have not been seriously affected during the crisis.[17] Political populism in Greece should not be confused with *controversial constitutional politics* or the *rule of law deficit* that naturally and inevitably flourished during the crisis. To put it simply, populism in Greece is often interpreted in an eventually misleading way: it is straightforwardly identified either to the dominant *clientelism* and the pathological relation between the Greek State and civil society or to the common *demagogy* of the political actors and their false promises to the people.[18] It is true that contemporary constitutionalism suffers from a profound tension between the *pragmatic* and *redemptive* face of democracy,[19] but in order to understand *precisely* the populist effect we shall not naively de-politicize politics; neither should we give an extreme emphasis and priority to liberalism over our democratic autonomy. To the contrary, we have to spot, with realism, the concrete interventions and threats to the constitutional and democratic regime, the institutional events that disrupt the constitutional continuity and undermine its stability. In this contribution I will argue that the legal and constitutional safeguards of Greek democracy (the rule of law) have been procedurally and substantially observed (section 2) despite few illustrative 'failures', such as the *referendum* of July 5th 2015 and certain signs of *jurisprudential* populism on identity matters (section 3).

---

15 Y Stavrakakis, 'How Did 'Populism' Become a Pejorative Concept? And Why is this Important Today? A Genealogy of Double Hermeneutics' (2017) POPULISMUS Working Papers 6, https://www.academia.edu/32641393 accessed 21 October 2019.

16 C Mudde and C Rovira Kaltwasser, 'Exclusionary vs. Inclusionary Populism: Comparing Contemporary Europe and Latin America' [2013] 48(2) *Government and Opposition* 158.

17 X Contiades and A Fotiadou, 'On Resilience of Constitutions. What Makes Constitutions Resistant to External Shocks?' [2015] 9(1) *Vienna Journal on International Constitutional Law* 3; A Manitakis, The impressive resilience of the Greek Constitution in the current financial crisis in Europe. in L Papadopoulou and I Pernice and JHH Weiler (eds), *Legitimacy Issues of the European Union in the Face of Crisis: Dimitris Tsatsos in memoriam* (Nomos 2017).

18 This extensive notion of populism is used Takis S. Pappas in his sophisticated book: TS Pappas, *Populism and Crisis Politics in Greece* (Palgrave Macmillan 2014).

19 M Canovan, 'Trust the People! Populism and the Two Faces of Democracy' [1999] 47(1) *Political Studies* 2; M Canovan, Taking Politics to the People: Populism as the Ideology of Democracy. in Y Mény and Y Surel (eds), *Democracies and the Populist Challenge* (Palgrave Macmillan 2002).

2 The Rule of Law Safeguards in Greece

In contemporary democracies, the balance between democracy and constitutionalism is not always stable, as politics may come in contrast with the constitutional rules. The rise of populism in Greek politics within the context of the financial crisis has (mostly) challenged our constitutional discourse and (rarely) tested the endurance of the main guarantees of the Greek constitutional order. In fact, the main interferences in our constitutional order have less to do with populism *per se* than with the standard *deficiencies* of the rule of law and, certainly, with the extreme pressure of crisis-law on the Greek constitutional and ordinary rules.

2.1 A short introduction to Greek Constitutionalism

The Greek Constitution of 1975 is a modern, democratic and liberal one. It has been for almost 40 years a major guarantee for the successful and peaceful function of Greek democracy. The text embraces the rule of law and all the principles of European constitutionalism, such as the protection of human rights and judicial review, and served as an institutional tool for the integration of the country in the EU and the advance into the direction of a welfare state and a modern democratic republic. It has been revised three times since 1975. In 1986, the revision aimed at a significant limitation of the powers of the President of the Republic. In 2001, an extensive and consensual constitutional amendment promoted civil rights protection and the welfare state, modernized the field of justice and upgraded the constitution for the new challenges of the 21st century. Within this context, the institution of a mechanism of concentration of the judicial review and the establishment of independent administrative authorities should be underlined. In 2008, the third revision of the Constitution focused on minor changes, such as the abolition, in compliance with the ECHR jurisprudence,[20] of the incompatibility of the parliamentary mandate with the exercise of a profession, which had been introduced in the 2001 revision. The Greek constitution, even if it can be reasonably criticized as a very long and restrictive one,[21] has been in line with the country's vast project of "modernisation"[22] between the mid-90s and until the economic collapse of the Greek State in 2009. Some constitutionalists have convincingly argued that the Greek bankruptcy is not a matter of constitutional policy.

The major political parties (Pasok and New Democracy) that ruled the country for 30 years simply failed to implement the right policies and reforms and have essentially

---

20 See: *Lykourezos v Greece* App no 33554/03 (ECtHR, 15 June 2006).

21 DJ Nardi and G Tsebelis, 'A Long Constitution is a (Positively) Bad Constitution: Evidence from OECD Countries' [2016] 46(2) *British Journal of Political Science* 457; G Tsebelis, 'The Greek Constitution From a Political Science Point of View' [2014] 42 *Greek Political Science Review* 145.

22 K Featherstone (ed), *Politics and Policy in Greece: The Challenge of 'Modernisation* (Routlegde 2006).

succumbed to the original sins of the Greek State and society: an anti-modern communitarianism, bureaucracy and the unbeatable establishment of clientelist networks which have resulted into the conflation of the ruling majority with the public service and the civil society.[23] For others, the Greek Constitution presents some emblematic 'irrational' provisions.[24] The constitutional text is perceived as an outdated set of rules which has proven unable to control the power of politics. Therefore, it shall be widely reformed in order to accommodate the new (European) economic government,[25] the normative context of austerity, the "Golden Rule",[26] and, furthermore, a more liberal perspective, such as the allowance of private universities and other structural reforms aiming at the urgent, under the circumstances, goal of economic growth.

In any case, it remains clear that constitutional rules have little to do with the rise or aggravation of populism in the Greek politics. On the contrary, the populist 'effect' of the economic crisis has been contained from the constitutional guarantees of the rule of law. During the crises, the alternation of different political parties (right and left-wing) in power and the function of the democratic institutions have proven the endurance of the Greek political regime and the strong democratic tradition of a country that throughout 20th century suffered from two World Wars, a civil war (1946-1949) and a dictatorship (1967-1974). The recent financial crisis, another turbulent episode in the modern Greek history, is, in reality, mostly a big failure of Greek politics, not of its constitutional rules and tradition.

2.2 *The rigid Constitution and the current constitutional debate*

The Greek Constitution is a very rigid one, in fact one of the most rigid world-wide Constitutions. The revision process requires two parliamentary terms in a row and is provided by Article 110 of the Constitution and Article 119 of the Standing Orders. According to Article 110, amending the constitution takes place in two distinct but interconnected phases, first:

> 2. The need for revision of the Constitution shall be ascertained by a resolution of Parliament adopted, on the proposal of not less than fifty Members of Parliament, by a three-fifths majority of the total number of its members in two ballots, held at least one month apart. This resolution shall define specifically the provisions to be revised.

---

23 TS Pappas, *Populism and Crisis Politics in Greece* (Palgrave Macmillan 2014) 43-70.

24 X Contiades, *The irrational Constitution* (in Greek, Sakkoulas 2017).

25 A Vlachogiannis, *The Constitution and the new European economic governance* (in Greek, Sakkoulas 2018).

26 That is a legal requirement that yearly budgets of the member States should be balanced. L Papadopoulou, Can Constitutional Rules, Even if 'Golden', Tame Greek Public Debt? in M Adams and F Fabrini and P Larouche (eds), *The Constitutionalization of European Budgetary Constraints* (Hart 2014).

The following and final step of the amending process belongs to the next Parliament which "shall, in the course of its opening session, decide on the provisions to be revised by an absolute majority of the total number of its members". In order for an amendment to pass "a proposal for revision of the Constitution" shall:

> receive the majority of the votes of the total number of members but not the three-fifths majority specified in paragraph 2, the next Parliament may, in its opening session, decide on the provisions to be revised by a three-fifths majority of the total number of its members.

In addition, the Greek Constitution has its own eternity clause, as Article 110 paragraph 1 stipulates that:

> 1. The provisions of the Constitution shall be subject to revision with the exception of those which determine the form of government as a Parliamentary Republic and those of articles 2 paragraph 1, 4 paragraphs 1, 4 and 7, 5 paragraphs 1 and 3, 13 paragraph 1, and 26

and finally "Revision of the Constitution is not permitted before the lapse of five years from the completion of a previous revision".

The text aims to draw a clear line between *constitutional* and *ordinary* politics, which prevents the arbitrary exercise of power and the frequent constitutional changes. In reality, formal constitutional change becomes extremely difficult in Greece and sometimes this constitutional rigidity seems to oppose to the adaptation of the text to the dynamic legal standards of the EU law,[27] notably during the years of the economic crisis. In other words, there is in Greece a certain sacred perception of the constitutional text that resembles the American constitutional tradition. On the other hand, given the fact that Greek politics are usually reduced to a two-parties majority game, the constitutional rigidity is per se a valuable check and balance to the arbitrary exercise and abuse of political power.

Currently, the Greek Constitution is in the first phase of its fourth amendment and strong voices have been raised in favour of the – in theory disputed – amendment of the amendment clause (Article 110), but without success. As far as the amendment procedure is concerned, the former government's initiative to organize and run a procedure of public deliberation and consultation prior to the parliamentary procedure (through an

---

27 See notably: Case C-213/07 *Michaniki AE v Ethniko Symvoulio Radiotileorasis and Ypourgos Epikrateias* [2008] ECR I-9999 about the compatibility with the general principles of Union Law of the aim pursued by the establishment of an incompatibility between the status of owner, partner, main shareholder or management executive of a media undertaking and that of owner, partner, main shareholder or management executive of an undertaking awarded a public works, supply or services contract.

electronic platform and the organization of open meetings with various civil society's organizations), in order to bring the Constitution closer to the people, has been denounced by the opposition as a populist jeopardy of the value of the text and as an indirect way to control the vote in Parliament. In any case, the people's participation did not meet the expected standards of the government and there was no interference with the abovementioned constitutional procedure of Article 110.

On the other hand, the recent constitutional debate in the first phase of the current revision of the Greek constitution has shown the tendency of the former Greek Government of Syriza-Anel to enhance the majoritarian features of the Greek democracy. Among the proposals of the government was the possibility of a direct election of the President of the Greek Republic. In addition, the former government proposed a series of amendments aiming at promoting institutions of 'direct democracy'. Specifically, it was proposed that a referendum should be held for any ratification of treaties transferring sovereign competences of the State and that, in addition, referenda on a "national issue" could be initiated by at least 500.000 citizens.[28] In other words, the revision of the Constitution, which will be completed or rejected or the most probably altered within the constitutional limits by the new Parliament and the former opposition and current Government of New Democracy, constituted a chance for Syriza to constitutionally express its political strategy and rhetoric on the elitist and democratically deficient character of the Greek Republic. This discourse has been, in fact, a constitutional echo of the new cleavage between the 'rule of the many' and the 'rights of the few'.

2.3 *An original system of judicial review and a flexible protection of rights*

Greek constitutionalism is an original mix of American and continental legal traditions. In this sense, the judicial review of legislative acts in Greece is a system of *diffuse review*, by all courts, like in the US, but there is no Constitutional Court and the most significant mechanism of concentration of the review is the jurisdiction of the Supreme Administrative Court. The court that declares the law unconstitutional sets it aside and declines to apply it in the particular case. The law still exists in the legal order but it remains inactive until the vote of a new law. The diffuse judicial review is an in *concreto* and *incidental* review, as the courts review the law contextually, in a given (and only for that) case.[29] The Greek system of judicial review has been inaugurated, by the Courts, in the late 19th century and has meaningfully contributed to the protection of

28 IN Grigoriadis, *Democratic Transition and the Rise of Populist Majoritarianism: Constitutional Reform in Greece and Turkey* (Palgrave Macmillan 2018) 48.

29 A Kaidatzis, 'Greece's Third Way in Prof. Tushnet's Distinction between Strong-Form and Weak-Form Judicial Review, and What We May Learn From It' [2014] *Jus Politicum* 13 https://ssrn.com/abstract=2548024 accessed 21 October 2019.

fundamental rights. It brings together elements of strong and weak forms of review and the courts seem to adopt a flexible position between judicial activism and judicial restraint, depending on the nature of the case.[30] The Supreme Administrative Court's jurisprudence, acting as a de facto 'constitutional' court, as the Court has the last word on significant constitutional matters, has proven its extreme importance for civil rights, but generally the Greek Courts express a certain 'timidity',[31] aiming not to take the place of the legislator, particularly in hard cases regarding what are called important "political matters", such as the economic and fiscal ones.

In this framework, during the last years of the financial crisis, the courts have implicitly recognized that the main responsible actor to deal (legally and politically) with the crisis is the political power: i.e. the elected, competent and legitimated legislator. The higher courts have mostly hesitated disregarding the Memoranda laws, unless they were obviously contrary to the Constitution. For instance, in its famous decision (668/2012) on the first Memorandum,[32] the Supreme Administrative Court underlined that the legislator's task had been notably difficult due to the unprecedented conditions of the economic crisis and the imminent danger of total budgetary derailment. In contrast to this sign of judicial restraint, the recent judicial activism of the Supreme Administrative Court in a series of cases concerning the constitutionality of legislation related to the 2nd Memorandum (essentially Law 4093/2012) and, in particular, the further cuts in pensions which have been found to be contrary to Article 22 paragraph 5 of the Greek Constitution (right of social security), has led to a different legal qualification of the crisis and social rights normative status. The Supreme Administrative Court (judgments 2287-90/2015) argued that the financial crisis should not justify any limitation of the right to social security and therefore should not constitute in this case a well-established and superior reason of public interest in the judicial review. The Court was of the opinion that the urgent phase of the crisis was definitely over and that no threat of immediate bankruptcy existed: as a certain normality within the crisis was being established and, given the fact that a large share of the State's fiscal adjustment measures had already been imposed on the Greek citizens, the usual reference of the legislator to the economic crisis as the justification for the new cuts should be overruled, being obviously disproportionate and inadequate.[33]

---

30 ibid.

31 ibid.

32 Regarding the constitutionality of the cuts on wages in the public sector and pensions. In this decision, the public interest clause prevailed heavily over the protection of constitutional rights. In other words, the judicial reception and interpretation of nonlegal facts, such as the economic and financial conditions, has led to a minimum amount of control being exerted over the Memorandum, via the application of the proportionality principle.

33 G Karavokyris, The Role of Judges and Legislators in the Greek Financial Crisis: A Matter of Competence. in L Papadopoulou and I Pernice and JHH Weiler (eds), *Legitimacy Issues of the European Union in the Face of Crisis: Dimitris Tsatsos in memoriam* (Nomos 2017).

Within this unprecedented political and financial context, we shall stress the fact that the Supreme Administrative Court is a well-respected and established institution in Greece and its jurisprudence during the crisis, even if it has been disputed in theory, notably by the anti-memorandum doctrine,[34] has guaranteed the new legal normality and protected the limits of the state interventions and the hard core of civil and social rights, mainly through the proportionality test and by advancing the rule of the public interest, in terms of the economic and fiscal balance of the country and the avoidance of an official bankruptcy. Therefore, it has shown a certain efficiency towards individual and social rights protection in very difficult, not to say extreme circumstances.[35]

The appointment of the higher courts judges according to the constitution is a privilege of the government, but the nomination is limited only to career judges. Specifically, Article 90 paragraph 5 of the Greek Constitution stipulates that:

> Promotion to the post of President or Vice-President of the Supreme Administrative Court, of the Supreme Civil and Criminal Court and of the Court of Audit shall be effected by presidential decree issued on the proposal of the Cabinet, by selection from among the members of the respective supreme court, as specified by law.

Recently, the promotion of the Presidents and the Vice Presidents of the Council of State has evolved into an important political issue, because of the high tension and cleavage of the crisis politics. For instance, the decision of the former Prime Minister to appoint the president of the Supreme Civil and Criminal Court as the head of his legal cabinet few days after her retirement has been severely criticized by the opposition as a symbolic compromise of the independence of the judiciary. The same objections were addressed to the new government of New Democracy for nominating as Deputy Minister of Justice the vice-president of the Supreme Court. It is in fact the procedure of the nomination itself that has been often criticized as a breach of the principle of separation of powers and an exercise of political control over the judiciary.

---

34 The so-called 'anti-memorandum' political and legal discourse has severely challenged not only the legality and the constitutionality of the crisis legislation but also its legitimacy, claiming that it has in fact been unilaterally imposed under the extreme pressure of the Troika and therefore should not be imputed to the Greek authorities and a fortiori to the Greek people. See notably G Katrougalos, The crisis and its way out (Athens, Livanis, 2012) (in Greek).

35 P Pikrammenos, 'Public law in emergency conditions from the point of the judicial review process' [2012] 2 Theoria kai Praxi Dioiktikou Dikaiou 97 (in Greek); G Karavokyris, *The Constitution and the crisis* (in Greek, Kritiki 2014) 17.

2.4 *The quality of democratic procedures*

Greece is a liberal democracy with all the traditional constitutional guarantees regarding the elections and the political party system, the financing and the terms of political campaigns. According to Article 54 paragraph 1 of the revised Constitution, the electoral system is determined by law, a statute which applies only once the next elections have been held, unless provision is made for an immediate enforcement of the electoral law just as long as a two-third parliament majority adopts it. In other words, the legislator holds the competence to determine the rules of the electoral game within a rather open constitutional provision, which leaves open the details of the election system. Until 2016, the electoral law stipulated an enhanced proportional system. Specifically, the law provided for electing 250 out of 300 of the MPs and the last 50 seats were granted to the majority party, in order to ensure the governmental stability. The ratio of this generous bonus of seats for the party that wins the majority is to allow the formation of a strong government. At the same time a threshold of 3% is (still) required for a party to be represented in Parliament. In any case, since 1975, there has never been a 'minority government', as Greek parliamentarism is a majoritarian one. Nevertheless, the new electoral law,[36] voted by the former governmental majority of Syriza-Anel, stipulates the application in the next elections of the simple 'proportional system'. This provision has incited a fierce reaction of the opposition, accusing the government of Syriza-Anel of 'political cynicism' and arguing, given the country's' non-consensual political tradition, that simple proportional representation will most probably lead to political instability.[37] Finally, the new electoral law has lowered the voting age from 18 years to 17 and has suppressed, as expected, the bonus of 50 seats.

The financing of the election campaign is based on public funds, but also on private donations. Public funding is the main source and establishes a strong connection between the state and the parties. Certainly, it is distributed to the latter in a proportional way, according to the votes received, but in order for a party to have access to the funding it must be represented in the national or the European Parliament or must have received at least 1.5 per cent of the vote in at least 70 per cent of constituencies. Donations from the private sector must be limited to EUR 20,000 per year to a political party and EUR 5,000 per year to a candidate. The parties usually take loans from banks, but cash donations are not allowed. They cannot also receive donations from owners of media outlets or other similar legal entities. During the elections, all candidates must report their finances and open an electoral bank account. The parties are obliged to designate a maximum of three bank accounts. The law provides for strict fines and sanctions in case of finance violations

36 Law 4406/2016.

37 Kathimerini, 'New electoral law approved by simple majority of MPs' *Kathimerini* (21 July 2016) http://www.ekathimerini.com/210662/article/ekathimerini/news/new-electoral-law-approved-by-simple-majority-of-mps accessed 21 October 2019.

(for instance the revocation of up to 50% of the funding). According to corruption experts there is a constant problem with the transparence and accountability of the financing, especially regarding the use of anonymous coupons for cash donations that have been reintroduced for amounts up to EUR 15, and a maximum ceiling of EUR 75,000 for parties that receive public funding and EUR 20,000 for those without funding.[38] The important challenge for the quality of democracy is the observation of the principle of equality in the electoral competition, which is always doubted, in the fields of finance and communication. The principle of a *proportional equality* in the financing of the parties shall also be observed for the new ones, the parties that enter the electoral campaign and shall preserve a certain *equality of chances*. In the same sense, the balance between public and private funding must be reviewed and the control of the financing shall be attributed to an independent authority, composed in majority by career judges.

The exact same democratic concern applies to the distribution of public and private media airtime during the campaigns, which, according to the jurisprudence of the Supreme Administrative Court, must follow the principle of (proportional) equality (based on parties' representation in parliament), without ignoring or marginalizing the new parties.[39] The airtime is decided by ministerial decisions and depends on the data provided by the media regulator (an independent authority). There are specific restrictions for the candidate's appearances on radio and TV during the election period and the opinion polls are free until one day before the election.

One of the most controversial cases in the media law landscape has been recently the Law 4339/2015, voted in the Greek Parliament in October 2015 and aiming to finally, after 30 years of political hesitation, grant licenses to the digital terrestrial television providers. Specifically, the new law stipulated that only four ten-year licenses would be granted through an auction held by the Secretariat General of Information and Communication. The opposition argued that the law violated frontally the Greek Constitution because it bypassed the independent regulatory authority, the National Council for Radio and Television. In addition, the limitation to 4 licenses was arbitrary and against the principle of pluralism. To the contrary, the media landscape would be under the States' custody. Finally, the law was declared contrary to the constitution by the Supreme Administrative Court because the National Council and not the Minister, should have been in charge of the licensing procedure.[40]

38 See the ODIHR report and proposals at: Office for Democratic Institutions and Human Rights, *Greece: Parliamentary Elections, October 2019: ODIHR Needs Assessment Report* (ODIHR 2019) https://www.osce.org/odihr/elections/greece/420839?download=true accessed 21 October 2019; For the legal framework see Law 3023/2002, 4304/2014 and 4509/2017.

39 Judgement of the Supreme Administrative Court no. 3427/2010.

40 Judgement of the Supreme Administrative Court no. 95/2017.

3 The Populist 'Failures' of the Greek Constitutionalism

As Nadia Urbinati puts it, populism is parasitical on representative democracy.[41] The very concept of representation is supposed to comply only with the pure interest of the representative and fatally ignore the people's 'real' will, the one that populist leaders claim to authentically express. The figure of the charismatic leader and its unmediated identification to the people is inherent to political populism. Therefore, populist politics emphasize the political necessity of referenda. The Greek referendum of July 2015 about the Greek reform program was highly contested and denounced, in political and constitutional terms, as a 'plebiscite' and a clear manifest of constitutional populism. On the other hand, populism is also about identity politics and the inclusion (left-wing populism) or exclusion (right-wing populism) of groups, especially minorities. During the last years and maybe as a *collateral effect* of the financial crisis, a certain *jurisprudential patriotism* has emerged which may qualify, *in extremis*, as *a populist sign*. Specifically, the higher court judges seem to embrace an exclusionary policy on crucial identity matters, such as citizenship and religious freedom.

3.1 The borderline Greek referendum of the 5th July 2015

According to Article 44 of the Greek Constitution:

> The President of the Republic shall by decree proclaim a referendum on crucial national matters following a resolution voted by an absolute majority of the total number of Members of Parliament, taken upon proposal of the Cabinet. A referendum on Bills passed by Parliament regulating important social matters, with the exception of fiscal ones shall be proclaimed by decree by the President of the Republic, if this is decided by three-fifths of the total number of its members, following a proposal of two-fifths of the total number of its members, and as the Standing Orders and the law for the application of the present paragraph provide.

Article 44 is supplemented by the implementing law 4023/2011 "on enhancing direct and participatory democracy through referendums."

---

41 N. Urbinati argues that 'populism is parasitical not so much on democracy but on representative democracy; it is *not* external to representative democracy but *does* compete with it about the meaning and use of representation as the way of claiming, affirming, and managing the will of the people. Populism's representative claim is the source of populism's radical contestation of parliamentary democracy'. See: N Urbinati, Populism and the Principle of Majority. in C Rovira Kaltwasser and others (eds), *The Oxford Handbook of Populism* (Oxford University Press 2017) 576.

In his address to the Greek people, the Prime Minister announced on 27th of June 2015 that the Cabinet decided to put the proposal of the EU/ECB/IMF institutions on Greece's bailout program to a referendum. Particularly, the electorate would vote on the "Reforms for the completion of the Current Program and Beyond" and the "Preliminary Debt sustainability analysis". The referendum was officially declared by the President of the Republic on June 28th, after a parliamentary vote. On June 28th the European Commission published these latest proposals "in the interest of transparency and for the information of the Greek people".

Several political and constitutional issues were raised by this controversial referendum. It goes without saying that it was a 'snap' referendum, which took place after an extremely limited amount of time for public deliberation, as only one week had passed between its official announcement and the election day. Given the fact that the referendum law stipulated a maximum period of 30 days for the referendum to take place, no reasonable time had been left for a rational campaign and the information of the electoral body on the proposals which were published in English and no Greek translation could be easily accessible to the citizens. In addition, according to the same law, the question of the referendum must be clear and precise. Nevertheless, at the exact time of the referendum the question was not valid anymore, as the proposals that were put into vote were withdrawn from the European institutions.[42] As the constitutionalists Contiades and Fotiadou have accurately summarised it:

> The ambiguity of the question is tremendous. The most obvious reading should be yes or no (or rather no or yes according to the ballot paper) to the implied question whether Greece should remain in the Eurozone. On June 29 Jean Claude Juncker addressed the Greek people asking them to vote "yes", since voting "no" would mean willingness to exit the Eurozone. Adversely, the Greek Prime minister has repeatedly and clearly stated that the "no" vote does not mean exiting the Eurozone -but it shall instead lead to a solution within the euro area. The "no" vote thus for some voters means yes to Europe but with a better deal, whereas to others "no" means Grexit. Referendum questions are not meant to be in application of the subjective reader response theory, according to which everyone can read their own things into the text. They are supposed to be understood in the same way by all voters. And after the vote, they are supposed to be understood in the same way by all actors. However, the

42 The question of the referendum was: Should the agreement plan submitted by the European Commission, the European Central Bank and the International Monetary Fund to the Eurogroup of 25 June 2015, and comprised of two parts which make up their joint proposal, be accepted? The first document is titled "Reforms For The Completion Of The Current Program And Beyond" and the second "Preliminary Debt Sustainability Analysis."

> "no" vote is open to multiple interpretations by voters, as well as by international actors and entities.[43]

Within an extremely polarized political context, the government pleaded for the 'no' and on the ballot paper, the 'no' box was above the 'yes' box. Furthermore, although the Constitution is not clear on this subject, there was a strong opposition in constitutional theory about the nature of the question, the fiscal character of the referendum and whether it is possible to be put as a "crucial national matter". Thus, the Government was blamed by the opposition to have organized a manipulative referendum, as the people were substantially unable to realize what was at stake and to decide on a rational ground. Furthermore, the legal framework of the referendum has been altered after its official proclamation by an (urgent) Act of Legislative Content (issued by the President of the Republic on proposal of the Cabinet),[44] a 'governmental act' that cannot be reviewed by the Supreme Administrative Court.[45]

Despite the fact that the referendum, from a *positivist* point of view, was not contrary to the Constitution and the law, it was still a borderline procedure, against all codes and good practices on referenda, an extreme political decision with no respect to the ethical and political conditions and prerequisites of a democratic vote.[46] In terms of political and constitutional populism, the referendum turned out to be a real 'plebiscite', a vote on the

---

43 X Contiades and A Fotiadou, 'The Greek Referendum: Unconstitutional and Undemocratic' (Constitution Making and Constitutional Change, 7 July 2015) https://constitutional-change.com/the-greek-referendum-unconstitutional-and-undemocratic accessed 21 October 2019; in addition, regarding the constitutional politics per se, the experience of the referendum "that shook Greek politics by bringing the country to the brink of exit from the European Union and the Eurozone further polarized an already deeply divided Greek society, and produces a result which the Tsipras government itself fail to respect was a defining one. In fact, it pointed not only against the proliferation of referendums as political instrument, but even against their use within the limits of the current constitution". See: IN Grigoriadis, *Democratic Transition and the Rise of Populist Majoritarianism: Constitutional Reform in Greece and Turkey* (Palgrave Macmillan 2018) 92: See also for a brief narrative of the referendum: C Mudde, *SYRIZA: The Failure of the Populist Promise* (Palgrave Macmillan 2017) 33.

44 Act of Legislative Content, 28/6/2015.

45 According to its decision in: Judgement of the Supreme Administrative Court no. 2787/2015.

46 According to the "Code of good practice on referendums" adopted by the Venice Commission (25/10/2018): "c. The question put to the vote must be clear; it must not be misleading; it must not suggest an answer; electors must be informed of the effects of the referendum; voters must be able to answer the questions asked solely by yes, no or a blank vote.
d. The authorities must provide objective information. This implies that the text submitted to a referendum and an explanatory report or balanced campaign material from the proposal's supporters and opponents should be made available to electors sufficiently in advance, as follows:
i. they must be published in the official gazette sufficiently far in advance of the vote;
ii. they must be sent directly to citizens and be received sufficiently far in advance of the vote;
iii. the explanatory report must give a balanced presentation not only of the viewpoint of the executive and legislative authorities or persons sharing their viewpoint but also of the opposing one.
The above information must be available in all the official languages and in the languages of the national minorities.". See: European Commission for Democracy through Law (Venice Commission), 'Code of Good Practice on Referendums' (CDL-AD(2007)008rev-cor, Venice Commission 2018).

legitimacy and the political survival of the former Government and the Prime Minister, verifying the link between 'the people' and the 'charismatic leader'. The result of the referendum, which has legally a consultative status, a clear 'no' of 61% was immediately after the ballot interpreted (in a manner that has been criticized as a violation of the people's will) by the Prime Minister as a clear mandate to renegotiate with the EU for a new 'austerity' program, the 3rd Memorandum.

4 A Judicial Populism? The Identity Politics of the Supreme Administrative Court's Jurisprudence

Constitutional populism promotes a compact and robust perception of the will of the 'people' or 'the nation' and gives emphasis on the famous 'majority rule', in the name of the democratic principle. The power of the 'many', as a dominant political and constitutional motive, has a significant institutional impact, leaving its trace also in the judicial field, especially in identity politics and hard cases regarding the 'constitutional identity' of the State. Actually, there is a high tension between the EU definition of the term[47] and its sovereign/national interpretation by the constitutional courts of the members of the Union.

In the Greek case, the recent jurisprudence of the Supreme Administrative Court, the ethnic and cultural identification of the 'nation' seems to gain a significant normative ground. A so-called 'constitutional patriotism' has emerged during the financial crisis, although the Supreme Administrative Court has accepted, in the vast majority of cases, the necessity and the proportionality of the memoranda crisis-law and their conformity with the public (fiscal) interest. This patriotism is not merely a procedural one (such as not asking a preliminary ruling in case 668/2012 of the first memorandum), but it seems to rise in response to the court's compliance with the requirements of the country's fiscal adjustment (for example in the decisions 668/2012 or PSI 1116/2014 of the Supreme Administrative Court).[48] In other words, the strict jurisprudential compliance with the economic austerity measures seems to have triggered the reaction of the Court on identity matters, on the preservation of a Greek original constitutional tradition. In its 100/2017 ruling about the new law 4427/2017 on voluntary operation of the shops on Sundays, the Court has underlined that Sunday's rest is essentially linked to the exercise of the freedom of religion. This reference of the Court seems of minor importance but, on the other hand, the recent decision 660/2018 of the Court on the constitutionality of the new program and material on religious teaching solemnly confirms that the dominant

47 P Faraguna, 'Constitutional Identity in the EU-A Shield or a Sword?' [2017] 18(7) *German Law Journal* 1627; D Gamba and D Lentzis, 'Crafting Constitutional Identity in the Era of Migration and Financial Crises – The Case of Greece' [2017] 18(7) *German Law Journal* 1683.

48 A Vlachogiannis, *The Constitution and the new European economic governance* (in Greek, Sakkoulas 2018) 194; C Yannakopoulos, *The impact of the EU law on the judicial review* (in Greek, Sakkoulas 2013) 459.

orthodox religion shall be recognized as part of 'the constitutional tradition of the country'. The Court argues that Article 16 paragraph 2 of the Greek Constitution stipulating that:

> Education constitutes a basic mission for the State and shall aim at the moral, intellectual, professional and physical training of Greeks, *the development of national and religious consciousness* and at their formation as free and responsible citizens.

imposes a majoritarian conception (the vast majority of Greek Christian-orthodox) of religious freedom and confirms the monophonic and catechetic character of religious education.[49] Few years before, in its decision 460/2013 on Greek citizenship, the court has underlined a *romantic* definition of the Greek nation, overruling the formal criteria of the disputed law and its provisions for granting the citizenship to the children of migrants, in compliance with their education status and their integration in Greek society. In fact, the court has assumed the role of the original interpreter of the constitutional concept of 'nation' and pointed to the legislator that its discretionary criteria of inclusion in the Greek community cannot bypass the mere fact that our nation is not an ephemeral but a durable in history community, with a precise and legally binding cultural background.[50]

In the abovementioned decisions, the Supreme Administrative Court crossed the line of judicial restraint and the minimum proportionality and constitutionality test and was self-proclaimed as the competent organ to define the terms of the formation and reproduction of our national and religious consciousness. The Court advanced an 'exclusionary' approach on migrants' rights as the significant 'other' (the migrant) must prove not only his sentiment of belonging to the Greek nation but also an 'authentic bond' with the Greek culture, language and society. In other words, the constitutional identity of the State, a sort of *mélange* of the religious and national consciousness of the citizens, is not a political 'construction' or a civil 'contract' but a prefixed community of values, a rather autoreferential and introvert 'natural law' state or condition.

---

49 G Stavropoulos, 'The course on religion under the light of the recent decision 660/2018 of the Supreme Administrative Court' (Constitutionalism, 10 June 2018) https://www.constitutionalism.gr/stavropoulos-mathima-thriskeutikon-ste-660-2018 accessed 21 October 2019 (in Greek).

50 I Koutsoukos, 'Citizenship, nation and rule of law' [2011] 1 Efimerida Dioikitikou Dikaiou 78 (in Greek).

5 Conclusion: The Rhetoric Force of Populism in Greek Constitutional and Political Discourse

Greek politics and constitutional debates have always been, since 1974 and the transition of the country to the democratic rule, widely influenced by the *majoritarian principle* and the overwhelming praise of *popular sovereignty*. The socialist government of Pasok and A. Papandreou in the 80's has claimed to have given again the (lost) power to "the people" against the 'establishment' (according to the slogan "Pasok in government, the people in power"), through the 'charismatic leadership' of an extremely powerful Prime Minister and in the conditions of an uninterrupted political polarization between the right and the left wing major parties (political scandals occurred, the 1989 penal trial of Papandreou etc.). Papandreou's narrative was simple and attractive: the dominant imperialist centre against the underdeveloped periphery, Greece was certainly belonging to the second and oppressed category. The 'non-privileged' Greeks against the 'establishment' was also a key phrase of his rhetoric, along with a moralist and hyper-ideological view of politics. Papandreou forged in Greece the idea of a single political entity, the people, ruling out the elites.[51] Consequently, Papandreou's impact on Greek politics, in terms of rhetoric and discourse, has marked the 'Metapolitefsi' era. In one of his famous speeches, Papandreou professed that in his view "there are no institutions, but only the people".[52] The constitutional amendment of 1986 and the suppression of the 'super-powers' of the President confirmed the hegemonic rule of the Prime Minister in the Greek parliamentary system. The government and its majority in Parliament turned into the real 'super-powers' holders. In the mid 90's the new Prime Minister of PASOK government K. Simitis departed from the populism of the 80s and Papandreou's heritage in order to set out the 'modernisation' of the Greek politics and society as basic motive and strategic objective of his political agenda. Simitis' rhetoric was a one of a moderate politician, in the steps of Giddens' and Tony Blair's 'third-way', a shift to a more professional and less passionate and sentimental perception of politics. The constitutional impact of its policy has been depicted in the extensive constitutional revision of 2001, notably in the strengthening of the independent authorities and the enhancement of the catalogue of civil rights, tackling corruption and the constitutionalization of checks and balances against the majority rule.[53] As Giannis Voulgaris has well defended,

> Undoubtedly, populism(s) has been a constant feature of Greek politics. We could say that it has been the shadow of Greek democracy after 1974.

51 TS Pappas, *Populism and Crisis Politics in Greece* (Palgrave Macmillan 2014) 24-26.

52 ibid 28.

53 IN Grigoriadis, *Democratic Transition and the Rise of Populist Majoritarianism: Constitutional Reform in Greece and Turkey* (Palgrave Macmillan 2018) 59.

> However, it has appeared under various circumstances, with various contents and various actors. It has been mainly national populism as a result of the powerful nationalistic ideology and the "politicians populism", to misuse Canovan' s term; a kind of populism, in other words, that has been endogenous to catch-all politics in an antagonistic party system. However, populism as a synonym of demagogy and manipulation of the people has been also constantly present. But that does not mean that we can raise populism to the key explanatory tool of all the political, economic and cultural transformations in Greece from the last quarter of the 20th century to the international economic crisis of 2008.[54]

According to Voulgaris, Greece is a peculiar example of a State that has developed into a modern liberal democracy, while populism has been inherent in politics. In fact, he reasonably argues that "what can help us understand Greece today is the concept of national populism".[55] This concept is the one that allows us to understand how left-wing parties (like Anel) and right wing (like Syriza) can form a mixed political sign of meta-communism beliefs, social and welfare state defence and nationalistic proudness. Moreover, this national populism, stemming from the deep 80s and presented as a catch-all political message throughout the 'Metapolitefsi' (for the two dominant parties, Pasok and New Democracy), with certain exceptions and interruptions, allows us to recognize today's significant rhetoric force of populism, expressed by Syriza in its anti-austerity polemic campaign. A similar observation, with less intense than the previous, applies to certain members of the party of New Democracy for their opposition to the 'Prespes Agreement' regarding the long-time unsolved issue of the name of Northern Macedonia. Put simply, national populism is a *leitmotiv* of Greek politics that emerges in conflictual matters and divides the electoral body. In this sense, again as Voulgaris concludes, it is difficult to find in Greece a 'progressive' version of populism, in terms of Mudde and Kaltwasser, as the populist discourse defends, in a retro and nostalgic sense: either the reproduction of the pre-crisis society, with all the well-known pathologies that, in fact, lead to the economic crisis,[56] or a nationalistic fantasy of the sovereign and powerful Greece.

Greek constitutional discourse has equally been impregnated by populist rhetoric during the financial crisis. The memoranda agreement with the institutions has often been identified as unconstitutional agreement and the cabinets that have adopted them accused to have been atypically disguised in 'parliamentary dictatorships', whose 'coups d'État' were interpreted as the symbolic and legal symptom of the country's 'sovereignty

---

54 G Voulgaris, Populism Harms Politics. in C Mudde, *SYRIZA. The Failure of the Populist Promise* (Palgrave Macmillan 2017) 77.

55 ibid 78.

56 ibid 79.

alienation'. Even if this constitutional doctrine, which in fact was reproducing political statements, was attributed to a minority of scholars and with significant degradations, the constitutional terms have been highlighted in the political debate. In other words, the political argument and the constitutional interpretation were not, if possible in such circumstances, clearly or even relatively distinguished and the debate between constitutionalists became as rough as the one between the political parties and leaders. Nevertheless, Greek constitutionalism has not been institutionally transformed or utterly weakened, as the constitutional guarantees have preserved the legal normality and frequent elections took place from 2009 to 2019, allowing the major parties to alternate in power. This can sound too little for many, but has been, to be accurate, a success of the Greek politics and their constitutional framework during a crisis that has not yet ended. Populism in Greece turned out to be what the concept implies, a thin-centered ideology, routed in its modern constitutional and political history, that is always present and parasitical to our liberal institutions. In the Greek example, its rhetoric force was decisive for the rise of parties in power but on the other hand rather weak to seriously threaten the liberal and democratic acquis of the political regime and the constitutional order of the country.

Hungary – Protecting the Liberal Constitution

*Petra Gyöngyi**

1 Introduction

The April 2010 parliamentary elections appeared as a defining moment for the liberal Constitution in Hungary. Fidesz-KDNP secured a two-thirds majority of votes, unprecedented in the country's history since the fall of communism in 1989. Moreover, Fidesz established itself as a populist party, understood in its large sense as a thin-centered "ideology that considers society to be ultimately separated into two homogenous and antagonistic groups, 'the pure people' versus 'the corrupt elite' and which argues that politics should be an expression of the volonte general (general will of the people)".[1]

Indeed, since the 2010 parliamentary elections, Fidesz relied on a rhetoric using the two-thirds majority of popular votes as a justification to represent the "Hungarian people" against *inter alia* the "elite" of opposition political parties, the judiciary, civil society, EU Institutions, and foreign-funded universities. Fidesz-KDNP relied on its legislative majority and populist rhetoric to adopt a new and renamed Fundamental Law in 2011,[2] replacing the 1989 modifications of the Constitution.[3] In addition, the governing majority modified the legal framework governing democratic processes, including the election system, referenda, political campaigning and campaign finance, as well as rules governing political parties.

This chapter will analyze the constitutional and legal safeguards of democratic constitutionalism in Hungary since a two-thirds parliamentary majority was secured by Fidesz-KDNP in the national parliamentary elections in April 2010, and retained in the

---

* Petra Gyöngyi is a Postdoctoral Fellow within the Judges under Stress project at the Department of Private Law. Her ongoing research focuses on the historical legacies of current rule-of-law and judicial independence challenges in Hungary and Romania.

1 C Mudde, 'The Populist Zeitgeist' [2004] 39(4) *Government and Opposition* 543. B Stanley, 'The thin ideology of populism' [2008] 13(1) *Journal of Political Ideologies* 95-110. J-W Müller, *What is Populism* (University of Pennsylvania Press 2016).

2 Fundamental Law of Hungary as in force on 29 June 2018, https://www.kormany.hu/download/f/3e/61000/TheFundamentalLawofHungary_20180629_FIN.pdf accessed 24 September 2019 official translation including the Sixth Amendment.

3 Act XXI of 1989 on the amendment of the Constitution. See also Act XX of 1949 The Constitution of Hungary as amended 1989-1990 and subsequent amendements Official Journal 150 (2009 October 23) 38614-38633.

2014 and 2018 elections. The analysis will focus on the content of the 2011 Fundamental Law of Hungary and related legislative acts. It will assess the extent to which the constitutional safeguards of democratic constitutionalism have been effective in light of the legal framework in force until 2010, having the 1989 constitutional modifications at its basis. Two case studies concerning court packing and specific circumstances contributing to the rise of populist, illiberal rhetoric in Hungary complement the analysis.

2 THE CONSTITUTIONAL AND LEGAL SAFEGUARDS OF DEMOCRATIC CONSTITUTIONALISM AND THE RULE OF LAW IN HUNGARY

2.1 Barriers to constitutional amendment and replacement

The main principles and rules related to the democratic form of governance and the rule of law in Hungary are laid down in a written constitution. Following a landslide victory of Fidesz-KDNP in 2010, the governing majority adopted a controversial new Fundamental Law, which entered into force in 2011 and has subsequently been amended seven times.[4]

2.1.1 Procedural rules for amendments

The Hungarian legal order knows a constitution with low barriers for constitutional amendment and for the adoption of a new Fundamental Law.[5] According to the rules laid down in the Fundamental Law, the President of Hungary, the Government as well as any parliamentary committee of the National Assembly or any member of the National Assembly have the possibility to submit a proposal for the amendment of the Fundamental Law or the adoption of a new Fundamental Law. The amendment or

4 Fundamental Law of Hungary as in force on 29 June 2018, https://www.kormany.hu/download/f/3e/61000/TheFundamentalLawofHungary_20180629_FIN.pdf accessed 24 September 2019 official translation including the Sixth Amendment; A Jakab and P Sonnevend, 'Continuity with Deficiencies: The New Basic Law of Hungary' [2013] 9(1) *European Constitutional Law Review* 102; G A Tóth, *Constitution for a Disunited Nation: On Hungary's 2011 Fundamental Law* (Central European University Press 2012); K Kovács and G A Tóth, 'Hungary's Constitutional Transformation,' [2011] 7(2) *European Constitutional Law Review* 183-203; A Arato and G Halmai and J Kis (eds), *Opinion on the Fundamental Law of Hungary*; Z Körtvélyesi and B Majtényi, 'Game of Values: The Threat of Exclusive Constitutional Identity, the EU and Hungary' [2017] 18(7) *German Law Journal* (2017) 1722-1744; G A Tóth, 'Constitutional Markers of Authoritarianism' [2019] 11(1) *Hague Journal on the Rule of Law* 37-61.

5 J Bryce, Flexible and Rigid Constitutions. in J Bryce, Studies in History and Jurisprudence vol I (Oxford University Press 1901) 124-213; Z Elkins and T Ginsburg and J Melton, *The endurance of national constitutions* (Cambridge Universtiy Press 2009); T Ginsburg and J Melton, 'Does the Constitutional Amendment Rule Matter at All? Amendment Cultures and the Challenges of Measuring Amendment Difficulty' [2015] 13(3) *International Journal of Constitutional Law.*

adoption of the Fundamental Law requires the vote of two-thirds of the Members of the National Assembly.[6]

The rules concerning the majority required for the adoption of a new constitution was modified following the 2010 parliamentary elections. The previous Constitution of Hungary required two-thirds majority vote for the amendment of the constitution and a four-fifths majority vote for the adoption of a new constitution.[7] However in 2010, the governing majority introduced a constitutional amendment, which lowered the rules for the adoption of the constitution from four-fifth the two-thirds. This was followed by the adoption of the new Fundamental Law of Hungary. With a two-thirds majority secured in Parliament, the governing majority did not have to consult with the opposition parties regarding a new Fundamental Law.[8] With an easy constitutional amendment rule, the old Constitution could have been simply amended with a two-thirds majority until it *de facto* became a new Constitution. However, the adoption of a completely new Constitution by the governing majority, renamed Fundamental Law, had a symbolic effect.

Apart from the new rules on the adoption of a new Constitution, the Fundamental Law contains further procedural guarantees concerning constitutional amendments. Accordingly, the Speaker of the National Assembly has to sign within five days the newly adopted Fundamental Law or the adopted amendment of the Fundamental Law and must send the document to the President of Hungary. The President has the role to sign the Fundamental Law or the amendment within five days and to order the promulgation in the Official Gazette. In case of any procedural errors, the President of Hungary must request the Constitutional Court to examine the matter at hand. In case the Constitutional Court does not find a violation of the procedural rules, the President must sign the amendment or the new Fundamental Law without further delay.[9]

The review possibilities by the Constitutional Court also represent a new element, which have been formalized through the Fourth Amendment of the Fundamental Law.[10] This role was introduced following tensions between the legislature and the Constitutional Court after the Court pointed out in a series of decisions[11] that, despite

6 Fundamental Law of Hungary, Art. S para 2, https://www.kormany.hu/download/f/3e/61000/TheFundamentalLawofHungary_20180629_FIN.pdf accessed 24 September 2019 official translation including the Sixth Amendment.

7 1989/1990 Constitution, section 24 (3,5).

8 Cf. P Sonnevend, Preserving the *Acquis* of Transformative Constitutionalism in Times of Constitutional Crisis: Lessons from the Hungarian case. in A von Bogdandy and others (eds), *Transformative Constitutionalism in Latin America. The Emergence of New Ius Commune* (OUP 2017) 123-148.

9 Fundamental Law, Art. S para 3, https://www.kormany.hu/download/f/3e/61000/TheFundamentalLawofHungary_20180629_FIN.pdf accessed 24 September 2019 official translation including the Sixth Amendment.

10 Fourth Amendment of the Fundamental Law, 25 March 2013, Section 2.

11 Constitutional Court of Hungary, Decision 184/2010 (X.28.) AB concerning a retroactive tax of 98% of severance bonuses of member of the previous government. See *NKM v Hungary* Applic. No. 66529/11 (4 November 2013). See also Decision 61 of 2011 (VII.13) AB. Decision 45/2012 (XII.29.) AB.

the lack of an explicit power in the constitutional framework to review constitutional amendments,[12] it would review the content of amendments if these were contrary to the rule of law or the Fundamental Law.[13] The Constitutional Court also pointed out that the use of constitutional amendments by Parliament to serve its political interest was highly problematic due to its incompatibility with the rule of law and constitutional stability.[14] However, with the Fourth Amendment of the Fundamental Law, such a substantive review possibility was explicitly excluded. The subsequent case law of the Constitutional Court followed this new constitutional role. In Decision 12 of 2013, reviewing the constitutionality of the Fourth Amendment to the Fundamental Law, the Court declared that it will review whether the procedural requirements were met and that its powers do not extend to substantive review.[15]

Ultimately, in the current political context and with the current supermajority, the governing party does not appear to be bound by any limits with regard to the amendment of the Fundamental Law or adoption of a new constitutional text. This situation makes it possible for the ruling party or coalition to promote their own views without any constraints.[16]

2.1.2 Eternity clauses and bans on certain amendments

The Fundamental Law of Hungary does not contain an explicit eternity clause[17] or any bans on specific constitutional amendments. In this sense, the new Fundamental Law maintains the approach of the previous constitutional frame of reference. However, this traditional silence of the Fundamental Law concerning eternity clauses motivated both the Constitutional Court and legal scholars to reflect on the possible existence of certain provisions in the Hungarian Constitution, which cannot be amended.[18]

The long-standing position of the Hungarian Constitutional Court has been that the lack of explicit eternity clauses and bans on amendment of certain constitutional provisions entails that every provision can be amended and there is no hierarchy between constitutional norms.[19] Notwithstanding this general position of the Constitutional Court, the constitutional case law is more nuanced. For instance, the

12 Constitutional Court of Hungary, 293/B/1994 CC ABH 1994, 362. Constitutional Court of Hungary, Decision 1260/B/1997, ABH 1998, 819-826.

13 Constitutional Court of Hungary, Decision 45/2012 (XII.29.) AB.

14 Constitutional Court of Hungary, Decision 61 of 2011 (VII.13) AB. For a critical analysis see G Halmai, 'Unconstitutional Constitutional Amendments: Constitutional Courts as Guardians of the Constitution' [2012] 19(2) *Constellations* 182-203.

15 Constitutional Court of Hungary, Decision 12 of 2013 (V. 24.) AB.

16 Cf. R Uitz, 'Can You Tell When an Illiberal Democracy Is in the Making? An Appeal to Comparative Constitutional Scholarship from Hungary' [2015] 13(1) *International Journal of Constitutional Law* 288.

17 See Y Roznai, *Unconstitutional Constitutional Amendments* (OUP 2017) Appendix.

18 G Halmai, 'Silence of transitional constitutions: The "invisible constitution" concept of the Hungarian Constitutional Court' [2018] 16(3) *International Journal of Constitutional Law* 969-984.

19 Constitutional Court of Hungary, Decision 39/1996 (IX.25.) CC ABH 138.

Constitutional Court suggested that specific provisions would be of a high constitutional value. Already in 1990 in a key decision concerning the death penalty, the Constitutional Court established that human life interpreted together with human dignity is a basic value of the Hungarian constitutional order. Moreover, the Constitutional Court stipulated that certain rights such as freedom of expression or the right to human dignity could be a source of further fundamental rights. Nevertheless, these findings did not result in the establishment of a higher value of certain rights against other type of rights in the Hungarian constitutional order or specific bans on amending certain provisions.[20] Despite the lack of explicit provisions regarding bans on certain types of amendments, legal scholarship has argued that constitutionalism entails a certain extent of unamendability, which could be legitimately declared through "judicial discovery" by the Constitutional Court.[21] However, this academic position has no mirroring in positive law.

2.2 Constitutional jurisprudence and the role of the judiciary in protecting constitutionalism

In the Hungarian legal order, the Constitutional Court is the main institution with the explicit task to protect constitutionalism. Indeed, Article 24(2) of the Fundamental Law stipulates the Constitutional Court as the guarantor of the Constitution.[22] Established in 1990, the Constitutional Court is the court with the exclusive competence to review constitutional questions. The rules pertaining to the selection and appointment of Constitutional Court judges as well as the rules concerning access to constitutional justice are laid down in the Fundamental Law. Further rules can be found in Act CLI of 2011 on the Constitutional Court.[23] However, the amendment of the rules concerning the selection and appointment of Constitutional Court judges as well as the rules concerning access to constitutional justice, taking place since 2010, significantly limited the possibility of the Constitutional Court to check the legislature.

---

20 For a more extensive analysis see F Gárdos-Orosz, Unamendability as a Judicial Discovery? Inductive Learning Lessons from Hungary. in R Albert and B E Oder (eds), *An Unamendable Constitution, Unamendability in Constitutional Democracies* (Springer 2018) 236-238.

21 ibid 231-258. See also A Bragyova and F Gárdos-Orosz, 'Vannak-e megvátozhatatlan normák az Alaptörvényben?' (Are there unamendable norms in the Fundamental Law?) [2016] *Állam és Jogtudomány* 57.

22 Fundamental Law of Hungary, Art. 24, https://www.kormany.hu/download/f/3e/61000/TheFundamentalLawofHungary_20180629_FIN.pdf accessed 24 September 2019 official translation including the Sixth Amendment.

23 ibid Art. 24(9).

2.2.1 Selection and appointment of Constitutional Court judges

The Fundamental Law of Hungary and its subsequent amendments introduced important modifications to the selection and appointment of Constitutional Court judges. According to Article 1(e) of the Fundamental Law the National Assembly elects the members and the President of the Constitutional Court.[24] These are new rules, which transferred significant appointment competences to the National Assembly with the amendment of the Constitution of 5 July, 2010. According to the previous constitutional rules, the National Assembly elected the judges of the Constitutional Court and the judges of the Constitutional Court elected the President of the Court, responsible for coordinating the activities of the Court, including scheduling decisions, the appointment of a given Member of the Constitutional Court to rapporteur, as well as the submission of proposals on the composition of panels and the presiding judges of the panels.[25] Due to these modifications, the decision about a key position within the Constitutional Court was transferred from the Members of the Court to the Parliament.

Moreover, under the previous constitutional rules, the Parliamentary committee responsible for nominating constitutional court judges had been based on parity between the government and opposition parties. In contrast, under the new rules, the committee's composition is proportional to the parties represented in Parliament.[26] The candidates proposed by the committee are then elected by Parliament with a two-thirds majority vote. Given the majority of Fidesz in Parliament since 2010, the governing majority has a determining role in the committee and can secure the vote without the opposition. Further novel constitutional elements are the removal of the possibility of the reelection of constitutional court judges and the extension of the term from nine to twelve years.[27] Nonetheless, despite these additional modifications the ruling coalition could significantly reshape the composition of the Constitutional Court.[28]

In a similar vein, the National Assembly elects with two-thirds of votes, the President of the Constitutional Court, who will serve in this position until the end of the term of office as a judge of the Constitutional Court.[29] Under the previous regulation, the Constitutional Court justices elected the President of the Constitutional Court.[30] As

24 ibid Artts. 1(e) and 24(9).

25 Act CLI of 2011, Section 17(1), https://www.venice.coe.int/webforms/documents/default.aspx?pdffile=CDL-REF(2012)017-e accessed 22 February 2020.

26 Z Szente, 'The Political Orientation of the Members of the Hungarian Constitutional Court between 2010-2014' [2016] 1(1) *Constitutional Studies* 130.

27 Fundamental Law of Hungary, Art. 24(8), https://www.kormany.hu/download/f/3e/61000/TheFundamentalLawofHungary_20180629_FIN.pdf accessed 24 September 2019 official translation including the Sixth Amendment.

28 See below section 4.1.

29 Fundamental Law of Hungary, Art. 24(8), https://www.kormany.hu/download/f/3e/61000/TheFundamentalLawofHungary_20180629_FIN.pdf accessed 24 September 2019 official translation including the Sixth Amendment.

30 Z Szente, 'The Political Orientation of the Members of the Hungarian Constitutional Court between 2010-2014' [2016] 1(1) *Constitutional Studies* 123-149.

such, these constitutional modifications further enhance the powers of the National Assembly in the selection and appointment of members of the Constitutional Court.

Furthermore, the Fundamental Law has also changed the composition of the Constitutional Court. Subparagraph 8 of Article 24 raised the number of Constitutional Court judges from eleven to fifteen members.[31] Thus, the new Constitutional Court judges could be appointed on the basis of the newly introduced selection procedure.[32]

The effects of these legal modifications become apparent with regards to the composition of the Constitutional Court. Due to these legal modifications right-conservative parties selected the majority of constitutional court judges.[33] Moreover, this change in the ideological position of the Constitutional Court judges seems to be visible in the case law of the Court following the legal modifications in cases related to populist tactics such as the anti-immigration legislation against the EU relocation scheme[34] and "Stop Soros" legislative package criminalizing NGO's providing legal aid to asylum seekers.[35]

2.2.2 Access to constitutional justice

Another significant modification introduced by the new Fundamental Law concerned the rules pertaining to access to constitutional justice.

The Hungarian Constitutional Court has ex-ante and ex-post review competences. Through these the Government, one-quarter of the Members of the National Assembly, the President of the Curia (the highest court in Hungary), the Prosecutor General, the Commissioner of Fundamental Rights, courts and individuals directly affected by an unconstitutional legal decision as well as the President of Hungary have access to the Court under the conditions described below.

One possibility to have access to constitutional justice is through abstract review. Accordingly, the Hungarian Constitutional Court has the power to examine acts not yet promulgated for their accordance with the Fundamental Law. This possibility is open to the Government, one-fourth of the MPs, the President of the Curia, the Prosecutor General or the Commissioner for Fundamental Rights.[36] However, in 2017

31 Fundamental Law of Hungary, Art. 24(8), https://www.kormany.hu/download/f/3e/61000/TheFundamentalLawofHungary_20180629_FIN.pdf accessed 24 September 2019 official translation including the Sixth Amendment.

32 See below section 4.1.

33 Z Szente, 'The Political Orientation of Members of the Hungarian Constitutional Court between 2010 and 2014' [2016] 1(1) *Constitutional Studies* 123-149.

34 Constitutional Court of Hungary, Decision 22/2016 (XII.5.) AB.

35 Constitutional Court of Hungary, Decision 3 of 2019 (III.7.) AB. See below section 4.1.

36 Fundamental Law of Hungary, Art. 24(2), https://www.kormany.hu/download/f/3e/61000/TheFundamentalLawofHungary_20180629_FIN.pdf accessed 24 September 2019 official translation including the Sixth Amendment; Act CLI of 2011, Section 24(1), https://www.venice.coe.int/webforms/documents/default.aspx?pdffile=CDL-REF(2012)017-e accessed 22 February 2020.

only 4 out of 461 cases were based on these types of petitions; in 2018 3 cases out of 391.[37]

Another possibility to access constitutional justice is open to judges. Upon the request from a judge, the Constitutional Court has the power to review the constitutionality of any law applied in a particular case.[38] This review has to take place as a matter of priority and no later than ninety days following the request by a judge. However, this possibility is also rarely used in practice. In 2017, judges requested only 48 out of the total number of 461 cases at the Constitutional Court; in 2018 judges requested 44 cases out of 391.[39]

Thirdly, via a constitutional complaint, the Constitutional Court has the power to review the constitutionality of any judicial decision. The constitutional complaint is a new review mechanisms introduced by the 2011 Fundamental Law.[40] It replaced the so-called *actio popularis* proceedings through which anyone could address a constitutional complaint to the Court.[41] This mechanism limits the group of stakeholders with access to constitutional justice, as the basis of the complaint must be a decision by a court. Furthermore, individuals can only contest the application of a legal act, whereas previously it was possible for individuals to directly challenge the constitutionality of a legal act. Despite these limitations, constitutional complaints represent the largest group of cases submitted to the Constitutional Court. In 2017, 330 out of 460 cases represented constitutional complaints; in 2018 the total number of individual complaints was 341 out of 391 cases.[42]

Subparagraphs 4 and 5 of section 24 of the Fundamental Law introduced two limitations with respect to the Constitutional Court's powers. Firstly, in case of legal provisions not explicitly requested to be reviewed, the Constitutional Court may only extend the scope of review in case of a "close substantive connection" between the requested constitutional provision and the non-requested provision. Secondly, The

37 The caseload of the Constitutional Court (2018), https://alkotmanybirosag.hu/uploads/2019/01/2018_12_31_ab_ugyforgalom.pdf accessed 24 September 2019.

38 Fundamental Law of Hungary, Art. 24(2), https://www.kormany.hu/download/f/3e/61000/TheFundamentalLawofHungary_20180629_FIN.pdf accessed 24 September 2019 official translation including the Sixth Amendment; Act CLI of 2011, Art. 25(1), https://www.venice.coe.int/webforms/documents/default.aspx?pdffile=CDL-REF(2012)017-e accessed 22 February 2020.

39 The caseload of the Constitutional Court (2018), https://alkotmanybirosag.hu/uploads/2019/01/2018_12_31_ab_ugyforgalom.pdf accessed 24 September 2019.

40 Fundamental Law of Hungary, Art. 24(2), https://www.kormany.hu/download/f/3e/61000/TheFundamentalLawofHungary_20180629_FIN.pdf accessed 24 September 2019 official translation including the Sixth Amendment; Act CLI of 2011, Art. 26(1).

41 See e.g. F Gárdos-Orosz, 'The Hungarian Constitutional Court in Transition: From Actio Popularis to constitutional complaint,' [2012] 53(4) *Acta Juridica Hungarica* 302-315. G Spuller, 'Transformation of the Hungarian constitutional court: tradition, revolution and (European) prospects' [2014] 15(4) *German Law Journal* 637-692.

42 The caseload of the Constitutional Court (2018), https://alkotmanybirosag.hu/uploads/2019/01/2018_12_31_ab_ugyforgalom.pdf accessed 24 September 2019. See K Kovács and K L Scheppele, 'The fragility of an independent judiciary: Lessons from Hungary and Poland – and the European Union' [2018] 51(3) *Communist and Post-Communist Studies* 192.

Constitutional Court may review the amendment of the Fundamental Law or the new Fundamental Law only with regards to possible procedural errors.[43]

Moreover, there are two further significant substantive limitations in the new constitutional framework. The Constitutional Court may only review budgetary and tax matters from the perspective of possible fundamental rights violations, such as right to life and human dignity, protection of personal data, freedom of thought, conscience and religion, right to Hungarian citizenship.[44] Furthermore, the Fourth Amendment of the Fundamental Law nullified the entire case law of the Constitutional Court adopted under the previous constitutional frame of reference between 1990 and 2011.[45]

Overall, these constitutional modifications changed the composition of the Constitutional Court, and significantly limited the possibility of the Constitutional Court to review the constitutionality of legislation and to rely on its case law. At the same time, these modifications mark the transition from the role of the Constitutional Court as a check on the legislative power to an individual-rights based institution. Protecting individual rights may also check the legislature. Indeed, in other legal orders this is the only way for courts to check legislation. However, it must be noted that the protection of individual rights was not the main role of the Hungarian Constitutional Court. Therefore, in the national context, due to the abrupt shift in competences, this role cannot be regarded as an automatic strong check.[46]

2.3 *Constitutional and statutory rules governing democratic processes*

The Fundamental Law and further statutory provisions establish the rules governing democratic processes in Hungary. These rules pertain to the election systems, referenda, political campaigning and campaign finance, as well as rules governing political parties. Remarkably, all these legal rules have been subject to the wider institutional reforms taking place in Hungary since 2010.[47]

---

43 Fundamental Law of Hungary, Art. 24(4-5), https://www.kormany.hu/download/f/3e/61000/TheFundamentalLawofHungary_20180629_FIN.pdf accessed 24 September 2019 official translation including the Sixth Amendment.

44 Act CXX of 2010. Fourth Amendment of the Fundamental Law, Art. 37(4). The modifications followed the Constitutional Court's decision striking down the retroactive 98% severance tax. See above section 2.1.

45 Fourth Amendment of the Fundamental Law, Art. 12, https://www.kormany.hu/download/f/3e/61000/TheFundamentalLawofHungary_20180629_FIN.pdf accessed 24 September 2019 official translation including the Sixth Amendment.

46 Cf. F Gárdos-Orosz, 'The Hungarian Constitutional Court in Transition: From Actio Popularis to constitutional complaint' [2012] 53(4) *Acta Juridica Hungarica* 302-315.

47 M Bánkuti and G Halmai and K L Scheppele, 'Hungary's Illiberal Turn: Disabling the Constitution' [2012] 23(3) *Journal of Democracy* 143-145.

2.3.1 Election systems

Hungary employs a mixed election system, consisting of the election of candidates in single-member constituencies as well as votes cast for national party lists. Candidates in single-member constituencies may secure a parliamentary mandate with the majority of votes, whereas party lists must secure at least five percent of all valid votes cast for party lists and national minority lists.[48] The main rules are laid down in the Fundamental Law, Act CCIII of 2011 on the election of Members of Parliaments and Act XXXVI of 2013 on electoral procedure. In addition, Act CXIII of 2003 contains rules on the election of Members of the European Parliament.

Article 2 of the Fundamental Law establishes the main rules governing national elections. In line with the constitutional rules, Members of the National Assembly are elected through universal and secret suffrage in a direct and secret ballot. The elections guarantee the free expression of the will of the voters.[49] Subparagraph 2 of Article 2 guarantees the participation of national minorities living in Hungary in the work of the National Assembly by stipulating that the specific rules in this sense are regulated via Cardinal Act, referring to the type of legal acts the adoption or amendment of which requires two thirds of the Members of the National Assembly present.[50] Moreover, subparagraph 3 establishes that elections are held in the month of April or May of the fourth year following the election of the previous National Assembly – with the exception of the National Assembly dissolving itself or being dissolved.[51]

Act CCIII of 2011 on the election of Members of Parliaments lays down the fundamental rules regarding the number of Members of Parliament, the establishment of single-member constituencies and the nomination of candidates in single-member constituencies, the determination of national election lists as well as the rules pertaining to voting and the determination of election results. This legislation entered into force in 2012 and replaced the 1989 legislation on elections.[52]

The 2011 Election Act introduced a number of new provisions. The Election Act establishes a one-round system instead of a two-round system installed by the previous legislation.[53] In parallel, the number of seats in the National Assembly was reduced from

48 Act CCIII of 2011, Art. 11, https://www.venice.coe.int/webforms/documents/?pdf=CDL-REF(2012)003-e accessed 23 February 2020.

49 Fundamental Law, Art. 2, https://www.kormany.hu/download/f/3e/61000/TheFundamentalLaw ofHungary_20180629_FIN.pdf accessed 24 September 2019 official translation including the Sixth Amendment.

50 ibid Section 2(2). For the rules concerning Cardinal Acts *see* Section T(4).

51 Fundamental Law of Hungary, Art 2, https://www.kormany.hu/download/f/3e/61000/TheFundamentalLaw ofHungary_20180629_FIN.pdf accessed 24 September 2019 official translation including the Sixth Amendment.

52 1989 Act XXXIV on Elections of Members of Parliament. See G Tóka, Seats and Votes: Consequences of the Hungarian Election Law. in G Tóka, *The 1990 Elections to the Hungarian National Assembly* (Sigma 1995) 41-66.

53 Act CCIII of 2011, Art. 11, https://www.venice.coe.int/webforms/documents/?pdf=CDL-REF(2012)003-e accessed 23 February 2020.

389 to 199. Out of the 199 Members of the National Assembly, 106 MPs are voted in individual districts and 93 members through national election lists.[54] Hence, the number of seats that can be gained based on the majority of votes were raised from 45,6% to 53,3%.[55] According to simulations between the old rules and the new rules, provided that the geographic distribution of the vote for major parties remained similar, the new rules would benefit the governing majority.[56]

Furthermore, the rights to vote of citizens living abroad without a permanent residence in Hungary have been extended.[57] Indeed, voting rules for the mixed election system are established on the basis of the existence of a residence in Hungary of the voters as well as national minorities. Residents may cast a vote for a candidate in a single-member constituency and one party list. Whereas voters with residence in Hungary registered as national minority voters, may cast a vote for one candidate in a single-member constituency as well as the list of their national minority. In case no such national minority list exists, national minority voters may vote for a party list.[58] In contrast, voters with no residence in Hungary may cast a vote for the national party list.[59] The Election Procedure Act introduced new interconnected procedural rules. Accordingly, citizens living abroad with no established residence in Hungary may vote by mail upon prior registration. No such possibility is open to citizens living abroad with an established residence in Hungary.[60] According to National Election Office data, 378.449 citizens with no primary residence in Hungary have been registered for the April 2018 elections.[61] The majority of these voters seem to support the governing majority, due to the fact that the 2010 amendment of the Citizenship Act introduced the preferential naturalization of persons belonging to the Hungarian minorities living abroad – a legal amendment that failed under the left-liberal government in 2004.[62]

---

54 ibid Art. 3(1-2).

55 A Jakab and S Emese, 'Sarkalatos törvények a magyar jogrendben' ('Cardinal Acts in the Hungarian legal order') [2015] 2 MTA Law Working Papers 2015/32, 265. G Halmai, 'A választójog szabályozásának átalakulása 2010-2013' ('The transformation of the regulation of election rights 2010-2013') [2014] 2 MTA Law Working Papers 57.

56 G Tóka, Constitutional Principles and Electoral Democracy in Hungary. in E Bos and K Pócza (eds), *Constitution Building in Consolidated Democracies: A New Beginning or Decay of a Political System?* (Nomos Verlag 2014) 4-6.

57 Fundamental Law Art. XXIII (4), https://www.kormany.hu/download/f/3e/61000/TheFundamentalLawofHungary_20180629_FIN.pdf accessed 24 September 2019 official translation including the Sixth Amendment.

58 See Act CLXXIX of 2011 on the rights of national minorities, Art. 53, njt.hu/translated/doc/J2011T0179P_20171221_FINrev.pdf accessed 23 February 2020.

59 Act CCIII of 2011, Art. 12(3), https://www.venice.coe.int/webforms/documents/?pdf=CDL-REF(2012)003-e accessed 23 February 2020.

60 Election Procedure Act, Section 274, 266(2) Constitutional Court *Decision* 3086/2016 (IV.26 AB). 3048/2014 (III.13) AB.

61 OSCE, 'Hungary Parliamentary Elections 8 April 2018' ODIHR Limited Election Observation Mission Final Report (27 June 2018) 9.

62 See below section 2.3.2 Referenda.

In addition, electoral constituencies were modified.[63] With regard to single-member constituencies, the Election Act explicitly states that in single-member constituencies one Member of Parliament may be elected. With regard to the establishment of single-member constituencies, the Election Act determines *inter alia,* that the constituencies cannot cross county borders or borders of the capital city and must form a contiguous area. Nonetheless, the Election Act stipulates that the "districts of Budapest or any town or village may be subdivided in two or more single-member constituencies" provided that the number of voters in the district exceeds the national average.

The Election Act explicitly sets the upper limit at 15 percent by which single-member constituencies may deviate from the national average and also taking into account "geographical, ethnic, historical, religious and other local characteristics and of any migration of population." The purpose of this provision is to comply with the main territorial rules prohibiting crossing county borders.[64]

Moreover, the legal act stipulates for the specific single-member constituencies to be established as Annex 1 to the legal act. The serial numbers of the single-member constituencies, their territorial division and seats are contained in Annex 2. Section 4(6) contains a possibility for Parliament to amend Annex 2 in case of a deviation of the number of voters in a single-member constituency that exceeds 20% of the national average. However, such modification is not possible between the first day of the year preceding the general election of Members of Parliament and the day on which the elections are held, with the exception of the voluntary or mandatory dissolution of Parliament. Part of these rules were introduced following the detailed criticism by the Venice Commission of the election system.[65] However, despite these new rules, the Election Act reshaped the map of election districts seemingly to the governing majority's benefit.[66]

Finally, the 2011 Election Act also modified the calculation of surplus votes from single-member constituencies and in case of party lists. Starting from the 2011 legislation, the calculation basis of surplus votes not only includes the votes for candidates in single-member districts who did not secure a mandate, but also the votes cast for winning candidates which are beyond securing the majority. The Constitutional Court reviewed the winner-compensation, resulting from adding the surplus votes of winning candidates to national party lists. At a fundamental level, the Court acknowledged that the principle of equality of votes is a constitutionally embedded

63 E Bodnár and J Mécs, 'A választójog védelme az Alkotmánybíróság legújabb gyakorlatában' ('The protection of the right to election in the recent case law by the Constitutional Court') [2018] *2-3 Fundamentum* 17-27.

64 Act CCIII of 2011, Art. 4(4), https://www.venice.coe.int/webforms/documents/?pdf=CDL-REF(2012)003-e accessed 23 February 2020.

65 See Venice Commission, CDL-AD(2012)012-e.

66 G Tóka, 'The Assessment of Partisan Bias in District Plans Outside of the US Context', Paper prepared for presentation at the 2016 Annual Meeting of the American Political Science Association, Philadelphia, PA, 1-4 September 2016, 22-31.

principle. However, the Constitutional Court held that while formal equality and the relatively equal weight of votes is a constitutional requirement, the principle of equality of vote does not mean full equality of votes.[67] As such, according to the Constitutional Court there are no barriers for strengthening the majoritarian elements of the election system.[68] Overall, the above-discussed modifications of the Electoral Act, although declared constitutional by the Constitutional Court, seem to benefit the governing majority in maintaining political power.

2.3.2 Referenda

Relevant safeguards concerning the organization of referenda are established in the Fundamental Law and Act CCXXXVIII of 2013 on referenda, EU citizen initiatives, regulate rules concerning national referenda. Related procedures are laid down in the election law.[69] This new regulatory framework, having the Fundamental Law at its basis, for the most part maintained the previous regulation of national referenda. However, the new regulation also introduced some important modifications strengthening the formal legal effects of referenda and changing direct democracy mechanisms in Hungary.

Article B of the Fundamental Law allows the organization of referenda by establishing that, in exceptional circumstances, public power may be exercised via direct vote. More specifically, Article 8 of the Fundamental Law empowers the National Assembly to order a national referendum. This may take place upon the initiative of at least two hundred thousand voters, in which case ordering a referendum by the National Assembly is mandatory. In addition, the National Assembly has the possibility to order a referendum at the initiative of the President of the Republic, the Government or one hundred thousand voters.

Furthermore, Article 8 guarantees at a constitutional level that a decision on a valid and conclusive referendum is binding for the National Assembly. This provision represents a novel element introduced by the Fundamental Law formally strengthening referenda. In contrast, the 1989 constitutional frame of reference allowed for the possibility of organizing consultative referenda, with non-binding legal effects. Moreover, the possibility of popular initiative, an additional direct democracy tool

---

67 Constitutional Court of Hungary. Decision 3141/2014 (V.9.) AB. Decision 22/2005 (VI.17) AB.

68 For criticism starting from the 2014 elections, OSCE, Hungary Parliamentary Elections 6 April 2014 OSCE/ODIHR Limited Election Observation Mission Final Report.

69 Act CCXXXVIII of 2013 on Initiating Referendums, the European Citizens' Initiative and Referendum Procedure, https://www.legislationline.org/download/id/7685/file/Hungary_Act_referendums_2013_en.pdf accessed 23 February 2020.

under the Hungarian constitutional frame of reference, is not part of the constitutional system anymore.[70]

In terms of content of referenda, Article 8 establishes that national referenda can be held on "any matter falling within the function and power of the National Assembly." However, the Fundamental Law introduced certain areas concerning which no referendum can be held. This limitation includes the amendment of the Fundamental Law, the modification of the central budget, the modification of the Election Act and Election of Members of the European Parliament Act, obligations arising from international treaties, personal and organisational matters falling within the competence of the National Assembly, the dissolution of Parliament or of a representative body, the declaration of the state of war and matters related to military operations as well as the granting of amnesties. Out of these, the limitation concerning the amendment of the constitution and the election system represent novel elements introduced by the Fundamental Law. While, the Constitutional Court has declared before that questions concerning the amendment of the constitution should not be subject to referenda, the Hungarian constitutional framework did not contain before a limitation on election legislation. Notwithstanding this difference, the governing majority has relied extensively on constitutional amendments and the election system has been subject to reforms since 2011.

Finally, sub-section 4 of Article 8 of the Fundamental Law, a national referendum is valid if more than half of all voters have cast valid votes and a referendum is conclusive if more than half of those who have cast valid votes opt for the same answer. This requirement also represents a novel element in the regulation of referenda.

The Referendum Act contains provisions concerning national referendums, local referendums and European Citizens' Initiatives. The rules concerning national referendums regulate the initiation stage and the national referendum procedure. The initiation rules stipulate the group of actors who may organize national referenda, the submission of the proposed referendum question as well as its certification by the National Election Commission, the collection and verification of signatures as well as the ordering of referenda, legal remedies and the binding force of national referenda.

Since 1989, seven national referenda were held on important political and social decisions. In 1989 the so-called "four yeses" referendum was held, containing questions referring to: the timing of the election of the President of the Republic; the dissolution of party militia; the prohibition of party organisations at workplaces; and the report on the state-socialist party's property. In 1990 a referendum was held concerning the manner of selecting the president (directly or by Parliament). In 1997, a referendum was held concerning Hungary's membership of the North Atlantic Treaty Organization (NATO).

70 See 1989 Constitution, Article 28/D. At least 50.000 voting citizens could require the National Assembly to place a matter on its agenda. The National Assembly had the obligation to discuss the subject requested through popular initiative.

This was followed by a referendum in 2003 on the accession to the European Union. The 2004 referendum contained two questions: the citizenship of native Hungarian's living outside the country's borders and the privatization of hospitals. While the 2008 so-called "social referenda" contained three questions related to social policies: daily inpatient fees in hospitals; outpatient medical consultation fees and university tuition fees. The last referendum was held in 2016 upon the initiative of the Government concerning the European Union's refugee relocation scheme. The question asked by the Government was: "Do you want for the European Union to be able to mandate the obligatory resettlement of non-Hungarian citizens into Hungary without the approval of the National Assembly?" Since the voter turnout was below fifty percent (41.32%), the referendum was not valid.[71]

Although the number of legally binding national referenda did not surge significantly since 2010, the Hungarian Government employed a different means of direct democracy, namely the so-called "popular consultations." These refer to political questionnaires initiated by the Government and distributed by the National Election Commission to citizens' postal address. Popular consultations are not regulated by legislation. As such, unlike national binding referenda, popular consultations are not subject to the above-discussed legal control mechanisms, such as review of the proposed question by a higher court, rules regulating the independence of bodies conducting the process, rules pertaining to the casting and counting of votes, as well as monitoring and complaint mechanisms. Nor are the political campaigning rules applicable to these consultations, such as guaranteeing the equal representation of different political opinions.[72]

Indeed, since 2010 the Hungarian Government has used popular consultations seven times, issuing: a pension questionnaire (September 2010), a citizens' questionnaire on the Fundamental Law (2011), social questionnaire (2011), economic questionnaire (2012), questionnaire on migration and terrorism (2015), the "Stop Brussels" questionnaire (April 2017) and the "Stop Soros" questionnaire (October 2017). It remains to be noted that the 2015 national consultation was used as a tool of legitimization for the construction of a wired fence on the Hungarian border and modifications of the penal code resulting in harsher punishments for border crossing.[73] The two national consultations of 2017 were issued after the failed referendum concerning the EU refugee relocation scheme and were followed by the adoption of the Stop Soros legislation package.

Ultimately, this reliance by the Government on national consultations renders the constitutional and legal guarantees for the organization of referenda ineffective. The

71 Á Bocskor, 'Anti-immigration Discourses in Hungary during the 'Crisis' Year: The Orbán Government's National Consultation Campaign of 2015' [2018] 52(3) *Sociology* 551-568.

72 See Z Pozsár-Szentmiklósy, 'Direct Democracy (1989-2016): from Popular Sovereignity to Popular Illusion' [2017] 6(1) *Acta Univ. Sapientiae, Legal Studies* 114-115.

73 See Á Bocskor, 'Anti-immigration Discourses in Hungary during the 'Crisis' Year: The Orbán Government's National Consultation Campaign of 2015' [2018] 52(3) *Sociology* 551-568.

Government can avoid compliance with the constitutional guarantees and initiate its own, unregulated consultation, the nature of which may be misleading for voters. The results can be claimed as popular support for the Government's initiatives.

2.3.3 Political campaigning

Rules pertaining to political campaigning in particular campaign period and campaign methods are contained in the Election Procedure Act.[74] The Election Procedure Act defines in section 140 campaign methods as "all methods capable of influencing or used in an attempt to influence voters' choices" with explicit reference to posters, direct contact by the nominating organization or the candidate, political advertisements and election rallies.[75] Section 144 provides a definition of and special rules applicable to posters. Accordingly, the notion of poster refers to "election placards, legends, flyers, projected images, and emblems regardless of size and the surface they are placed upon."[76] According to the Election Procedure Act during the campaign period, nominating organizations and candidates have the possibility to produce posters without "express permission or notification" and as a general rule during the campaign period posters may be placed without any limitations.[77] Further limiting rules are stipulated at the level of Governmental Ordinance[78] The Constitutional Court rejected to review a constitutional complaint contesting this legal situation in light of freedom of expression.[79]

Furthermore, the Election Procedure Act defines political advertisements as "a political message in the media as defined in section 203 (55) of Act CLXXXV of 2010 on Media Services and Mass Media with the difference, that "party", "political movement" and "Government" shall be interpreted as nominating organization and independent candidate."[80] In addition, the Election Procedure Act further clarifies that political advertisement refers to "any content published in the press or in a cinema in return of consideration promoting or advocating support for a nominating organization or independent candidate, or promoting the name, objectives, activities, slogan or emblem of such entities."[81]

The Election Procedure Act also stipulates rules concerning broadcasting political advertisements, such as the obligation of media providers to allow political

74 Act XXXVI of 2013 on electoral procedure, https://www.valasztas.hu/documents/538536/548702/Act+XXXVI+of+2013+on+Electoral+Procedure.pdf/2e82a257-b592-4819-923f-eac4a18cfec6 accessed 23 February 2020.

75 ibid Section 140.

76 ibid Section 144(1).

77 ibid Section 144(3).

78 Governmental Ordinance 5/2014 (I.17.) concerning the placement of billboards along public roads.

79 Constitutional Court of Hungary, Decision 3036/2014 (III.13.) AB. Seven dissenting opinions.

80 Act XXXVI of 2013, Section 146(a), https://www.valasztas.hu/documents/538536/548702/Act+XXXVI+of+2013+on+Electoral+Procedure.pdf/2e82a257-b592-4819-923f-eac4a18cfec6 accessed 23 February 2020.

81 ibid Section 146(b).

broadcasting under equal conditions and the prohibition to accept payments for broadcasting such advertisements.[82] Special rules are applicable to public media services, which must broadcast political advertisement in the order determined by the National Election Commission. The Election Procedure Act sets the specific number of minutes that must be dedicated to organizations nominating party lists at 470 as well as organizations nominating national minority lists at 130. Further rules determine the number of times political advertisement must be broadcast (3) as well as the timeframes: 6-8, 12-14, and 18-20. According to the legal act these provisions also apply for European Parliament elections, with a total of 300 broadcasting minutes.[83]

Although the Election Procedure Act lays down legal rules applicable to campaign periods and campaign methods, a particular problem in practice in Hungary since 2010 has been that official Government campaigns and the governing party's election campaigns were run in parallel. This is due to the fact that there are no legal limitations on Government campaigns during the election periods.[84] Consider, for instance, the 2018 elections. The OSCE monitoring of the elections noted explicitly that the state and the governing party were campaigning in tandem. As a result, in the opinion of the OSCE the elections were free but not fair. Indeed, the State's information campaign consisted of billboards, leaflets, television advertisements and mass mailings through which the governing majority depicted "Brussels" and "George Soros" as "enemies of Hungary."[85] At the same time, the content of the advertising campaign slogans of Fidesz matched the parallel State campaign. While the party campaign financing is capped, no such limit applies to State campaigns.

---

82 ibid Section 147. Originally the first version of the Election Procedure Act only allowed national channels to broadcast advertisements. This was struck down by the Constitutional Court by Decision 1/2013(I.7.) AB. The Fourth Amendment of the Fundamental Law incorporated the rules at the level of the constitution, Article 5. Following inter alia the Venice Commission's Opinion on the Fourth Amendment of the Fundamental Law, 37-47, the Fifth Amendment partially modified the constitutional rules and annulled the limitation to public broadcasters. However, it maintained the requirement of broadcasting political advertisements without any costs. In practice, this resulted in the situation that commercial broadcasters did not participate in the political campaign broadcasting. Zoltán Pozsár-Szentmiklósy, 'Alapjogok az új választójogi szabályozásban' ('Fundamental Rights in the new election regulation') MTA Law Working Papers 2014/2016, 4-5.

83 Act XXXVI of 2013, Section 147/A and B, https://www.valasztas.hu/documents/538536/548702/Act+XXXVI+of+2013+on+Electoral+Procedure.pdf/2e82a257-b592-4819-923f-eac4a18cfec6 accessed 23 February 2020.

84 Z Pozsár-Szentmiklósy, 'Alapjogok az új választójogi szabályozásban' ('Fundamental Rights in the new election regulation') MTA Law Working Papers 2014/2016.

85 OSCE, Hungary Parliamentary Elections 8 April 2018, ODIHR Limited Election Observation Mission Final Report.

2.3.4 Campaign finance

Explicit rules referring to campaign finance are laid down in the Fundamental Law, the Act on the transparency of campaign costs and the Election Procedure Act.[86]

With regard to political campaigning and party financing, subparagraph 3 of Section IX of the Fundamental Law guaranteeing the freedom of expression stipulates that in order to guarantee the delivery of information as necessary during the "electoral campaign period for the formation of democratic public opinion, political advertisements may only be published in media services free of charge, under the conditions guaranteeing equal opportunities, laid down in a Cardinal act."[87]

Further rules are set out legislation. Act LXXXVII of 2013 establishes rules pertaining to the transparency of campaign costs related to the elections of Members of the National Assembly.[88] Moreover, the Act on Electoral Procedure contains further rules related to campaign financing. Both of the above-mentioned legal acts contain safeguards against abuse of financial resources.

The Campaign Finance Act limits the amount of money that can be spent by parties during the campaign periods for general elections. The new legal act raised the cap on campaign spending to five times of the previous limit, from 1 million HUF to 5 million HUF.[89] However, the number of parliamentarians was reduced from 386 to 199.[90] As a result, the new rules allow a total spending limit of 995 HUF to parties as compared to the previous 386 million HUF.[91]

A further legal limitation concerns the amount of money directly available to candidates. According to the legal rules, 1 million HUF out of the total 5 million is made directly available to candidates from the state treasury, on a treasury card.[92] Candidates may only use the card for transfers. Thus, no direct cash withdrawals are allowed.[93] Furthermore, candidates must give a full account of their spending.[94] In addition, to these safeguards, the campaign finance act adds a risk element to the

86 See in general Z Enyedi, 'Accounting for Organisation and Financing. A Comparison of Four Hungarian Parties' [2006] 58(7) *Europe-Asian Studies* 7 1101-1117.

87 Fundamental Law of Hungary, Art. IX, https://www.kormany.hu/download/f/3e/61000/TheFundamentalLawofHungary_20180629_FIN.pdf accessed 24 September 2019 official translation including the Sixth Amendment.

88 Act LXXXVII of 2013 on the Transparency of Campaign Costs related to the Election of the Members of the National Assembly, https://www.legislationline.org/download/id/5101/file/Hungary_Act%20LXXXVII%20of%202013%20on%20Camapign%20Finance_en.pdf accessed 23 February 2020.

89 ibid Section 5(1).

90 First amendment to the Fundamental Law of Hungary.

91 Transparency International, Campaign spending in Hungary: Total Eclipse. The Monitoring of Campaign Spending at the Parliamentary and Municipal Elections of 2014 https://transparency.hu/wp-content/uploads/2016/02/Total-Eclipse-Campaign-Spending-in-Hungary-Study.pdf accessed 24 September 2019.

92 Act LXXXVII of 2013, Section 1(1), 2(2), https://www.legislationline.org/download/id/5101/file/Hungary_Act%20LXXXVII%20of%202013%20on%20Camapign%20Finance_en.pdf accessed 23 February 2020.

93 ibid Section 1(5).

94 ibid Section 1(6).

financing of candidates' campaign. Accordingly, if a candidate fails to win 2% of the total votes cast, the full amount of the directly available support (1 million HUF) must be paid back to the State Treasury.[95] This guarantee protects against the risk of running for office solely for the purpose of obtaining the amount of money available as campaign financing.

The 2013 legal act on electoral procedures contributes to determining legal safeguards by defining election campaign periods and election methods and tools.[96] According to the electoral procedure act the campaign period starts from the 50th day before voting and lasts until the end of the Election Day.[97] This represents the exclusive period when state campaign support can be used. Furthermore, the legislation posits the obligation for political parties to report to the State Audit Office the prices of political advertisement to be published in the printed press as well as the actual amount paid by political parties for publishing these advertisements.[98] However, the Electoral Procedural Act does not set such a reporting requirement for outdoor billboards and posters.[99] Political advertisements can be published in the electronic media free of charge.

Once again, the effects of these legislative modifications have been most beneficial to the governing majority. Indeed, as discussed above, the Government has used extensive billboard campaigns as part of populist tactics concerning *inter alia* the anti-immigration, "Stop Brussels", and "Stop Soros" public campaigns. Moreover, a concern raised during the 2018 national elections campaign was that the Government billboards could be not easily dissociated from the Fidesz campaign billboards, due to their similar content.[100]

2.3.5 Political parties

Rules regulating political parties are contained in a legislation dating to 1989 on the functioning and financing of political parties.[101] The most recent modification of the Political Parties Act was adopted in 2014. The legal act contains rules on the formation and registration of new political parties, the functioning of political parties, situations in which political parties cease to exist, as well as rules regarding the assets and financial management of political parties, including permitted sources for party financing, from fees paid by party members, state subsidies and contributions from private persons or

95 ibid Section 8(4, a).
96 Act XXXVI of 2013, Chapter VIII, https://www.valasztas.hu/documents/538536/548702/Act+XXXVI+of+2013+on+Electoral+Procedure.pdf/2e82a257-b592-4819-923f-eac4a18cfec6 accessed 23 February 2020.
97 ibid Section 139.
98 ibid Section 148.
99 See below section 4.
100 OSCE, Hungary Parliamentary Elections 8 April 2018, ODIHR Limited Election Observation Mission Final Report.
101 Act XXXIII of 1989 on the functioning and financial management of political parties, https://www.legislationline.org/download/id/5879/file/Hungary_financial_management_political_parties_asof2012.pdf accessed 23 February 2020.

companies without legal personality, with the explicit exception of companies with state ownership, other states and unanimous donations;[102] permitted economic activities.[103]

Moreover, since the 2014 amendment, section 9(1) requires political parties to publish their financial records in the Official Journal of Hungary every year by the 31st of May. Political parties operating their own websites must also publish on that platform the financial details of their operation. The financial records must disclose contributions exceeding five hundred thousand HUF, including the name of the contributor and the specific amount of the financial contribution. Since 2014, the legal act contains an Annex with the model financial record to be disclosed by the parties.

The legal act also includes monitoring rules. According to Section 10 the State Audit Office is responsible for monitoring the financial management of political parties. The State Audit Office inspects every two years the financial records of those political parties that regularly receive state subsidies. In case of any irregularities, the State Audit Office notifies the political party. If the unlawful situation in light of the financing rules persists, the State Audit Office notifies the Prosecutor's Office. A modification in 2014 changed the notified organ from courts to the Prosecutor's Office. Although the legal modifications enhancing transparency could be a check on the functioning of political parties, the transfer of inspection competences from courts to the prosecutorial services joins the observed broader legal trends of centralizing political power. In legal orders with no established rule of law conventions, such modifications can become prone to political manipulation.

3 THE INEFFECTIVENESS OF CONSTITUTIONAL SAFEGUARDS

Possible explanations for the ineffectiveness of the constitutional safeguards against the rise of populist and illiberal ideology promoted by Fidesz since 2010, which will be discussed in the next section, can be found in the political history and context at the time of the adoption of the constitutional safeguards. The original constitutional safeguards incorporated in the previous constitutional frame of reference of 1989 were adopted during the peaceful transition process towards a democratic form of government, characterized by party pluralism and a commitment to integrating rule-of-law values.[104] The centralization of power within one political party was not a threat during this period of peaceful democratic transitional period. Indeed, at the roundtable discussions ultimately leading to the significant amendment of the communist

102 ibid Section 4.

103 ibid Section 6.

104 A Bozóki, 'Hungary's Road to Systemic Change: the Opposition Roundtable East European Politics and Societies' [1993] 7(2) *East European Politics and Societies*. A Arato, Post-Sovereign Constitutional Making. Learning and Legitimacy. in M Rosenfeld, *The Identity of the Constitutional Subject: Selfhood, Citizenship, Culture, and Community* (Routledge 2009).

constitution, several parties participated.[105] Although as the Preamble of the 1989 significant amendment of the Constitution indicated, the text of the constitution was not meant to be definitive,[106] due to the lack of political consensus and the achievements of the new constitutional order, a new Constitution was not adopted at that time.[107] The creation of a new constitutional order in this manner raised legitimacy concerns, which were captured as part of populist tactics to adopt a new Fundamental Law.[108]

The position of the Constitutional Court also was closely connected to these original aspirations. The establishment of a Constitutional Court with extensive competences in 1990 was also inspired by Western democracies, in particular by the German model of constitutional justice.[109] Indeed, the Constitutional Court by design was meant to serve as a main check on the unicameral Parliament.[110] In line with this important constitutional mandate, the Constitutional Court delivered in its early years key decisions establishing rule of law values in the Hungarian legal order.[111] Through the concept of "invisible constitution"[112] the Sólyom Court within the first nine years of the Constitutional Court's functioning, sought to establish a liberal-democratic constitutional identity, by filling in the gaps of the text of the Constitution.[113] This role has also led to tensions between the legislature and the Constitutional Court. Although after the first nine years

---

105 Z Szente, 'The Political Orientation of Members of the Hungarian Constitutional Court between 2010 and 2014' [2016] 1(1) *Constitutional Studies.*

106 1989/1990 Constitution, Preamble"[i]n order to facilitate a peaceful political transition to a constitutional state, establish a multi-party system, parliamentary democracy and a social market economy, the Parliament of the Republic of Hungary hereby establishes the following text as the Constitution of the Republic of Hungary, until the Republic's new Constitution is adopted."

107 L Sólyom and G Brunner, *Constitutional Judiciary in a New Democracy: The Hungarian Constitutional Court* (University of Michigan Press 2000) 118-138. See also A Arato, 'Parliamentary Constitution Making in Hungary,' East European Constitutional Review (1995) 4(4). On the legitimacy see A Arato, *Post-Sovereign Constitution Making - Learning and Legitimacy* (OUP 2016) 170-186. G Szoboszlai, The Politics of Constitutional Amendment: Hungary's Lasting Transitory Constitution. in M Andenas (ed), *The Creation and Amendment of Constitutional Norms* (BICCL 2000) 174.

108 See e.g. C Klein and A Sajó, Constitution making: Process and Substance. in M Rosenfeld and A Sajó, *The Oxford Handbook of Comparative Constitutional Law* (OUP 2012) 419; A Arato, 'Continuity and Its Crisis *Constitution and Continuity in the European East Transitions* [1993-4] 3(4) *Tilburg Foreign Law Review* 352.

109 G Halmai, Grundlagen und Grundzüge staatlichen Verfassungsrecht: Ungarn. in A Bogdandy, and P Cruz Villalón and PM Huber (eds), *Handbuch Ins Publikum Europaeum* (C.F. Müller 2007) 693.

110 Szente (2006). Ran Hirschl, *Towards Juristocracy: The Origins and Consequences of the New Constitutionalism* (Harvard University Press 2004).

111 László Sólyom and Georg Brunner, *Constitutional Judiciary in a New Democracy: The Hungarian Constitutional Court* (University of Michigan Press 2000) 118-138. Catherine Dupre☒, *Importing the Law in Post-Communist Transitions: The Hungarian Constitutional Court and the Right to Human Dignity* (Hart 2003) 65-157.

112 Constitutional Court of Hungary Decision 23/1990 (X.31) AB.

113 G Hamai, The Hungarian Approach to Constitutional Review: The End of Activism? The First Debate of the Hungarian Constitutional Court. in W Sadurski (ed), *Constitutional Justice, East and West, Democratic Legitimacy and Constitutional Courts in Post-Communist Europe in a Comparative Perspective* (Kluwer International Law 2002) 189-211; H Schwartz, *The Struggle for Constitutional Justice in Post-Communist Europe* (The University of Chicago Press 2000) 87-101.

the Constitutional Court took less an activities stance, it continued to remain an effective check on the legislative power in accordance with its original constitutional role.[114]

This constitutional setting was completely reshaped in 2010 when Fidesz KDNP gained a two-thirds parliamentary majority, allowing essentially one political party to control the National Assembly and adopt a new Constitution.[115] Indeed, with this unprecedented majority the governing majority explicitly took up the role to modify the Constitution.

4 THE FAILURE OF NATIONAL SAFEGUARDS TO PROTECT DEMOCRATIC CONSTITUTIONALISM AGAINST CHALLENGES POSED BY POPULIST POLITICAL ACTORS SINCE 2010 IN HUNGARY

4.1 *The issue of court packing – Modifying the composition and functioning of courts*

A particularly visible aspect of "disabling"[116] the previous Hungarian Constitution constitutes the issue of court packing, which affected both the Constitutional Court and the ordinary judiciary in Hungary. As a result of the new Fundamental Law and the modifications introduced to the act on the Constitutional Court, the composition of the Constitutional Court has been significantly reshaped. In conjunction with the cyclical vacancies occurring at the Court, eight new judges were appointed to the court following the new selection procedural rules. During these selection procedures, the opposition parties were not consulted.[117]

These new rules reflect the division of political parties nominating the Constitutional Court judges. Indeed, before 2010 the division was four judges nominated by the left-liberal parties, one consensual judge and four judges nominated by the right-conservative parties. In contrast, since July 2010, there are three judges nominated by the left-liberal parties, one consensual judge and 11 judges nominated by the right-conservative parties.[118] This has been compounded by a surge in Members of the Constitutional Court with a direct link to Fidesz, for instance by being members of the first Orbán-Government (1998-2002) and serving as MPs previously. This is possible because the incompatibility rules only refer to government members and leading politicians.

---

114 See above section 3.

115 See above section 2.

116 See M Bánkuti and G Halmai and K L Scheppele, 'Hungary's Illiberal Turn: Disabling the Constitution' [2012] 23(3) *Journal of Democracy* 143-145.

117 Z Szente, 'The Political Orientation of Members of the Hungarian Constitutional Court between 2010 and 2014' [2016] 1(1) *Constitutional Studies* 123-149.

118 Z Szente, 'The Political Orientation of Members of the Hungarian Constitutional Court between 2010 and 2014' [2016] *Constitutional Studies* Table 1, Table 2, 132.

The modifications in the composition of the Constitutional Court incrementally became visible also in the case law of the Court.[119] In 2016, the Constitutional Court approved the government's anti-immigration legislation against the EU relocation scheme.[120] In 2019, the Constitutional Court upheld certain elements of the Stop Soros legislative package criminalizing NGO's which provide legal aid to asylum seekers.[121]

The new constitutional order not only significantly reshaped the functioning of the Constitutional Court, but also modified the functioning and management of the ordinary judiciary. Firstly, institutional reorganizations affected the Supreme Court. The guaranteed tenure of the President of the Supreme Court, who was also the President of the judicial self-governing body and critical towards reforms, was prematurely discontinued.[122]

Secondly, significant modifications also affected the composition and the management of the ordinary judiciary. The retroactive reduction of the retirement age of Hungarian judges in 2012 forced into retirement more than 10 percent of judges occupying court leadership positions. Despite European criticism and subsequent legal modifications, in practice these judges were not reinstated.[123] Moreover, the central administration of courts was completely reorganized. Instead of the judicial council of Hungary, composed of judges, a new judicial administration model was introduced, unprecedented in Europe. The administration is divided between a National Judicial Office, headed by a President, selected and appointed by the National Assembly and holding powers related to the selection and promotion of judges, overseeing the functioning of courts, publicly representing the judiciary and regulating the communication of the judiciary with the media. Although, a collegial body, the

---

119 See e.g. B Eszter and F Gárdos-Orosz and Z Pozsár-Szentmiklósy, Hungary. The State of Liberal Democracy. in R Albert and D Landau and P Faraguna and S Drugda (eds), *2017 Global Review of Constitutional Law (I-CONnect – Clough Center 2018)* 129-133. Z Szente, 'The Political Orientation of Members of the Hungarian Constitutional Court between 2010 and 2014' [2016] *Constitutional Studies.*

120 Constitutional Court of Hungary, Decision 22/2016 (XII.5.) AB. See also above. The decision of the Court followed referendum of October 2, 2016. The failed seventh amendment of the Fundamental Law of 8 November 2016, which fell two votes short. Following these events, the Constitutional Court put on its docket a previously filed complaint by the Commissioner for Fundamental Rights. See also Decision 2/2019.

121 Constitutional Court of Hungary, Decision 3 of 2019 (III.7.) AB.

122 ECtHR, *Baka v Hungary*, Applic. No. 20261/2012 (ECtHR [GC], 23 June 2016). A Vincze, 'Dismissal of the President of the Hungarian Supreme Court: ECtHR Judgment Baka v. Hungary' [2015] 21(3) *European Public Law*; D Kosař and K Šipulová, 'The Strasbourg Court Meets Abusive Constitutionalism: Baka v Hungary and the rule of law' [2018] 10 *Hague Journal on the Rule of Law* 1-28.

123 Case C-286/12 *Commission v Hungary* [2012] ECR I. T Gyulavári and N Hős, 'Retirement of Hungarian Judges, Age Discrimination and Judicial Independence: A Tale of Two Courts' [2013] 42(3) *Industrial Law Journal* 289-297; G Halmai, The Early Retirement Age of the Hungarian Judges. in F Nicola and B Devis (eds), *EU Law Stories: Contextual and Critical Histories of European Jurisprudence* (Cambridge University Press 2017); U Belavusau, 'On Age Discrimination and Beating Dead Dogs: Commission v Hungary' [2013] 50(4) *Common Market Law Review* 1145-1160.

National Judicial Council has a formal role in the field of judicial discipline and in reviewing the functioning of the President of the NJO, a parliamentary complaint was rejected.[124]

Overall, an important lesson from these developments appears that when constitutional safeguards are ineffective, the Constitutional Court and the ordinary judiciary, can be easily captured. A particularly effective way of capturing the ordinary judiciary appears to be the reorganization of the central management of the judiciary, especially in legal orders where this institution holds extensive competences.

4.2 *The rise of the Hungarian populist movement as a consequence of specific problems*

Next to the issue of court packing, political changes taking place in Hungary remain notable due to the specific economic and internal and external political circumstances, which propelled the governing coalition into gaining unprecedented majority. Firstly, the 2010 elections took place against the background of the 2008 financial crisis. The crisis affected significantly Hungarian households and the economy. The International Monetary Fund provided support, however, in exchange the Bajnai Government (MSZP) had to impose strict austerity measures.[125] Before the 2010 elections, improving economic performance was a major point in the Fidesz campaign. Indeed, following the 2010 victory the governing majority called off connections to the IMF and set on their own financial policies and rhetoric concerning economic performance. The improved economic performance achieved since the 2010 elections remains a major aspect of the political messaging. Indeed, by 2017 the governing majority emphasized a 4 percent economic growth, with a stabilized budget and national debt. In addition, the IMF loans were repaid; real income exhibited a 10 percent growth between 2016 and 2017 with lower inflation and lower unemployment rates.

Notwithstanding the economic developments, other aspects must be noted. This economic performance was possible by re-nationalizing pension funds estimated at eight percent of the GDP, a decrease in welfare spending, lowered research and education spending as well as levying taxes. In addition, this increase was possible due to the EU funds from which Hungary continues to benefit and the 4 percent growth

124 K Kovács and K L Scheppele, 'The fragility of an independent judiciary: Lessons from Hungary and Poland – and the European Union' [2018] 51(3) *Communist and Post-Communist Studies* 191-198.

125 P Sonnevend, Preserving the *Acquis* of Transformative Constitutionalism in Times of Constitutional Crisis: Lessons from the Hungarian case. in A von Bogdandy and others (eds), *Transformative Constitutionalism in Latin America. The Emergence of New Ius Commune* (OUP 2017) 133-134.

represents a smaller amount than the value of EU transfers, accounting for approximately 6-7 percent of the GDP.[126]

In addition, at the national level specific political factors contributed to the favorable position of the governing majority. In 2006, an audio recording was revealed in which Prime Minister Gyurcsány of the governing Socialist party confessed during an annual party gathering that the Government failed to accomplish any of its promised goals and has been dishonest in the public discourse concerning their activities.[127] The release of these recordings resulted in a major backlash. Since these setbacks the opposition had difficulties in organizing a sufficiently strong system. The 2018 national elections exhibited initiatives of coalitions of the opposition parties nominating joint candidates in the single-member districts. Nonetheless, the nomination deadlines continue to place the opposition parties in unfavorable position.[128]

Finally, a major contributing factor behind dismantling the Hungarian liberal constitution has been the 2015 immigration crisis. The governing majority effectively captured this event as a powerful tool for furthering their own political aims, already disclosed in 2014 as building an illiberal democracy "and to part from the dogmatics of Western Europe".[129] Images from the 2015 immigration crisis were displayed on billboards as part of the efforts to undermine the European Union and depict the institutions in Brussels as irresponsible. The 2015 migration crisis was also used to first attack civil society organisations, and, later on to target specifically the Open Society Foundation and the Central European University, founded by George Soros. Ultimately, these campaigns culminated in the widespread "Stop-Soros" campaign and resulting legislation, upheld by the Constitutional Court with respect to financing of human rights organisations.[130] Furthermore, since the Fourth Amendment of the Fundamental Law and relying on a continuous threat to the Hungarian security since the 2015 events, the Government of Hungary has uninterruptedly prolonged a state of emergency. All these appear more than contributing factors to the rise of populist rhetoric in Hungary. As it has been explained above, these problems have been actively used as tools to further promote the populist rhetoric adopted by Fidesz.

---

126 P Krekó and Z Enyedi, 'Explaining Eastern Europe: Orbán's Laboratory of Illiberalism' [2018] 29(3) *Journal of Democracy* 43-45.

127 Á Bocskor, 'Anti-immigration Discourses in Hungary during the 'Crisis' Year: The Orbán Government's National Consultation Campaign of 2015' [2018] 52(3) *Sociology*; V Glied and N Pap, 'The 'Christian Fortress of Hungary' – The Anatomy of the Migration Crisis in Hungary' [2016] 19 *Yearbook of Polish European Studies.*

128 See above section 2.

129 Speech of 26 July 2014 at Baile Tusnad, available at http://budapestbeacon.com/public-policy/full-text-of-viktor-orbans-speech-at-baile-tusnad-tusnadfurdo-of-26-july-2014

130 See above.

5 CONCLUSION

Based on the foregoing analysis, it can be concluded that the governing majority entrenched its non-pluralist values at the level of the Fundamental Law and legal acts. The safeguards of the previous constitution failed to stop this. In light of these changes, Hungary appears as a testing ground for populist ideas under the specific form of building an illiberal democracy. In this new context, the governing majority equated the majority of votes gained in the national elections as democratic legitimacy emerging from the entire population, which empowers them to reshape the constitutional order without consulting the opposition.[131]

Looking back, there are certain constitutional features that might have stopped these developments. For instance, more rigid constitutional amendment rules, the existence of eternity clauses or bans on certain amendments might have stopped the significant constitutional changes. Moreover, a less prominent role of the Constitutional Court, might have stopped the appearance of the Court as a fundamentally elitist institution, which requires significant modifications. Because of the possibility to adopt a new Fundamental Law, the governing majority did not violate any national laws, since all subsequent legal modifications were in line with the new Fundamental Law. Moreover, the Constitutional Court has the role to uphold the modified constitutional frame of reference. Given the unchecked possibility of Fidesz-KDNP to modify the Fundamental Law and any legislation, legal tools were not effective in stopping these modifications.

Finally, the Hungarian experience provides an example for other countries, mostly in the Central and Eastern European region, for strengthening values and constitutional norms. The Hungarian example shows that the formal acknowledgement of democratic principles and rules are not enough for securing democratic quality in legal orders with no long-standing traditions in this sense. In order to effectively protect the Constitution, these norms must benefit from a context-specific national conceptualization – enjoying wider democratic legitimacy.

131 Cf. P Sonnevend and A Jakab and L Csink, The constitution as an instrument of everyday party politics: the basic law of Hungary. in A von Bogdandy and P Sonnevend (eds), *Constitutional Crisis in the European Constitutional Area: Theory, Law and Politics in Hungary and Romania* (Nomos Verlagsgesellschaft 2015) 33-110; G Halmai, 'Populism, Authoritariasm, Constitutionalism' [2019] 20(3) *German Law Journal* 296-313. A L Pap, *Democratic Decline in Hungary: Law and Society in an Illiberal Demcoracy* (Routledge 2018).

The Italian Paradox – Is There Such a Thing as *Too Strong* Constitutional Safeguards?

*Matteo Bonelli**

1 Introduction

It is a daring task to write today a chapter on the theme of 'constitutional resistance' to populism in Italy. Even in a time of populists' growing successes, in Europe and elsewhere, Italy was recently the theater of a unique populist experiment: the coalition government between the Five Stars Movement and the League. Running on competing platforms before the groundbreaking parliamentary elections of 2018, the two parties joined forces[1] after few months of negotiations and agreed to indicate Giuseppe Conte, a university professor and lawyer, as President of the Council of Ministers. The experiment was unique in several senses.

First, the two parties do not share the same ideological background: the League (*Lega*), previously known as Northern League (*Lega Nord*), has evolved from a secessionist movement into a nationalistic, far-right party;[2] the Five Stars Movement (*Movimento Cinque Stelle*), created by comedian Beppe Grillo and tech guru Gianroberto Casaleggio, has constantly presented itself as a post-ideological movement,[3] difficult if not impossible to classify on the left to right spectrum.[4] What the two parties truly had

* Matteo Bonelli is Assistant Professor at the Faculty of Law of Maastricht University.

1 The two parties did not however form a stable coalition. They continued to run on different and competing lists in all local and regional elections and sit in different groups at the European Parliament: the League is part of the newly created right-wing 'Identity and Democracy' group, while the Five Stars have so far failed to form a new group after the demise of the 'Europe of Freedom and Direct Democracy' group, which mainly consisted in an alliance between the Five Stars and Nigel Farage's UKIP.

2 The Northern League was already in power in 1994, from 2001 to 2006, and then from 2008 to 2011 as a junior partner in the four Berlusconi's governments. On the qualification of the League as 'far right', see e.g. C Mudde, *The Far Right Today* (Polity 2019).

3 For a constitutional analysis of the Five Stars Movement and further references, see L Corso, 'When anti-politics becomes political: what can the Italian Five Star Movement tell us about the relationship between populism and legalism' [2019] 15(3) *European Constitutional Law Review* 462-487. See also N Urbinati, 'The Italian Five Star Movement for foreigners' *Il Mulino* (1 March 2018) https://www.rivistailmulino.it/news/newsitem/index/Item/News:NEWS_ITEM:4272 accessed 3 February 2020.

4 More specifically, in the first years of its existence, the Five Star Movement was often considered an example of left-wing populism, along the lines of Podemos and Syriza. Yet, from the outset the Five Stars ran on an eclectic mix of left (especially on economic issues) and right-wing proposals, and arguably progressively shifted to the right on themes such as migration and European integration, as also highlighted by the alliance with UKIP in the European Parliament.

in common, even more than concrete policies proposals[5] – during the Conte I government, they disagreed on a large number of issues, from infrastructures to taxation and regional autonomy – was the populist approach described by Jan-Werner Müller:[6] anti-elitist, critical of the functioning of liberal democratic institutions,[7] and at least skeptical towards European integration.

A second remarkable element of the experiment was the choice of the President of the Council of Ministers, Giuseppe Conte. Conte was a figure external to both parties – but considered to be closer to the Five Stars' positions – who did not even run as a candidate in the general elections, and had a 'non-political' profile more similar to a technocrat than to a prototypical populist leader. Third, even the form of the coalition agreement between the two parties was peculiar: the agreement was presented as a private law contract (*contratto di governo*) between the two parties and their leaders. The contract even envisaged the creation a 'conciliation committee' for resolving disputes between the two parties.[8]

The Five Stars – League populist experiment was always instable, and the brewing tensions between the two parties grew even more after the 2019 European Parliament elections, which saw a large success of the League and a resounding defeat for the Five Stars Movement.[9] Trying to capitalize on his growing popularity, League's leader Matteo Salvini decided in Summer 2019 to end the experiment and called for early elections, with the goal to gain an autonomous majority in the Italian parliament. Much to his surprise, however, archenemies Five Stars and center-left Democratic Party agreed to avoid new elections and form a new government, still led by President Conte but with a radically different parliamentary support and outlook.

The truly surprising turn of events leaves questions of constitutional resistance very much open. On the one hand, while the political impact of the experiment will be felt for years, the League-Five Stars government left no deep scars on the Italian constitutional

5 In this sense, Cassese defined the Conte I government as a 'government of the opposites': see S Cassese, 'Con il governo è cambiata anche la forma di governo?' [2019] 1(2019) *Quaderni Costituzionali, Rivista italiana di diritto costituzionale* 118; T Fournier, 'From rhetoric to action, a constitutional analysis of populism' [2019] 20(3) *German Law Journal* 363 argues that the League – Five Stars coalition was an 'unnatural alliance'.

6 J-W Müller, *What is Populism?* (University of Pennsylvania Press 2016).

7 On the inherent tension between populism and constitutionalism (defined by the author also as "democracy under the rule of law"), see also L Corrias, 'Populism in a Constitutional Key: Constituent Power, Popular Sovereignty and Constitutional Identity' [2016] 12(1) *European Constitutional Law Review*. For a different view, B Bugaric, 'The two faces of populism: Between authoritarian and democratic populism' [2019] 20(3) *German Law Journal* 3, arguing that populism and constitutionalism are not necessarily incompatible, and that populism can have two faces: next to the authoritarian face, it can also be emancipatory.

8 See e.g. C Pinelli, 'Uno strano contratto', *Il Mulino* (22 May 2018) https://www.rivistailmulino.it/news/newsitem/index/Item/News:NEWS_ITEM:4367 accessed 3 February 2020.

9 The League came first with 34.26% of the votes, the Five Star Movement only third with 17.06%, Results by national party: 2019-2024 https://europarl.europa.eu/election-results-2019/en/national-results/italy/2019-2024 accessed 3 February 2020.

system. There has simply been no structural undermining of institutional safeguards and democratic and rule of law institutions. This might suggest at least a timid optimism when assessing the Italian constitution's resistance. On the other hand, polls consistently indicate that the League will be favorite to win a majority in the next elections, which could come at any point in time due to the enduring instability of the new scenario. A League dominated government, perhaps in coalition with the far-right partner 'Brothers of Italy' (*Fratelli d'Italia*) that has recently gained ground in the polls, would most probably be an harsher stress-test for the Italian constitutional framework. To further complicate things, one should not forget that despite the recent change of tones, and to a lesser extent of policies, the Five Star Movement remains a typical populist party, and is still not only in power, but the governing coalition's leading party.

The scenario is thus rapidly evolving, in directions that are difficult to foresee: both the deal between the League and the Five Stars, and more recently that between the Five Stars and the Democratic Party were considered little realistic by most observers before they quickly came through. Any assessment of the degree of resistance of the Italian constitution is thus necessarily a snapshot taken at a certain point in time, and hardly a prediction on the future. Yet, reflecting on the topic is certainly a much-needed exercise, precisely because there might soon be a need to find new solutions and counter-measures to possible attacks to constitutional safeguards and institutions. Some indications of what works and what does not in the Italian constitutional system can furthermore be offered by the previous experiences under the Berlusconi governments. While Berlusconi and *Forza Italia* cannot be easily associated to the Five Stars – League coalition government or to other populist experiences discussed elsewhere in this volume, it would be difficult to deny that they also made use of populist rhetoric and approaches, and that at least on some fronts – most notably, media pluralism and freedom of information – they presented a challenge to the Italian constitutional order.[10]

The fact that at least three[11] different – in term of degree, kind, and political orientation – populist movements have been in power in Italy in recent years may already suggest something very crucial for the present contribution. First and obviously, populist movements *have* been successful in Italy, perhaps even more than anywhere else in the Western world, or at least for a longer period. Thus, in terms of 'preventing' the

---

10 As acknowledged also at the European level: see e.g. European Parliament, *Resolution on the risks of violation, in the EU and especially in Italy, of freedom of expression and information* (Article 11(2) of the Charter of Fundamental Rights) (22 April 2004 Strasbourg Doc. 2003/2237(INI)); High Level Group on Media Freedom and Pluralism, *A free and pluralistic media to sustain European democracy* (January 2013) www.ec.europa.eu/information_society/media_taskforce/doc/pluralism/hlg/hlg_final_report.pdf.

11 Another example, though the party was far less influential than Forza Italia, the League, and the Five Stars, was the *Italia dei Valori* of former prosecutor Antonio di Pietro, a peculiar brand of left-wing, anti-corruption populism that joined the ruling coalition between 2006 and 2008. In general, on populism in Italy, M Tarchi, Italy: A Country of Many Populisms. in D Albertazzi and D Mcdonnell (eds), *Twenty-First Century Populism* (Palgrave Macmillan 2008); P Blokker and M Anselmi (eds), *Multiple Populism – Italy as Democracy's Mirror* (Routledge 2019).

populist' success, the Italian constitutional and political order has proved to be quite weak and ineffective. On the contrary, it even seems a fertile ground for different breeds of populism. Yet, and at least until today, the story has been different as regards 'reacting' to populism in power, that is to say that the constitutional system and safeguards have been able to adequately constrain populist when they are in power. Constitutional tools and bodies have proved to be sufficiently robust and capable to offer protection against any possible move towards a less liberal system, they adequately fought cases of abuses of power, and offered protection to minorities, showing a high degree of resilience.

This, however, might be the 'Italian paradox' that I refer to in the title of this chapter and that I wish to discuss in the following pages. As provocative as this might sound, the constitutional safeguards in place might actually be *too* strong and *too* strict: while they form robust obstacles against possible threats to democratic constitutionalism, at the same time they may also be a factor in the rise of populism,[12] as they contribute to create an institutional system that is perceived as inefficient, corrupt, and ultimately unable to address the outstanding social, political and economic problems of the country. Thus, the same constitutional safeguards that are able to effectively constrain populists once they reach power may also be one of the reasons for the rise of populism itself. It is against the background of this paradox, of this contradiction (strong constitutional safeguards – strong populism) that this chapter discusses the Italian case.

The chapter is structured as follows: the first section identifies and analyses existing constitutional safeguards, starting from the historical context in which the 1948 Constitution was adopted and then moving to the concrete mechanisms it contains; section two begins reflecting on whether safeguards have been successful, looking at the 'preventive' function and arguing that they have so far failed in that respect; the following section analyses, on the other hand, the ability of the Italian constitutional system to 'react' to populism, for which there are more positive results so far; and finally, the fourth and last section reflects on the Italian paradox and possible lessons for other constitutional systems.

2 The Italian constitutional safeguards

2.1 *The historical context*

The Italian Constitution was drafted in the aftermath of World War II and the end of the Fascist *ventennio*. A little more than a year after Liberation Day (April 25th, 1945), the Italian electorate was called to the polls on June 2nd, 1946, first, in order to decide in a

12 Of course, they are by no means the only, or even the decisive factor in the rise of populism in the country. Just to offer a couple of examples, the economic and migration crises of the past decade are other key elements that can explain the rise of the Five Stars and the League.

general referendum on the form of the state – monarchy or republic – and second, to elect the members of the Constituent Assembly entrusted with writing the new constitutional text. In the first vote, the Republic narrowly prevailed, forcing the royal family to leave the country; in the second, the Christian-Democrat came out on top with 35.2% of the votes, followed by the Socialist party (20.6%) and then the Communist party (18.9%). It then took eighteen months for the Constituent Assembly to agree on the text of the new constitution, which was finally approved in December 1947 by a vast majority of the assembly and entered into force on January 1st, 1948.

The Italian Constitution of 1948 is the result of a compromise between three political forces: the Christian-democrats; the socialist and communist left; and finally, with a more limited impact, the liberals. These three forces had been the main actors of the Italian resistance movement, working together in the National Liberation Committee (CNL) that fought behind the lines against the occupying German forces and the fascist Repubblica di Salò in the North, and cooperated with the monarchy in governing the already liberated South. In this sense, the Resistance movement is said to be the 'founding myth' of the Italian constitution.[13] In contrast to the German or Japanese experience, there was very little external influence in the drafting of the Italian constitution.[14]

Seen in this historical context, it is not surprising that one of the key goals, if not the main one, of the new drafters of the new constitution was creating a system that could prevent a return of the authoritarian past. The Constituent Assembly rejected not only (and obviously) the experience of the Fascist period, both in terms of its institutional setting and of the values and principles expressed by the regime,[15] but also the previous constitutional model that had allowed Mussolini to gain power and then transform the

---

13 See C Mortati, Lezioni sulle forme di governo (Cedam 1973) classifying the Italian as a 'resistance constitution'; and the widely celebrated speech by P Calamandrei, prominent jurist and member of the constituent assembly, 'Discorso ai giovani sulla Costituzione nata dalla Resistenza' (delivered in Milan, 26 January 1955) 'If you want to go on a pilgrimage to the place where our Constitution was born, go to the mountains where the partisans fell, to the jails where they were imprisoned, to the camps where they were hanged' (own translation).

14 See C Pinelli, 'The 1948 Italian Constitution and the 2006 Referendum: Food for Thought' [2006] 2(3) *European Constitutional Law Review* 331, underlining that the Italian constitution was 'written in a vacuum', also because there was no historical tradition to which the members of the constituent assembly could go back.

15 In contrast to the Fascist period, 'openness' is one of the key values of the new text: see G Martinico and B Guastaferro and O Pollicino, The Constitution of Italy: Axiological Continuity Between the Domestic and International Levels of Governance? in A Albi and S Bardutzky (eds), *National Constitutions in European and Global Governance: Democracy, Rights, the Rule of Law* (Asser Press 2019).

country into a dictatorship.[16] The 1948 Constitution stood therefore in clear opposition to the 1848 Albertine Statute, which worked as the basic constitutional text since the unification of Italy in 1861 until the entry into force of the new constitution, and remained formally in force even during the Fascist regime.[17] The Albertine Statute was an *octroyée* constitution, conceded by Charles Albert, King of Sardinia, to the citizens of the Kingdom and later extended to the entire country after the unification, and clearly showed all the main features of that constitutional model. For example, it put the King at the head of the executive, envisaged a Senate directly nominated by the monarchy, and only offered protection to individual liberty rights. Most importantly, it was a flexible constitution, which could be modified by ordinary laws, and did not provide any mechanism of constitutional review. In the 1920s, it proved too weak to resist to Mussolini and the Fascist party, which were able to revolutionize the system while maintaining the Statute formally in place. Well aware of the shortcomings of the previous constitutional model, the members of the Constituent Assembly thus drafted the 1948 Constitution in clear contrast to the Statute: the current constitution is a rigid text, which creates a clear hierarchy between the constitution and ordinary laws, entrusts a constitutional court with the task of monitoring compliance with constitutional norms, and contains reinforced amendments procedures.[18]

There is a second aspect of the historical context that is however worth noticing as well. If the main and explicit goal of the constitution was to prevent return to authoritarianism and to fascism in particular, more implicitly some of the features of the 1948 text were also a guarantee for each of the three main forces drafting the constitution against each other.[19] Fearing a possible future electoral victory of the Marxist left, the Christian Democrats considered more prudent, despite being in the majority at the time, designing a central government with fairly limited and strictly-defined powers. The left, on the other side, fought to ensure that political minorities could still actively contribute to political and institutional life, for example pushing for a high threshold for constitutional amendment. Many of the safeguards included in the 1948 system can thus be seen in both directions: opting for a fairly weak executive, in this sense, was both a way to reduce the risk of a return to the fascist past *and* a guarantee against the partners in the constitutional drafting process. The two goals contributed therefore to the creation of a rigid constitution that multiplied the number of

16 At the same time, there was a fairly high degree of institutional continuity between the two periods, especially when it comes to the (ordinary) judiciary and bureaucracy: see also D Tega, 'The Constitution of the Italian Republic: Not revolution, but principled liberation' [2019] 17(2) *International Journal of Constitutional Law*, debating Bruce Ackerman's discussion of the Italian constitution as a revolutionary one: see B Ackerman, *Revolutionary Constitutions – Charismatic Leaderships and the Rule of Law* (Harvard University Press 2019).

17 For an overview, R Martucci, *Storia costituzionale italiana. Dallo Statuto Albertino alla Repubblica* (1848-2001) (Carocci 2002).

18 See sections 2.3. and 2.4 below.

19 See e.g. G Bognetti, *La Divisione dei Poteri* (Giuffrè 2001) 128.

institutional actors and of possible veto players, with the goal to prevent any possible attempt to centralize control over public power: two chambers with identical powers, the President of the Republic, the Constitutional Court, but also the regions, when it comes to the vertical distribution of powers.

2.2 *The political-institutional setting*

As mentioned above, the choice on the form of the state was resolved before the constituent assembly began operating, in the referendum of June 2, 1946, with the republic narrowly prevailing on the previous monarchical system. The key decisions on the form of government and the key institutional actors were then taken during the eighteen months of constitution-making process. In most of these decisions, it is possible to see the influence of the historical background that led to the drafting of the constitution and that called for distributing public power between many different actors and for preventing any possible (re)centralization of authority in a single figure or party, as happened during the Fascist period.

The first of these decisions, and one of the explicit lines of continuity between the Albertine Statute and the Constitution of the Republic, was the choice for a bicameral parliamentary system, composed of a lower chamber (*Camera dei Deputati*) and of a higher chamber (*Senato*). Not only did the drafters opt to maintain a bicameral parliament, but they also opted for a form of 'perfect bicameralism' (*bicameralismo perfetto*) that has few equivalents around the world.[20] The two chambers have in fact identical powers, their mandates are perfectly aligned,[21] and the electorates are only marginally different.[22] Thus, for any piece of legislation to be validly adopted by the Italian Parliament, the two chambers need to agree on the very same text;[23] furthermore, the Government must receive and maintain the confidence of both chambers.[24]

---

20 Even the US Congress is not a perfect comparison, both because it obviously acts in a different (presidential) institutional setting, and because the Italian Senate does not truly serve and represent regional and local interests.

21 See Art 60 of the Italian Constitution: 'The Chamber of deputies and the Senate of the Republic are elected for five years'. It should however not be forgotten that the original text of the provision actually envisaged a six years mandate for the Senate. The norm was modified in 1963 (L.Cost. 2/1963) in order to reflect the already developed practice of shortening the mandate of Senate and allowing for parallel elections of the two chambers.

22 All citizens above the age of 18 elect the Chamber; only citizens above the age of 25 elect the Senate (although a constitutional reform bill proposing to align the two electorates is now under discussing in Parliament). Furthermore, the Senate has 'life members': former Presidents of the Republic and other figures who are nominated by the President of the Republic.

23 On the legislative process, see Art 70 of the Constitution: 'The legislative function is exercised collectively by both Houses'.

24 See Art 94 of the Constitution.

As for the executive, the constituent assembly designed a fairly weak government. Once again, this was not a mistake or the accidental outcome of the negotiations, but a clear constitutional choice: the risks inherent in having inherently weak executives were considered to be lower than the risks of a too strong executive that could again produce an authoritarian regime. Better to err on the side of caution, to put it in lay terms. The choice is most evident in the figure of the President of the Council of Minister (*Presidente del Consiglio dei Ministri*), who is not a true prime minister but a *primus inter pares* figure: the constitution does not design a clear formal hierarchy between the President and the other ministers.[25] Thus, the President does not directly nominate the ministers – this is a competence assigned to the President of the Republic[26] – and cannot remove them. The government, at least until the legal and political landscape changed in the 1990s, worked on the basis of the principle of collegiality. It was then established, as already mentioned, that the government must hold the confidence of both chambers, a choice that has contributed, as shall be seen, to governmental instability over the decades, as even a small minority in either chamber can precipitate a governmental crisis. Furthermore, the government has few mechanisms to push its legislative agenda: there is no formal preference assigned to legislative proposals coming from the executive, or mechanisms that can ensure that a final decision on a governmental proposal is taken before a certain date.[27]

A figure created *ex novo* by the 1948 Constitution was that of the President of the Republic, the Head of State of the new Italian republic. The text of the constitution does not however offer a detailed discipline on the President's role and functions, leaving the figure itself and the concrete powers assigned to her flexible, if not ambiguous.[28] There is no doubt, though, that the constitution, by linking the President to all other key institutions – the President is involved in the formation of the government, decides on the dissolution of the parliamentary chambers, nominates judges of the Constitutional Court, and so forth – foresees the President as a non-partisan figure, standing above party

25 Only much later Law no 400/1988 and Legislative Decree no 303/1999 affirmed – but still not in the constitutional text – the political superiority of the President.

26 See Art 92: 'The President of the Republic appoints the President of the Council of Ministers and, on his proposal, the Ministers'. On the issue, see the discussion of the 'Savona affair' in the following pages.

27 This has led to wide use of mechanisms originally meant for different use, such as urgency decrees or 'confidence votes' that can stop the parliamentary discussion and ask the chambers to reach a final decision.

28 For a brief overview of the debate in English, F Fabbrini and O Pollicino, Constitutional Identity in Italy: Institutional Disagreements at a Time of Political Change. in C Callies and G van der Schyff (eds), *Constitutional Identity in a Europe of Multilevel Constitutionalism* (Cambridge University Press 2019). In practice, we have seen more and less activist presidents; and then in any event the President's role constantly shifts in view of political landscape, generally increasing in clear of crises, and then returning to 'normal'. As noted by F Clementi, 'I-CONnect Symposium – The Aftermath of the Italian General Election of March 4, 2018 – The Italian Political Elections: A Definitive Back to the Past? [2018] Part II http://www.iconnectblog.com/2018/08/i-connect-symposium-the-aftermath-of-the-italian-general-election-of-march-4-2018-the-italian-political-elections-a-definitive-back-to-the-past, the influence of the President largely depends on the strength or the weakness of the political party system.

politics, working as a guarantor of the integrity of the state and of the constitution itself, and guaranteeing balanced relationships between state organs.[29] For an example of a situation in which the President can fulfill that 'guarantor' role, one could refer to the President's power to send back laws to Parliament after their approval,[30] if she considers that there are serious doubts on the constitutionality of the legislation in question. This is however not a veto power: the President can stop the adoption of a law only temporarily and if the Parliament decides to adopt again the same legislative text, the President is obliged to promulgate it. The President of the Republic can however have an even more influential role, especially in times of crises, in the moment of formation of a new government.[31] The constitution provides that the President of the Republic is responsible for nominating the President of the Council of Ministers and then, on her proposal, the ministers. After a parliamentary election or the fall of a government the President conducts rounds of consultations – a procedure not explicitly mentioned in the constitutional text but created by praxis – with the major political forces: if the result of the elections is clear, then the role of the President is minimal; however, in case the results are more mixed, the President's influence, thanks to practices such as the 'exploratory mandates' (*mandate esplorativi*) or pre-appointments (*pre-incarico*) can be much more decisive and shape the choices of the political parties.[32]

In order to guarantee the autonomy of the President vis-à-vis the daily political game, the Constitution designed a long mandate (seven years) and an indirect election system, where the President is elected by the two chambers together, (integrated, after 2002, by regional representatives) at a qualified majority. It is to be underlined, however, that the rules on the election of the President are not extremely demanding: while a two-thirds majority is required in the first three ballots, an absolute majority is sufficient from the fourth round onwards.[33] Nonetheless, the custom that presidents should not be first lines politicians and that the majority should at least try to involve the opposition has so far resisted. For example, even if the two most recent Presidents, Napolitano (in his first mandate) and Mattarella, have actually been elected by relatively small majorities, they were both senior figures whose political standing and experience was recognized also by the opposition, even when it did not contribute to electing them. There is however no guarantee that this custom will remain in place in the future: a determined populist coalition with a strong majority in parliament could easily decide to elect a more

29 See also Judgment 1/2013 Corte Costituzionale holding that the President of the Republic is the 'supreme guarantor of the equilibrium between the branches of state'.

30 See Art 74 of the Constitution: 'The President of the Republic may send Parliament a reasoned opinion to request that a law scheduled for promulgation be considered anew. If such law is passed again, it shall be promulgated'.

31 See also C Fusaro, *Il Presidente della Repubblica* (Il Mulino 2003).

32 For an explanation of the different pratices, see e.g. P Caretti and U De servio, *Diritto Costituzionale e Pubblico* (3rd edn, Giappichelli 2017).

33 See Art 83 of the Constitution.

partisan or easily controllable figure that would likely be unwilling or unable to play the role of guarantee of the constitution that the 1948 text envisages.[34]

2.3 *The Constitutional Court and the judiciary*

The other key new institution and other key safeguard of the new constitutional system is the Italian Constitutional Court.[35] The Court was one of the main relevant innovations brought by the 1948 Constitution and it was given the task to protect the rights and values enshrined in the new constitution, as well as key competences in deciding on possible conflicts between the other institutional actors. Together with the President of the Republic, the Court is therefore on the two crucial '*organi di garanzia*' – an expression that can be loosely translated as 'institutional guarantees' – of the constitutional system.[36]

In order to fulfill this ambitious mission, the Court needed robust autonomy and independence from the political institutions. The drafters made sure to grant these features to the new body first of all through the rules on composition and membership of the Court. From an institutional perspective, the constitution protects the Court from external interferences by granting it administrative, regulatory, and disciplinary autonomy: for example, only the Court itself can decide on the removal of some of its members, in strictly confined cases. Members of the Court furthermore cannot be prosecuted for their opinions or actions as judges.

As for the selection process, the Constitution divides the tasks between three different organs: Parliament, the President of the Republic, and the ordinary judiciary. Each of these organs selects five of the fifteen judges. As for the Parliament, the two chambers sitting together elect the five judges at a qualified majority. More precisely, a two-third majority is required in the first three votes, and then a three-fifth majority after that. In an ordinary scenario, i.e. excluding an unlikely landslide victory of one political party, an agreement between the majority and the minority is therefore required for a successful election; furthermore, there is a convention that elections should reflect the majority-minority balance in parliament,[37] that is to say that when the mandate of a judge of a certain political area terminates, another judge with similar political orientations[38] should be nominated, unless the political balance has shifted in the meantime. While the practice has so far resisted, in the last years it has become more and more difficult to find common

34 This could qualify as a case of 'constitutional hardball', as defined by MV Tushnet, 'Constitutional Hardball' [2004] 37 *John Marshall Law Review*: playing by the rules (absolute majority for the election of the President) but pushing their boundaries (electing a strongly partisan figure).

35 The Constitutional Court however began operating only in 1956, after the adoption of the Constitutional Law 1/1956 that gave concrete implementation to the constitutional text.

36 See G Silvestri, *Le Garanzie della Repubblica* (Giappichelli 2009).

37 See e.g. P Caretti and U De servio, *Diritto Costituzionale e Pubblico* (3rd edn, Giappichelli 2017) 426-427.

38 Judges are rarely, if ever, affiliated with a certain political party, yet it is often clear whether they belong to the (center)left or (center)right of the political spectrum.

nominations and there have often been delays in the election of new judges.[39] Similarly, the President of the Republic, who also nominates five judges, always tries to balance the representation of different political and cultural groups. The last five judges are elected by the judiciary, and more specifically by ordinary and administrative supreme courts: three by the Court of Cassation, one by the Council of State, and one by the Court of Auditors.[40] Finally, the Constitution opted to assign a very long mandate to the judges of the court – nine years – and excluded that they could be re-elected.[41] This long mandate allows even the judges nominated through the political channels the possibility to emancipate themselves from the political area that indicated them. Finally, the constitution establishes specific requirements for elections: only (former) judges of higher courts, university law professors, and lawyers with more than 20 years of experience can be elected to the Court.[42]

Along with the creation of the constitutional court, the 1948 Constitution also had the goal to put in place a strong, independent judiciary, in order to fulfill the promise posed by Article 104: 'The Judiciary is a branch that is autonomous and independent of all other powers'. On the individual level, Articles 101 and 107 offers robust guarantees of independence. The former affirms that 'Judges are subject only to the law' (and not to political power); the latter states that 'judges may not be removed from office' and that 'they may not be dismissed or suspended from office or assigned to other courts or functions unless by a decision of the High Council of the Judiciary'. Institutionally, it is in particular the High Council of the Judiciary (*Consiglio Superiore della Magistratura*, CSM) that guarantees judicial independence. The new body was assigned powers that had been traditionally in the hands of the Ministry of Justice.[43] In particular, the Council has crucial competences on careers and disciplinary measures. It is a mixed body, composed by a majority of judges (sixteen) but also by lay members (eight), and is presided by the President of the Republic, though in practice her functions are taken over by the vice-president of the CSM. The Parliament, with the two chambers sitting together, elects the eight lay members at a three-fifths majority of the members in the three votes, and then at a three-fifths majority of the votes after that moment, thus, as is the case for constitutional court's judges, the election always requires an agreement between the majority and the opposition.

39 See e.g. A Marin and M Paris, 'Consulta, per il giudice mancante Camere verso un ritardo da record' (Il Sole 24 Ore, 8 March 2018) https://www.ilsole24ore.com/art/consulta-il-giudice-mancante-camere-un-ritardo-record-AEd4cokE accessed 7 February 2020.

40 On the concrete election procedures, see Constitutional Law no 2/1967.

41 See Art 135 Italian Constitution, third sentence.

42 See Art 135 Italian Constitution, second sentence.

43 On the creation and evolution of the CSM, see S Benvenuti, 'The Politics of Judicial Accountability in Italy: Shifting the Balance' [2018] 14(2) *European Constitutional Law Review*.

2.4 Constitutional amendment

As is typical of post-war constitutions, the Italian constitution is a rigid one: it cannot be amended by ordinary laws, but only through the special and reinforced procedure that can be found in Article 138. The procedure works as follows: both chambers have to adopt the amendment bill twice, with the second deliberation taking place no less than three months after the first. In the second reading, Article 138 requires at least an absolute majority in both chambers. There is then another eventual step, namely a constitutional referendum in which the citizens are called to confirm or reject the amendments approved by Parliament. The referendum takes place if, in the second reading, the majority approving the amendment does not reach the threshold of two thirds of the members in both chambers.[44] In contrast to the ordinary referendums established by Article 75, which demands the participation of more than 50% of the electorate for the referendum to be valid, there is no quorum to be reached in constitutional referendums.

In comparative perspective, the amendment procedure is not excessively difficult or cumbersome.[45] It does not require extremely high thresholds – an absolute majority is sufficient – or approval by two different terms of parliament, and does not involve regional authorities in the amendment process, if not for the possibility of five regional councils to call for the confirmative referendum. Ultimately, an ordinary political majority is technically able to push forward a constitutional reform if it wishes to do so. While for many years there was an implicit agreement between the main parties that the constitution should have not been changed without a wider agreement of political forces, the custom was broken for the first time in 2001, when the center-left, by a slim majority, reorganized the competence of regions and local authorities (Title V of the Constitution). It is however to be said that the reform came after several unsuccessful attempts to reach a broader consensus.[46] Then, other two times, in 2006 and 2016, the constitution was again amended by a small majority, but in both cases the reforms were rejected in the following referendums. The additional guarantee of the final confirmation of the electorate has thus proved to be a powerful tool against changes that do not have a broad consensus in the political arena and eventually in society at large. In particular, and regardless of the merits of the reform itself, the last referendum shows that

44 The confirmative referendum is however not automatic, but on a request of one fifths of the members of one chamber, 500.000 electors, or five regional councils.

45 This is shown also by the relative frequency of amendments: the text has been changed fifteen times until today, and other two reforms approved by Parliament have been rejected in constitutional referendums (2006 and 2016). A new reform, reducing the number of MPs, has been approved in the last months of 2019 and will be subject to a new confirmative referendum in 2020.

46 See C Pinelli, 'The 1948 Italian Constitution and the 2006 Referendum: Food for Thought' [2006] 2(3) European Constitutional Law Review 337 arguing that the decision 'marked a precedent in terms of parliamentary convention, in the sense that the other coalition, once in power, would not feel obliged to seek the opposition's consent on constitutional reform either'.

constitutional referendums are an excellent opportunity to mobilize different oppositions against the government: the 'No' front in the last constitutional referendum brought together the left, the populist Five Stars Movement, the traditional center right and the far right against the center left government led by Matteo Renzi that had pushed for the reform.[47]

In terms of the content of possible constitutional amendments, the Constitution itself provides an explicit limit in Article 139, which is 'a typical example of explicit unamendability'.[48] The provision states that 'the Republican form of the State is not subject to revision'. This is the only formal eternity clause – which has its historical roots in the decision to leave the choice between monarchy and republic to the 1946 referendum – and a quite vague one, which could be read in narrow formal sense or a more substantive one, as to include the 'values' of the republic. In any event, there has always been wide agreement between commentators that, along with Article 139, there are other implicit limits to amendability, namely the supreme principles (*principi supremi*) expressed in the first part of the constitution. The Constitutional Court endorsed this theory on implicit limits with its 'supreme principles' doctrine: according to the Court, the essential content of these principles cannot be altered even by the Article 138 procedure; and those principles also pose a limit to European integration, in the sense that any conflicting EU provision cannot be applied in the Italian legal order: this is the core of the famous *controlimiti* doctrine.[49] The Court has however never offered a full list of those principles.

2.5 *The political system and the democratic process*

If, from an institutional point of view, the constitutional safeguards against illiberalism and authoritarianism are numerous and robust – as it was already suggested, they might be even in certain respects *too* strong – the framework concerning the rules of the

---

47 On the 2016 referendum, see the special issue of the Italian Law Journal, P Passaglia (ed), 'The 2016 Italian Constitutional Referendum: Origins, Stakes, Outcome' [2016].

48 See P Faraguna, 'Unamendability and Constitutional Identity in the Italian Constitutional Experience' [2019] 21(3) *European Journal of Law Reform* 7.

49 Judgment 1146/1988 Corte Costituzionale: 'The Italian Constitution contains some supreme principles that cannot be subverted or modified in their essential content, either by laws amending the Constitution, or by other constitutional laws. … those principles that even though not expressly mentioned among those principles not subject to the procedure of constitutional amendment, belong to the essence of the supreme values upon which the Italian Constitution is founded'. See P Faraguna, 'Unamendability and Constitutional Identity in the Italian Constitutional Experience' [2019] 21(3) *European Journal of Law Reform*; P Faraguna, Ai confini della Costituzione – Principi supremi e identità costituzionale (Franco Angeli 2015).

political game is much weaker. In the first place, the Constitution does not regulate the electoral system,[50] despite a clear preference for proportional representation in the constituent assembly's works.[51] In any event, the choice was left to the 'ordinary' political actors. Until the 1990s, Italy maintained a strictly proportional system.[52]

The proportional system was however often criticized for contributing to party fragmentation and undermining governability. In the beginning of the 1990s, a tumultuous period for the Italian political landscape for a number of reasons – the end of the historical parties dominating the post-war period and the rise of new actors and movements, including Silvio Berlusconi and the Northern League, the *Tangentopoli* corruption scandal, as well as economic and financial turmoil – the electoral system was radically modified. The elections of 1994, which opened the door of *Palazzo Chigi*, for the first time, to Silvio Berlusconi, were fought under a complex mixed system (*Mattarellum*), but the higher proportion of seats were assigned by a first past the post majoritarian system. Since then, there has been growing instability on the electoral laws' front. The system was again dramatically changed in 2006: the ruling center-right coalition opted for a proportional system with a big majority prize for the winning coalition. Then, the Constitutional Court intervened, for the first time in 2014,[53] eliminating the majority prize that was found to be unconstitutional, and then again in 2017,[54] after a new system (the *Italicum* law) had been put in place.[55] After the latter ruling of the Court, which found some key aspects of the new system to be in conflict with the constitution,[56] the Parliament approved yet another electoral law (the *Rosatellum* law) that again envisages a mixed system. A majority of the seats (61%) is assigned through proportional representation in a national district; the rest of the seats (37%)[57] are divided in smaller districts and assigned by a first past the post scheme, which envisages coalitions between different parties in support of the same candidate. The new Democratic Party – Five Stars majority is however proposing to reshuffle the system yet

50 The text of the Constitution leaves the question of the electoral law 'open-ended': see E Longo and A Pin, 'Judicial Review, Election Law, and Proportionality' [2016] 6 *Notre Dame Journal of International & Comparative Law* 105.

51 On September 13rd, 1947, the Constituent Assembly affirmed in a non-legally-binding order its preference for a proportional system, stating that 'the Constituent Assembly holds that the election of members of the Chamber of Deputies shall be based on a proportional representation system'.

52 The majority prize briefly put in place for the 1953 elections was never concretely assigned, as the Christian Democrats failed reach the required threshold, and it was soon abolished in 1954 after it received harsh attacks from the oppositions, which labeled the new regulation 'fraud law' (legge truffa).

53 See Judgment 1/2014 Corte Costituzionale.

54 See Judgment 25/2017 Corte Costituzionale. For an analysis see P Faraguna, 'Do You Ever Have One of Those Days When Everything Seems Unconstitutional?': The Italian Constitutional Court Strikes Down the Electoral Law Once Again'[2017] 13(4) *European Constitutional Law Review.*

55 For an overview of the 'electoral law saga' and the interventions of the Court, see A Baraggia and L P Vanoni, 'The Italian Electoral Law Saga: Judicial Activism or Judicial Subsidiarity?' [2017] STALS Research Paper 2/2017.

56 In particular, the 'second round' format that would have assigned the majority prize.

57 The remaining 2% is reserved to candidates elected abroad.

again, and the proposal discussed in the first months of 2020 is loosely inspired by the German system.

The unstable, constantly shifting landscape has certainly not helped in restoring the already declining trust in political parties and institutions. On the contrary, it might have further widened the distance between citizens and the political system, both because it created confusion in the electorate, and because instruments such as the institution of 'closed lists', with no preference voting, and the possibility of multi-candidatures in several districts loosened the link between electoral districts and their representatives. This weakness and instability may have fostered populist movements and especially the Five Stars Movement that since its creation has campaigned on a platform of distrust towards established representative institutions[58] and proposed to rely in the alternative on forms of direct democracy.[59]

The instability of the electoral system mirrors the instability of the Italian party system, and the two phenomena are certainly interrelated. This is true both in purely political terms – to offer a quick picture, all the parties represented in the current parliament have less than thirty years of history, and many have a far shorter history – and in terms of the legal framework that regulates party politics. Rules on party financing, which have been amended several times in the last thirty years, are arguably the most notable example. Recently, direct financing has been completely abolished and replaced by a system of private contributions and indirect financing,[60] with the decision widely seen as an attempt to respond to the rise of the 'anti-political' Five Star Movement, which has always been vocal on cost-reduction and anti-corruption issues. More structurally, there is no detailed constitutional or legislative framework on political parties. Article 49 of the constitution simply states that "Any citizen has the right to freely establish parties to contribute to determining national policies through democratic processes", but Parliament never adopted an ordinary law implementing that constitutional provision. Only recently, the new regulation on party financing just mentioned put in place a public registry of political parties, requiring for their registration that parties adopt and publish a formal statute with transparent rules on internal democracy. These rules, however, are

58 As an example, the Five Stars have long campaigned (and the proposal was also included in the 2018 'contract of government') for modifying or abolishing Article 67 of the Italian Constitution, which ensures that MPs can carry out their duties 'without a binding mandate', arguing that MPs should be bound to follow party-lines and that they should not be allowed to switch parties during their mandate. Internally, Five Stars' leaders have asked their candidates to sign a private law agreement that forces MPs to pay a penalty if they switch parliamentary group.

59 L Corso, 'When anti-politics becomes political: what can the Italian Five Star Movement tell us about the relationship between populism and legalism' [2019] 15(3) *European Constitutional Law Review*. Here reference can be made to the constitutional reform bill proposed by M5S that would modify Artt 71 and 75 of the Constitution, introducing a 'propositional referendum' that would allow for the adoption of legislation even bypassing parliament, and lowering the quorum required for abrogative referendums. Approved in first reading by the Chamber of Deputies, the bill is still pending before the Senate.

60 See Law no 13/2014.

only applicable for those parties that wish to receive the indirect public financing, while they can still run in national and local elections even with no formal registration.

Finally and crucially, the Italian constitutional framework does not provide for 'militant democracy'[61] mechanisms. The only exception is the prohibition to recreate the Fascist party dissolved after the end of the regime,[62] but otherwise the constitutional framework allows anti-establishment and anti-system parties to participate to the political game. It has thus been defined as a 'tolerant' framework.[63] Recently, even parties inspired by the fascist ideology have been able to participate to the elections: neo-fascist movements Forza Nuova and Casapound fell however well short of the 3% threshold in the latest general elections and do not have parliamentary representation.

Before moving to the second part of the chapter, a final consideration needs to be reserved to the mechanisms of direct democracy provided for by the Italian constitution. The constituent assembly was evidently very prudent in this respect: it opted to include direct democracy procedures in the constitutional texts, but within very strictly defined limits. Most importantly, while the constitutional framework did establish a referendum system, first, it only allows – along with the confirmative referendums on constitutional amendment described above – for abrogative referendums; and second, it limits the substantive scope of referendums: budgetary and taxation laws, criminal amnesty, or the authorization to ratify international agreements[64] cannot be subject to referendums, and the Constitutional Court is in charge of monitoring admissibility of referendum questions.[65] Finally, the constitution requires a fairly significant number of signatures to officially request a referendum (500.000),[66] and then provides for a high quorum for the referendum's validity: at least 50% of the electorate must participate in the vote for the referendum to be valid, out of which a majority is needed to repeal the law in question.

---

61 On militant democracy, see generally K Loewenstein, 'Militant Democracy and Fundamental Rights' [1937] 31(3) *The American Political Science Review* and A Sajó (ed), *Militant Democracy* (Eleven International Publishing 2004).

62 Point XII of the Transitional and Final Provisions attached to the constitutional text affirms that 'It shall be forbidden to reorganise, under any form whatsoever, the dissolved Fascist party'.

63 See M Bassini, 'Rise of populism and the Five Stars model: an Italian case study' [2011] 11(1) *Italian Journal of Public Law* 1. See also Judgment 114/1967 Corte Costituzionale, which held that bodies that pursue the 'mutation of existing political order' are still covered by freedom of association's guarantees, as long as there is 'democratic method' and no direct or indirect use of violence.

64 Thus, membership of the EU could not be subject of a binding referendum. Yet a consultative referendum could probably be envisaged: see R Bin, 'Italexit? Come si potrebbe fare (se si può fare)' [2018] 4 *Quaderni Costituzionali*.

65 See Constitutional Law no 1/1953, implementing the constitutional provisions on referendums. The Court opted for an expansive reading of this admissibility control, see e.g. judgement 16/1978 Constitutional Court.

66 See Art 75 of the Constitution.

3 The failure of prevention

Regardless of the precise definition of populism one adopts, it would be hard to deny that populist parties and movements have been very successful in Italy in the last thirty years, with the coalition government between the League and the Five Stars being not only the most recent, but arguably the best and most salient example of such success. Defining that coalition as populist is certainly not a partisan, one-sided accusation: Five Star and League's leaders themselves have not rejected the 'populist' label and actually at times explicitly endorsed it.[67] During his first stint as President of the Council, even the President of the Council of Ministers Giuseppe Conte in a speech at the United Nations General Assembly did not disagree with the definition and attempted to 'constitutionalize' populism[68] by linking it to Article 1 of the Constitution, affirming in its second sentence that 'Sovereignty belongs to the people and is exercised by the people in the forms and within the limits of the Constitution'.[69] Furthermore, as already mentioned before, in the recent past Berlusconi and his *Forza Italia* also used populist rhetoric,[70] and so did their allies and in particular the then Northern League. And the (center)left was certainly not immune to populist tones either.[71]

It is beyond the scope of this contribution to analyze all the various reasons that have led to the electoral successes of populist movements in Italy, and certainly the phenomenon can hardly be explained by a single factor, but only by a combination of political-institutional, economic, and societal reasons. This section wants rather to stress two main points. First and quite evidently in light of the electoral results, existing constitutional safeguards did not prevent the success of populism. Second and perhaps more controversially, they might have enabled it, creating an institutional and political environment that has been fertile ground for populist movements.

As for the first point, one could even legitimately wonder whether constitutional safeguards *should* have that function, i.e. whether a constitutional structure should marginalize populist even before elections or at least strive to avoid that they reach the highest offices. Irrespectively, choices like opting for proportional electoral laws, or

---

67 See e.g. Salvini claiming to be "proudly populist": Ansa, 'Salvini, sono orgogliosamente populista' (ANSAit, 30 December 2017) http://www.ansa.it/sito/notizie/topnews/2017/12/30/salvini-sono-orgogliosamente-populista_3c6ae45b-134c-4945-a3c3-4e10056764b4.html accessed 7 February 2020.

68 According to Martinico, this is an example of the 'mimesis' strategy, in the sense that populist leaders seek legitimacy by relying on constitutional texts and concepts, rather than directly attacking them: see G Martinico, 'Fra mimetismo e parassitismo.
Brevi considerazioni a proposito del complesso rapporto fra populismo e costituzionalismo' [2019] 2019(1) *Questione Giustizia.*

69 See https://www.ilpost.it/2018/09/27/giuseppe-conte-nazioni-unite/. This interpretation of Art 1, according to Martinico (ibid 69) is however rough and selective.

70 For some examples, see J-W Müller, *What is Populism?* (University of Pennsylvania Press 2016) used Berlusconi as one of the prototypical examples of populist leaders.

71 Some scholars argue that even Renzi was, at least to some extent, a populist leader: see e.g. M Revelli, *Populismo 2.0* (Einaudi 2018).

limiting the scope of direct democracy instruments such as referendums, and in the most extreme cases even introducing and implementing militant democracy tools, may have the function of narrowing the chances that populist movements gain positions of power or more generally influence in decision making processes. While many of these choices were made in Italy, as described in the previous section, they still could not stop the rise of populist movements. Again, the more controversial second point is that they might have even enabled it.

During the so-called 'first republic' (1946-1994), the combination of perfect bicameralism and proportional representation with a low electoral threshold, led to a situation in which small parties, or even different fractions (*correnti*) within the main parties, had a disproportionate influence on legislation or government negotiations and could easily extort concessions from the majority, making their consent conditional upon the defence of often small and particular interests. This multiplication of veto powers on the one hand significantly slowed down decision making processes, and on the other contributed to governmental instability: between 1946 and 1994, Italy experienced a constant turnover and reshuffling of cabinets, often lasting for few months or even weeks. When the little transparency in the party financing system and generally the absence of effective regulation of political parties is added to the picture, it is clear that the emerging picture is that of an inefficient, and even worse, corrupt political system. Ironically, however, proportional representation also made sure that populist movements could be easily isolated during this phase.

The situation reached the boiling point in the early 1990s, with the *Tangentopoli* scandal further exposing the level of corruption of the political system and especially of the Christian Democrats and of the Socialist party. Radical changes took place also on the left, as the communist party, always in the opposition in the post-war period, had to rebrand itself as a European social-democrat movement after the collapse of the Berlin wall and of socialist regimes in Central and Eastern Europe. Populist movements exploited the fairly chaotic situation. The Northern League scored its first electoral successes. Two referendums, promoted by the Radical party and other small political groups, attacked key pillars of the party system, abolishing party financing and parts of the electoral laws, in the attempt to move from a proportional to a majoritarian system, and also abolished several ministries (agriculture, state holdings, and tourism) with a view to reducing public spending. Then, Silvio Berlusconi decided to enter the political arena and within few months, with his brand-new party Forza Italia, won the elections of 1994, forming his first government.

On top of economic and social dynamics, the environment that enabled the first populist successes was thus produced by a combination of two elements: first, an institutional system that generated quite cumbersome decision-making procedures and unstable governments, and that structurally failed to provide for effective accountability and responsibility mechanisms; second, a weak framework to regulate the political process, which contributed to the fall of the old parties, once corruption scandals were exposed, and facilitated the rise of new (populist) movements. In the 1990s and then early 2000s, Berlusconi and the Northern League could exploit the situation and gain power promising a transformation of the institutional system and running against the old elites, on the one hand, and the 'danger' of the left, which they continued to associate to its communist past, on the other.

Neither Berlusconi nor the center-left managed to address the shortcomings of the institutional system in the two decades of the 'Second Republic': constitutional reforms meant to simplify the institutional setting and speed up decision making procedures, differentiating the roles of the Chamber and the Senate – roughly transforming the latter in a regional chamber comparable to the Bundesrat – and, to a different extent, strengthening the powers of the central government, failed in the constitutional referendums of 2006 and 2016. The perceived inability to reform the institutional and political system, combined with the effects of the economic crisis of 2008-2012, contributed to further political instability in the 2010s. The instability was exploited this time by the Five Stars Movement – in this sense, as argued by Urbinati, the success of the Five Stars shows 'the party system's ineptitude to amend itself and stop its corrupting decline'[72] – and then by the League, the latter especially after the migration and refugee crisis.

In this sense, thus, the system designed in 1948, which spread responsibilities as much as possible across different actors, both vertically and horizontally, with a view to prevent a possible return to fascism and authoritarianism, might have perversely facilitated today's populist successes. This is not to accuse the members of the constituent assembly: if blame is to be assigned, it would rather be with the following generations of politicians that have been unable to reform the system and sufficiently respond to the challenges emerging in the most recent decades. Yet, choices that were perfectly reasonable in 1948 and motivated by a rational 'fear of the dictator' might today contribute to creating fragmentation, instability, and ultimately open the door to populist.

As an example, the lack of stability in the figure of the President of the Council of Ministers is a weakness that has been particularly exploited by populists.[73] As seen in section 1.2, the constitution designs a weak figure in comparison to most European prime ministers. The President has few means to push forward a strong autonomous political programme and can easily become hostage of her own majority. During the first republic, this institutional setting produced weak leaderships, easily replaceable, and in constant competition with other party leaders within the dominant Christian Democrat party.

72 N Urbinati, 'The Italian Five Star Movement for foreigners' *Il Mulino* (1 March 2018) https://www.rivistailmulino.it/news/newsitem/index/Item/News:NEWS_ITEM:4272 accessed 3 February 2020.

73 See also M Bassini, 'Rise of populism and the Five Stars model: an Italian case study' [2011] 11(1) *Italian Journal of Public Law*.

When the political system began crumbling and the electorate strived for radical changes, the charismatic figure of Silvio Berlusconi emerged as a successful alternative proposing a new leadership model. The weaknesses of the previous system thus paved the way to the emergence of a stronger figure, not reluctant to using populist tones, who stood politically, but also rhetorically and even visually, in opposition to the 'grey' leaders of the past and sought to modernize, or even revolutionize, the Italian system.

More recently, the new populists of the 2010s and especially the Five Stars again have exploited the weaknesses of the constitutional framework with the electorate. Criticizing the ineffectiveness and inefficiency of representative institutions, the Five Stars campaigned on a platform of radical direct democracy that, according to its proponents, would guarantee better and more legitimate decisions. On the other hand, Salvini and League suggest again a strongly centralized leadership model that is seen as a solution to the incapacity of representative institutions to take rapid and radical decisions.

4 The successes of reaction

The electoral successes of populist movements in the last twenty-five years have however not caused any major constitutional breakdown. There is no structural crisis of democratic constitutionalism in Italy: despite the fact that populists not only scored well in the elections, but also gained power on more than one occasion, the Italian democratic and rule of law situation has mostly remained stable, even if some negative effects, especially on specific fundamental rights, could hardly be denied.[74] Even when controversial measures were adopted, existing safeguards were by and large able to remedy the single problems before any true breakdown occurred.[75] This suggests that while the framework cannot prevent electoral successes of populism, and might even contribute to them, it works much better when populist are in power. In this sense, and at least so far, the Italian constitution has thus proved remarkable resilience.[76]

Paradoxically, the reasons for this resilience are, to some extent, precisely the same reasons that contribute to the success of populist parties. When they gain power, populists struggle as much as other politicians to bring forward their agenda. Even for populist parties, for example, the legislative process remains cumbersome and it is difficult for the government to push forwards its legislative proposals. A good example,

74 See again the situation of freedom of expression under Berlusconi, as well as restrictions to migrants' rights under the Conte I government.

75 An example is the 'Lodo Alfano' case, with the Constitutional Court striking down the immunity law adopted by the Berlusconi government in order, according to critics, to save the President of the Council from criminal proceedings pending against him. See Judgment 262/2009 Corte Costituzionale.

76 On 'constitutional resilience', see Verfassungsblog debate available at https://verfassungsblog.de/category/debates/constitutional-resilience-debates/promising.

in the current legislative term, is the fate of 'citizenship income' (*reddito di cittadinanza*), the flagship proposal of the Five Stars before the 2018 elections. Despite being the senior partner of the Five Stars – League coalition and the larger group in both chambers, the Five Stars struggled a great deal to push the reform through parliament and, compared to the original proposals, the scope of the measure ultimately adopted was far narrower.

The presence of several different institutional actors, which can negatively lead to a lack of general accountability for political actors and create difficulties to assign precise responsibility for political choices, also produces veto-like powers that can be used to put to stop populist leaders, or at least make life more difficult for them. The contradiction is perhaps best evident in the 'Savona affair' of spring 2018. After the League and the Five Stars finally reached a deal on the formation of a coalition government, Giuseppe Conte, the President of the Council indicated by the two parties, went to the President of the Republic with the proposed list of ministers. The Constitution, as already illustrated above, provides that the President of the Republic nominates the ministers 'on a proposal' of the President of the Council. Mattarella and Conte clashed on the indication of Paolo Savona, a figure close to the League with strong anti-Euro views, and who argued in favor of Italy's exit from the common currency, as minister of economic affairs. President Mattarella *de facto* put a veto on the nomination, although is at least debatable that Article 92 of the Constitution ('The President of the Republic appoints the President of the Council of Ministers and, on his proposal, the Ministers') goes as far as creating such power.[77] The governmental talks then collapsed and only re-started a few days later, when the League and the Five Stars agreed to propose another minister for the same post. On the one hand, the Savona affair demonstrates that the constitutional setting can put meaningful obstacles to the populist agenda: the intervention of Sergio Mattarella blocked the nomination of an anti-Euro and anti-Europe minister – the subsequent minister had a much more nuanced position on the topic of Italy's membership of the Euro – especially considering that the two parties did not explicitly campaign on a Euroexit platform before the 2018 elections. For some, Mattarella's intervention had a positive influence: as argued by Fabbrini and Pollicino,

77 There are however previous examples of Presidents vetoing ministerial indications: in 1994, President Scalfaro stopped Berlusconi's nomination of his lawyer, Cesare Previti, as minister of justice; and in 2014 Napolitano pressured Renzi to modify the indication once again of the minister of justice. In both cases, the Presidents of the Council immediately accepted the President's intervention and indicated a replacement. Arguing that Mattarrella's decision was within the boundaries of his powers, D Tega and M Massa, 'Why the Italian President's Decision was Legitimate' (Verfassungblog on constitutional matters, 28 May) https://verfassungsblog.de/why-the-italian-presidents-decision-was-legitimate/#primary_menu_sandwich accessed 7 February 2020; M Fichera, 'The People vs. the Elite: Italian Dialectics and the European Malaise' (Verfassungsblog on constitutional matters, 28 May) https://verfassungsblog.de/the-people-vs-the-elite-italian-dialectics-and-the-european-malaise accessed 7 February 2020; and G Piccirilli, 'Part II: Is the institutional crisis in Italy over? Surely a storm, maybe indicating a climate change' (IACL-AIDC Blog, 8 June) https://blog-iacl-aidc.org/blog/2018/6/8/part-ii-s-the-institutional-crisis-in-italy-over-surely-a-storm-maybe-indicating-a-climate-change accessed 7 February 2020.

it 'constrained and rechannelled anti-European forces within the constitutional perimeter'.[78]

At the same time, the fact that a figure with no direct electoral legitimacy, such as the President of the Republic, could *de facto* veto a political choice of two of the largest parties may have further fostered populist feelings in the electorate. The Five Star Movement in particular strongly criticized Mattarella's decision, even calling for the impeachment of the President, and only later opted to lower its tone and agreed to put forward a new candidate for the post. Such attacks to the President hardly contribute to re-create trust in the institutional system and even if the situation has been recomposed in the meantime, the wounds of the Savona affairs could be felt in the future and be further exploited by populist movements, often keen to criticize 'unelected' institutions when they allegedly take decisions that should rest with directly representative bodies.[79]

In any case, there is no doubt that creating strong independent institutions such as the President of the Republic, but also the constitutional court, has greatly contributed to the resilience of the Italian constitutional system, resilience that is best shown when populist parties gain power. As for the President, however, it is necessary to acknowledge that the capacity of the President to act as a guarantor of the constitution has also been the result of fortunate circumstances. In section 1.2, it was noted that the constitution does not necessarily require for an agreement between the majority and the opposition for the election of the President. The custom that the President of the Republic should not be a too explicitly partisan figure has so far survived, even after the election of some presidents by narrow majorities. Yet, there is no formal guarantee that the custom will remain in place; so far it has worked because, for purely contingent reasons, Presidents of the Republic have been always elected when populists were not in power.

As for the constitutional court, there has been no attempt of court packing or to undermine the independence of the judges. Here, the constitutional framework seems in any case to be more robust. First, the constitution requires an agreement between parties for the election of the five judges selected by parliament. In this manner, and providing that there is no supermajority of one party (or a coalition of), it is very difficult, if not impossible, to create a completely unbalanced court. Second, even in the case in which the parliament pushes forward controversial nominations, the fact that other judges are chosen by other actors make any packing plan even more complicated.

---

78 F Fabbrini and O Pollicino, Constitutional Identity in Italy: Institutional Disagreements at a Time of Political Change. in C Callies and G van der Schyff (eds), *Constitutional Identity in a Europe of Multilevel Constitutionalism* (Cambridge University Press 2019). More generally, they read Mattarella's intervention as motivated 'by the intention to protect Italy's constitutional commitments towards the EU'. His intervention 'confirmed that Italy's commitment toward the process of European integration and the limitations of sovereignty encapsulated in Art 11 of Italian Constitution constitutes a core element of the state's constitutional purpose' (page 8).

79 See also C Pinelli, 'Populismo, diritto e società. Uno sguardo costituziônale' [2019] 2019(1) *Questione Giustizia* 33.

A Hungarian or Polish situation in which the constitutional court becomes the expression of the political majority seems thus unlikely. In contrast to those experiences,[80] thus, the Italian model could be a suitable candidate for export. So far, both under the Berlusconi's governments and under the League-Five Stars coalition, the constitutional court has constantly proved its independence and its ability to stop controversial points of the reforms.[81] And the judiciary at large has offered resistance too, both under Berlusconi – perhaps sometimes even overstepping the boundaries of its mandate – and more recently for example reacting to the controversial League's initiatives on migration, with courts limiting the possible negative effects on fundamental rights.[82]

The events of August 2019 – the collapse of the Five Stars-League government and its replacement with another peculiar, but, all things considered, at least less explicitly populist coalition between the Five Stars and the Democratic Party – could be seen as further proof of the resistance of the Italian constitutional framework. The attempt of League leader's Salvini to take 'full powers' badly backfired, and the robust parliamentarism created by the 1948 constitution, facilitated by the presence of the President of the Republic acting as its guarantor, allowed the Five Stars and the Democratic Party to overcome their differences and agree on a new coalition government. Yet, populism did not suddenly disappear. Just to offer an example, few weeks after the new government took power, Parliament, under the impulse of the Five Stars approved a constitutional reform reducing the number of MPs. While the reform itself is not revolutionary and could hardly be considered a strong blow to democratic constitutionalism, the rhetoric used to explain and promote the reform was typically populist. Further tests are thus undoubtedly on the horizon.

5 Conclusion: The Italian paradox and lessons

What the Italian case shows, thus, is therefore and in the first place a paradox. Constitutional safeguards constructed to prevent a return to authoritarian forms of the past – in Italy, as is obvious, with a specific eye to the fascist experience – might have actually contributed to create an environment in which current populist movements thrive. This scenario materializes if public power is too sparse and if the system, in

---

80 See W Sadurski, 'On the Relative Irrelevance of Constitutional Design: Lessons from Poland' [2019] Sydney Law School Research Paper no 19/34 19, depicting the Hungarian and Polis systems as 'bad', because 'the parliamentary winner can appoint judges to all of the vacancies that open up during the parliamentary term, so that the compromise-oriented election of judges depends largely on the political culture and goodwill of the ruling party/parties rather than being compelled by institutions'.

81 See again the Lodo Alfano case, mentioned *supra* 76.

82 See e.g. the decision of the Cassation Court holding that the 'Salvini decree' on migration is not retroactive: Judgment 9460/19 Corte di Cassazione.

order to avoid authoritarian-like centralization, ultimately fails to provide clear mechanisms of political accountability and responsibility, as well as swift and efficient decisions-making processes. In these circumstances, democracy becomes so dysfunctional that runs the risk of becoming a 'vetocracy', giving to the citizens the impression that traditional parties and institutions are inefficient and thus useless. This a context in which populism can prosper, and it prospers even more when the answer to the inefficiency of traditional parties is technocracy, as happened between 2011 and 2013 with the Monti government, and to a lesser extent after the failed constitutional referendum of 2016.[83] In both cases, 'technocrats' fared badly in the following elections, and populist won convincingly. In this respect, as correctly argued by Müller, technocracy can pave the way to populism (and vice versa), as they are both based on a similar belief: debate and disagreement are not needed, and there is always one and only one correct solution, either based on a technical analysis of the problem, or because it expresses the only authentic will of the people.[84]

A second lesson is that shortcomings in regulating the political arena can be costly. The lack of a clear framework on political parties, the constant changes to the financing regime, and the instability of the electoral law regime have all contributed to the successes of populism and the failure of the 'preventive' function of constitutional safeguard. This is not to say that a 'tolerant' attitude towards anti-establishment parties, as it was described by Bassini, cannot work, and that militant democracy mechanisms should be preferred; but that a tolerant attitude still requires clear and stable regulation of the political process.[85]

On a more positive note, the Italian case also shows that well designed constitutional safeguards can limit populists (or populist parties) even when they have reached power. A constitutional court that is difficult to capture thanks to clever appointment rules, a solid framework for the independence of the judiciary, a robust and widely accepted doctrine on the limits to constitutional amendments, supra-partes presidents of the republic able to act as 'guarantors' of the constitution, have so far been able to defend democratic constitutionalism even in a time of strong political conflict, when the rules of the game do not always seem to be shared by all political actors.[86] Yet, as noted above, the challenges are growing, and recent experiences around the globe show that even

---

83 While the Monti Government was a typical technocratic government, the Gentiloni government that took however from Renzi in 2016 was a more political one, but still often sought political legitimacy in the 'competence' of its ministers.

84 In this sense, technocracy and populism are 'mirror images of each other': see J-W Müller, *What is Populism?* (University of Pennsylvania Press 2016). In similar fashion, see also D Kosař and J Baroš and P Dufek, 'The Twin Challenges to Separation of Powers in Central Europe: Technocratic Governance and Populism' [2019] 15(3) *European Constitutional Law Review*.

85 See M Bassini, 'Rise of populism and the Five Stars model: an Italian case study' [2011] 11(1) *Italian Journal of Public Law*.

86 On the importance of 'unwritten democratic norms', see S Levitsky and D Ziblatt, *How democracies die* (Crown 2019).

allegedly robust and resilient constitutional systems can be swiftly attacked and even dismantled. It is yet to be seen whether and how the Italian constitutional safeguards would react to a direct attack by populist leaders: the timid reasons for optimism presented in this chapter need also to acknowledge the inherent fragility of any legal safeguard against raw political power.[87]

87 See W Sadurski, 'On the Relative Irrelevance of Constitutional Design: Lessons from Poland' [2019] Sydney Law School Research Paper no 19/34 19 and T Ginsburg and A Z. Huq and M Versteeg, 'The Coming Demise of Liberal Constitutionalism [2018] 85(2) *University of Chicago Law Review* 253, arguing that in the best case 'constitutional design features serve as speed bumps to slow the agglomeration and abuse of political power; they cannot save us from our worst selves completely'.

Spain – Constitutional Safeguards and Populism

*Juan Antonio Chinchilla Peinado** *and Mónica Domínguez Martín***

1 Introduction

Populism[1] is not a new phenomenon, neither in Spain or in the rest of the world. However, the last years, this phenomenon has a clear process of expansion. In this context, it is worth considering what instruments or mechanisms of safeguards have the law and the Spanish democratic system to limit these movements. Specifically, this work presents the constitutional and legal safeguards related to constitutional reform procedures, the role of constitutional jurisprudence and the judiciary in the protection of constitutionalism, the regulation of the electoral system and political parties and the effectiveness of the safeguard mechanisms. Finally, we expose two relevant case studies tha represent the main threats that have been raised to the Spanish State in recent years have been presented since the phenomenon of populism. The first of them refers to secessionist movements and identity populism in Spain; specifically, the cases of the Basque Country and Catalonia. Finally, the second of the case studies focuses on the appearance of the so-called "new" political parties (Podemos and Vox), which are classified as left and right populisms within the ideological spectrum.

The following lines analyze both the reality of these movements, and the response adopted by the State to protect constitutional principles.

2 Constitutional and Legal Safeguards of Democratic Constitutionalism and the Rule of Law in Spain

2.1 *Barriers to constitutional amendment and replacement*

Title X of the Spanish Constitution (SC) is dedicated to constitutional reform and sets forth two reform procedures. Article 167 of the Spanish Constitution especially protects

---

* Juan Antonio Chinchilla Peinado is a Lecturer in Administrative Law at the Universidad Autónoma of Madrid (Spain).

** Mónica Domínguez Martín is a Lecturer in Administrative Law at the Universidad Autónoma of Madrid (Spain).

1 In the term proposed by J-W Müller, *What is populism?* (University of Pennsylvania Press 2016).

certain parts of the Constitution: Preliminary Title (Articles 1-9)[2]; Chapter Two, Section One of Title I (Fundamental rights and public liberties), and Title II (the Monarchy), as well as the Constitution as a whole (to approve a new Constitution). The remainder of reforms, not included under Article 168 SC, should be conducted through the modification procedure provided for in Article 167 SC. The Spanish Constitution has chosen not to establish an intangibility clause. A limitation is placed only on the possibility of a constitutional reform "in the event of war or any of the conditions foreseen in Article 116" (Article 169 SC). These are the states of alarm, exception or siege, under the terms of Organic Law 4/1981, of 1 June.

Article 166 SC, in defining who has the right to initiative for constitutional reform, refers to the provisions of Articles 87.1 and 2 of the Constitution, attributing that right to the Government, Congress of Deputies, the Senate and the Autonomous Regions. This effectively excludes popular initiative. When the initiative is taken by the Congress, constitutional reform proposals may be adopted, as per Article 146 of the Rules of Congress, when signed by two parliamentary groups or one fifth of the members. In the case of the Rules of the Senate, the right to initiative for a proposal is held, as set forth in Article 152, by fifty senators who are not members of the same parliamentary group.

With regard to the procedure for constitutional reform foreseen in Article 167, in general terms, the legislative procedure is applicable, albeit with certain specialities. The end result **is** the existence of a procedure that is more complex than usual. Article 167 of the Spanish Constitution requires such reform to be effected by a three-fifths majority in the Congress and the Senate. In the event of disagreement between the Houses, a Commission would be set up composed equally of deputies and senators, establishing a special procedure to resolve any further disagreement between the Houses on the text drafted by the joint Commission. Lastly, the reform is to be ratified by referendum, but only when requested by one tenth of the members of either House.

To date, only two instances of constitutional reform have taken place, both following the ordinary reform procedure and by parliamentary initiative. The first of these was the reform of 1992, at the initiative of all the parliamentary groups in the Spanish Congress. As a consequence of Spain's accession to the European Union, it was necessary for the Spanish legal order to recognise the right of all EU citizens residing in a Member State of which they are not nationals to be voters and eligible at the municipal elections in their Member State of residence, under the same conditions as the nationals of said State. It was imperative that Article 13 SC should incorporate a reference to the right to passive suffrage. The second reform took place in 2011, in the context of the economic crisis affecting Spain and the rest of the EU, to alter Article 135 and include a reference to

2 About: definition/model of State ("Social and Democratic Rule of Law"), national sovereignty, monarchy, unitary State, language, flag, capital of the country (Madrid), political parties, labor unions and business organizations, Army, principles relating to the Rule of Law.

the mechanisms for budgetary stability. This reform was backed by the Socialist and Popular Parliamentary Groups in Congress.

The aggravated reform procedure in Article 168 requires, first of all, the approval of the reform by a two-thirds majority in both Houses, following which the Houses are automatically dissolved and elections convened (and subsequently held). Besides, the newly elected Chambers must ratify the previously adopted reforms, for which no pre-set quorum is required (the Rules of the Senate, however, require ratification of the proposal for reform by absolute majority). Following this, the Houses are obliged to submit the reform proposal through the ordinary legislative procedure, with the requirement of a favourable vote by two-thirds of the members in each House. And, finally, Article 168.3 establishes that "the reform having been approved by the Cortes shall be ratified by referendum". Therefore, the subsequent ratification by referendum is mandatory, with no qualified majority for such ratification or any demand regarding participation being specified.

The Spanish Constitution has been criticised for the excessive rigidity of this reform procedure includes in Article 168 SC, such that it prevents, de facto, the reform from being implemented. It has also been criticised for the scarce rationality of its implementation rationale, which includes in this procedure matters of minor import but excludes its use in major issues that severely impact our constitutional system.[3] However, the issues for whose modification this aggravated procedure was actually established are the same as (or very similar to) those which other constitutional texts declare as unreformable.

Moreover, this reform system has undeniably given stability to a Constitution born in a highly specific and uncertain context. In addition, this has avoided the temptation of the approach of populist reforms that could threaten the democratic system itself and the State model: the head of state (monarchy versus republic), secession of parts of the territory, the elimination of the Autonomus Communities, Civil and social rights, the role of the Army, the electoral system, special funding conditions for certain Autonomus Communities, the elimination of the principle of budgetary stability, the elimination of the privileged jurisdiction for members of Congress and the Senate and for the King...In recent years, utilitarian accounts of constitutional deficiencies are frequent to support the political programs of the respective political parties and, simultaneously, to propose a constitutional reform. It includes populist elements, namely the political system as a problem, financial adjustments as a consequence of the economic crisis, politics falling into disrepute for being ineffective or corrupt, the political class failing to represent a virtuous population. And the political forces (especially the nationalist parties and those political parties that we can qualify as populist, as we will see in section 5) have responded by attributing their consequences to alleged weaknesses or

3 F Rubio Llorente, De la reforma constitucional'. in ME Casas Bassmonde and M Rodríguez y Bravo (eds), *Comentarios a la Constitución Española* (Vol. II, BOE 2018) 1863.

inconsistencies in the constitutional text. With this, the obvious democratic and social advances that Spain has experienced in its democratic stage by the hand of the Spanish Constitution of 1978 are ignored or undervalued. In this context, the need and the possibility of deep reforms have become a dangerous populist rhetoric. And, of course, the existence of a complex and difficult constitutional reform procedure has prevented these proposals from succeeding until now.

2.2 Constitutional jurisprudence and the role of the judiciary in protecting constitutionalism

The Spanish democracy is not a militant democracy, and therefore does not impose a positive adhesion to the legal order and to the Constitution.[4] Consequently, in the Spanish political-constitutional system, any political position can be maintained, as it does not require a normative nucleus that is inaccessible to constitutional reform procedures. Any citizen, the political parties and, indeed, any autonomous region organ is entitled to defend and express the political position deemed appropriate. The limit set by Spanish Constitutional case-law is strict: any idea may be defended, but always respecting the constitutional system. It is thus mandatory to respect the constitutionally established channels to translate dissident political will against the system into a legal reality. Democratic principles exist only as a result of acknowledging the unconditional primacy of the Constitution and observing the principle of the Rule of Law. A hypothetical democratic legitimacy cannot oppose to constitutional legality. The democratic concept of power has no other legitimacy than the legitimacy grounded on the Constitution. The Spanish Constitution, and the entire legal order, does not stand as a limitation to democracy but rather, precisely, as its foundation and guarantee. The sole political option that is prohibited by the Spanish constitutional order is the endorsement of terrorism, which leads to the outlawing and dissolution of any political party that includes it in its ideology or justifies it (Article 9 Organic Law 6/2002, on Political Parties (LOPP)).[5] The decision to adopt such prohibition is the remit of a special division of the Supreme Court, and is controlled through the corresponding appeal for protection focused on protecting the right of association, particularly with regard to the right to create political parties (Articles 6 and 22 SC), in relation to rights to freedom of thought (Article 16.1 SC), to the freedom of expression (Article 20.1.a) SC) and of political participation (Article 23.1 SC). Similarly, on the basis of the right to education

4 Judgment of the Constitutional Court 136/2018 (ECLI:ECLI:ES:TC:2018:136).

5 Judgments of the Constitutional Court 138/2012 (ECLI:ES:TC:2012:138); 5/2004 (ECLI:ES:TC:2004:5); 48/2003 (ECLI:ES:TC:2003:48), where it is specified that the control of whether the defining purposes of a party's political ideology, in principle constitutionally free, are pursued by means compatible with the constitutional functions to which parties serve as an instrument must be verified at a time subsequent to their constitution.

recognised in Article 27.2 SC, constitutional case-law bars the existence of private educational centres inspired by totalitarian or anti-democratic educational ideologies. Ideological indoctrination is not contemplated, whereas the opposite is true of the higher values of freedom and pluralism. Nevertheless, constitutional case-law is far from neutral, and positively encourages the dissemination of constitutional values.[6]

From these premises, jurisdictional protection of the constitutional State is twofold, entrusted fundamentally to the Constitutional Court. On the one hand, vis-à-vis the proposals of nationwide nationalist populist movements and their re-centralising tendency, the Constitutional Court stands, as guarantor of the constitutionally guaranteed condition of autonomy (both in the Autonomous Regions – political, administrative and financial autonomy – and in local entities – administrative autonomy –). The constitutional instruments are the appeal of unconstitutionality (Articles 161.1.a and 164.1 SC; 27.1 and 33.2 Organic Law 2/1979 of the Constitutional Court (LOTC)),[7] positive conflict of competence (Articles 161.1c and 60-72 LOTC),[8] and conflict in defence of local autonomy (Articles 75 bis to 75 quinquies LOTC).[9]

On the other hand, and addressing proposals of pro-independence populisms (right-wing or left-wing, nationwide or only regional), the Constitutional Court affirms the existence of a single sovereignty. The unilateral rupture of the constitutional order by an Autonomous Region allows the State, exceptionally, to adopt coercive measures that imply interference in the autonomy of the Autonomous Region, rendering the latter temporarily constrained to a greater or lesser degree (Article 155 SC). That a 'right to decide' exists in the Spanish system as a right that is inherent to a partial political community and that allows said community to separate itself from the remainder of

---

6 Judgment of the Constitutional Court 31/2018 (ECLI:EN:TC:2018:31). However, it allows education differentiated by sex as a pedagogical option of voluntary adoption by schools and free choice by parents and students. The Constitution recognises the right to establish an ideology in the educational center, although with the additional limitation of respect to the constitutional principles and values, orienting its activity towards the full recognition of the human personality.

7 Through this process, the Constitutional Court guarantees the supremacy of the Constitution and judges the conformity or non-conformity with it of the laws, regulations and acts with the force of law of the State or of the autonomous Regions that may affect the scope of autonomy recognized to the Regions or state competences. The President of the Government, the Ombudsman, fifty Deputies and fifty Senators, as well as the executive and legislative bodies of the autonomous Regions are entitled to file an appeal of unconstitutionality.

8 Through this process, the Constitutional Court controls the provisions, resolutions or acts without legal value of the State or of the autonomous regions, or the omission thereof, that may affect the constitutional order of competences established in the Constitution, in the Statutes of Autonomy or in the organic laws dictated to delimit the competences between the State and the autonomous regions. The central government and the executive bodies of the autonomous regions are entitled to intervene in conflicts.

9 According to Judgment of the Constitutional Court 107/2017 (ECLI:ES:TC:2017:107), this procedure is subject to a strict legitimation regime, since only those local entities that are directly affected by the challenged norm and reach a certain representativeness among all affected entities can access it. In addition, the object of the appeal is exclusively the violation of local autonomy, without the possibility of alleging on the occasion of the same other violations other than the constitutional text

the political community is rejected. In the event of unilateral actions that blatantly violate the constitutional order and severely undermine the general interests of Spain, and that cannot be remedied through ordinary control channels, the Central Government may, with prior authorisation given by the Senate, modify the political autonomy in the community by means of adopting the necessary measures. These measures may even include the assumption by the Government of the nation of the powers of the autonomous government, or simply the issuing of mandatory instructions to the autonomous bodies. State coercive measures shall not, in any event, lead to the indefinite suspension of autonomy, nor to the institutional suppression of the Autonomous Regions in question.[10] The scope of the Constitutional Court is fully focused on compliance with the formal requirements for the coercive procedure (Article 155 SC: prior order, issued by the Government to the president of the Autonomous Region, to cease non-compliance with constitutional and legal responsibilities, or to cease any actions contrary to the general interest; and, should this order not be complied with, the approval by the Senate, by absolute majority, of the coercive measures deemed appropriate in the light of the prior proposal made by the Government.) On the content and scope of the measures adopted, the Constitutional Court restricts its control to an external judgment of reasonableness, not of the measure itself, but of the rationale adopted by the Government and the Senate regarding the appropriateness of the measure to the circumstances triggering the implementation of Article 155 SC.

Given the central position of the Constitutional Court, the rules for selecting its members are of particular interest. The Court is composed of twelve members, selected and appointed among Spanish citizens who are judges, prosecutors, university professors, civil servants or lawyers, all of whom are proven jurists with over fifteen years of professional experience or in office in their respective capacity (Article 18 LOTC). Of these, four are chosen by Parliament, by a majority of three fifths of deputies; four by the Senate, chosen from the candidates put forward by the Legislative Assemblies of the Autonomous Regions, with a majority of three fifths of its members; two at the proposal of the Government; and two at the proposal by the General Council of the Judiciary, by a majority of three fifths of its members. Appointment as Magistrate of the Constitutional Court entails a nine year tenure, while one third of the Court is renewed every three years. No Magistrate may be proposed for another consecutive period, unless the incumbent had only held the post for a term not exceeding three years (Article 16 LOTC). The protagonism of the majority political parties in the appointment of members of the Constitutional Court is manifest.

---

10 Judgment of the Constitutional Court 89/2019 (ECLI:ES:TC:2019:89).

2.3 *Constitutional and Statutory rules governing democratic processes*

2.3.1 The political parties

By virtue of the Constitutional provisions contained specifically in Article 6 SC and also generically in Article 22 SC, political parties are a type of association[11] as referred to in Article 23 SC, on the grounds that party membership falls within the right to public participation. From the baseline of this constitutional configuration, it may be stated that political parties are the expression of political pluralism, which is one of the highest values in the legal order (Article 1 SC), and that they embody the fundamental instrument for political participation which, in the Spanish legal order, is rooted in the idea of representative democracy.[12]

Their appearance in Article 6 SC under the Preliminary Title (included in the instances of aggravated constitutional reform listed in Article 168 SC) expresses the importance given to political parties within the constitutional system and as the key to political pluralism.[13]

The foundation of political parties and the exercise of their activity are unrestricted, within the limits of respect for the Constitution and the Law. This is likewise established in Article 1 of LOPP. The Constitution only demands that the internal structure and operations of political parties are democratic, as a constitutional pattern of organization and operation. The constitutional demand for democracy in operations "translates as a subjective right or set of rights and powers attributed to members with regard to their party, that tend toward safeguarding their participation in decision-taking and controlling the internal operations within said parties".[14]

The above would appear to prevent any control beyond the boundaries stated in the Constitution itself and (by means of the interpretation embedded in Article 6 and Article 22 SC) would exclude, therefore, any political parties pursuing ends or using means classified as a criminal offence, or those of a secret or paramilitary nature (Article 22.5 SC).

The law does, however, require the inscription of legal political parties in the Political Parties Register of the Ministry of the Interior, on presentation of the foundation charter subscribed by its promoters and accompanied by documentation to accredit compliance with the formal requirements foreseen in the Organic Law on Political Parties. The effects of said inscription are to make public the constitution of the party and its statutes[15] and the acquisition of legal personality, as established in Article 3, LOPP. This system of prior inscription in a public register only allows formal, strictly regulated external control to be

11 More in Organic Law 1/2002 of March 22 Regulating The Right Of Association, Art.1.3.
12 Judgment of the Constitutional Court 31/1993 (ECLI:ECLI:ES:TC:1993:31); 32/1985 (ECLI:ECLI:ES:TC:1985:32); 119/1990 (ECLI:ECLI:ES:TC:1990:119).
13 Judgment of the Constitutional Court 85/1986 (ECLI:ECLI:ES:TC:1986:85).
14 Judgment of the Constitutional Court 56/1995 (ECLI:ECLI:ES:TC:1995:56).
15 Judgment of the Constitutional Court 138/2012 (ECLI:ECLI:ES:TC:2012:138).

exerted by the administrative authority.[16] Political control it is not allowed. Government control over political parties consists of "simple verification of the legal and formal aspects of the documentation presented on inscription".[17]

In the Spanish system, a political party may be declared illegal by a reasoned court ruling if found to pursue ends or use means typified as a criminal offence, or to be of a secret or paramilitary nature (Article10.2.a) LOPP). As set forth in Article 515 of the Criminal Code:

> The following are punishable as illicit associations:
> 1) those whose purpose is to commit a criminal act or that, following their constitution, promote the commission of such acts;
> 2) those that, despite having a legal purpose, employ means that are violent, or cause personality alteration or control, for its fulfilment;
> 3) organisations of a paramilitary nature;
> 4) those that directly or indirectly foment, promote or incite hate, hostility, discrimination or violence against people, groups or associations on the grounds of their ideology, religion or beliefs, some or all of its members' belonging to an ethnia, race or nation, their sex, sexual orientation, family status, illness or incapacity.

Similarly, a political party may be dissolved if it infringes regularly, repeatedly and severely the requirement for a democratic internal structure and operation (compliant with Article 10.2.B) LOPP in relation to Articles 7 and 8 LOPP) or if its activities, repeatedly and severely, violate democratic principles or seek to deteriorate or destroy the regime of freedoms or to eliminate or render the democratic system impossible by means of the behaviours referred to in Article 9[18] in the law of political parties (Article 10.2.c) LOPP).

In Spain, political parties are supported through mixed funding, including both private and public funds, but with a clear predominance of public funding, fundamentally in the form of subsidies for electoral expenditure. During the entire election period, from the moment elections are convened up to the proclamation of the elected, election expenses arise that are reviewed "ex post" by the electoral administration and the Court of Audit (Articles 132, 133 and 134 of the General Electoral System Law (LOREG)). In controlling election expenditure, the law holds candidacy administrators

16 Judgment of the Constitutional Court 3/1981 (ECLI:ECLI:ES:TC:1981:3).

17 Judgment of the Constitutional Court 85/1986 (ECLI:ECLI:ES:TC:1986:85).

18 Among the behaviours included in Art. 9.2 of the LOPP we can mention: systematic violation of rights and freedoms; promoting, justifying or exculpating attacks against life or integrity, or the exclusion or persecution of ideology, religion, beliefs, nationality, race, sex, or sexual orientation; promote or legitimize violence as a method to achieve political objectives, or eliminate the conditions for democracy, pluralism or freedoms; support to terrorist organizations.

accountable for election accounts (Article 121 LOREG). From a substantive angle, the law encompasses both private financial contributions and advance payments of public subventions. Private contributions are limited to ten thousand euros per individual. As for public funding, in the form of subventions, Article 127 bis LOREG establishes a scale of percentages for advance payment, based on the results obtained by the parties, coalitions or federations in previous elections, thus favouring consolidated parties.[19]

It is mandatory for political parties to keep accounts that correspond with the Court of Audit. Political parties are under the obligation to keep detailed accounts, treasury book, inventories and balance sheets, and to publish on their websites their profit-and-loss accounts, balance sheets, outstanding credit, nominative subventions and donations greater than 25000 euros. Similarly, the parties must publish the report issued by the Court of Audit on their websites.

These measures of transparency and control of the financing of political parties have been especially important in recent years. And, to a large extent, this is the result of the debate opened by the so-called "new parties", which have appeared recently and are frequently qualified as populists (see section number 4). Traditional parties have often been accused of corruption, of having opaque financing or of being subjected to the influence of lobbies or economic agents.

2.3.2 The electoral system

The Spanish electoral system is regulated fundamentally through the LOREG and through the constitutional provisions relating to the principles of democracy (Article 1.1 SC) and the fundamental rights to active and passive suffrage: Article 23.1 and 2 SC. In addition, provisions are also given in the Statutes of Autonomy (the main Law of the Autonomus Communities, approved by the Cortes Generales). Lastly, the electoral system also incorporates governmental regulations and 'instructions' dictated by the Central Electoral Commission.

The Constitution does not regulate the electoral system directly, but does, nevertheless, contain two fundamental rights that condition and give meaning to its legal regulation.[20] These are the fundamental right of every Spanish national to take part in public affairs by proxy (Article 23.1 SC) and the fundamental right to act as a representative (Article 23.2 SC). These two rights exclude any limitations to active or passive suffrage that are not directly provided for in the (organic) law, or that, despite being legally provided for, are deemed unnecessary or disproportionately restrictive.[21] Fundamental electoral rights are exercised through the procedures set forth in the LOREG.

19 M Pérez-Moneo and M Garrote De Marcos and E Pano Puey, *Derecho electoral español* (Juruá 2019) 241.
20 Judgment of the Constitutional Court 136/1999 (ECLI:ECLI:ES:TC:1999:136).
21 Judgment of the Constitutional Court 24/1989 (ECLI:ECLI:ES:TC:1989:24).

Firstly, this contains (Title I) a standard regulation for all elections, including elections within the autonomous regions (Additional Provision 1.2 LOREG). It likewise contains specific rules for the various types of 'general' elections, including elections for the Spanish Parliament (Title II), the European Parliament (Title VI) and local elections: municipal (Title III), 'Cabildos' in the Canary Islands (Title IV) and provincial Councils (Title V).

For the fifteen-day election campaign period, a full range of propaganda activities for the purpose of attracting votes is allowed (Article 50.4 LOREG) and public bodies are tasked to collaborate by providing spaces for staging electoral communication events (arts. 54.3, 55.1, 56.1, 57.1 LOREG). Free broadcasting time for political parties' electoral purposes is provided by public radio and television media (Article 64 LOREG, mainly), according to results obtained in previous elections. A code of conduct is likewise imposed on the private communication media. Thus, private fees for electoral publicity are capped (Article 58 LOREG) and private television channels are barred from reaching agreements with the political parties for broadcasting electoral publicity (Article 60.1 LOREG). In addition, during the last five days of the campaign before voting day, all public or private communication media are prohibited from publishing, disseminating or reproducing polls or surveys (Article 66.7 LOREG). The above prohibition is often criticised as being outdated and paternalistic.[22] It is the duty of the electoral commissions (Central Electoral Commission and those local to each area) to ensure that the electoral campaign unfolds in accordance with these rules.

The allocation of seats to each candidate (according to the votes obtained) is performed as per the electoral system, known as the D'Hondt system, consisting of a modified proportional system that favours candidacies receiving the most votes.

The proclamation of elected candidates may be challenged before the contentious-administrative jurisdiction by means of a special procedure (Articles 110 et seq., LOREG) and, having exhausted ordinary judicial channels, through an appeal for protection to the Constitutional Court (Article 114 LOREG).

Regarding the composition of the Congress of Deputies, or Spanish Parliament, Article 68.1 SC establishes a margin between the three hundred seats and the four hundred deputies, and dictates their determination by law. This is accomplished by the LOREG:Aarticle 162.1 LOREG indicates that 'Congress is made up of three hundred and fifty Deputies'. Suffrage is necessarily universal, free, direct and secret (Article 68.1 SC) and the LOREG allows postal ballots as well as voting in person.

Article 68.2 SC establishes that the province is the constituency. Each constituency must have a 'minimum initial representation', the remainder of seats being distributed 'in proportion with the population'. The initial minimum number is two Deputies per

22 M Pérez-Moneo and M Garrote De Marcos and E Pano Puey, *Derecho electoral español* (Juruá 2019) 241; F Velasco Caballero, Sistema electoral. in F Velasco Caballero (ed), *Tratado de Derecho Local* (Marcial Pons 2020).

province, and the rest are distributed following a proportional procedure on a highest remainder system (Articles 162.2 and 3 LOREG). Furthermore, an electoral barrier is imposed: to obtain seats, candidates must gain at least three per cent of valid votes cast within the corresponding constituency (Article 163 LOREG).

The current Law benefits the big parties (the Socialist Partie, PSOE, and the Popular Partie, PP) with national implementation and the parties that concentrate their representation in a certain territory (nationalist parties). Even in this normative context, have been able to appear the 'new parties' and of the parties considered populist, with differences: some of the parties of the ideological environment of Podemos (left), have only been presented in some territorial constituency; the new right-wing parties, however, have chosen to attempt their national implementation.

With regard to mandate duration, Article 68 SC indicates a duration of four years for members of Congress. However, the duration of a legislature is not fixed, being liable to early dissolution (Article 115 SC) either due to the organisation of early elections or the tabling of a vote of censure (Parliamentary loss of confidence) by at least one tenth of the Deputies (Article 113.2 SC). This is a constructive motion of censure and the proposal should, therefore, include a candidate for President of the Government (Article 113.2 SC). Such a proposal is voted only in the Congress of Deputies (not in the Senate) and absolute majority is required for it to prosper (Article 113.1 SC). Should Congress not approve the vote of no confidence, the signees may not table another during the same period of sessions (Article 113.4 SC). To date, four motions of censure have been tabled of which only one was approved (in 2008), leading to the replacement of President Mariano Rajoy by President Pedro Sánchez.

After holding general elections (for members of Parliament and senators to the Senate), Article 99 SC sets forth the procedure for the appointment of the President of the Government by means of securing a vote of absolute majority by the members of the Congress of Deputies (hence only one of the Chambers). The King, after consultation with the representatives appointed by the political groups represented in Parliament, and through the presiding officer of the house of Parliament, proposes a candidate for President of the Government. The candidate thus proposed presents before Congress the political programme for government he or she intends to set up, and asks for the confidence of the Chamber. If the Congress of Deputies, by absolute majority vote of its members, grants confidence to the proposed candidate, the King proceeds to appoint the latter as President. Should such a majority fail to be reached, the same proposal will be subjected to a fresh vote forty-eight hours after the first, and confidence will be deemed granted with a simple majority. In the event that, within two months of the first vote of appointment, no candidate has received Parliamentary confidence, the King will dissolve both Chambers and convene new elections with the approval of the presiding officer of the Congress of Deputies. On one single occasion, in the 11th Legislature, the candidate for President of the Government (Pedro Sánchez) failed to obtain the support of the

House in the first and in the second vote, leading to the dissolution of the Cortes Generales two months after the first vote. In the 12th Legislature (October 2016) a second vote was necessary to appoint Mariano Rajoy as President of the Government. Similarly, in the current 13th Legislature (July 2019) a second vote was needed to appoint Pedro Sánchez as President of the GovernmentFinally, he failed to obtain the support of the House also in the second vote and had to dissolve the Cortes Generales for voting again (November 2019). The results of the last general elections (November 2019) again shows a House with a very fragmented representation, with a high number of political parties with representation (sixteen political parties). For the first time since the 1978 constitutional regime was established, a coalition Government has been formed, with Pedro Sánchez as President of the Government. This Coalition Government has been constituted between the Socialist Party and Podemos, with the support in the investiture of eight political parties, some of them with an independence ideology, in addition to the abstention of Bilde (political party whose ideology of origin supports the actions of the terrorist organization ETA).

This shows how difficult it is currently to obtain enough support (in the General Courts) to be invested President of the Government. The traditional Spanish bipartisanship of the beginning of the democratic period, has been breaking down little by little. Currently, there is a strong fragmentation of the political forces and an important number of political parties obtain representation in the Congress. Many of them are populist and / or nationalist parties, which become decisive and essential forces to give enough support that the president of the Government needs. The result is the growing importance of these parties that have increased their ability to impose their political program.

3 Effectiveness of Legal Safeguards

The effectiveness of the unconditional supremacy of the Constitution, and its values, has been proved, initially, by means of the legal statement of public powers' obligation to comply with the decisions of the Constitutional Court (Article 87.1 LOTC: "All public authorities are obliged to comply with what the Constitutional Court decides"). This legal statement has been assumed uncontestedly by all political actors, in line with the recommendations of the Council of Europe's Venice Commission (Criteria for verification of the rule of law adopted by the Venice Commission at its 106th Plenary Session (Venice, 11-12 March 2016).

In addition to this, the architecture of the Spanish constitutional system establishes as a final safeguard for the Rule of Law, in the event of blatant violation by the autonomous authorities, the possible suspension of the political and administrative autonomy granted to (Article 155 SC) or the dissolution of the administrative bodies comprised in the local entities (Article 61 Law 7/1985).

Similarly to the corresponding procedures established in other national constitutions (Germany, Article 37 GG[23]; Italy, Article 126 IC[24]) and the TEU (Article 7), despite this being an eminently political decision, a number of procedural requirements are laid down to guarantee the non-arbitrary use of this mechanism. In both cases, the initiative lies with the state Council of Ministers, on recording gross infringement of constitutional or legal duties, or actions that seriously undermine the general interest within an Autonomous Regions or a local entity. Approval by absolute majority is required in the Senate, as the House of territorial representation, which will authorise the necessary measures to be adopted to enforce compliance by the Autonomous Region with said duties or the dissolution of the local entity's organs and call for elections within that entity.

However, in the face of the constant challenge posed by Catalan pro-independence populism, the procedural law has been expressly modified (Article 92 LOTC[25]) by means of enforcement proceedings[26] with the aim of verifying whether the public authorities have honoured their duty to observe the Constitutional Court's decisions, authorising the latter to declare null and void any decisions that are contrary to those given in the exercise of its jurisdiction. In addition, the Constitutional Court may adopt any other enforcement measures as deemed fit, establishing sufficient guarantees to safeguard for the bodies responsible for the acts or resolutions liable to be annulled. The aim of these proceedings is not to monitor the constitutionality of a legal text, but to preserve the effectiveness of the Constitutional Court's decisions, thus protecting its jurisdictional

---

23 Article 37 GG [Federal execution]: "(1) If a Land fails to comply with its obligations under this Basic Law or other federal laws, the Federal Government, with the consent of the Bundesrat, may take the necessary steps to compel the Land to comply with its duties. (2) For the purpose of implementing such coercive measures, the Federal Government or its representative shall have the right to issue instructions to all Länder and their authorities.".

24 Art. 126 Constitution of Italy states that "The Regional Council may be dissolved and the President of the Executive may be removed with a reasoned decree of the President of the Republic in the case of acts in contrast with the Constitution or grave violations of the law. The dissolution or removal may also be decided for reasons of national security. Such decree is adopted after consultation with a committee of Deputies and Senators for regional affairs which is set up in the manner established by a law of the Republic. The Regional Council may adopt a reasoned motion of no confidence against the President of the Executive that is undersigned by at least one-fifth of its members and adopted by roll call vote with an absolute majority of members. The motion may not be debated before three days have elapsed since its introduction. The adoption of a no confidence motion against a President of the Executive elected by universal and direct suffrage, and the removal, permanent inability, death or voluntary resignation of the President of the Executive entail the resignation of the Executive and the dissolution of the Council. The same effects are produced by the simultaneous resignation of the majority of the Council members".

25 In accordance with the wording given by Organic Law 15/2015.

26 Decision of the Constitutional Court 123/2017 (ECLI:ES:TC:2017:123A), which specifies that its purpose is to guarantee the defence of the institutional position of the Constitutional Court and the effectiveness of its judgments and resolutions, protecting its jurisdictional scope against any subsequent interference by a public authority that might undermine it.

scope against any ulterior intromission by public authorities seeking to undermine it. These proceedings also check whether any constituted authority should make a pronouncement contrary to the previous ruling and other findings of the Constitutional Court or attempts to undermine the legal or material effectiveness of the decisions taken therein.

4 Case Studies: Secessionist Movements and Identity Populism. The Cases of the Basque Country and Catalonia

Two of Spain's historic regions, governed by nationalist parties whose ideology advocates independence (Basque Country and Catalonia) have each made an attempt to reach such independence, albeit on a different route.

The Basque case was articulated on a Draft Political Statute for the Autonomous Region of Euskadi presented by the Basque Government and approved by the Basque Parliament in December 2004, the purpose of which was to reform the Organic Law on the Statute of Autonomy for the Basque Country. This proposal was received with 39 votes in favour (PNV, EA and EBB), and 35 against (PP and PSOE). Said Statute sought to reform the current Statute in force since 1979 through the mechanims established in Article 46 of the above-text, which expressly recognises the right to self-determination to the Basque people (comprising the Spanish regions of the Basque Country and Navarre, and the French region of Iparralde), which acknowledges Basque nationality to its citizens and the obligation of the State to respect and abstain from interfering in the new Statute. This Statute would furthermore not be subject to control by the Constitutional Court. Having submitted this proposal to the Congress of Deputies with the purpose of discussing the modification of the Organic Law on the Statute of Autonomy, the proposal was rejected in 2005 by 313 votes against (PSOE, PP, IU, CC and CHA), 29 in favour (PNV, ERC, CiU, EA, NaBai and BNG) and 2 abstentions (ICV). The rejection was accepted by the Basque political parties and constitutional order was maintained.

Here a nationalist party seeks to achieve independence, always with respect for the rule of law. There is no populist drive in its program beyond racial diversity. On the contrary, the Catalan case does incorporate populist elements, channeling and assimilating the protests derived from the movement against the austerity policies imposed by the central government.

The Catalan case features a manifest breach of the constitutional order. The criminal implications for the political actors involved have been determined by the Criminal Division of the Spanish Supreme Court.[27] In summary, the Catalan nationalist political parties (JxC, ERC and CUP) and the autonomous institutions, supported by two pro-independence associations (ANC and OMC) set out on the self-proclaimed 'proceso constituyente' with the purpose of creating an independent Catalan State in the form of a Republic. To this end, the Catalan Parliament enacted a number of laws whose aim was the unilateral segregation of Catalonia from the territory of Spain, by means of calling a referendum for a decision on this separation, for which the date was set on 1 October 2017. In concrete terms, on 6 September 2017, the Catalan Parliament, steamrolling the political rights of the parties in the opposition (CC, PSOE and UP) approved law 19/2017, known as the "referendum for self-determination", which established the result of said referendum as legally binding and that if, of the votes cast, the number of positive votes should be greater than the number of negative votes, the result would imply the independence of Catalonia, regardless of the total number of votes cast. Following the action of unconstitutionality before the Constitutional Court brought by the Central Government, it was agreed to suspend the law as a cautionary measure and to declare illegal the organisation and holding of the mentioned referendum. On 8 September 2017, the Autonomous Region of Catalonia enacted law 20/2017 known as "*ley sobre el proceso de transición jurídica y de fundación de la República*", in which the foundation for a new state was established, articulated as an illiberal democracy, envisaging the direct appointment of judicial authorities by the regional Government and the removal of those not supporting the cause for independence (existing judges are purged by forcing them to go through a new selection process); the absolute immunity of the President of the Government during his term of office is established; and an amnesty is approved for all prisoners for cases related to the independence process. The identity base of the Catalan secessionist movement has been overwhelmed by the populist component of the economic crisis of 2011, which has surpassed the Catalan political parties themselves, replacing them with social movements. In a dangerous feedback, the pro-independence political parties have directed the social response to the economic crisis towards the separation of Spain. The independence of one of the richest areas would allow the recovery of the welfare state for the middle and lower classes. But at the same time, social organisations have promoted and favoured the actions of these political parties, denying territorial solidarity and perceiving the rest of the State as a threat to their way of life. Even its voters, less than half of the electorate, are identified with the entire Catalan people, denying the identity and political rights of the non-separatists.

27 Judgment of Criminal Division of the Spanish Supreme Court, Octobre, 14th, 2019 (ECLI:ES:TS:2019:2997), have convicted the main politicians defendants of sedition, misuse of public funds and/or contempt of constitutional court. The Supreme Court clarifies that they are politicians who have committed crimes, not political prisoners.

Today the so-called Committees for the defence of the Republic, with a strong anti-system component, lead the social response, leaving the action of political parties in the background. Indeed, the pro-independence association ANC justifies the violent response as a measure that makes the conflict visible at the international level. At the same time, the President of the Generalitar justifies the commission of violent acts in the protests, considering that the citizens detained for such violent acts are political prisoners. Fortunately, the tumultuous and violent behaviour of the RDCs (burning of containers, fierce confrontations with the regional police and roadblocks) has been diluted to the point of disappearance.

Following the action of unconstitutionality before the Constitutional Court brought by the Central Government, the Constituional Court agreed to suspend the app lication of 20/2017 law as a cautionary measure. Having ascertained that the decreed cautionary suspension of the law was breached, the Constitutional Court called on the elected representatives to comply with their duty to enforce its resolutions. Despite this, however, the referendum was held without the necessary formal guarantees and with a non-existent electoral administration. Following this, at the session of the Catalan Parliament on 10 October 2017 a formal declaration of independence from Spain, in the form of a republic, was made by the President of the Autonomous Region (but immediately inviting the Parliament to suspend the effects of the mentioned declaration), ignoring the Constitutional Court's suspension of the plenary.

The Spanish State responded through two channels. On the one hand, by declaring the unconstitutionality of the Laws 'of disconnection' approved by the Catalan Parliament,[28] and of the declaration of independence made by the Catalan Parliament.[29] Nothing prevents the Catalan Parliament to promote, through a request or a proposal, the hypothetical reform of the Constitution, as the possibility of subjecting any matter of general interest to political discussion is inherent in the democratic parliamentary system. This said, however, laws cannot be adopted by the autonomous parliaments to amend the Constitution in deliberate disregard of the procedures expressly provided for that purpose in the Constitution, as parliamentary autonomy cannot serve as a pretext for an autonomous region's parliament to assume the power to violate the constitutional order on which its own authority rests. Parliamentary Assemblies, in their condition as constitutional authority, should ensure that their decisions are at all times compliant with the Constitution and all other

---

28 The Judgment of the Constitutional Court 114/2017 (ECLI:ES:TC:2017:114) declared unconstitutional and annulled regional Law 19/2017, while the Judgment of the Constitutional Court 121/2017 (ECLI:ES:TC:2017:121) declared unconstitutional and annulled the regional Decree of the Generalitat 140/2017, of 7 September, of complementary norms for the celebration of the referendum of self-determination. Finally, the Judgment of the Constitutional Court 144/2017 (ECLI:ES:TC:2017:144) declared unconstitutional and annuled regional Law 20/2017.

29 Judgment of the Constitutional Court 46/2018 (ECLI:EN:TC:2018:46). Judgment of the Constitutional Court 46/2018 (ECLI:ES:TC:2018:46).

components of the legal order (Article 9.1 SC). Furthermore, in no case may such decisions infringe the right of individuals representing politicians in non-nationalist groups to exercise their functions as representatives (Article 23 SC).

On the other hand, through the exceptional, restricted and punctual intervention of autonomous political and administrative bodies. Under the authority granted by the Senate (Article 155 SC), the national Government agreed to the cessation of the president of the *Generalitat de Cataluña*; the cessation of the vice-president and the ministers integrating the Governing Council of the *Generalitat de Cataluña*; the appointment of organs and authorities to give effect to the measures applied to the Catalonian Government and the Administration of the *Generalitat*; the adoption of a range of measures affecting the organization of the *Generalitat de Cataluña* and the removal from office of various of its members; and to convene elections to the Catalan Parliament and its dissolution. The Constitutional Court has deemed these measures to be strictly designed to re-conduct the autonomous community to its proper constitutional framework; they are partial measures, that guarantee the autonomous legal order and the organisation of the autonomous community. They were considered necessary, being viewed as proportionate in the interpretation adopted by the Government and the Senate, in that they meet the severity of the breach in the constitutional order conducted by the Autonomous Region. To date, these decisions are corroborated by the European Court of Human Rights, which has found the coercive measures adopted by the Constitutional Court to enforce the effectiveness of its decisions to be consistent with the Convention. Indeed, the European Court of Human Rights considers that a political party is entitled to run a campaign seeking a change of legislation on or a modification in the legal or constitutional structures of the State. This entitlement is subject to two conditions: 1) the means employed in this regard must be legal and democratic on all counts; 2) the proposed change must be compatible with the fundamental principles of democracy. Hence, the suspension of laws and actions taken by the Catalan Parliament should be viewed as a reasonable interference, necessary within a democratic society, particularly for maintaining public security, defending public order and safeguarding the rights and freedoms of others.[30]

All subsequent measures adopted by the Parliament of Catalonia aimed at reiterating the right to self-determination have been annulled by the Constitutional Court. Thus, for example, by agreement of the Bureau of the Parliament of Catalonia of 22 October 2019, the motion for a resolution "in response to the Supreme Court's ruling on the events of 1 October" was admitted for processing. The resolution states that "Parliament reiterates and will reiterate as many times as Members wish the defence of the right to self-determination and the claim to sovereignty of the people of Catalonia to decide their political future". The Constitutional Court considers that such a decision by the Bureau

30 Judgments of the European Court of Human Rights of 28 May 2019 (ECLI:EC:ECHR: 2019:0507DEC007514717) and 11 September 2018 (ECLI:EC:ECHR:2018:0911DEC007021917).

of the Regional Parliament is manifestly unconstitutional.[31] And that unconstitutionality does not derive from its content, but from the express will of the latter to dispense with constitutionally permissible procedures and channels for achieving its objectives. The election as MEPs of several members of the Catalan government who fled from Spanish justice, under both the option allowed by Spanish law and the decision[32] of the European Court of Justice, does not affect the illegalities committed. At this time, the Spanish justice system has made a request to the European Parliament and processed the corresponding European arrest warrants.

5 Case Studies: Populist Political Movements and the "New" Political Parties

Ever since the first democratic elections held in Spain (1977), the Spanish system has been characterised by a clear two-party system, with governments formed of the two major Spanish political parties; centre-left (*Partido Socialista Obrero Español*, PSOE) and centre-right (UCD, at the first elections and subsequently *Partido Popular*, PP, up to the present), in many cases obtaining absolute majority of deputies supporting the party in question. However, in recent years, the Spanish political system has undergone major changes and a clearly visible fragmentation, to the detriment of the previous two-party system fortitude, and with the emergence of new political parties (*Ciudadanos*, *Podemos* and other parties of a similar leaning, *Vox*, and previously also UPyD), as well as an increase in the representation within the Congress of Deputies of regionalist and pro-independence parties (*Coalición Canaria, Partido Nacionalista Vasco, Bildu, Esquerra Republicana de Cataluña, Junts pel Cat*, etc.).

The appearance in Spain of political forces self-qualified as 'populist' is very recent.[33] Of course, this does not mean that Spain's two leading political parties (PSOE and PP), at certain times, mainly when they are in the opposition, have refrained from employing a populist discourse to criticise their political adversary and mobilise their electorate or followers; however, neither of these parties has resorted to populism as a central feature in their political strategy.[34]

31 Decision of Constitutional Court of 28 January 2020 (ECLI:ES:TC:2020:12A).

32 Jugdment of the Court of Justice of the European Union of 19 December of 2019 (ECLI:EU:C:2019:1115).

33 In this sense, see: A Rivero, Populismo: ¿cómo destruir la democracia en nombre de la democracia? in A Rivero and J Zarzalejos and J Del Palacio (eds), *Geografía del populismo. Un viaje por el universo del populismo desde sus orígenes hasta Trump* (Tecnos 2017) 31.

34 M Álvarez Tardío, El populismo en la democracia española: del GIL a Podemos. in A Rivero and J Zarzalejos and J Del Palacio (eds), *Geografía del populismo. Un viaje por el universo del populismo desde sus orígenes hasta Trump* (Tecnos 2017) 260-261; that considers, from this idea, that the emergence of populism is not something recent in the Spanish democratic period. Specifically, the author refers to significant precedents, with a strong media presence and who obtain votes in the European elections. These are the cases of businessmen (with problems with judicial power): José María Ruiz Mateos and Jesús Gil y Gil, in addition to the case of the financier Mario Conde.

This late emergence of populism, when compared to the European context, together with the existence of left-wing populism, are the two distinguishing features of this phenomenon in Spain. In Spain, in contrast with the rest of Europe, first a left-wing populist political group appeared: Podemos, and other parties or groups ideologically and influentially within the same sphere, stemming from the 15-M popular movement (May 2011). And only at the last general, municipal and regional elections (2019) did a populist political group with its roots in the right/ultra-right wing (Vox).

The political party *Podemos* has appeared under different denominations and formations across the Spanish State. Today, it is called *Unidas Podemos* as a nationwide political party. This group became a clear political reference after the previous elections (general, regional and municipal), although in recent election processes (held between entre 2018 and 2019) it has suffered setbacks. In 2015 it stood for the national elections and obtained 20% of votes and 69 deputies. Similarly, at the local elections in 2015 this party achieved (under a different name) the government of major cities such as Madrid, Barcelona or Cádiz. Compared to their 69 deputies in the previous legislature, this party obtained 42 deputies at the general elections in May 2019. Likewise, at the municipal elections of 26 May 2019, they suffered a further drop in the number of votes obtained, leading to the loss of the government in Madrid, for instance, where they had governed for the last four years.

The political groups belonging to the *Podemos* party or its environment do not actually reject the European Union (although with major configuration differences and expressing strong criticism, without proposing separation)[35] and do not conceal (at least at the time of their appearance, though this is not so clear at present) their positive relations with Latin American leaders such as Rafael Correa, Evo Morales and, most especially, Hugo Chávez, political regimes they have been linked to in the past.[36]

This political group first emerged from the 2010 economic crisis and in the wake of the '15-M movement' (2011). On 15 May 2011 a demonstration took place at Plaza del Sol, in Madrid, that began as a social and citizens' movement. Over the following days the demonstrators remained camped on the streets and public squares (especially Madrid's Plaza del Sol), with the communication media out in force. Stated briefly, we can say that this movement was intended to represent the victims of the economic crisis, 'the outraged': the unemployed, pensioners, immigrants, the homeless or evicted, civil servants whose salaries were cut, etc. Typically, populism is a term associated with emotions such as indignation, frustration, suffering or resentment.[37]

35 J-W Müller, *What is populism?* (University of Pennsylvania Press 2016) 1; the author states that Podemos shows an opposition to EU austerity policies in response to the Eurocrisis.

36 ibid 1; that affirms the identification of Podemos with these Latin American populist leaders.

37 ibid 1.

In sum, it began as a social movement that later solidified as a political party springing up in the University environment (the Faculty of Political Science and Sociology, Universidad Complutense de Madrid).[38]

Their ideological foundations are rooted in extreme left-wing discourse, anticapitalistic in nature and contrary to liberal democracy, and include populist elements, namely the political system as a problem, financial adjustments as a consequence of the economic crisis, politics falling into disrepute for being ineffective or corrupt, the political 'caste' failing to represent a virtuous population, etc..[39] An appeal is made to the 'real' people, the 'real' popular will, over and above representative democracy,[40] sometimes with internal decision-taking on the basis of assembly votes or through calls to clearly led consultations. A further defining trait is the presence of hyper-leadership by these parties' leaders; in particular, by Pablo Iglesias, whose leadership has been cultivated and intensified over time, while alternative figures or adversaries within the party disappeared. In sum, these groups adopt a discourse centred on political and moral regeneration in the face of a democracy that is described as false or ailing.[41]

The emergence of Vox on the Spanish political scene has been quite a different matter. It has brought about the fragmentation of the monolithic dominance, up to now, of the Spanish right-wing by Partido Popular, which is finding its far-right votes flocking to Vox while, at the same time, Ciudadanos is taking away its votes from the centre or centre-right.

---

38 More information in: A Rivero, Antipolítica y populismo: del "no nos representan" a "democracia real ya". in A Rivero and J Zarzalejos and J Del Palacio (eds), *Geografía del populismo. Un viaje por el universo del populismo desde sus orígenes hasta Trump* (Tecnos 2017) 42; About the university roots of Podemos, see: J López Alós, 'El debate sobre el populismo en España (2014-2017). Un estado de la cuestión' [2017] 7 *Pensamiento al margen* 149.

39 Similar reasons and more in: A Rivero, Populismo: ¿cómo destruir la democracia en nombre de la democracia? in A Rivero and J Zarzalejos and J Del Palacio (eds), *Geografía del populismo. Un viaje por el universo del populismo desde sus orígenes hasta Trump* (Tecnos 2017) 31; M Álvarez Tardío, El populismo en la democracia española: del GIL a Podemos. in A Rivero and J Zarzalejos and J Del Palacio (eds), *Geografía del populismo. Un viaje por el universo del populismo desde sus orígenes hasta Trump* (Tecnos 2017) 263-264 and more information in 266-269. Also see: C Rovira Kaltwasser and C Sandoval, 'Populismo inclusionario en España: analizando la evolución del discurso político de Podemos' [2017] Congreso Latinoamericano de Ciencia Política; J-W Müller, *What is populism?* (University of Pennsylvania Press 2016) 2-3 argues that it is necessary but not sufficient condicition to be critical of elites in order to count as a populist. Otherwise, anyone criticizing the status quo would by definition be a populist. In addition, populist are always antipluralist. Populist clam that they, and they alone, represent the people.

40 ibid. Also see: S Gherghina, *Contemporary Populism: a controversial concept and its diverse forms* (Cambridge Scholars Publishing 2013) 67.

41 A Rivero and J Zarzalejos and J Del Palacio, ¿Cómo se ha de tratar el populismo en democracia. in A Rivero and J Zarzalejos and J Del Palacio (eds), *Geografía del populismo. Un viaje por el universo del populismo desde sus orígenes hasta Trump* (Tecnos 2017) 395-396, make these claims, in general, in relation to populisms. This feature common to the populist phenomenon is exposed by S Gherghina, *Contemporary Populism: a controversial concept and its diverse forms* (Cambridge Scholars Publishing 2013) 6-7; J-W Müller, *What is populism?* (University of Pennsylvania Press 2016) 1 also notes that "anti-system" is a term regularly used as a synonym for populism.

Despite Vox having gained considerable media and political protagonism over recent months, this political group is not new but has been in existence for more than five years (December 2013) with almost no electoral support. Its political elite and leadership (and its grassroots) united with a substantial splinter group from Partido Popular, its rise and current strength have played a decisive role in the Catalan pro-independence movement. Vox, in its electoral programme for the general elections in April 2019, maintained that the Spanish Constitution has been 'ignored and scorned' and, therefore, proposed 100 measures designed to recover what the party deems to be 'the living Spain'. In its endeavour to strengthen the Spanish State, the party plans to eliminate or reduce the Autonomous Regions and to 'bestow maximum protection' to national symbols (the national flag, fundamentally, the army and the security forces and corps of the State). It is therefore not a party with an 'anti-system' creed or that seeks to destroy the legal and political order (which could call into question the use of the populist label).[42] To the contrary, they are ardent supporters of the Spanish Constitution of 1978 and all it represents.

In addition to the above, this party also plays a key role in Partido Popular's in-house crisis and its image as a weak party that is unable to address its severe internal problems or those of the country (corruption, unemployment, immigration, the 'Catalan problem', or the integrity of Spain). Further elements to bear in mind in their view are the defence of the traditional family (as opposed to homosexual marriage), of cultural and religious traditions (bullfights, Easter processions and religious events), lower taxation, derogation of the law against gender violence and women's quota policies ('gender ideology'), tougher treatment of illegal immigrants (encouraging immigration from American countries and reducing Muslim immigration), fighting Islamic fundamentalism, protection for hunting activities, extension of the right to carry arms, etc.

Although failing to reach their own (perhaps somewhat unrealistic) expectations, Vox obtained 24 deputies in the general elections in May 2019, clearly a successful achievement for a political force making its debut in national parliamentary representation. And, most importantly, it has become a decisive force in supporting the formation of governments under right-wing leadership. This has already occurred in the Autonomous Region of Andalusia (elections on 2 December 2018), governed for the first time in democracy by the right (Partido Popular) with the support of Ciudadanos, whose inauguration was possible only thanks to the support received from Vox. The same is being observed in other regions and municipalities (Comunidad y Ayuntamiento de Madrid, Región de Murcia, Comunidad de Castilla y León), following the local and regional elections on 26 May 2019, although they have raised more difficulties and set higher demands for their votes to facilitate right-wing parties to form governments.

---

42 S Gherghina, *Contemporary Populism: a controversial concept and its diverse forms* (Cambridge Scholars Publishing 2013) 6-7.

6 Conclusion

The Spanish Constitution does not establish a militant democracy, with ideological limitations. The rule of law principle allows dissent from constitutional purposes and values, always respecting the formal channels established by the Constitution itself. The broad protection provided by the Constitution and legislation to the creation and existence of political parties, as well as the electoral system, have allowed and facilitated the creation of political parties with a wide ideological diversity and that obtain representatives in democratic institutions. There are two elements of tension that Spanish democracy currently faces, derived from the populisms that are on the rise. On the one hand, the Catalan secessionist challenge. The identity base of the secessionist movement has been overwhelmed by the populist component of the economic crisis of 2011, which has surpassed the Catalan political parties themselves, replacing them with social movements that deny the rights of that part of the population that does not share their ideology. Two expressions, "the democratic mandate of the ballot boxes" and "the streets will always be ours", agglutinate their ideology. On the other hand, the incorporation into the national political space of two new parties, located on both sides of the political spectrum, with strong populist tendencies that reject to a greater or lesser extent the Constitutional model established by the so-called "political transition of 1978".

In the final balance, it can be stated that although the right-wing/left-wing dichotomy has not turned out to be a useful guide in addressing an analysis of populism, owing to the ease with which populism can attract voters who are in diametrical opposition,[43] in Spain this phenomenon has appeared in parties at the extreme poles of the ideological spectrum. In both cases they are stigmatised and both are accused of being degenerate forms of democracy, as a pathology requiring radical resection, or as a crisis in democracy in which populism is seen as a form of protest.[44]

It is early still to assess the role played – or that will be played – by right-wing populism in Spain, as it is only a few months since it has begun to reach public institutions. Our only close reference (although quite distant from an ideological point of view) are the consequences of Podemos' accession to the institutions and, indeed, to the government. Despite their initial approach (on maximum values, rejecting the liberal system and capitalism, rejecting the Spanish democratic transition and the Constitution, advocating an assembly-based democracy...) and the catastrophist accounts of their political adversaries, and frequently being called 'anti-system', to this day they have neither departed from the system nor caused the destruction of the democratic institutions (at the locations where they have governed). Currently (2020), Podemos even be part of the first coalition Government that has been formed since the approval

43 ibid 5.

44 ibid 6-7.

of the Spanish Constitution of 1978, with two Vice Presidents and Ministers of Podemos integrated into the Spanish Government. In like manner, Vox has given its support to the formation of local and autonomous governments by Partido Popular, displaying a clear willingness to enter the institutions and take up decision-making positions.

Although it would certainly be an error to assume that leaders who come to power through the institutions can neither modify nor destroy those same institutions (even when this is precisely what they have proclaimed they will do),[45] these political groups, with their idiosyncrasies and profiles of their own, have adapted and accepted the rules of the game within the democratic system configured by the Spanish Constitution. Time will tell which role they will play in the democratic institutions.

It is equally hard to forecast whether these parties will remain stable over time. These are often phenomena with a meteoric rise but little long-term development.[46]

The secessionist populist movements deserve a different analysis, especially those that are inserted into Catalan secessionism with features of a national-populist and segregationist movement and with a strong component of media and social propaganda (national and international). In the first place, we can affirm that this movement also includes the whole ideological spectrum: from the most radical, anti-capitalist left to elements of the bourgeois right, even with a segregationist, xenophobic and racist discourse (written and published by the current President of Catalonia).[47]

In the previous paragraphs we have stated that populist parties at the national level, even when they question the structural principles of the constitutional system, assume the rules of the game of the democratic system configured by the Spanish Constitution for its hypothetical reform: they have had a relatively loyal behaviour with the system, even where they have acceded to the corresponding government. We cannot say the same in the case of the Catalan independence nationalist movement: from the Catalan public institutions themselves and with the support of a strong social movement, they have posed a challenge to the Spanish State, to the current legal system and to the Spanish Constitution, with a clearly rupturist vocation. The result is the convocation of an illegal referendum, without any democratic guarantee, the proclamation of the independence of Catalonia. All this has culminated, in October 2019, with a criminal conviction of the

45 Literally: T Sneyder, *Sobre la tiranía. Veinte lecciones que aprender del siglo XX* (Galaxia Gutenberg 2017) 24.

46 S Gherghina, *Contemporary Populism: a controversial concept and its diverse forms* (Cambridge Scholars Publishing 2013) 5.

47 According to Quim Torra, the current President of Catalonia, a "non-independence Catalanist" is not acceptable. In March 2012 he published a paper entitled "The language and the beasts" in which he identifies Catalans who do not speak Catalan with beasts (quote): "Now you look at your country and see the beasts speak again. But they are of a different kind. Scavengers, snakes, hyenas. Beasts with human form, that distill hatred (...). "They are here, among us" (...) "they are repulsed by any expression of Catalanity. It is a sick phobia. There is something Freudian about these beasts. Or a little shudder in their DNA chain. Poor individuals!".

main leaders (political and social) of the Catalan independence movement for crimes of sedition and embezzlement of public funds.

Another differentiating feature of this phenomenon, as opposed to what has been said in relation to the new national populist parties, is that, in the case of Catalan nationalism, it does not seem that we are dealing with an ephemeral movement. On the contrary, it has a broad and solid popular implantation, around 43 % of the population, according to data published by the autonomous government. It is true that it may increase in the future, above all due to the control of the educational system and the public media. It has recently incorporated a progressive radicalization and violence. Frequently, its political leaders, in coordination with social leaders, call for civil disobedience, appealing to the real will of an abstract subject, the Catalan people, over and above the current constitutional system, and ignoring dissidents, around 48% of the population, who are considered non-authentic Catalans. The strong response of the Spanish state, together with the clear indication that this is an internal matter both by the authorities of the European Union and the other Member States, seems to have stopped the attempts at unilateral break-up by the Catalonian pro-independence parties. Perhaps this is best appreciated in the position adopted by ERC in relation to the new government. Its indirect support (abstention) has enabled the first coalition government in Spain under the current constitutional regime. The counterpart sought is to articulate an institutional dialogue, within the constitutional framework.

Faced up with this serious challenge, the Spanish constitutional system has been severely strained. The legal and political instruments of the rule of law have been formally effective in dealing with a threat that comes from the (Catalan) public institutions themselves, which show institutional disloyalty and which have made opposition and disobedience to the Spanish state and their flag. But they have not resolved the underlying political and social problem.

The United Kingdom and Populism

Alison L Young[*]

1 Introduction

It is both true and almost trite to conclude that the rise of populism in the UK is connected to Brexit and, in particular, the referendum on the UK's continued membership of the EU. On 23 June 2016, 51.9% of those participating voted to leave the EU and 48.1% voted to remain. Referendums in the UK require legislation. The European Union Referendum Act 2015, which empowered the holding of the Brexit referendum, did not provide a legally binding obligation on the Government to implement the referendum outcome. Consequently, the referendum outcome was only 'politically advisory'.[1] Nevertheless, it has become the touchstone of UK politics. Although the then Prime Minister, David Cameron, and most of the members of the Government, campaigned to remain in the EU, the Government was quick to adopt the outcome of the referendum. The people had spoken. They had spoken clearly and definitively on one specific issue, where the turn-out for the referendum had been particularly high when compared with the turn-out for general elections. Westminster was also quick to adopt the outcome of the referendum in a series of motions in the House of Commons.[2] Not only had the people spoken, but they had spoken with one voice. As such, the Government saw itself as under a mandate to implement the will of the people, with the will of the people being the desire to leave the EU as expressed in the outcome of the referendum.

In addition to being silent as to any legal obligation to be imposed on the executive following the referendum, the 2015 Act also did not expressly provide the Government with a legal power to inform the European Council of the UK's intention to leave the EU. This silence gave rise to the so-called 'constitutional case of the century', *Miller,* which concluded that the Prime Minister did not have a prerogative power to notify the European Council of the UK's intention to leave the EU, thus triggering the process

---

* Alison L Young, Sir David Williams Professor of Public Law, University of Cambridge, and Fellow of Robinson College, Cambridge. This chapter draws upon the arguments made in two prior publications: AL Young, 'Populism and the UK Constitution' (2018) 71(1) Current Legal Problems 17; AL Young, 'Populism and Parliamentary Sovereignty: The Goldsworthy Solution' in L Burton Craven and P Emerton and D Smith (eds), *Law under a Democratic Constitution: Essays in Honour of Jeffrey Goldsworthy* (Hart 2019) 175.

1 *R (Miller) v Secretary of State for Exiting the European Union* [2017] UKSC 5, [2017] 2 WLR 583.

2 See, in particular, the Opposition Day motions: HC Deb 12 October 2016, vol 618, cols 323-415; HC Deb 7 December 2016, vol 618, cols 220-336.

found in Article 50 TEU in order to facilitate the UK's withdrawal from the EU Treaties.[3] The reaction to the *Miller* decision provides two further illustrations of the equation of the will of the people with the outcome of the referendum, and the political force of this equation.

First is the criticism of the members of the judiciary. The three members of the first instance court – technically a decision of the Divisional Court, despite being populated by three members of the bench, all of whom were distinguished members of the Court of Appeal – were infamously characterised by one newspaper as 'Enemies of the People'.[4] The members of the Supreme Court were also criticised for denying the democratic will of the people, although this criticism was not worded as strongly. Second, the consequence of the *Miller* decision was that the UK Parliament would need to enact legislation. Lord Carnwath noted in his judgment that this would put Parliament in a position where it could place conditions on the exercise of this power. Nevertheless, no conditions materialised in the European Union (Notification of Withdrawal) Act 2017.[5] Section 1 of the Act merely states that '[t]he Prime Minister may notify, under Article 50 (2) of the Treaty on European Union, the United Kingdom's intention to withdraw from the EU'. Duly empowered, the Prime Minister wrote to Donald Tusk on 29 March 2017, thereby notifying the European Council of the UK's intention to withdraw from the European Union.

It is almost as difficult to predict if, and if so when, the UK will leave the EU as it is to determine the UK's future relationship with the EU. The original intention was that the UK would leave the EU at 11pm on 29 March 2019. However, following the inability to obtain a vote in favour of the Withdrawal Agreement and the Framework for the Future Relationship with the European Union in the House of Commons – as required by section 13 of the European Union (Withdrawal) Act 2018 – the UK sought, and obtained, an extension to the two year period set out in Article 50 TEU. The first extension, granted by a decision of the European Council on 22 March 2019, allowed for an extension to 22 May 2019 should the House of Commons approve the Withdrawal Agreement by 29 March 2019.[6] Failing that, the Council was only prepared to grant an extension until 12 April 2019. Having failed to obtain a vote in favour of the Withdrawal Agreement by 29 March, the UK then sought, and was granted, a further extension to the Article 50 period. The Council decision of 10 April 2019 provides for an

3 *R (Miller) v Secretary of State for Exiting the European Union* [2017] UKSC 5, [2017] 2 WLR 583.

4 J Slack, 'Enemies of the people: Fury over 'out of touch' judges who have 'declared war on democracy' by defying 17.4m Brexit voters and who could trigger constitutional crisis' *Daily Mail* (3 November 2016) https://www.dailymail.co.uk/news/article-3903436/Enemies-people-Fury-touch-judges-defied-17-4m-Brexit-voters-trigger-constitutional-crisis.html accessed 16 November 2019.

5 European Union (Notification of Withdrawal) Act 2017.

6 European Council Decision taken in agreement with the United Kingdom, extending the period under Article 50(3) TEU (EUCO XT 20006/19, BXT 26, 22 March 2019) https://data.consilium.europa.eu/doc/document/XT-20006-2019-INIT/en/pdf accessed 19 November 2019.

extension for as long as is necessary to ratify the Withdrawal Agreement, with a final deadline of 31 October 2019.[7] Following the failure to obtain the consent of the House of Commons for the Withdrawal Agreement, Theresa May resigned as leader of the Conservative Party on 7 June 2019. After winning the Conservative Party leadership contest, Boris Johnson assumed the office of Prime Minister on 24 July 2019. He successfully negotiated a new Withdrawal Agreement, most notably with a modification to the Northern Ireland backstop in order to avoid a hard border in Northern Ireland.

Boris Johnson made it clear that he was prepared for the UK to leave on the 31 October with no deal. However, following the enactment of the European Union (Withdrawal) (No 2) Act 2019, this did not take place. Rather, given that the House of Commons failed to vote in favour of the Withdrawal Agreement, or in favour of leaving the EU with no deal by 19 October 2019, Boris Johnson was required by the 2019 Act to seek a further extension of Article 50 until 31 January 2020. The Prime Minister complied with this obligation. However, he made it clear that the request for an extension was not Government policy and that it was still the intention of the Government to leave on 31 October 2019. However, this did not take place, following the defeat of the programme motion of the European Union (Withdrawal Agreement) Bill 2019 – the legislation designed to implement the Withdrawal Agreement into English law in order to fulfil the requirements of section 13 of the European Union (Withdrawal) Act 2018 for the ratification of the Withdrawal Agreement. This prompted Boris Johnson to seek an early parliamentary general election under the provisions of the Fixed Term Parliaments Act 2011. However, having failed to obtain the necessary votes of two thirds of all MPs, the Prime Minister initiated legislation to hold an early parliamentary general election.

Following the enactment of the Early Parliamentary General Election Act 2019, a general election was held on 12 December 2019. This election produced a stronger Conservative majority Government. Consequently, at the time of writing, it seems likely that the UK will leave the EU under the terms of the new Withdrawal Agreement. It remains to be seen whether the UK will be able to negotiate a future trade agreement with the EU by the end of the implementation period. It is still possible that the UK could effectively leave the EU with no trade agreement at the end of the implementation period on 31 December 2020.

It is undeniable that the referendum and the Brexit process has had an impact on the UK constitution. Indeed, there have been arguments that the whole process may be the catalyst that prompts the UK to change from a system of parliamentary sovereignty to one of constitutional sovereignty, with the UK adopting a codified Constitution that has a

---

7 European Council Decision taken in agreement with the United Kingdom extending the period under Article 50(3) TEU (EUCO XT20013/19, BXT 38, 11 April 2019) https://data.consilium.europa.eu/doc/document/XT-20013-2019-INIT/en/pdf accessed 19 November 2019.

higher status than ordinary legislation.[8] However, it would be wrong to see populism in the UK as only occurring due to our recent use of referendums, or because of Brexit alone. The UK has held other referendums which have not had the same effect of fuelling populism in the same manner as the Brexit referendum. Indeed, it can be argued that the referendum on Scottish Independence in 2014 facilitated deliberative democracy, allowing for fair and rational debate rather than witnessing a move from political argument to emotionally charged debates. Moreover, the Brexit referendum acted as a catalyst for populism because of a convergence of two possible pressure points that may generate populist movements. First, it concerned a boundary issue, determining whether the UK wished to identify itself as sharing sovereignty with the EU, or as a separate and distinct state that was no longer wishing to share sovereignty through its membership of the EU. This is amply illustrated by the referendum campaign with its focus on 'taking back control' from the EU. Second, it came at a time of austerity, when there were both perceived and real failures of representative democracy, particularly amongst communities living in more deprived areas who felt out of touch with the Westminster Parliament.

Nevertheless, the on – going Brexit saga provides a useful lesson for the UK constitution, as well as illustrating more generally how constitutions may be vulnerable to populist movements. The Brexit referendum, in combination with other circumstances, has placed pressure on the assumptions on which the UK constitution is based, and on weaknesses in the UK's constitutional and political arrangements. It illustrates how the self-correcting mechanisms which may ensure that populism remains a temporary as opposed to a permanent state of affairs may fail. Moreover, it explains how, given the wrong combination of circumstances, the UK constitution may become a catalyst for populism. This chapter will first explain the relationship between Brexit, referendums and populism. It will then explain how this combination of circumstances undermined the self-correcting mechanisms that may prevent populist movements from obtaining or maintaining political power, as well as explaining how this combination meant the UK constitution became a catalyst for populist movements. It will conclude by suggesting possible reforms to help shore up the UK constitution from populism.

2 Brexit, Referendums and Populism

It is hard to deny that the Brexit referendum played a role in the perceived move towards populism in the UK. Nor is it unsurprising that this is the case. Historically, referendums have not played a role in the UK constitution. Moreover, earlier arguments for their adoption focused on their role as a means of facilitating a veto of the people over

8 V Bogdanor, *Beyond Brexit: Towards a British Constitution* (Bloomsbury 2019).

proposed constitutional reforms, rather than as a trigger for constitutional reform.[9] Despite their growing use in the UK constitution, referendums still continue to be criticised due to their potential to undermine as opposed to facilitate deliberative democracy.[10] More specifically, referendums can be used by populist movements.

Populism is characterised, inter alia, by the way in which it homogenises the will of the people, pitching this will of the people against the will of political elites.[11] A referendum can provide an effective tool through which to create a homogenised will of the people. The electorate are asked to form an opinion on one issue, channelling their will into either the acceptance or the rejection of a particular option. Should the UK leave or remain in the EU? Although there may be a range of possible arguments in favour of or against Brexit, these arguments are channelled into one outcome – leave or remain. The outcome of the referendum becomes the will of the people as expressed on this one issue, homogenising a range of views into one, followed by defining the will of the people as the winning side. If more people vote leave then remain, then the will of the people becomes the will to leave the EU. Referendums can also fuel populism by presenting complex ideas as a simple choice. This over-simplification, in turn, can lead to the replacement of deliberative democratic debate with emotional responses. This can enable charismatic leaders to further homogenise the will of the people, suppressing democratic deliberation. Once the choice is made, any voice of opposition can be silenced due to its opposition to the will of the people as expressed in the referendum outcome.

However, whilst this may be true of referendums, it is not true of all referendums. The same criticism is not made, for example, as regards the Scottish independence referendum, held on 18 September 2014.[12] Exploring the differences between these two referendums can provide further insight into why the Brexit referendum led to populist movements that were not as present in the Scottish independence referendum. Referendums prioritise votes over voices.[13] In other words, they tend to prioritise majoritarianism over deliberation. It is this tendency that may make them prone to being used by populist movements. However, although referendums have this tendency, they can be structured in a manner that facilitates deliberative democracy. The contrast

9 Most pertinently as regards the UK Constitution, see: AV Dicey, *An Introduction to the Study of the Law of the Constitution* (8th edn, Macmillan 1915); AV Dicey, 'Democracy in Switzerland' [1890] 171 *Edinburgh Law Review* 113; AV Dicey, 'Ought the Referendum to be Introduced into England?' [1890] 57 *Contemporary Review* 489.

10 See, for example: S Tierney, *Constitutional Referendums: The Theory and Practice of Republican Deliberation* (Oxford University Press 2012); L LeDuc, 'Referendums and deliberative democracy' [2015] 38 *Electoral Studies* 139; R Levy, 'Deliberative Voting': Realising Constitutional Referendum Democracy' [2013] *Public Law* 555; E Daly, 'A republican defence of the constitutional referendum' [2015] 35(1) *Legal Studies* 30.

11 See: J-W Müller, *What is Populism?* (University of Pennsylvania Press 2017).

12 See: S Tierney, 'Popular Constitutional Amendment: Referendums and Constitutional Change in Canada and the United Kingdom' [2015] 41(1) *Queen's Law Journal* 41.

13 L LeDuc, 'Referendums and deliberative democracy' [2015] 38 *Electoral Studies*.

between the Brexit referendum and the Scottish independence referendum would tend to suggest that, the more measures are in place to facilitate deliberative democracy, the less likely it is that referendums will give rise to populism.

This argument is made most clearly by Stephen Tierney.[14] Tierney argues that there are three main criticisms of referendums which detract from their ability to facilitate deliberative democracy: elite control; deliberative deficit and the majoritarian danger. Each of these criticisms could provide a means of facilitating populism. Elite control occurs when those in power are able to select when to use a referendum, and to dictate the question. A populist government in power could use referendums as a tool to further homogenise the will of the people, cutting out democratic debate and thus making it easier for a populist movement to collapse into an authoritarian regime. LeDuc refers to this as the intrusion of politics, where political groups can manipulate referendums so they become popularity contests, rather than a vote on the issues raised in the referendum.[15] Second, through favouring votes over voices, referendums can give rise to a democratic deficit. Although referendums can be a means of engaging with the people and facilitating deliberative democracy, they can also be used to undermine deliberation, replacing democratic deliberation with emotive responses to divisive issues. Moreover, referendums require a yes or no response. They may fail to provide a means of compromise and promote divisiveness. Again, this may make them an effective tool for populism. Finally, referendums give rise to the majoritarian danger. They may fail to provide a means to facilitate minority voices, helping to form a 'will of the people' that is expressed as conclusive, even if this is only backed by a relatively small majority.

Tierney's analysis demonstrates how the Scottish Independence referendum was structured in a manner that minimised these dangers, helping the referendum to facilitate deliberative democracy. First, issues arose as to whether Scotland had the power to hold a referendum on independence, or whether this was a constitutional matter that would be reserved to Westminster. Rather than enacting an Act of the Scottish Parliament to hold a referendum, and facing a potential legal challenge, the Scottish Government sought a specific transfer of power to hold the referendum from the UK Government under section 30 of the Scotland Act 1998.[16] This meant that conditions of the referendum were not determined solely by the Scottish Government or by the Westminster Government, but through negotiation between the two Governments. These negotiations made it harder for one elite to take control of the

---

14 S Tierney, The Scottish Independence Referendum: A Model of Good Practice in Direct Democracy? in A McHarg and others (eds), *The Scottish Independence Referendum: Constitutional and Political Implications* (Oxford University Press 2016).

15 L LeDuc, 'Referendums and deliberative democracy' [2015] 38 *Electoral Studies*.

16 'Agreement between the United Kingdom Government and the Scottish Government on a referendum on independence for Scotland' (Agreement, 15 October 2012) https://webarchive.nationalarchives.gov.uk/20130102230945/http://www.number10.gov.uk/wp-content/uploads/2012/10/Agreement-final-for-signing.pdf accessed 17 November 2019.

terms and conditions of the referendum so as to potentially skew the result in favour of the outcome desired by the elites.

A different story arises when we examine the Brexit referendum. Prior to the 2015 referendum, the UK was governed by a coalition composed of the Conservative Party and the Liberal Democrats, with David Cameron, the then leader of the Conservative Party, as the Prime Minister and Nick Clegg, the then leader of the Liberal Democrats, as the Deputy Prime Minister. During the coalition, tensions continued to rise in the Conservative Party concerning the UK's continued membership of the EU. Whilst some factions in the Conservative Party were strongly in favour of remaining in Europe, others were deeply distrustful of the EU and wished to leave. Moreover, there was growing support for UKIP – the United Kingdom Independence Party – whose main aim was to seek the UK's exit from the EU. This was evident in their rise in support in the 2014 European Parliament election. A lot of these concerns – valid or otherwise – stemmed from fears over immigration. Particularly in areas of the UK affected by adversity, there were concerns that too many immigrants from other EU countries were using scarce social services, placing so much pressure on these services that UK citizens were unable to have access.[17]

In the face of these divisions in the Conservative Party, and growing support for UKIP, the Conservative Party manifesto included a promise to hold a referendum on the UK's continued membership of the EU.[18] Following the success of the Conservative Party in the 2015 general election, David Cameron, returning as Prime Minister of a Conservative government, announced that measures would be put in place to hold a Referendum on EU membership. The elites in power used the referendum, at least in part, for political purposes, both to fend off a perceived challenge from an emerging political party and to strengthen the Conservative Party by providing a definitive resolution to an issue which threatened to split the party.

The referendum was regulated by the European Union Referendum Act 2015. This Act enabled the holding of the referendum, set the question[19] and its possible responses,[20] in addition to determining the franchise.[21] The Act also empowered Ministers to enact regulations regarding the regulation of the referendum,[22] and provided information as to the regulation of the campaign and financial controls over

17 See the manifesto of UKIP: UKIP, 'Believe in Britain: UKIP manifesto 2015' (UKIP, 2015) https://d3n8a8pro7vhmx.cloudfront.net/ukipdev/pages/1103/attachments/original/1429295050/UKIPManifesto2015.pdf?1429295050 accessed 17 November 2019.

18 Conservatives, '2015 Conservative Party Manifesto' (*Conservatives*, 2015) https://www.conservatives.com/manifesto2015 accessed 17 November 2019.

19 European Union Referendum Act 2015, s 1(4).

20 European Union Referendum Act 2015, s 1(5).

21 European Union Referendum Act 2015, s 2.

22 European Union Referendum Act 2015, s 4.

campaign expenditure.[23] As discussed above, it failed to provide any legal obligation on the Government to implement the outcome of the referendum.

The enactment of legislation may appear to provide a means of controlling elite-dominance of referendums, given that legislation requires the consent of the House of Commons, the House of Lords, and royal assent. However, given the dominance of the law-making process by the Government, even when it has a relatively small majority, it is often the case that the legislature can place little restraint on the will of the Government. This may make it difficult to ensure the maintenance of constitutional principles such that referendums are designed in a manner that can facilitate deliberative democracy. Again, the enactment of the European Union Referendum Act 2015 provides an illustration of these difficulties. Alex Salmond had proposed an amendment to require a 'quad lock' on the referendum outcome during the second reading of the Bill in the House of Commons. The quad lock would have required a majority vote to be determined not just in terms of whether more votes were cast for leave or remain, but would also require that this outcome represented a majority of the component nation states.[24] His amendment failed. Moreover, debate on the amendment was curtailed as time allocated for debate was limited by the Government, and the amendment was discussed in tandem with other amendments.[25] The amendment regarding the quad lock was heard at the same time as the amendments regarding the extension of the franchise to 16- and 17-year olds in addition to the inclusion of EU nationals.[26] The stronger the dominance of the Government, the easier it is for referendums to be used as a tool for the Government, who may enact conditions for referendums which favour the outcome the Government desires. This leaves referendums vulnerable to populism, either when a Government is enticed by a populist movement or a populist party is in Government. The Brexit referendum may well be regarded as the former.

Tierney argues that there is evidence that the Scottish Independence Referendum also helped to overcome the deliberative deficit of referendums, as there is evidence of citizen engagement surrounding the referendum. This was also added to by the inclusion of 16- and 17-year olds in the referendum – a further proposed amendment that was rejected during the enactment of the European Union Referendum Act 2015. The inclusion of 16- and 17-year olds meant that issues concerning Scottish independence and its consequences were debated in schools, furthering deliberative democracy. The Scottish Government also produced detailed White Papers setting out the consequences of independence. There was also evidence of high turn-out for the Independence Referendum.

23 European Union Referendum Act 2015, schedule 1.

24 HC Deb 16 June 2015, vol 597, col 190; Similar arguments were made by Ms Ahmed-Sheikh: HC Deb 16 June 2015, vol 597, cols 260-261.

25 European Union Referendum Bill (Programme)(No 2); HC Deb 7 September 2015, vol 599, col 71.

26 ibid; European Union Referendum Bill (Programme)(No 3); HC Deb 8 December 2015, vol 603, col 864.

The same conclusion could not be reached as concerns the Brexit referendum. There was a high turnout. Also, the question put to the voters was clear – 'Should the United Kingdom remain a member of the European Union or leave the European Union?'[27] as were the possible responses of the electorate – 'Remain a member of the European Union' or 'Leave the European Union'.[28] High turnout suggests good engagement with the question by votes. In addition, a simple question and response can help to further facilitate engagement. However, when it came to the Brexit referendum this clarity failed to fully facilitate deliberative democracy. As demonstrated after the referendum outcome, though not as greatly during the debates on the referendum, there are a number of possible interpretations of 'leave'. Political statements following the referendum also failed to provide clarity. The infamous statement of the Prime Minister that 'Brexit means Brexit' did little to explain and continued in the trend of replacing deliberation with rhetoric. It also added to the homogenisation of the will of the people.

Nor can we point to evidence of campaigns during the Brexit referendum that were designed to facilitate deliberation, despite the production of a leaflet from the Government. The referendum campaign of 'Vote Leave' – one of the groups campaigning to leave the EU – focused predominantly on the need for Britain to remain independent and regain its sovereignty, and on the need for the UK to control its border against a perceived flood of immigrants[29] This message of the need to leave the EU in order to control immigration was then used by more mainstream politicians – e.g. Boris Johnson and Michael Gove – in their pro-leave campaigning prior to the referendum. These sentiments were also echoed in pro-leave newspapers. Those in the Remain campaign, however, focused predominantly on the economy, setting out the way in which leaving the EU would cause economic damage as opposed to focusing more clearly on economic benefits. Media outlets that were 'pro-Leave' characterised these campaigns as 'Project Fear'. The main focus of the Leave campaign was to 'take back control'. This use of slogans, and the general lack of education in the UK as to how the EU works, meant that it was easy for political campaigns to focus more on emotion than reason, with Leave campaigners appealing to an idealised notion of the people which homogenised the will of the people, to the exclusion of immigrants and the elite who wished to remain in the EU. There was no role of the Electoral Commission during the campaign to act as a fact-checker for information.

Given these differences, it is easier to argue that the Brexit referendum provides a stronger illustration of the majoritarian danger inherent in the use of referendums than

27 European Union Referendum Act 2015, s 1(4).

28 European Union Referendum Act 2015, s 1(5).

29 Vote Leave, 'Why Vote Leave' (*Vote Leave*) http://www.voteleavetakecontrol.org/why_vote_leave.html accessed 17 November 2019.

the Scottish referendum. This is reinforced by concerns, which arose later, as to spending irregularities amongst certain Leave campaigners.[30] The greater the possible imbalance in spending, or the tipping of the balance of campaigning in favour of one side or the other on social and other forms of media, the greater the possibility of majoritarianism. This not only undermines democracy, but also can provide a means for populism to use referendums as a tool to achieve their agenda.

These differences also illustrate that it is not just the specific regulation of referendums that may influence the extent to which referendums may fuel populism. The specific issue raised by the referendum may also be relevant. The referendum, in part, required voters to balance a desire for self-determination against possible economic consequences.[31] Not only are these competing values incommensurable, but they are hard to predict. Forecasting economic consequences is difficult at the best of times, and is made even harder by the lack of knowledge as to the UK's future relationship with the European Union. Moreover, it is difficult to separate Brexit from austerity. No claim will be made in this chapter that Brexit was purely decided on austerity issues. However, it is hard to deny that austerity played a role. This is particularly true as regards those voters who felt disenfranchised or ignored by Westminster.[32] A feeling of disenchantment with politics and with those in power, combined with persistent austerity are further factors that may influence the use of referendums to fuel a populist movement.

In addition, it could also be argued that the Brexit referendum is a culmination of a process of change in the UK constitution, with a move away from parliamentary sovereignty towards an incorporation of popular sovereignty, evidenced through the growth in the use of referendums.[33] Referendums have been used for a move to proposed alternative voting, in addition to continued EU membership and devolution. Legislation now incorporates referendums on important constitutional issues. The Northern Ireland Act 1998 provides for the people of Northern Ireland to determine by referendum whether to seek unification with Ireland, placing the UK government under a legal obligation to begin to implement the will of the people should they vote in favour of reunification.[34] Legislative provisions state that both the Scottish Parliament and Government, and the Welsh Assembly and Government are a 'permanent part of the United Kingdom's constitutional arrangements', the purpose of this statement being to

30 Investigation, Vote Leave Ltd, Mr Darren Grimes, BeLeave and Veterans for Britain https://www.electoralcommission.org.uk/who-we-are-and-what-we-do/our-enforcement-work/investigations/investigation-votee-leave-ltd-mr-darren-grimes-beleave-and-veterans-britain.

31 J Allan, 'Democracy, Liberalism and Brexit' (2017) 39 Cardozo Law Review 879.

32 IL Koch, Democracy as Punishment: Brexit and Austerity Politics. in IL Koch, *Personalizing the State: An Anthropology of Law, Politics and Welfare in Austerity Britain* (Oxford University Press 2018) chapter 7.

33 B Wellings and E Vines, 'Populism and Sovereignty: The EU Act and the In-Out Referendum, 2010-2015' [2016] 69(2) *Parliamentary Affairs* 309.

34 Northern Ireland Act 1998, s 1.

'signify the commitment of the Government of the United Kingdom' to these institutions.[35] In the light of this, neither can be abolished unless there is a decision of the people of Scotland, or Wales respectively, voting in favour of their abolition in a referendum.[36] Some modifications to the structure of local government – including the election of a mayor – also require a local referendum.[37] In addition, the European Union Act 2011 imposed referendum locks as regards the ratification of EU Treaties amendments and modifications that could have resulted in the transfer of power from the UK to the EU. The UK constitution appears to be moving towards regarding referendums as an aspect of constitutional change, particularly when this change is related to the UK's relationship with the EU.

This section has explained that there is no necessary link between referendums and populism. Referendums can, in certain circumstances, help to facilitate deliberative democracy. However, the institutional arrangements surrounding the Brexit referendum, the nature of the question asked, the link to growing feelings of austerity and disenfranchisement coupled with a growing acceptance of the use of referendums to institute constitutional change may all explain why the Brexit referendum may have been used as a tool for populist movements in the UK. The next section will reflect on more abstract issues, looking at the more general connection between populism and the UK constitution. It will argue that the UK constitution may have weaknesses, which mean that it is less capable of preventing referendums from being used to facilitate populism.

3 POPULISM AND THE UK CONSTITUTION

It seems easy to conclude that, to the extent populism has become a feature of the UK constitution, it has been caused by a specific set of circumstances that are unlikely to be replicated: austerity; a feeling amongst some members of the UK that the political elites were failing to represent their interests; and a growing use of referendums for constitutionally important issues, particularly as regards EU membership. As such, it may also seem obvious that any problems of populism in the UK are merely temporary. It is not the case that there are problems with the UK constitution that may make it prone to populism, but rather the UK's normally robust constitution may face a combined series of pressure points that make it vulnerable to populism in these extreme circumstances. This section will argue that this conclusion is too simplistic. It is based upon a misunderstanding of the causes of populism and the circumstances under which populist movements may give rise to authoritarianism. When these causes are understood more fully, it becomes clear that the UK's constitution has weaknesses that

35 Scotland Act 1998, s 63A (1) and (2); Government of Wales Act 2006, s A1(1) and (2).
36 Scotland Act 1998, s 63A (3); Government of Wales Act 2006, s A1(3).
37 Local Government Act 2000, s 9M.

mean that, rather than stopping populism, the UK's constitutional arrangements may provide a further catalyst for populism.

The previous section examined how referendums could be a tool of populist movements and hinted at some of the causes of populism. Populism can be difficult to define. This collection uses the definition of Jan Werner Müller, which focuses on how populism arises when an appeal is made to the people whose views are not represented by the current political elites who hold power.[38] Populism builds on this discontent, but it does so in a manner that homogenises the will of the people. This was illustrated by the Brexit referendum. Although the referendum delivered a relatively narrow majority in favour of leave, this was transformed into the will of the people, homogenising not just those who wished to remain as well as leave, but also those who had different reasons for voting to leave the EU or who believed in a range of possible future relationships between the UK and the EU once the UK had left the EU. Second, Müller argues that populism deploys emotion as opposed to reason in political debate, appealing to feelings of morality, often over-simplifying complex political debate. Again, this is amply demonstrated by the Brexit referendum.

This understanding of populism suggests some of the causes of populism. Appeals to the people only work when it is possible to identify a group who feel disenfranchised and under-represented. This suggests that populism occurs when representative democracy fails to work effectively. This can be because of failures in the political system. In addition, this may arise because of problems resolving two deeper issues which exist in democratic societies. First, liberal democracies strive to balance democratic decision-making with a protection of human rights and civil liberties.[39] Difficulties may arise when this balance is struck in a manner that produces a perception that the political elites are protecting values that do not reflect those of the majority of people in society. This may occur in particular as court cases which protect civil liberties often protect minority rights. With regard to Brexit, this arose when courts used legal principles to determine the means through which the Government could notify the EU of its intention to leave the EU. This was portrayed by some of the media as a decision of the legal elites to ignore the wishes of the people to leave the EU as expressed in the referendum.

Second, a perceived incorrect resolution of the boundary problem may also trigger populism.[40] The boundary problem arises when determining how to identify the group or

38 J-W Müller, *What is Populism*? (University of Pennsylvania Press 2017).

39 M Canovan, *The People* (Polity 2005) chapter 5; P Taggart, *Populism* (Oxford University Press 2000) chapter 9-10; C Rovira Kaltwasser, 'The Responses of Populism to Dahl's Democratic Dilemmas' [2014] 62(3) Political Studies 474-477; M Canovan, 'Trust the People! Populism and the Two Faces of Democracy' [1999] 47(1) *Political Studies* 2.

40 C Rovira Kaltwasser, 'The Responses of Populism to Dahl's Democratic Dilemmas' [2014] 62(3) Political Studies 472-474; P Taggart, *Populism* (Oxford University Press 2000) chapter 8; M Canovan, "People', Politicians and Populism' [1984] 19(3) *Government and Opposition* 314; M Canovan, 'Populism for political theorists?' [2004] 9(3) *Journal of Political Ideologies* 247-250; M Canovan, *The People* (Polity 2005) chapter 4.

groups of individuals who are then governed by a particular state or a particular set of governmental institutions. Tensions arise when it is perceived that boundaries are being drawn in the wrong place, or that political institutions are governing those who others do not feel belong in that particular society. The boundary issue is not one that can be resolved by rational political debate. It appeals to emotion and a sense of belonging. This potential trigger of populism is also present in the Brexit referendum. Appeals were made to the emotions of UK citizens, suggesting that they were being governed by European institutions that failed to represent UK nationals, in addition to the UK becoming a country with too many European immigrants. Whether these appeals were based on rational arguments was irrelevant.

When the causes of populism are analysed in this manner, it lends support to the argument that it was the particular circumstances of Brexit which caused populist movements to gain power in the UK. Moreover, when understood in this manner, populism is often regarded as self-correcting.[41] Populist movements may come to power. However, once populist movements gain power, they become part of the political elite. They too may face criticism of their actions from others, who appeal to groups who feel under-represented. Any populist group that becomes part of the political elites may face future criticism from other groups who appeal to direct democracy. As such, populist movements may come and go, each new movement gaining power perhaps for a short while, before being replaced by another group.[42]

The nature of the UK's constitution fits this transient nature of populism, which may explain why populism normally fails to take hold in the UK, reinforcing our understanding of Brexit as a rare occurrence, where a series of circumstances combined to allow populism to take hold more convincingly than would normally be the case. First, the Westminster Parliament is elected on a first-past-the-post system, with smaller constituencies each voting for one Member of Parliament to represent that particular constituency in Parliament. This means that it can be hard for populist movements to challenge the more established political parties. This is particularly true for populist movements who may have widespread support across the country, but who do not have enough support in particular constituencies to win seats in Parliament.

Second, Parliamentary terms are currently fixed at five years,[43] although this may be cut short following a vote of no confidence in the Government,[44] or when there is a two-

41 P Taggart, *Populism* (Oxford University Press 2000) chapter 9.

42 For further discussion of how populism may act as a corrective, see: F Decker, 'The Populist Challenge to Liberal Democracy' [2003] 3 *International Politics and Society*; M Canovan, *The People* (Polity 2005); M Canovan, 'Trust the People! Populism and the Two Faces of Democracy' [1999] 47(1) *Political Studies*; M Canovan, 'Populism for political theorists?' [2004] 9(3) *Journal of Political Ideologies*; C Rovira Kaltwasser, 'The Responses of Populism to Dahl's Democratic Dilemmas' [2014] 62(3) *Political Studies*; C Mudde and C Rovira Kaltwasser, *Populism: A Very Short Introduction* (Oxford University Press 2017).

43 Fixed Term Parliaments Act 2011, s 1.

44 Fixed Term Parliaments Act 2011, s 2(1) and 2(4).

thirds majority of the whole House voting in favour of an early general election.[45] As recently demonstrated, it is also possible for an early parliamentary general election to be called following the enactment of specific legislation calling an early general election.[46] This minimises the amount of time any Government can hold power and means that a populist Government managing to gain power could be replaced relatively quickly.

Third, the Government is formed from the political party that has the most seats in the House of Commons and so is normally able to maintain the confidence of the House. Standing Order 14 prioritises Governmental business, effectively allowing the Government to control legislation. The Government initiates most legislation and can propose programme motions which restrict the amount of time spend by the Commons scrutinising legislation. There are examples of these processes being circumvented. The clearest example is the recent enactment of the European Union (Withdrawal) Act 2019 and the European Union (Withdrawal) (No 2) Act 2019. The first Act was initiated by opposition and backbench MPs, with a vote in the House of Commons to disapply Standing Order 14, enabling instead debate on this Bill, which was enacted quickly through Parliament. The second occurred when backbench and opposition MPs used Standing Order 24 to propose an emergency debate to suspend Standing Order 14, proposing an alternative programme which saw the act passing through its stages in the House of Commons in one day. However, this may well be regarded as the exception that proves the rule, given the specific set of circumstances which enabled this legislation to be enacted.[47]

Fourth, the Political Parties, Elections and Referendums Act 2000 regulates political parties, election expenditure during general elections and referendums, and donations to both individual candidates and political parties. These provisions are overseen by the Electoral Commission. In addition, political advertising is highly regulated. It is unlawful to broadcast political advertising in the UK.[48] Instead, a series of party political broadcasts is permitted during an election, again regulated through the provisions of the Political Parties, Elections and Referendums Act 2000. These regulations are designed to maintain parity between political parties.

Fifth, the UK balances liberal principles of human rights and democracy through the provisions of the Human Rights Act 1998. Whilst this places courts under an obligation to read and give effect to legislation in a manner compatible with Convention rights, so far as it is possible to do so, it does not empower courts to strike down legislation that is incompatible with Convention rights.[49] Courts of the level of the high court or above may only declare legislation incompatible with Convention rights. Declarations of

45 Fixed Term Parliaments Act 2011, s 2(1) and 2(2).

46 Early Parliamentary General Election Act 2019.

47 AL Young, 'Taking (Back) Control?' (*UK Constitutional Law Blog*, 23 April 2019) https://ukconstitutionallaw.org/2019/04/23/alison-young-taking-back-control accessed 17 November 2019.

48 Communications Act 2003, s 333. These provisions are regulated by OFCOM.

49 Human Rights Act 1998, s 3.

incompatibility do not affect the validity, legal force or continuing effect of legislation declared incompatible with Convention rights.[50] Although tensions may still arise between democratically enacted legislation and declarations of incompatibility, particularly when this gives rise to decisions of the European Court of Human Rights concluding that UK legislation has breached Convention rights, these tensions are not as great as arise in constitutions where courts do have a strike-down power. In addition, pre-legislative scrutiny, particularly by the Joint Committee on Human Rights, minimises conflicts.[51] Moreover, the continued reliance on parliamentary sovereignty makes it difficult, if not impossible, for any populist movement which gains power to entrench its beliefs so as to make it harder for a future Parliament to overturn its legislation.

This would seem to suggest that there are no reasons why populism should be anything other than a temporary problem for the UK constitution. It may even suggest that populism is something that the UK constitution is able to easily withstand. The structure of the UK constitution may mean that it is less likely to produce situations which may cause populist movements and any populist movement that were to arise would be short-lived. However, this section argues that this conclusion is overly optimistic. It fails to fully account for the causes and consequences of populism. Moreover, when these are more fully understood, it appears that features of the UK constitution may act as a catalyst for populism.

Canovan argues that populism is not caused by the tension between liberalism and democracy, but instead arises from tension between what she refers to as the pragmatic and redemptive aspects of democracy,[52] drawing on Oakeshott's distinction between the politics of faith and the politics of scepticism.[53] The pragmatic aspect of democracy regards democratic decision-making as a mechanism of dispute resolution. Democracy provides solutions, a means for government to achieve its objectives. The redemptive aspect of democracy focuses on the normative value of democracy. It is not just a means of resolving conflict, but a legitimate means. Democratic decision-making provides a justification for those who would have otherwise disagreed to adhere to the decision of the majority.[54] Difficulties arise when too much focus is placed on the pragmatic as opposed to the redemptive aspects of democratic decision-making. When this occurs, society may lose its justification for adhering to democratically determined decisions, leading those who feel they are in the minority to reject the outcomes of democratic decision-making. Populism, with its focus on an appeal to emotions, can use the disconnection between the redemptive and the pragmatic aspects of democracy.

---

50 Human Rights Act 1998, s 4.

51 Human Rights Act 1998, s 19.

52 M Canovan, 'Trust the People! Populism and the Two Faces of Democracy' [1999] 47(1) *Political Studies*; M Canovan, 'Populism for political theorists?' [2004] 9(3) *Journal of Political Ideologies* 89-90.

53 M Oakeshott, *The Politics of Faith and the Politics of Scepticism* (Yale University Press 1996) 21-38.

54 M Canovan, 'Trust the People! Populism and the Two Faces of Democracy' [1999] 47(1) *Political Studies* 9-10.

It appeals to those who feel disenfranchised. It focuses on these groups to reject decision-making by the political elites, calling for direct as opposed to representative democracy.[55]

This possible further cause of populism may be more problematic for the UK constitution, which tends to focus more on pragmatic than redemptive justifications. This explains, in part, why so much of the UK constitution is formed of, and regulated by, political as opposed to legal rules. The UK constitution has evolved over time, changing in response to practical problems. It has not had a recent constitutional moment, establishing a redemptive justification.[56] The manner in which the UK constitution has adopted referendums provides an illuminating illustration. As the House of Lords Select Committee on the Constitution noted in its report on referendums, their use in the UK is under-theorised, with 'little consistency'; referendums taking place on 'an ad hoc basis, frequently as a tactical device rather than on the basis of constitutional principle'.[57] This is clearly illustrated by the Brexit referendum, as discussed above.

The Westminster Parliament is also cited as the *locus classicus* of an arena legislature.[58] Strong cohesive control over political parties, an electoral system that tends to return a Government with a strong majority, and the Government's dominance over parliamentary business are all cited as explanations for why it can be difficult, although not impossible, for back bench and opposition MPs to initiate or amend legislation. There is a perception that the Government is elected on a mandate from the people as set out in its manifesto, the job of the opposition being to propose an alternative mandate for possible future election. Success is measured in rhetoric rather than reason. This can provide a further means through which the UK constitution may become a catalyst for populism. Populism favours appeals to emotion over appeal to reason. Such appeals may be more effective in an arena legislature, where the political culture already appears to favour political rhetoric.

In addition, although Westminster's position is justified by the principle of parliamentary sovereignty, there is little discussion as to why this principle has legitimacy, beyond a bare mention of democracy. This lack of appeal to legitimacy meant that it was difficult for appeals to parliamentary sovereignty to resist the challenge that came from calls to popular sovereignty. Again, this is illustrated by the Brexit referendum, as politicians moved from relying on the sovereignty of Parliament,

55 ibid 10-11.

56 B Ackerman, *We the People, Volume 1: Foundations* (Belknap Press 1993); B Ackerman, *We the People, Volume 2: Transformations* (Belknap Press 2000).

57 HL Select Committee on the Constitution, *Referendums in the United Kingdom* (HL 2009-10, 99) para 205.

58 NW Polsby, 'Legislatures' in FI Greenstein and NW Polsby (eds), *Handbook of Political Science* (Addidson-Wesley 1975) 277-296.

citing instead the need to uphold the will of the people.[59] When implementing the European Union (Notification of Withdrawal) Bill in the House of Commons, David Davis MP, the then newly appointed Secretary of State for Exiting the European Union, focused on the need to enact the legislation in order to implement the will of the people as expressed in the referendum.[60] During the enactment of the European Union (Notification of Withdrawal) Bill, the House of Lords proposed, and voted in favour of, an amendment which would have placed the Government under a legal obligation to hold a vote in Parliament to approve the first draft of the Withdrawal Agreement between the UK and the European Union. When voting against this amendment on the return of the Bill to the House of Commons, emphasis was placed on how this amendment, whilst designed to strengthen the powers of Parliament, effectively prevented the Government from having a free hand in the negotiations with the EU in order to implement the will of the people.[61] Even when discussion in the House of Commons focused on the extent to which this amendment would preserve parliamentary sovereignty,[62] or preserve the proper constitutional process,[63] it was countermanded by the need to ensure that the UK Parliament respected the outcome of the referendum.[64] The House of Lords voted to withdraw both amendments in the face of defeat in the House of Commons.[65] Again, this demonstrates how the UK constitution almost becomes a catalyst for populism. This preference for the pragmatic as opposed to the redemptive aspect of democracy means it can be harder to argue against populist movements.

This argument is exacerbated when we focus more clearly on the consequences of populism. Populism has a negative impact on political debate due to the way in which it homogenises the will of the people and its replacement of deliberation and reason with rhetoric and emotion, undermining deliberative democracy. The arena nature of Westminster, with its preference for rhetoric provides little means for deliberative democracy and reason to challenge populist claims. Whilst deliberation may be more present in the House of Lords, its status as an unelected, predominantly nominated chamber, means that its conclusions can often be trumped by the assertion of the

59 See: M Gordon, 'Brexit: a challenge for the UK constitution, of the UK constitution?' [2016] 12(3) *European Constitutional Law Review* 415-416; See also the debates surrounding the opposition day motions on Brexit on 10 October 2016 and 7 December 2016.

60 HC Deb 31 January 2017, vol 620, cols 818-9.

61 HC Deb 13 March 2017, vol 623, col 38.

62 See: Kier Starmer, HC Deb 13 March 2017, vol 623, cols 47-49; Hilary Benn, HC Deb 13 March 2017, vol 623, col 62; Emma Reynolds, HC Deb 13 March 2017, vol 623, cols 65-66; Chris Leslie, HC Deb 13 March 2017, vol 623, cols 67-68; Helen Goodman, HC Deb 13 March 2017, vol 623, col 69; Caroline Lucas, HC Deb 13 March 2017, vol 623, cols 71-72.

63 See: Dominic Grieve, HC Deb 13 March 2017, vol 623, cols 66-67.

64 See: Mr Baron, HC Deb 13 March 2017, vol 623, col 49; Seema Kennedy, HC Deb 13 March 2017, vol 623, cols 62-63; Sir William Cash, HC Deb 13 March 2017, vol 623, col 65; Gisela Stuart, HC Deb 13 March 2017, vol 623, col 70.

65 HL Deb 13 March 2017, vol 779, cols 1709-1736.

greater legitimacy of the elected House of Commons over the House of Lords. Although measures exist to regulate political advertisements that are broadcast, there is less control over social media. This lack of regulation may make it harder for populist movements to be challenged by deliberation. In addition, there is little focus on providing education as to the value of living in pluralist societies. Without this understanding, there is little that can be used to challenge the homogenisation of the will of the people.

4 Conclusion

This chapter recognises that the causes and consequences of populism can be complex and varied. Referendums in and of themselves may not cause populism. Indeed, in certain circumstances they may facilitate deliberative democracy. However, as the Brexit referendum demonstrates, they can also be tools of populism. Moreover, given the structure of the UK constitution, in particular its preference for pragmatic as opposed to redemptive justifications of democracy and its arena style legislature, the UK constitution may act as a catalyst for populism, particularly when combined with a referendum.

The easy solution would appear to be to suggest that the UK needs major constitutional reform. However, it is important to recognise that there are no easy solutions, and that reform needs to focus specifically on remedying those features of the UK constitution that may fuel populist movements. To move from a system of parliamentary to constitutional sovereignty may not remedy these difficulties. Instead, there are specific issues that the UK constitution needs to address. First, the UK constitution needs to redress the imbalance between redemptive and pragmatic aspects of democracy. Initiating a process of constitutional reform may prompt discussions as to why the UK has adopted parliamentary sovereignty. In addition, more needs to be done to explain the values of a pluralist society. More needs to be done to ensure that representative democracy works effectively in the UK, in particular to ensure that there is investment in the poorer as well as the wealthier areas of the UK. In particular, there is a need to think more carefully about the use of referendums and the role they should play in the UK constitution.

Political reform may also be needed in the House of Commons. It may be time to question the values of a traditional Westminster arena-style legislature. This may require further bolstering the role of select committees, allowing more avenues for the Commons to challenge the Government's dominance over programme motions, or even rethinking the way in which the Commons determines its order of business. In addition, it may be time to revisit how we elect MPs to Westminster, moving away from first-past-the-post to alternative voting mechanisms. Moreover, there is a need to investigate how we regulate social media, both in terms of ensuring that rules designed to create parity in political debate surrounding elections or referendums and to determine how social media can play a part in facilitating deliberative democracy without replacing reasoned debate with heated rhetoric.

These are only suggestions. They do not form a clear plan. The most important lesson to learn from the UK's experience of Brexit is that populism can have an effect even in otherwise stable democracies, whose constitutional structure may have appeared to provide a means of immunising the effects of populism. The experience of Brexit illustrates the naïveté of this view. It was based on a misunderstanding of populism and of the UK constitution in the light of the causes and consequences of populism. The UK constitution needs to find the time, post Brexit, to reflect on these issues if it is to evolve further in the light of this experience.

Indonesia – Preserving Democracy Against the Rise of Populism

Rosa Ristawati and Radian Salman***

1 Introduction

Populism is closely linked with democracy. It may be a movement, usually in politics, in which a politician claims to represent the sentiments of the people, and wherein the populist claims to represent rightfully the claims of the (oppressed) population. On the other hand, democracy is a form of government that requires every citizen to participate in the government process, and in which the elected legislative assembly should represent the whole people. According to Rousseau, democracy is a form of government in which the sovereign may put the government in the hands of the whole people or of a majority of them.[1] The term populism is derived from the Latin word populus which has the meaning of "people".[2] Populists usually deny that majoritarian will formation may be limited by the rule of law. Debate over the populism movement actually has been started as a concept of the state developed in Ancient Greek history. Polybius who was famous with the "cycle of Polybius" came up with a theory that a democratic government might transform into a 'bad' sort of government of democracy with lawless ferocity and violence.[3] The concern about bad government is when the will of the majority of the people would undermine minorities or infringe upon human rights and liberties. Similarly, populism is where politics is conducted through a relatively direct relationship between a charismatic leader and the people.[4] In modern times, Cas Mudde argued that populism is about creating a schism between the elite and the people.[5] It is a movement against established authority, against both the private and government sector and the distrusted elites who hold the power and cannot claim to

---

* Rosa Ristawati is Assistant Professor of Constitutional Law at Airlangga University Surabaya. She holds a PhD from Maastricht University and a LL.M from the University of Groningen.

** Radian Salman is vice dean III of the faculty of law of Airlangga University, Surabaya. He holds a PhD from Airlangga University and a LL.M from Utrecht University.

1 J-J Rousseau (2017). Social Contract. (Online) (2017) www.earlymoderntexts.com 33.

2 M Rooduijn, *A Populist Zeitgeist?: The Impact of Populism on Parties, Media and the Public in Western Europe* (Dissertation 2013) 6.

3 Polybius translated by E S Shuckburgh, The History of Polybius Book Six (In parentheses Publication Greek Series 2012) 355.

4 O Törnquist, Stagnation or Transformation in Indonesia? [2014] 49(50) *Economic and Political Weekly* 23.

5 C Mudde, The Populist Zeitgeist [2014] 39(4) Government and Opposition 544.

represent the people.[6] Populism may be progressivism. Both may have a moralistic tone with the intention of reforming government and society, populism distrusts representative government and seeks to constrain it. The progressives have the intention to serve as an additional check on representative government in order to improve the quality and effectiveness of the government, whereas, the populist tends to have a radical vision in order to undermine representative government by shifting power to the people or himself.[7] However, progressivism recognizes the legitimacy of representative government but requires better progress for society. It demands changes that fit with the development and global changes in the community.

The rise of populism in European countries and the US may be a reflection as well as an alert for Indonesia to protect its democracy values and rule of law from the excesses of populism. This chapter will deal with three different issues. The first issue is the character of populism in Indonesia. The second issue is whether populism will be a threat that potentially undermines democracy in Indonesia. The third is the role of the courts, in particular the Constitutional Court in defending its judicial independence against populist movements. The fact that democracy in Indonesia has been well-established requires Indonesia to improve and protect democracy from any deviation of values including populism. This article finds that the law is essential to protect democracy against populism in Indonesia. In this sense, the courts have an important role to put forward judicial independence instead of being intimidated by the majority will of the people. The article starts by exploring the rule of law in the Indonesian Constitution and assessing whether the Constitution has provided a mechanism to prevent populism. The article describes particular legal issues which may trigger the rise of populism in Indonesia and how the Court has resolved such phenomena.

1.1 Populism in Indonesia: characteristics

For Indonesia, populism may present a potential intimidation to the representative democracy system specifically where elites in bureaucracy and the oligarchic system are merged within the system. In this context, people may realize that representative government does not represent the interests of the people and the process of government is merely reflecting the interest of particular groups such as political parties in the political system. This situation threatens democracy system while democracy in Indonesia is susceptible to such threats. One common political situation is an indication that political parties change their program significantly from what had been offered to the

6 A E Hara, 'Populism in Indonesia and its Threats to Democracy' (Third International Conference on Social and Political Sciences (ICSPS 2017) Advances in Social Science, Education and Humanities Research (ASSEHR) Atlantic Press 2018) 106.

7 K P Miller, Symposium, Constraining Populism: The Real Challenge of Initiative Reform [2001] 41(4) *Santa Clara Law Review* 1037.

electorate during the campaign. It may often be classified as normal political phenomena in Indonesia. Politicians, and figures in a political party, have a tendency of defending their own interests rather than contesting for the public interest. In this situation, these phenomena may provoke the emergence of a populist movement which claims to represent the people. Here the populist movement claims to defend the neglected group. Experiences show that populism in Indonesia is mostly driven by political parties, organizations, or a candidate for the presidency in order to gain popularity to compete with and beat the opponents.[8] In Indonesia, a public figure could arise to be a populist figure when s/he promotes and advocates causes for the people. However, it is difficult in Indonesia to have one dominant and strong figure emerge on behalf of populism. Several different groups advocating populism, give populism in Indonesia a character of convergence rather than dominance and centralization. As in other countries, populism in Indonesia is claimed as an alternative mechanism representing the people's will.

Populism in Indonesia might be seen in the momentum of the fall of the New Order (the authoritarian Soeharto's regime) in 1998. The fall of the authoritarian regime and the anti-democratic regime at the time marked the rise of the alternative transitional regime which manipulated the power with democratic system and openness. However, the alternative transitional regime at the time, the political tension, the representative political failure, and the euphoria openness gave rise to the alternative leadership idea in Indonesia. In the phase of finding alternatives of leadership, populism offers an alternative of leadership which promoted anti-establishment, against the former authoritarian regime and encouraged the public participation to determine the direction and development of the state. At that moment, the new alternative regime promoted by populism gave rise to shifting the authoritarian elite and building a new reformist system based on the people's consensus. In this context, populism in Indonesia had a positive impact.

In general, the issue of populism is actually not very significant in the whole political system in Indonesia. It is because the populist movements often do not have substantive issues and are not that concrete in controlling the political system in Indonesia. However, the indications and the potential significant movement of populism have been shown by several political parties, and mass organizations, as well as individuals (such as a presidential candidate) in recent political campaigns within the last decade. It is mostly perceptible in how the populists behaved in an election campaign. For instance, in a way a political elite figure speaks in a simple way and is easy to be understood by common people and by the constituents. This is the opposite of the elite government to which they mostly speak in rhetorical phrases and in a more complicated way, such as how

8 A E Hara, 'Populism in Indonesia and its Threats to Democracy' (Third International Conference on Social and Political Sciences (ICSPS 2017) Advances in Social Science, Education and Humanities Research (ASSEHR) Atlantic Press 2018) 108.

commonly bureaucrats communicate. In this sense, an Indonesian populist is usually a figure who has charisma and attracts people with simple language in advocating people's will. However, just like in other countries, populism in Indonesia shows itself to be a movement that is against a complicated representative government system.

From the historical perspective, populism in Indonesia could be phenomenally traced back. It was not only that the political setting obliged the government to involve people in policy making. The organized mob mobilization, for instance in Solo within the "*Keraton*" regime under the Dutch colonization, might reflect two types of people resistance; namely the individual and sporadic actions against plantation controllers in order to protect the lands, and the popular mobilization that was more organized by marching to the local leader's offices at the time.[9] In the more modern era, according to Mietzner, the experience of populism in Indonesia reappeared when President SBY introduced an extensive cash program for the poor, suggesting that economic populism may become a constant feature in elections and new pro-poor policies of social welfare initiative in his second term of office.[10] In this context, populism in Indonesia emerged as a choice of form in administering the state using subsidies to the majority of the people (which are poor and marginalized).

Other scholars identify the characters of populism in Indonesia in other ways. Törnquist argues that populism in Indonesia may be characterized as conservative national populism with strong leadership with the representative figure of Prabowo and participatory and welfare oriented populism of Jokowi with its basis firmly rooted in territorial citizenship, with the special feature of anti-corruption, public services, public education, social security and the negotiated groups of business, middle classes, workers, and the urban poor in order to deal with problems of urban development.[11] The characters of populism according to both scholars may be susceptible to particular issues of religion. However, the fact that Indonesia is a state where issues on religion may also drive the political system, may significantly indicate that any movement on the basis of religion may be a populist movement.

In a different argument, Eby Hara indicates there are at least three kinds of populism in Indonesia, namely radical left-wing populism, radical right-wing populism, and the populism of Islamic parties.[12] Similar to Eby Hara, Ehito Kimura figured out the characters of populism in Indonesia, namely technocratic populism, demagogic

9 P Pratikno and C Lay, From Populism to Democratic Polity: Problems and Challenges in Surakarta, Indonesia [2011] 3(1-2) *PCD Journal* 46.

10 M Mietzner, 'Indonesia's 2009 Elections: Populism, Dynasties and the Consolidation of the Party System' [2009] *Lowy Institute for International Policy*.

11 O Törnquist, Stagnation or Transformation in Indonesia? [2014] 49(50) *Economic and Political Weekly* 26.

12 A E Hara, 'Populism in Indonesia and its Threats to Democracy' (Third International Conference on Social and Political Sciences (ICSPS 2017) Advances in Social Science, Education and Humanities Research (ASSEHR) Atlantic Press 2018) 107.

populism, and Islamic populism.[13] The three have been influencing the political system in Indonesia recently. Technocratic populism is represented in the way that Jokowi promotes pro‐poor reformist policies in areas such as healthcare, education, welfare, infrastructure and pro‐investment.[14] Whereas, demagogic populism is reflected by Prabowo in his campaigns against the establishment and against-corruption; he is a proponent of economic-nationalism and "firm leadership" and the view that the global economy and foreign powers are the perpetrators in their own economic malaise.[15] On the other hand, Islamic populism is more expressing a populist response to the tensions and contradictions of global capitalism.[16] The experience of the Islamic populism has brought forward the issue of religion such as mobilizing mobs to resist the Chinese Christian incumbent DKI Jakarta's Governor as conflicting with or aggressively confrontational to economic and spiritual welfare in 2016.[17] In a further development, Islamic populism emerged on the wave of right-wing populism with the formation of what was called the "411" movement and the "212" movement as a result of a problem of Moslem marginalization combined with militarism in Indonesia.[18] However, Hadiz observed that Islamic populism in Indonesia is still quite vulnerable, and has a tendency of being conservative in response to the needs of the allied establishment consisting of different groups but having the same interests and through the solidarity with Islamic symbols.[19] Meanwhile, technocratic populism is a different form of populism which reflects the pragmatism of populism in terms of prioritizing the improvement of day to day services over grand political visions and the promise to maintain democracy.[20] Such populism shows itself to be inclusive, non-confrontational and supportive to the democratic status quo.[21]

In 2014 Indonesian Presidential elections, Jokowi advanced a new form of technocratic populism that was inclusive, non-confrontational which primarily focused on improving the quality of public service delivery as well as pragmatic populism which

---

13 E Kimura, 'Populist Politic in Indonesia' [2007] *Asia Pacific Bulletin* 407.
14 ibid.
15 ibid.
16 V R Hadiz, 'Indonesian Political Islam: Capitalist Development and the Legacies of the Cold War' [2011] 30 (1) *Journal of Current Southeast Asian Affairs* 7.
17 E Kimura, 'Populist Politic in Indonesia' [2007] *Asia Pacific Bulletin* 407.
18 L A Savitri and D Adriyanti, 'The Demise of Emancipatory Peasant Politics? Indonesian Fascism and The Rise of Islamic Populism' (ERPI Conference papers Emancipatory Rural Politics Initiative (ERPI) 2018 Conference: "Authoritarian Populism and the Rural World 2018).
19 R Gunadha, Interview with V R Hadiz, Populism Islam dan Kaum Oligarkis pada Pilpres 2019 https://www.suara.com/wawancara/2019/02/25/072000/vedi-r-hadiz-populisme-islam-dan-kaum-oligarkis-pada-pilpres-2019 (Senin, 25 February 2019).
20 M Mietzner, 'Reinventing Asian Populism: Jokowi's Rise, Democracy, and Political Contestation in Indonesia' [2015] 72 Policy Studies XIII.
21 ibid.

promised rapid improvements in the workings of government and the way it delivers its services.[22] During the 2019 presidential election, the situation still portrayed the two characters of populism in Indonesia, namely demagogic populism and technocratic populism. The two candidates for the presidency were populist figures in ways that they were campaigning with a populist policy, and used the populist campaign to attract voters. The Islamic parties were also still having a significant contribution of Islamic populist phenomena in the 2019 general election. Jokowi also represents a desire for local negotiations in increasingly chaotic and ungovernable urban areas between, on the one hand, business and the middle classes who want plots for commercial ventures and space for cleaner cities, and, on the other hand, subordinated classes being dispossessed of land, housing and livelihood.[23] After the presidential election, populism in Indonesia may be potentially driven by populist figures who are in the government through the pursuit of government policies. Such an indication would potentially undermine the process of democratic development in Indonesia. If the figure is the president-elected supported by the majority of political parties sitting in the parliament, the situation may even more provoke the emergence of a potential authoritarian regime, while it increases the dangerous effect of populism in Indonesia in a way that populism may constrain freedom with the result that the government is setting the policy driven by populist provocation.

2 THREATENING DEMOCRACY IN INDONESIA

As a democratic state according to Article 1 section (2) of the Indonesian Constitution (the Amendment), Indonesia evolves as a mature democratic state showing positive progress through direct general elections. The political atmosphere is quite calm. Recently, populism emerges as a threat to democratic life in Indonesia in a way that it drives the elite government into setting policy or delivering their decisions. In the democratic system of Indonesia, the movement to express majority will of the people on behalf of particular religious group may significantly influence the government policy. For example when there was a big rally in December 2016 which demanded the DKI Jakarta's Governor to step down. The movement was conducted by one of the religious mass organization which was called the "212" people movement. Furthermore, as populism shows the tendency of exclusiveness in a way that most of the movement is intolerant and racist, the populist in Indonesia is mostly justifying the exemption of other groups that may not be suitable to be people in the populist view. It strictly distinguishes

22 B R Nikku and A Azman, 'Populism in the Asia: What role for Asian Social Work?, Social Dialogue' [2017] 17 *Populism & Social Work, Social Dialogue, Free Magazine of the International Association of Schools of Social Work (IASSW).*

23 O Törnquist, Stagnation or Transformation in Indonesia? [2014] 49(50) *Economic and Political Weekly* 24.

between allies and enemies. Such a tendency is shown in Indonesia by the phenomenon of political parties competing to discredit their political opponents in the recent general election by using populism as propaganda. In reality, there is a political party that often opposes laws which relate to Islamic values on the basis that this party is represented in the multi-cultural and pluralistic society. Such issues generate a situation of conflict, which is not conducive to an acceptance of a democratic outcome. In other situations, the rise of populist parties, especially parties with an exclusive and radical perspective, may give rise to the provocation of racism since it may put a framework of influence on the people and its political actors. This issue gives Indonesia the experience that populism threatens the democratic atmosphere through the intimidation of the concept of democracy within the state. It may be delivered as a populist mobilization of ethnic and religious issues.

Within a democratic system, populism may trigger violence and conflict when it sets high expectations which fail to be manifested. One of the weaknesses of populism is that in the name of the people's will, policy has to be determined right away. This situation makes the decision makers urgently push forward the process. The decision that is made in a very short time with the insistence and high pressure without carefully observing the consequences will lead to more complicated and negative effects in its implementation. This may happen in particular policy making processes and several institutions in Indonesia, especially when they are under pressure by public opinion and public mood. Furthermore, populism decreases principles of transparency and unity because it is mostly about skepticism, intolerance or partisanship, religiosity, and self-approval. In Indonesia, as an example can serve when there was a successful broad alliance rally between labor unions and various popular organizations and civil society groups in around 2010 targeted against the repeal of a progressive social security law.[24]

At this context, with regard to the Indonesian political strategy, populism would potentially obstruct the democratic development process in Indonesia, in particular on the issue that Indonesia still has some institutional problems to be fixed in order to protect the government regime against any kind of authoritarian tendency, majority dominance and the distortion of some basic principles of democracy, such as the principle of equality and pluralism. Those are the issues that may drive populist movement, which will be a threat to democracy. Moreover, since populism is relevant to the mobilization of people on the basis of specific issues, it may potentially cause conflict and violence as a democratic deviation. In this sense, there might be a distortion of democratic values and principles. For instance, on the distortion of fairness as one of the democratic principles during the election campaign. Campaign on particular religious issues may significantly influence the voters but sometimes creating an unfair competition among the candidates. This situation may happen in Indonesia

24 ibid 23.

since religion has become the most majority and dominant issue in the political system in Indonesia. Candidates with more support from the big religious organizations (Islamic organization) find it easier to gain votes.

Furthermore, as according to Théo Fournier that populism may be a threat for democracy in a way that populism may be parasitic to the ecosystem of constitutional democracy,[25] the argument would become an actual fact since in Indonesia the potency that majority will take control over the minority is inevitable. In this context, populism manipulates constitutional democracy principles through the populist rhetoric of majority manipulation, by creating a unitary and uncompromising majority and the manipulation of the rule-of-law pillar.[26] The manipulation of the majority as unitary and homogenous is because the majority is assumed to be undivided or undifferentiated, but such an assumption is a fiction considering that the majority in a democracy is an accumulation of different minority expectations.[27] In Indonesia, such a situation in the election would eliminate the non-conformist group.

Furthermore, populism may be a threat to the electoral process before the actual elections, and during the process after the election. Before the election, populism used the promotion of the rule of law for a particular agenda by the populist to make sure that the objective of constitutional democracy will be to protect the majority from the tyranny of minorities by the will of the majority which takes precedence over the rule of law.[28] In this situation, the populist claims that minority protection has to be be achieved. After the election, populism may transform into populist opposition and a populist government.[29] After the election process, populism promotes that the rule of law is useless and the constitution is just a tool for majoritarian expression and no longer a safeguard against majoritarian abuses.[30] In this context, populism is manipulating the majority with the claim that all people would accept choices which have been made by a majority of people. In Indonesia, such populist manipulation may be shown at the electoral process in the presidential campaign during the recent election. Both presidential candidates may usually show the tendency of being used to the majority manipulation in most of the proposed agendas. This definitely has the purpose to attract voters in order to gain majority votes in the election. But problems may arise after the election when a populist candidate gains victory in the election and deviates from the campaigned agenda.

---

25 T Fournier, 'From Rhetoric to Action – A Constitutional Analysis of Populism' (2019) EUI Working Paper LAW 2018/08, 4 https://cadmus.eui.eu/bitstream/handle/1814/51725/LAW_2018_08.pdf?sequence=1&isAllowed=y accessed 9 February 2020.

26 ibid 3.

27 ibid.

28 ibid 4.

29 ibid 5.

30 ibid 5.

However, concern that constitutional democracy would vanish or be destroyed by populism is not entirely correct. The constitutional structure with its checks and balances and with the human rights framework may only be down-graded and become slower because populism gradually changes the regulations; for example, values such as political pluralism, transnational solidarity and protection of minorities would be incompatible with populist interests.[31] In this context, a proper and firm legal framework would protect democratic values from negative tendencies in order to strengthen the foundation of democracy. A firm legal framework has to give alternative solutions to anticipate conflicts. For example, when Indonesia conducts elections, the Election Commission has to make sure enforcement on the basis of the Election Law to minimize conflicts during a presidential election. It is because there is always a potential populism propaganda threat during the election which may become conflicts. Mostly, the situation before, during and after the election, in particular the presidential election, shows the tendency of friction and clash among the presidential supporters. If the legal framework does not provide solutions, further friction may develop into conflict and potentially provoke a campaign of intolerance and racism which are mostly promoted by the populists in particular issues of religion.

While demagogic populism may potentially consist of authoritarianism, the technocracy populism, which employs strategic political communication using simple language and programs for the people, might provoke tendencies that the policies will be more than just implementation of what the majority of people supported. However, people who support the demagogic populist will argue that a leader has to be a firm leader to protect the country and to organize Indonesian multicultural pluralism. Both demagogic and technocratic populism may provoke authoritarianism. For example when the government enacted a Law on Mass Organization which had some articles as a legal basis to cripple the opposition groups and critics in society during the first period of the Jokowi administration, the enforcement of such a Law would be similar to the Law of anti-subversion during the New Order which was used to bring down freedom and silence of dissidents and the opposition.

On the other hand, Islamic populism would be a potential threat to democracy in Indonesia in a way that Islamic populism has potentially emerged as a result of the majority of religions in Indonesia. However, the use of ethnicity and religion in politics has actually not been a political culture in Indonesia. Religion, in particular Islam, does not constrain pluralism and democracy which is being protected by the Constitution. But in several cases, the issue of religious fanaticism in Indonesia was significant to fight off political opponents. The most recent case was the case of Governor DKI Jakarta (BTP) who was the incumbent DKI Jakarta governor. There was also a significant provocation during the DKI Jakarta head of government election. The issue of religion was used to

31 ibid 6.

discourage one of the governor candidates. In the end, it was giving significant contribution for the election result of the Governor of DKI Jakarta election in 2016. Another current issue reflected populism in Indonesia was the movement against the revision of the Anti-Corruption Law which eventually resolved in a judicial review process at the Constitutional Court.

3 The Rule of Law and the Role of Law: Courts to preserve Democracy

We discussed in the previous section that the use of ethnicity and religious issues as a basis for a populist movement may intimidate or even endanger democracy in Indonesia as a pluralist state. Populism on the basis of Islamic populism for instance, may be more about racism. Moreover, as an example may serve a case that showed that mass mobilization and can lead to overruling the law by what was called ed by the people "majority will". This case concerning the former Governor of DKI Jakarta in 2016-2017 might be a significant example that people have power to directly influence the courts. The movement of mob mobilization was also on behalf of an ethnic and religious issue in order to deliver a message from the people impinging upon the independence of judiciary power. This experience created a precedent that the law which set a democratic framework has been overruled by public pressure on behalf of the will of a majority of the people. This showed that the people's power through the movement has went against the Constitution and the Laws. The Constitution and the Laws must be considered as expressing the majority will of the people. Thus, this provides a negative excess of populism in Indonesia and a violation of constitutional values.

The Indonesian Constitution provides for the guarantee of judicial independence in Article 24 (1) the Indonesian Constitution (Amendment). Furthermore, the Laws need to have a legal basis for institution building, specifically making the Executive branch must be consistent in dealing with justice and security service delivery more efficiently.[32] The role of Laws have to be understood as the legal basis in the long-run processes of state development and the political nature of legal interactions.[33] As one of the roles of the Constitution is as a legal instrument to establish a democratic framework and rule of law standards, the Indonesian Constitution in this context sets the primary rule by providing mechanisms of protection to accommodate pluralism and minority. The Constitution provides solutions to restrain excessive populism. The role of the Constitution is also a legal instrument providing fundamental controls for the state political system. The Indonesian Constitution upholds the basic constitutional rules of the amendment in Article 37 or at least a demand of particular majorities as one of democratic

32 UNDP, Strengthening the Rule of Law in Crisis-affected and Fragile Situation, Global Programme Annual Report, 2011.

33 ibid.

mechanism while it also secures the Court's independence in particular the Constitutional Court and Supreme Court in interpreting the Constitution and the Laws, and sets up and protects the standards framework of rule of law.[34] In this sense, the design of the Indonesian Constitution has already accommodated values on pluralism and minority safeguards.

Under the Indonesian Constitution, democracy is living in co-existence with the rule of law under Article 1 of the Indonesian Constitution. Democracy, as it is stipulated in Article 1 (2) of the Indonesian Constitution (the Amendment) confirms that the Constitution recognizes that sovereignty is in the hands of the people and is implemented according to the Constitution. The Article emphasizes that democracy in Indonesia is a constitutional democracy. On the other hand, Indonesia is a state according to the rule of law. The Constitution emphasizes that the rule of law is the basis for Indonesia as a state in Article 1 (3) of the Indonesian Constitution (the Amendment). This article provides a constitutional basis that any government actions as well as any solutions for any kind of issues have to be in accordance with the law. Rule of law is the fundamental framework in any democratic society. Without the principles of the rule of law, democracy would not be well implemented. The legal framework protects democratic values in the Constitution. Such protection as implied in Article 1 (2) of the Indonesian Constitution stipulates that sovereignty is in the hands of the people and is implemented according to this Constitution. This article gives a strong commitment to protect democracy by giving the sovereignty to the people but its implementation has to be in accordance to the Constitution, thus the Laws.

The Laws have essential roles as tools to prevent populist threats. They control and limit the rise of populism from becoming excessive and superior to constitutional democracy since the Law making processes are regulated in the Constitution and rule of law. On the first role, the Laws provide alternative legal solutions to minimize potential threats of populism. In this context, the role of legal institutions, in particular the courts (the Supreme Court and the Constitutional Court) as the legal institution holding judiciary powers has to be consistent with their independence. Judges a the Court have to uphold the judicial independence and when it is necessary daring to be counter-majoritarian and decide according to the Laws. In controlling and limiting the rise of populism from being superior to constitutional democracy, the Laws have to provide

34 N Walker, 'Populism and Constitutional Tension, Symposium: Public Law and The New Populism' (2017) Jean Monnet Working Paper 15/17 www.JeanMonnetProgram.org: "In functional terms, a constitution typically involves a 'triple lock' control of the political system. The first and most fundamental lock involves the entrenchment of the basic constitutional rules of the game against amendment or replacement, or at least a requirement of special majorities. The second lock concerns the independence of the constitutional court or other apex courts in interpreting the constitution and the laws made under it. The third lock involves the basic 'rule of law' requirement that government be conducted according to laws that have been duly passed under the widely-endorsed foundational constitutional pact and interpreted by a judiciary insulated from executive or other partial interference".

more opportunities and mechanisms for minorities to express their will. The Laws have an important role because of the fact that constitutional democracy and populism coincide and have to be reconciled. In this context, the Laws in Indonesia ensure that the minority interests are accommodated in all aspects of state. Public participation in the law making process is one of the mechanisms to gain aspiration from minority. The Indonesian Constitution actually has already provided a constitutional basis for minorities. Meanwhile, the law facilitates effective control of the parliament as the people's representation and as the government branch which has the power to make laws. In the Indonesian Constitution, the Constitution has to facilitate effective control by setting a mechanism of checks and balances. In a presidential system as in Indonesia, the law has to prevent the rise of tyranny by preserving the relation between the President as the executive and the Parliament as the legislative. The Laws have to ensure the mechanism of checks and balances among both institutions.

The Indonesian Constitution has shown a tendency to retrench populism through its provisions. In line with the Constitution, the Laws have the strength to hold up populism. For instance, the Electoral Law sets a threshold for political parties and presidential candidates to participate in the election when at the same time it makes it more difficult to establish a new political party reducing opportunities for a populist movement to enter the electoral arena.[35] This tendency may show that the Indonesian democratic by-laws are trying to limit populism. In order to deal with a technocratic populism which mostly requires improvement instead of replacing the existing policy, any efforts for improvement have to be in according to the Constitution.

Populism may arise because of the demands from the people which are commonly reflected and represented by an individual populist figure. The law has to provide facilities to transform populism by institutionalizing the populist figure into a more democratic representative figure so that the populist figure could act constitutionally instead of only speaking on behalf of the people outside of the system.[36] However, in the process, pressure from the people makes the process subject to the will of the people or interest groups. In this situation, it is important to gain more organized support not only from the parliament which holds the legislative power to make laws but also from all groups within the community. Such support will come by gaining cooperation through the ability of disseminating popular organizations and civil society activists to give new energy to extra-parliamentary alliances and work with progressive politicians to press a core set of demands for public services, social rights, decent

35 M Mietzner, 'Reinventing Asian Populism: Jokowi's Rise, Democracy, and Political Contestation in Indonesia' [2015] 72 *Policy Studies* 58.

36 P Pratikno and C Lay, From Populism to Democratic Polity: Problems and Challenges in Surakarta, Indonesia [2011] 3(1-2) *PCD Journal* 55.

employment relations, inclusive growth and democratic participation in public governance.[37] On the other hand, the courts, and in particular the Constitutional Court, are the pivotal actor in the process of shielding democratic values from any threats. The courts, in particular the Constitutional Court, have the role of reinforcing constitutional restraints for democracy values, and of hindering negative manifestations of populism, even when facing the dilemma of being counter-majoritarian. As long as the Court delivers a justified-reasoning of judgment, judges may confront populism. The Court could act as an intermediate institution when the legislative or executive become populist. In this context, the Courts have to act according their nature, applying the law and holding the ground of legalism and the core values to keep its legitimacy, upholding judicial objectivity as well as its independence and acting according to its basic mandate to adjudicate disputes even when the judgment is in contradiction with the will of the people. It is in accordance with Article 24 (1) of the Indonesian Constitution on the constitutional basis for judicial independence in Indonesia.[38]

4 Against Populism: The Role of the Constitutional Court in Indonesia

Populism in Indonesia is not only a political issue but also may be of concern as a judicial issue. The question is about how populism could infiltrate justices under the judicial branch, the Court. In its decision and judicial process, the Court has to show its independence as an independent and impartial institution. As the general role of the judicial branch, the Constitutional Court is from its nature the counterpart of other branches, the executive and legislative. In Indonesia, the Constitutional Court is one of the branches which has the role as an institution which must conduct the checks and balances mechanism by such judicial mechanisms as a judicial review. In this context, the Court has the key to the counterpart whenever there is a populist executive or populist legislative. However, it would be a dilemma when the Court has to decide according to the majoritarian will rather than deciding what legally mandated the Court has to decide.

Under Article 24C (1) of the Indonesian Constitution, the Court has several competences including the competence of judicial review, dispute settlement of the state institutions, and dispute settlement of the election process.[39] On the competence

---

37 A E Hara, 'Populism in Indonesia and its Threats to Democracy' (*Third International Conference on Social and Political Sciences (ICSPS 2017) Advances in Social Science, Education and Humanities Research (ASSEHR) Atlantic Press 2018*).

38 Art. 24 of the Indonesian Constitution stipulates: "The judicial power shall be independent and shall possess the power to organize the judicature in order to enforce law and justice".

39 Art. 24 of the Indonesian Constitution stipulates: "The Constitutional Court shall have the power to try a case at the first and final level and shall have the final power of decision in reviewing laws against the Constitution, determining disputes over the authorities of state institutions whose powers are given by this Constitution, deciding over the dissolution of a political party, and deciding disputes over the results of general elections".

of judicial review, the Court has a vital role to protect democracy by preserving constitutional values by controlling the political product of the President and the DPR. On the Court's competence to determine disputes between state institutions, the Court may have the opportunity to protect the political system from populists. On the other issue of the Court's competence to decide disputes over the result of general elections, the Court is about defending democracy while confirming the majority. To this extent, the Court may potentially affirm the populist figure resulting from the direct election.

In the judicial making process, the Constitutional Court has the key to resist the majoritarian will and oppose populism through judicial independence. The populist character of the Court could emerge as a consequence that the Court may overrule the President and the DPR as the people's representatives in Indonesia. In such a situation, the people's representative has a negative image of being elitist and to mostly put forward its individual interest and tending to be corrupt. In the Court's experience, the independence of the Court has been challenged several times.

In a case concerning the notion that 20% of the national budget had to be spent on education, the character of populism may be reflected in the Court's decision. The Constitution requires that 20 % of the state budget has to be allocated for the national education budget. This constitutional obligation has the character of progressivism in its realization, meaning that the budget would have to become 20% according to the situation of the state's financial situation. However the 2005 – 2008 state budget did not meet the 20% criterion. The Court decision No. 13/PUU-VI I 2008 entailed that this was unconstitutional and that therefore, the 20% had to be immediately met. In this decision, the Court may be assumed as proponent to the populist pretention from the people since the Court affirms the people's will and decided taking side to accommodate the populist policy and against the DPR and the President's political decision in the realization of the national educational budget.

In another case concerning Law No. 42/2008 Article 28 and Article 111, the Court decided that the application of the Indonesian national identity card "the KTP" in the presidential election was constitutional. Under the pressure of the majority of the people, the Court delivered a new norm on the application of the rights to vote for voters who are not registered on the voter list (the DPT). The Court decision was decided right before the Election Day under pressure from the people who was manipulated by most of political parties as the partisan in the election.

In another Court's decision, the Court defended the existence of the Corruption Court, even though it was unconstitutional, when assessing the Anti-Corruption Law. The Court said in its decision that on the basis of constitutional importance, the establishment of an anti-corruption court (as a judicial institution) under the anti-corruption commission is constitutionally important even though it is beyond the Constitution. The Court decided on what was called constitutional necessity on the basis of pressure from the people which was at the time an incessant anti-corruption movement.

In other issues, the Court has the function to mitigate the people movement systematically in order to counter-balance the government regime. The Court's function is shown by two cases concerning economic rights and political rights. In the issue of economic democracy, Indonesia has dealt with the issue of fuel prices. The main issue is that fuel is heavily subsidized and the question is whether it ought not to be market prices. This has always been difficult for the government and has always been a dilemma of parliament. Under the Law No. 22/2001 concerning Oil and Gas, the government issued a policy to implement the oil-fuel price through the market mechanism on the basis of the market competition. The government assumed that the private business actors will benefit from this policy and will therefore pay more taxes so as to reduce the subsidy burden of oil-fuel price. Here the government expected that the state budget will not be challenged by the subsidies. The subsidy will be only for particular fuels. The government policy was supported by the DPR but was challenged by judicial review by the Court. Several NGOs and Labor organizations were against the new policy relying on the argument that the government responsibility has to be in accordance to Article 33 of the Indonesian Constitution. In this case No. 002/PUU-I/2003, the Court decided that the government intervention in the price policy has significant impact on the life of the people. The government may consider several issues in the process of determining the price policy including the price offered by the market mechanism. However, the priority of market competition mechanism and the government intervention has to be limited only for the particular level of community on the basis of welfare level. In this context, the mechanism is not guaranteeing the principle of economic democracy. Therefore, the government policy determining the oil-fuel price by considering the market competition even on the basis of fairness and proportionality was said to be unconstitutional by the Court. The Court decision is based on its interpretation of Article 33 Paragraph (3) of the Constitution concerning the principle of people welfare and the state necessity. The Court reviewed that the principle of people welfare on the oil and gas production has the meaning that the definition is not only about the lower price but also has about the good quality, the availability, and distribution to all the people.

Concerning political rights, the Court decided in July 2009 with respect to voting rights. The case was about the mechanism to invoke voting rights. It was regulated that in order to use the voting rights, the citizen has to be registered as the voter in the voting list. In fact, there were many citizens who were eligible to use their voting right but did not register in the voting list because of administrative matters including problem with the resident identity card. Such situation was assumed as a state violation to the right to vote and right to have equal position in law and government. Meanwhile, the government makes an effort to establish the service office in order to provide the identity card for the people. However, the effort had several obstacles. It made the General Election

Commission had to deal with the validation issue of voters. In the Court decision No, 102/PUU-VII/2009, the Court was responsive to the factual situation and issued its decision that the use of identity card or Indonesian Passport could be used to invoke the voting right. This Court decision was delivered as the populist group which manipulated speaking to represent the people. The Court decision enforced the General Election Commission to implement the Court decision.

5 Conclusion

In Indonesia, populism and democracy may co-exist. Populism may be within constitutional democracy. The Indonesian Constitution and the Laws have their role to maintain the improvement process and balance with the constitutional democracy principles. The rule of law facilitates democratic life in Indonesia. It is an effective instrument promoting responsibility, accountability, reciprocity and trust in democracy. Within the rule of law framework, the Law would regulate the people, *vice- versa*, the Law has to be obeyed by the people. At this point, the Law must be proportionally implemented, it has to be certain. Thus, any democracy deviations would be hindered. The rise of populism in Indonesia may give benefit to democracy in the sense that it could reconcile the process within the corridor of the democratic system in accordance to the Constitution and the legal framework. The Laws on the establishment of the democratic regime in Indonesia have precisely introduced a preventive measure for any negative excesses of populism.

The Indonesian Constitution and the Laws have the role to be an effective catalyst to resist populism by setting democratic standards, such as cultural identity, pluralism values, religion, human rights, economic prosperity, ethnicity, citizenship, the judicial independence, and system of government. Those standards must resist populist politics that are mainly based on division and rules. In this context, the Law has to be certain and has the role of giving guidance to people and the elite government on how to behave. The parliament involves in grassroots organizing and helping people to understand the party politics and politics of populist policies and form alternative policies to counteract the development. Hence there is a continued role for the Constitution and the Laws to provide people with legal protection and a legal framework so that people could make the right choices in electing their representatives who in turn are accountable, not only to their voter citizens but also to the entire population.

In the end, it is the courts which have the key role to uphold the Constitution and the Laws. The Constitutional Court, being a part of the judicial branch, has an important role to show its objectivity, impartiality and independence. This is important to minimize the negative risk of giving in to the majority people's will. In reaching its decisions, the Court has to put aside what the majority expresses as its desires and must decide on what is legal according to the Constitution and Laws.

The Case of the Philippine Judiciary – Guardian of Democracy or Enabler of Populism?

*Dante Gatmaytan**

1 Introduction

Populists view themselves as the exclusive moral embodiment of the People, and in so doing they take on the form of a "degraded form of democracy."[1] Populist leaders use the legitimacy conferred by democratic elections to consolidate power. They undermine the checks and balances that limit the leader's personal power.[2] They attack the basic principles of liberal and democratic constitutionalism because they want to consolidate power and entrench themselves in office.[3] They launch legal reforms that remove the checks on executive power, limit the challenges to their rule, and undermine the crucial accountability institutions of a democratic state.[4] Because they push their illiberal measures with electoral backing and use constitutional or legal methods to accomplish their aims, they can hide their autocratic designs behind legitimate legal forms.[5]

Faced with an assault on democratic constitutionalism, we look to the judiciary to preserve the constitutional order. Judges are regarded as the guardians of the Constitution, ensuring government will not overstep its powers or encroach on citizens' rights.[6]

However, in the Philippines, the Supreme Court has in the past years been ruling consistently in favor of President Rodrigo Duterte's administration on a variety of issues, including the use of emergency powers, and the removal of the Chief Justice.

---

* Dante Gatmaytan is Professor of Law at the University of the Philippines, College of Law. He graduated with a Bachelor's Degree from the Ateneo de Manila (B.S. Legal Management) and a law degree (LL.B.) from the University of the Philippines. He holds Masters Degrees from Vermont Law School (cum laude) and the University of California, Los Angeles. He is a professorial lecturer at the Department of Constitutional Law of the Philippine Judicial Academy.

1 J-W Müller, *What is Populism?* (University of Pennsylvania Press 2017) 6.

2 F Fukuyama, *Identity: The Demand for Dignity and the Politics of Resentment* (Profile Books 2018).

3 K L Scheppele, 'Autocratic Legalism' [2018] 85 *University of Chicago Law Review* 548.

4 ibid.

5 ibid.

6 A S Chilton and M Versteeg, 'Courts' Limited Ability to Protect Constitutional Rights' [2018] 85(2) *University of Chicago Law Review* 296.

Duterte, who has often been described as a textbook case of a populist politician,[7] has won every case where his acts were questioned, always at the expense of separation of powers.

The Supreme Court has been assisting the President and by implication, his populist agenda, even at the cost of its own independence.

In this Chapter, I will show that in a country with weak institutions[8] and where the judiciary defers to the executive branch, the courts will toe the populist line. The Philippine case is astonishing as the Supreme Court automatically implements the populist program even without any overt pressure.[9]

2 Populism

Populism is a way of perceiving the political world that sets a morally pure and fully unified people against elites who are deemed corrupt and morally inferior.[10] Populists claim exclusive representation to speak for the people as a whole.[11] Their core claim is that only some people are really the people.[12] Populists claim that "a part of the people is the people – and that only the populist authentically identifies and represents this real or true people."[13] The sentiment that gives rise to populism is that government serves only the elite and is too remote and uncaring about problems at the grassroots.[14]

Populism challenges principles such as the centrality of competitive elections to the constitutional form, the ideal of the rule of law, the primacy of judicial review in

7 See for instance R J Heydarian, *The rise of Duterte: A populist revolt against elite democracy* (Springer 2017).

8 Despite decades of American apprenticeship as a colony and decades more as an independent state, a "properly functioning democracy remains elusive" in the Philippines. See: C Sherrill, 'Promoting Democracy: Results of Democratization Efforts in the Philippines' [2006] 32(4) *Asian Affairs: An American Review* 211.

9 I leave out the role of Congress in defending the liberal constitution because it abdicated its role as a check on Executive power. Soon after Rodrigo Duterte was elected President of the Philippines, a vast majority of the members of the House of Representatives formed a coalition with his party which gathered 260 allies or 90 percent of the estimated 290 members. See: G C Cabacungan, 'From 3 to 300, PDP-Laban forms 'supermajority' in House' (*Inquirernet*, 26 May 2016) https://newsinfo.inquirer.net/787547/from-3-to-300-pdp-laban-forms-supermajority-in-house#ixzz5aN2G71jx accessed 13 February 2020; Mass defections are common in the Philippines where the political parties' policies and legislative behaviour are virtually indistinguishable and highly unstable over time. See: G R Montinola, 'Parties and Accountability in the Philippines' [1999] 10(1) *Journal of Democracy* 133-34; In fact, parties were merely temporary electoral and legislative alliances designed to maximize the election chances of individual politicians. Any discernible difference between the parties at any given time had nothing to do with party organizations at all. Such differences as there were depended solely on the policy preferences of their current standard-bearers, ibid 135.

10 J-W Müller, *What is Populism?* (University of Pennsylvania Press 2017) 19-20.

11 ibid 20.

12 ibid 21.

13 ibid 22-23.

14 A C Grayling, *Democracy and Its Crisis* (Oneworld Publications 2018) 116.

constitutional enforcement, and the force of individual rights.[15] Populism is democracy's natural antagonist.[16]

3 Populism and the Threat to Law

"Populism" emerged in the latter decades of the nineteenth century as a *protest movement* by political outsiders, composed mostly of distressed farmers, but also laborers, ranchers, and debtors of all types.[17] Populists constituted an unstable coalition but they agreed on three fundamental points: 1) the government needs to combat private economic power, which profits at the expense of the common person, but 2) it cannot be trusted to do so, and thus, 3) the "people" must gain control of the government. "Regaining control" led them to advocate, almost obsessively, direct legislation. For many populists, adoption of the mechanisms of direct democracy overshadowed nearly every other issue.[18] Populists sought to use the initiative power to undermine representative government and shift power to the people themselves.[19]

To populists, the problem of democratic government was the excessive domination of the political system by the corporate system and the danger they thought increasing concentrations of wealth posed to democracy. They also noted the lack of elections that reflected the popular will.[20]

There are many views on the reasons for the rise of populism today.[21] While there may be disagreement on the trigger, there is little disagreement on the impact of the rise of populism. The current populist wave is subverting democracy by leaders who are promising more democracy – but it is a democracy of a different kind. Populists embrace the "form" of democracy and claim to speak for the people themselves. At the same time, however, by undermining its liberal constitutional foundations, they erode the substance of democracy, and gradually transform it into various forms of illiberal and authoritarian regimes.[22]

---

15 A Z Huq, 'The People against the Constitution' [2018] 116(6) *Michigan Law Review* 1124-5.

16 ibid 1137.

17 K P Miller, 'Constraining Populism: The Real Challenge of Initiative Reform' [2001] 41(4) *Santa Clara Law Review* 1039-40.

18 ibid 1040.

19 ibid.

20 ibid.

21 One, for example, cites four central institutional challenges: first, the accelerated decline of political parties and other institutional forms of popular engagement; second, the paralysis of the legislative branches; third, the loss of a sense of social cohesion; and fourth, the decline in state competence. These four have a particular salience in theories of democratic superiority that make their decline or loss a matter of grave concern. Each of these theories states a claim for the advantages of democracy, and each faces worrisome disrepair. See: S Issacharoff, 'Democracy's Deficits' [2018] 85 *University of Chicago Law Review* 488.

22 B Bugaric, 'The Right to Democracy in a Populist Era' [2018] 112 *American Journal of International Law Unbound* 79.

The rise of populism is directed at non-majoritarian institutions such as courts and intergovernmental bodies. Populists attack non-majoritarian institutions because of their lack of democratic legitimacy. Once in office, populists claim that Parliament is the sole legitimate authority to be obeyed in a democracy, thus threatening the credentials of non-majoritarian authorities.[23] Populists claim that liberal norms and policies weaken democracy and harm the people. Thus, liberal institutions that prevent the people from acting democratically in their own interest should be set aside.[24]

Assaults on democracy shatter democratic institutions that constrain them slowly and imperceptibly with "baby steps", none of which appear to threaten democracy.[25] These steps receive a veneer of legality because they are approved by Congress or the courts.[26]

Would-be authoritarians also skew institutions that are designed to check the abuse of executive power such as the judiciary and law enforcement bodies. If these are controlled by the President then he can "break the law, threaten citizens' rights and even violate the constitution *without* having to worry that such abuses will be investigated or censured."[27]

Institutions that cannot be purged are hijacked. Judges who cannot be bought are impeached or neutralized through court packing.[28] More extreme cases involve the abolition of courts and the creation of new ones under the executive's control.[29] By capturing the referees, buying off or enfeebling opponents, and rewriting the rules of the game, elected leaders can establish a decisive – and permanent – advantage over their opponents. Because these measures are carried out piecemeal and with the appearance of legality, citizens are often slow to realize that their democracy is being dismantled.[30]

4 POPULISTS AND CONSTITUTIONS

Populists can write constitutions to keep themselves in power ostensibly to perpetuate "some supposed original and authentic popular will."[31] Populist constitutionalism is not an outright denial of liberal constitutionalism and the rule of law. It is a form of constitutional critique and 'counter-constitutionalism.'[32] Populist constitutionalism could be mistaken for a democratic project because of its alleged endorsement of

---

23 C Pinelli, 'The Populist Challenge to Constitutional Democracy' [2011] 7(1) *European Constitutional Law Review* 5.

24 W A Galston, 'The Populist Challenge to Liberal Democracy' [2018] 29(2) *Journal of Democracy* 5.

25 S Levitsky and D Ziblatt, *How Democracies Die* (Crown 2018) 77.

26 ibid 85.

27 ibid 78.

28 ibid 79.

29 ibid 80-81.

30 ibid 92.

31 J-W Müller, *What is Populism?* (University of Pennsylvania Press 2017) 102.

32 P Blokker, Populist Constitutionalism. in C de la Torre (ed), *Routledge Handbook of Global Populism* (1st edn, Routledge 2018).

popular rule. But, it has been argued that populism has to be qualified differently. "While populism draws on democratic principles, by drawing extreme, one-sided conclusions, it violates key dimensions of democratic constitutionalism, such as those of pluralism, inclusiveness, and actual civic participation in constitutionalism."[33]

The populists' constitution-writing project has three functions: (i) deconstructing the existing political regime, (ii) serving as an ideological critique that promises to overcome flaws in the prior constitutional order, and (iii) consolidating power in the hands of the populist leadership. These tendencies appear inherent in nearly all populist projects, and thus studying populist constitutional change is helpful in understanding populism in general. There are two possible responses to the challenge of populism for liberal-democratic constitutionalism: (i) block forms of constitutional change that allow populists to remain in power for long periods of time and thus have a particularly corrosive effect, and (ii) confront and respond to the weaknesses in liberal democracy that give legitimacy to populist constitutional projects.[34]

5 Courts and Populism

Another feature of populism is its attack on apex courts. From a democratic point of view courts guard the differentiation (separation and division) of powers. Populism, however, on its own interpretation of popular sovereignty must resist such differentiation, and any agency seeking to enforce it.[35]

Courts have already run into populist threats but have few success stories. The Colombian Constitutional Court, in two decisions in 2005 and 2010, the first allowed President Álvaro Uribe Vélez to set aside a one-term limit, but then barred him from abrogating a new two-term limit through constitutional amendment. In the latter decision, the court reasoned that a second extension of the presidential term would effectively be a "substitution" of the constitution, since it would allow the President to "name members of the central bank, the attorney general, the ombudsman, the chief prosecutor, and many members of the Constitutional Court." This second decision is thought to have "prevent[ed] a significant erosion of democracy by preventing a strong president from holding onto power indefinitely." In effect, the decision enabled other oversight institutions to operate effectively in ways that helped promote democratic practices. The decision, however, was only possible because the court had initially

33 P Blokker, 'Populism as a Constitutional Project' [2018] 17(2) *International Journal of Constitutional Law* 536.

34 D Landau, 'Populist Constitutions' [2018] 85 *University of Chicago Law Review* 521.

35 A Arato, 'Populism and the Courts' (Blog of the International Journal of Constitutional Law, 25th April) http://www.iconnectblog.com/2017/04/populism-and-the-courts accessed 26 September 2019.

avoided a confrontation with Uribe, and instead had delayed intervention until it would have maximum effect and might generate more public support.[36]

In March 2016, the Constitutional Court of South Africa ordered President Jacob Zuma to repay millions of rand used to refurbish a private residence. The decision was said to "de-legitimiz[e]" the president as a leader who relied on the spoils system.[37]

A survey of the performance of other courts shows few reasons to celebrate. In Hungary the Fidesz party in 2013 took advantage of an unexpected legislative supermajority to alter the constitution to abrogate prior judicial precedent *en masse* and limit judicial review to procedural, not substantive, questions of legality and constitutionality. More significantly, a system by which a majority of parliamentary parties had to endorse a candidate for the Supreme Court was abandoned in favor of one where Fidesz has plenary control of who sits on the Court.[38]

Hungary created a new court system that cements executive control over the judiciary.[39] Prime Minister Viktor Orban's justice minister will control the hiring and promotion of its judges, who will have jurisdiction over cases relating to "public administration" – including electoral law, corruption, and the right to protest. Hungary's existing judiciary will have a reduced mandate, and with no oversight of the parallel court system, known as the administrative courts.[40]

In Poland, the populist Law and Justice Party (PiS) won a plurality of seats in October 2015, and refused to seat the Constitutional Tribunal Justices who had been selected by other parties but awaited commissions; amended the statutory framework for judicial appointments to centralize control in the PiS-controlled Sejm, the lower house of the Polish Parliament, changed the voting rule in constitutional cases to make invalidations less frequent, and rejiggered the flow of cases to the court.[41]

In Venezuela, the government of Hugo Chávez relied first on its appointments power. When judges continued to resist his agenda, Chávez leveraged street protests against the court and "strong rhetoric" in public speeches to undermine the judiciary. In Turkey, the Constitutional Court in 2008 permitted criminal indictments against the ruling Justice and Development (AK) Party to proceed based on party leaders' public condemnations of

36 A Z Huq, 'Democratic Erosion and the Courts: Comparative Perspectives' [2018)] 93 *New York University Law Review* 23.

37 ibid 23-24.

38 ibid 25-26.

39 B Novak and P Kingsley, 'Hungary Creates New Court System, Cementing Leader's Control of Judiciary' (The Times New Roman, 12 December 2018) https://www.nytimes.com/2018/12/12/world/europe/hungary-courts.html accessed 26 September 2019.

40 ibid.

41 A Z Huq, 'Democratic Erosion and the Courts: Comparative Perspectives' [2018)] 93 *New York University Law Review* 26; F Zoll and L Wortham, 'Judicial Independence and Accountability: Withstanding Political Stress in Poland' [2019] 42(3) *Fordham International Law Journal* 889-898.

a ban on religious garb in public universities. But less than a decade later, a resurgent and popular AK Party was able to neuter the judiciary by rallying public opinion against it.[42]

So far, Courts' roles at moments of democratic erosion show various tactical options. At best, as in the Colombian and South African cases, courts delay backsliding. At worst, they are captured or eviscerated in backsliding's opening gambit. The literature suggests that a judiciary committed to democracy should carefully play a moderating function at pivotal moments in the course of democratic backsliding, in the hope, perhaps, that exogenous political developments enable rather than erode the presuppositions of democracy's continued operation.[43]

6 The Case of the Philippines

Rodrigo Duterte was elected in 2016, riding on a "law and order" campaign that exploited popular anxieties about social disorder.[44] He sustains his popularity by claiming that only the use of violent strongman rule can bring about reforms.[45] Duterte promised to restore "law and order" in three to six months largely through the extrajudicial killing of criminals. Besides promising a quick fix to the growing crime problem, he also pledged to rebuild crumbling infrastructure and to end corruption. This helps explain why Duterte's support was middle class-driven, particularly strong among taxi drivers, small shop owners, and overseas workers who were worried their fragile economic gains after years of growth would be threatened unless 'order' was restored by any means necessary.[46]

Duterte represents a new politician who promises to use violence and strong-arm tactics to solve social and political problems; a platform known as voting against disorder.[47] Voting against disorder entails the emergence, within a democratic system, of support for a political platform that either implicitly or explicitly promises to undermine the rule of law – and with it, democracy itself.[48]

Duterte and his allies have been brought before the Supreme Court, but they have never lost a single case. Rather than operate as the guardian of the Constitution, the

42 ibid 26.

43 ibid 27.

44 M R Thompson, 'Why Duterte Remains So Popular' (Foreign Affairs, 9 October 2018) https://www.foreignaffairs.com/articles/philippines/2018-10-09/why-duterte-remains-so-popular accessed 26 September 2019.

45 ibid. Duterte's "war on drugs" has been described as a form of genocide. See: D Simangan, 'Is the Philippine "War on Drugs" an Act of Genocide' [2018] 20(1) *Journal of Genocide Research* 68.

46 M R Thompson, 'The Moral Economy of Electoralism and the Rise of Populism in Thailand and the Philippines' [2016] 32(3) *Journal of Developing Societies* 258.

47 T Pepinsky, 'Southeast Asia: Voting Against Disorder' [2017] 28(2) *Journal of Democracy* 120.

48 ibid 122.

Supreme Court ruled in favor of the President, imperiling the separation of powers, and consolidating power in the Executive Branch.

The following sections will illustrate this point further through a number of sample cases.

6.1 *Baguilat, Jr. v. Alvarez, G.R. No. 227757, July 25, 2017*

The issue in this case was whether respondents may be compelled via a writ of mandamus to recognize Representative Teddy Brawner Baguilat as the Minority Leader of the House of Representatives. Baguilat failed in his bid to become Speaker of the House.

Petitioners hoped that as a "long-standing tradition" of the House – where the candidate who garnered the second-highest number of votes for Speakership automatically becomes the Minority Leader – Baguilat would be declared and recognized as the Minority Leader. However, Baguilat was never recognized as such. Instead, there was a motion to recognize Representative Suarez as the Minority Leader. Representative Lagman opposed this motion on the ground that Suarez was a member of the Majority as he voted for Speaker Alvarez. However, the opposition was overruled, and consequently, Suarez was officially recognized as the House Minority Leader.

The case was elevated to the Supreme Court but the Supreme Court declined to intervene, saying it was hard-pressed to find any grave abuse of discretion which would warrant its intrusion in this case. According to the Court, the case:

> concerns an internal matter of a coequal, political branch of government which, absent any showing of grave abuse of discretion, cannot be judicially interfered with. To rule otherwise would not only embroil this Court in the realm of politics, but also lead to its own breach of the separation of powers doctrine.

6.2 *Lagman v. Medialdea, G.R. No. 231658, July 4, 2017*

On May 23, 2017, Duterte issued Proclamation No. 216 declaring a state of martial law and suspending the privilege of the writ of *habeas corpus* in the whole of Mindanao for a period not exceeding 60 days. As required by the Constitution he submitted a written Report to Congress on the factual basis of Proclamation No. 216. According to the Report a government operation to capture high-ranking officers of the Abu Sayyaf Group (ASG) and the Maute Group was conducted. These groups confronted the government operation by intensifying their efforts at sowing violence aimed not only against the government authorities and its facilities but likewise against civilians and their properties.

The President's actions were challenged before the Supreme Court, principally on the ground that there was neither an invasion nor rebellion that would justify martial law.

The Petition also claimed that the declaration of martial law has no sufficient factual basis because the President's Report contained "false, inaccurate, contrived and hyperbolic accounts."

The Court first distinguished judicial and congressional powers of review: It held that the Court may strike down the presidential proclamation in an appropriate proceeding filed by any citizen on the ground of lack of sufficient factual basis. On the other hand, Congress may revoke the proclamation or suspension, which shall not be set aside by the President.

The Court weakened its power in the following paragraph saying that in reviewing the sufficiency of the factual basis of the proclamation or suspension, the Court considers only the information and data available to the President prior to or at the time of the declaration; it is not allowed to "undertake an independent investigation beyond the pleadings."

Congress, however, may take into consideration not only data available prior to, but also events supervening the declaration. Unlike the Court, which does not look into the absolute correctness of the factual basis, Congress could probe deeper and further and "delve into the accuracy of the facts presented before it."

The Court added that the Court's review power is passive and is initiated by the filing of a petition "in an appropriate proceeding" by a citizen. Congress' review mechanism is automatic in the sense that it may be activated by Congress itself at any time after the proclamation or suspension was made.

The Court would then restate the classic rationale for judicial deference: The President's power to declare martial law is a judgment call and the determination of this Court as to whether there is sufficient factual basis for the exercise of such, must be based only on facts or information known by or available to the President at the time he made the declaration or suspension. These facts or information are found in the proclamation as well as the written Report submitted by him to Congress. These may be based on the situation existing at the time the declaration was made or past events. How far the past events should be from the present depends on the President. Past events may be considered as justifications for the declaration and/or suspension as long as these are connected or related to the current situation existing at the time of the declaration.

What facts must be stated in the proclamation and the written Report is within the President's sole discretion, taking into account the urgency of the situation as well as national security. He cannot be forced to divulge intelligence reports and confidential information that may prejudice the operations and the safety of the military.

The Court also held that the Court should not expect absolute correctness of the facts stated in the proclamation and in the written Report because the President could not be expected to verify the accuracy and veracity of all facts reported to him due to the urgency of the situation. To require precision would impede the process of his decision-making. That would require the President to be on the ground to confirm the correctness of the reports submitted to him and would place the President in peril and defeat the very purpose of the grant of emergency powers that is to immediately put an end to the root cause of the emergency.

6.3 *Padilla v. Congress of the Philippines, G.R. No. 231671, July 25, 2017*

In *Padilla*, Petitioners assailed the failure and/or refusal of the Congress of the Philippines to convene in joint session and deliberate on Proclamation No. 216.

The Court ruled that Congress is not constitutionally mandated to convene in joint session except to vote jointly to revoke the President's declaration or suspension.

The case was concerned with the interpretation of the phrase:

> The Congress, voting jointly, by a vote of at least a majority of all its Members in regular or special session, may revoke such proclamation or suspension, which revocation shall not be set aside by the President.

According to the Court, the use of the word "may" is to be construed as permissive and operating to confer discretion on the Congress on whether or not to revoke, but in order to revoke, the same provision sets the requirement that at least a majority of the Members of the Congress, voting jointly, favor revocation.

It added that the provision only requires Congress to vote jointly on the revocation of the President's proclamation and/or suspension. The Houses of Congress already separately adopted resolutions expressing support for President Duterte's Proclamation No. 216. Given the express support of both Houses and their already evident lack of intent to revoke the same, the provision on revocation did not even come into operation and, therefore, there is no obligation on the part of the Congress to convene in joint session.

6.4 *Lagman v. Senate President, G.R. No. 235935, February 6, 2018*

These cases questioned the constitutionality of the extension of the proclamation of martial law and suspension of the privilege of habeas corpus in the entire Mindanao for an entire year from January 1, 2018 to December 31, 2018. The Supreme Court once more ruled in favor of the government and held that the only limitation to the exercise of these powers is that this extension should be at the President's initiative, that there is invasion, and rebellion, that it is required by public safety, and that it is subject to the Court's review of the factual bases.

6.5 *Lagman v. Medialdea, G.R. No. 243522, February 19, 2019*

By the time the third extension of martial law had come before judicial review, the Supreme Court had all but written itself out as a constitutional check. Here are excerpts:

> The Court need not make an independent determination of the factual basis for the proclamation or extension of martial law and the suspension of the privilege of the writ of habeas corpus. The Court is not a fact-finding body required to make a determination of the correctness of the factual basis for the declaration or extension of martial law and suspension of the writ of habeas corpus. It would be impossible for the Court to go on the ground to conduct an independent investigation or factual inquiry, since it is not equipped with resources comparable to that of the Commander-in-Chief to ably and properly assess the ground conditions.
> Thus, in determining the sufficiency of the factual basis for the extension of martial law, the Court needs only to assess and evaluate the written reports of the government agencies tasked in enforcing and implementing martial law in Mindanao [...].
> The Court need not delve into the accuracy of the reports upon which the President's decision is based, or the correctness of his decision to declare martial law or suspend the writ, for this an executive function. The, threshold or level (degree) of sufficiency is, all, an executive call. The President, who is running the government and to whom the executive power is vested, is the one tasked or mandated to assess and make the judgment call which was not exercised arbitrarily.

The Supreme Court goes on to devalue its own review powers, saying it is inferior to legislative review:

> In finding sufficiency of the factual bases for the third extension, the Court has to give due regard to the military and police reports which are not palpably contrived and untrue; the full complement or totality of the submitted, and not make a piecemeal or individual appreciation of the facts and the incidents reported. The President's decision to extend the declaration and the suspension of the Writ, when it goes through the review of the Legislative must be accorded a weightier and more consequential basis. Under these circumstances, the President's decision or judgment call is affirmed by the representatives of the People.

In its conclusion the Court simplified the approach to judicial review of emergency powers, once more, granting the Chief Executive the widest leeway:

> The Constitutional safeguards found in Section 18, Article VII do not demand that a city be first taken over or get killed and billions of properties go up in smoke before the President may be justified to use his options under Section 18. What the Constitution asks is only that there be actual rebellion, an existing rebellion in the territory where Martial rule is to be imposed. The declaration should not be arbitrary or whimsical, but its basis should not also be so accurate that there is no room for changes or correction. Considering the volatility of conflict, situations may change at the blink of an eye. And the Executive is burdened with such responsibility to act decisively.

6.6 Republic of the Philippines v. Sereno, G.R. No. 237428, May 11, 2018

On May 11, 2018, the Supreme Court of the Philippines promulgated a historic 8-7 decision, removing Chief Justice Maria Lourdes Sereno from office.

The Supreme Court has always interpreted the Constitution to mean that the public officials listed (which include the Chief Justice) can be removed only by impeachment. Jurisprudence also prohibits the circumvention of this rule. In *Cuenco v. Fernan*,[49] a disbarment case filed against then incumbent Supreme Court Justice Marcelo B. Fernan was dismissed because it would circumvent the constitutional mandate that his removal from office should only be by way of impeachment.[50]

To grant a complaint for disbarment of a Member of the Court during the Member's incumbency, would in effect be to circumvent the constitutional mandate that Members of the Court may be removed from office only by impeachment for and conviction of certain offenses listed in Article XI (2) of the Constitution.[51]

The Court also abandoned decades-old case law that barred the Solicitor-General from filing a *quo warranto*[52] case against public officers a year after they took office. The Supreme Court has always held that in actions of *quo warranto involving right to an office, the action must be instituted within the period of one year from the time the cause of action arose.*[53]

49 *Cuenco v Fernan* [1988] Supreme Court of the Republic of the Philippines No 3135 [1988] 241 Phil. 816.
50 *Re: Pamatong* [2013] A.M. No 12-11-14-SC (Notice).
51 *Cuenco v Fernan* [1988] Supreme Court of the Republic of the Philippines No 3135 (Resolution) [1988] 241 Phil. 816.
52 See *Topacio v Ong* [2008] G.R. No. 179895, [2008] 595 Phil. 491.
53 *Cristobal v Melchor* [1977] G.R. No. L-43203, [1977] 168 Phil. 328.

Preceding all this was an unprecedented spectacle where five of the Justices queued in the House of Representatives' committee hearings to shore up a weak impeachment case against the Chief Justice.

When the case for *quo warranto* was filed, not only did the Court entertain the petition some six years after Sereno assumed office, the Justices who appeared before the House of Representatives refused to recuse themselves, contributing five of the eight votes removing the Chief Justice.

To justify its ruling, the Court distinguished impeachment and an action for *quo warranto*. Impeachment is a proceeding exercised by the legislative, as representatives of the sovereign, to vindicate the breach of the trust reposed by the people in the hands of the public officer by determining the public officer's fitness to stay in office. Meanwhile, an action for *quo warranto*, involves a judicial determination of the eligibility or validity of the election or appointment of a public official based on predetermined rules.

A *quo warranto* proceeding is the proper legal remedy to determine the right or title to the contested public office or to oust the holder from its enjoyment. In case of usurpation of a public office, when the respondent is found guilty of usurping, intruding into, or unlawfully holding or exercising a public office, position or franchise, the judgment shall include the following: (a) the respondent shall be ousted and excluded from the office; (b) the petitioner or relator, as the case may be, shall recover his costs; and (c) such further judgment determining the respective rights in and to the public office, position or franchise of all the parties to the action as justice requires.

Quo warranto and impeachment are, according to the Court, not mutually exclusive remedies and may even proceed simultaneously because the causes of action in the two proceedings are different. In *quo warranto*, the cause of action lies on the usurping, intruding, or unlawfully holding or exercising of a public office, while in impeachment, it is the commission of an impeachable offense. The crux of the controversy in this *quo warranto* proceeding is the determination of whether or not the respondent legally holds the Chief Justice position and can thus be considered an impeachable officer in the first place. On the other hand, impeachment is for respondent's prosecution for certain impeachable offenses. The Chief Justice, according to the court, is not being prosecuted for such impeachable offenses enumerated in the Articles of Impeachment. Instead, the resolution of this case shall be based on established facts and related laws. Now, the Court ruled that the language of Section 2, Article XI of the Constitution does not foreclose a *quo warranto* action against impeachable officers. The provision reads:

> Section 2. The President, the Vice-President, the Members of the Supreme Court, the Members of the Constitutional Commissions, and the Ombudsman may be removed from office on impeachment for, and conviction of, culpable violation of the Constitution, treason, bribery, graft

> and corruption, other high crimes, or betrayal of public trust. All other public officers and employees may be removed from office as provided by law, but not by impeachment.

The provision uses the term "may" which denotes discretion and cannot be construed as having a mandatory effect. An option to remove by impeachment admits of an alternative mode of effecting the removal. The Court said:

> To subscribe to the view that appointments or election of impeachable officers are outside judicial review is to cleanse their appointments or election of any possible defect pertaining to the Constitutionally-prescribed qualifications which cannot otherwise be raised in an impeachment proceeding.

The courts should be able to inquire into the validity of appointments even of impeachable officers. Otherwise, the appointment of an impeachable officer cannot be questioned even when, for instance, he or she has been determined to be of foreign nationality or, in offices where Bar membership is a qualification, when he or she fraudulently represented to be a member of the Bar. To construe the Constitution as proscribing a *quo warranto* petition is to deprive the State of a remedy to correct a "public wrong" arising from defective or void appointments.

The Court declared that an action for *quo warranto* is not barred by prescription.

> A *quo warranto* action is a governmental function and not a propriety function, and therefore the doctrine of laches (originally a defence in equity, asserting that the claimed has unreasonably delayed the assertion of his claim, thereby putting the defendant in a detrimental position) does not apply. When the government is the real party in interest, and is proceeding mainly to assert its rights, there can be no defense on the ground of laches or prescription.

In removing the Chief Justice, the Court held that a member of the Judiciary must be a person of proven competence, integrity, probity and independence. Having filed an incomplete set of Statements of Assets and Liabilities (which is required by the Constitution), she could not rightfully claim to be a person of integrity.

In short, the Supreme Court crafted another avenue for the removal of a member of the Court. Despite its previous rulings on the use of impeachment as an *exclusive* remedy to remove, despite its previous rulings on the temporal limitations on the use of an action for *quo warranto,* despite its rulings on protecting impeachable officials from collateral attacks (disbarment, for example), despite the fact that the Chief Justices' qualifications have been assessed and not found defective by the Judicial and Bar Council, the Supreme Court still decided to handover its Chief to the Chief Executive.

The use of *quo warranto* against a judge is unusual and there were concerns this remedy was used instead of commencing impeachment proceedings against the Chief Justice. It was also very controversial, given that Sereno was well-known for her opposition to the policies of President Rodrigo Duterte, such as his 'war on drugs' policy. The granting of *quo warranto* in this instance is an example of the potential misuse of writs remedies for political advantage.[54]

7 Analysis

President Duterte has removed constitutional constraints in the use of Executive Power, thanks to a Supreme Court that refused to exercise its own powers as a check on the President's actions. All the cases cited in this study weaken "separation of powers" because they remove checks on the Administration's actions. The removal of the Chief Justice, who demonstrated independence, is the ultimate demonstration of the Court's subservience.

In the House of Representatives, Duterte's allies approved on third and final reading its version of a federal constitution.[55] This draft scraps the term limits for House members and other local officials in the present Constitution.[56] Unlike the draft commissioned by President Duterte, the House version does not have any provisions on the regulation on political dynasties, barely cloaking the attempt to keep themselves in power.

What is astonishing about the Philippine case is that the assault on the judiciary is self-inflicted. Without any overt threat, the Supreme Court has been ruling consistently for the President.

The Supreme Court's behavior might be due to fear of "court curbing" – that is, the "actual changes to the Court's institutional power – through jurisdiction stripping, court packing, or other legislative means." Such measures can be passed through constitutional reform, legislative measures, or the overturn of long-standing conventions. Regardless of the form, their goal is to limit courts' powers.[57] But the Court has never been threatened in this manner by the Duterte Administration and the only obvert act that threatened the Court was the removal of the Chief Justice. However, that legal remedy was well-within

54 M Crouch, 'The Prerogative Writs as Constitutional Transfer' [2018] 38(4) *Oxford Journal of Legal Studies* 659.

55 The Philippine Star, 'In final vote, House approves charter change' (The Philippine Star, 12 December 2018) https://www.philstar.com/headlines/2018/12/12/1876439/final-vote-house-approves-charter-change accessed 26 September 2019.

56 ibid.

57 A S Chilton and M Versteeg, 'Courts' Limited Ability to Protect Constitutional Rights' [2018] 85(2) *University of Chicago Law Review* 314.

the powers of the Court. In other words, the Court could have stood by its own rulings to deflect the assault on the judiciary.

The Court's behavior might also be due to competence concerns. Judges have identified certain questions as being inappropriate for judicial resolution, or have refused on competency grounds to substitute their judgment for that of another person on a particular matter.[58] However, the Constitution already gave the Supreme Court the power to rule on the exercise of emergency powers; it should not be allowed to duck behind its own insecurities to avoid exercising its powers.

Part of the reason for the Court's decisions may have to do with the weak institutions that are now operating in the Philippines. The western liberal concepts that underpin constitutionalism were ineffectively transmitted during colonization of the Philippines.[59] Separation of powers remains illusory as studies show that the judiciary in the Philippines defers to the Executive Branch.[60] Newer research is showing that informal networks put pressure on Chief Justices and influence decision-making in the Philippines.[61] These factors combined may explain why the Supreme Court has opted to toe the populist line.

It is also possible that the Court is biding its time, waiting for the right moment to assert its power in a manner that would have the greatest impact. Recall, the tragic consequence of Courts that decided to confront populist leaders.

But at the rate the Philippine Supreme Court is going, there will be nothing left of the Constitution by the time the Justices decide to act. If the Supreme Court continuously decides to concentrate power in the Chief Executive then there can be no time in the future to assert judicial independence. Judicial support for the populist agenda might even outlast the President's term. Before President Duterte's term ends in 2022, he would have appointed 13 of the 15-member Supreme Court.

In emerging Asian democracies, judicial review has been important to the survival of the constitutional system. Emerging democracies often face the risk that dominant

---

58 J A King, 'Institutional Approaches to Judicial Restraint' [2008] 28(3) *Oxford Journal of Legal Studies* 409.

59 D B Gatmaytan, 'Lost in Transmission: Rule of Law Challenges in the Philippines' [2017-2018] 8 *Impunity Watch Annual Review* 6.

60 D A Desierto, 'Judicial Independence: Evidence from the Philippine Supreme Court (1970-2003). in N Schofield and G Caballero (eds), *The Political Economy of Governance: Studies in Political Economy* (Springer 2015).

61 B Dressel and T Inoue, 'Informal networks and judicial decisions: insights from the Supreme Court of the Philippines, 1986-2015' (2018) 39(5) *International Political Science Review* 616. This study draws attention to how informal networks may have influenced the votes of justices on the Supreme Court of the Philippines in 47 high-profile cases. Based on analysis of university and work-related social network variables as applied to 618 individual votes between 1986 and 2015, the study provides descriptive evidence that political-presidential and hierarchical pressures via the Chief Justice exerted through networks did influence the voting behavior of individual justices. Thus, the results support a widely reported but understudied aspect of the behavior of Philippine Supreme Court justices: how informality on and off the bench may animate judicial votes.

groups will reject the constraint of unfavorable judicial rulings.[62] Paradoxically, the experiences of democratic near misses that we have explored underscore the role of political elites and non-elected institutions – courts, military commanders, and election administrators – in decisively repudiating authoritarian leaders bent on democratic erosion.[63]

A democracy under threat depends critically on support from unelected and non-majoritarian actors. Such support serves to slow down erosion, giving political parties and public movements time to regroup and reorganize in the face of threats.[64] Courts can win their battle against authoritarian populists as long as they have the strong support of initiatives within civil society. Civil society initiatives against populist regimes not only can re-enforce the role of courts, but can gain new strength for themselves in such effort.[65]

There are other issues already on the Court's docket that may be opportunities to hold the President accountable, such as the Philippines' decision to withdraw from the International Criminal Court (where cases against Duterte have been filed). A populist Supreme Court can further concentrate power in the Executive Branch by immunizing him from the International Criminal Court processes. Populist actors, however, can exhibit hostility towards international courts because they are international and because they are countermajoritarian. Populism offers an ideology that opposes the very idea that international courts should have authority over issues of distribution, identity, or other matters that fall within the normal provenance of democratic politics.[66]

8 Conclusion

Protecting the Liberal Constitution in a populist age is a losing battle in the Philippines. Congress allied itself with the President leaving only the judiciary as the only institution that check Rodrigo Duterte's government. Tom Ginsburg, et al., criticized too much optimism with regard to the fate of liberal constitutionalism, saying that comparative constitutionalists have focused on a small set of countries where courts have made a difference.[67] The Philippine case is a signal case that should alert the legal community on the inability of courts to defend against populism.

---

62 M C Davis, 'Strengthening Constitutionalism in Asia' [2017] 28(4) *Journal of Democracy* 158.

63 T Ginsburg and A Huq, 'Democracy's Near Misses' (2018) 29(4) *Journal of Democracy* 29.

64 ibid 29.

65 A Arato, 'Populism and the Courts' (Blog of the International Journal of Constitutional Law, 25th April) http://www.iconnectblog.com/2017/04/populism-and-the-courts accessed 26 September 2019.

66 E Voeten, 'Populism and Backlashes Against International Courts' [2019] *Perspectives on Politics* (forthcoming).

67 T Ginsburg and others, 'The Coming Demise of Liberal Constitutionalism' [2018] 85(2) *The University of Chicago Law Review* 239.

Scholars now acknowledge that courts are ill-equipped to deal with the tidal wave of populism that is sweeping the world.[68] Democratic governance works only when people accept assumptions about power and institutional limitations with recognized boundaries. In countries emerging from autocratic rule, the habits of incremental power and the legitimacy of the opposition are hard to inculcate. Populism puts these values as much at risk in mature democracies.[69] Refusing to abide by the rules, the liberal infrastructure is unable to deal with populist resurgence.

The most astonishing fact about the Philippines' experience with populism, however, is that it seems to be an unmitigated acquiescence to the populist agenda. Without any threat of court curbing, the Court immediately succumbed to populist pressure. The Constitution, written as a response to Executive abuse under the Marcos government, has been interpreted on every opportunity presented to the Supreme Court, in a way that erodes checks on Executive power.

The consequences of the Court's actions on democracy and the rule of law are ominous. Liberal democracy is able to rely upon the separation of powers and other constitutional mechanisms to restrain the translation of temporary and potentially destructive popular whims into political action. Yet there is no denying that liberal democracy ultimately depends on the will of the majority. If voters keep making poor electoral choices or unreasonable demands on their governments, especially ones that threaten to erode the liberal aspects of the regime, then liberal democracy cannot endure.[70]

68 S Choudry, Will Democracy Die in Darkness?: Calling Autocracy by its Name. in M A Graber and S Levinson and M Tushnet (eds), *Constitutional Democracy in Crisis?* (Oxford University Press 2018).

69 S Isaacharoff, Populism versus Democratic Governance. in MA Graber and S Levinson and M Tushnet (eds), *Constitutional Democracy in Crisis?* (Oxford University Press 2018).

70 M F Plattner, 'Liberal Democracy's Fading Allure' [2017] 28(4) *Journal of Democracy* 13.

Epilogue

Epilogue: Endangered Liberal Democracies and How to Safeguard Them

Aalt Willem Heringa and Hoai-Thu Nguyen***

1 Introduction

Are liberal democracies in danger in contemporary times and are we facing a real risk of liberal democratic erosion, or democratic backsliding, throughout the world? And if so, is this process of erosion linked to a populist *Zeitgeist*, an affinity to populist ideologies in the population that made possible the rise of populist groups and political parties? Or can we pinpoint flaws in our liberal democratic models that have come to the surface and that need remedying? The most obvious one being that liberal democracies may not always cater for the interests of all its citizens and their concerns. In that sense it is predominantly output related. And if there is indeed a real and imminent danger for liberal democracies in the form of populism, how can they defend themselves successfully without having to compromise on essential features of what a liberal democracy is? This is of course assuming that the liberal democratic model is by far to be preferred over other models because of their respect for liberty and democracy.

These are the questions that have dominated much of the scholarly debate on liberal democratic erosion in the current time and that also the contributions in this edited volume have in common. When attempting to find an answer to these questions from the different perspectives employed in this volume – both horizontally and topic-focussed, and from various national perspectives inside and outside of Europe – it becomes apparent that there is no clear-cut answer or solution to these questions. Populist threats to liberal democracies can differ significantly in nature, extent, and purpose, depending on the context and national system in which they are studied. This also means that there is no one-fits-all-answer to the question raised above. Instead, what we witness are very different suggestions for solutions as well as paradoxical tendencies, under which solutions can lead to biting one's own tail: attempting to save or preserve the state of liberal democracy can thus sometimes even lead to the strengthening of anti-democratic and populist sentiments.

We set out in this project with a 'thin' definition of populism, which Sascha Hardt describes in the introductory chapter of this volume, and the assumption that populism

* Professor of comparative constitutional law Faculty of Law Maastricht University.
** Assistant Professor of European and comparative constitutional law, Faculty of Law, Maastricht University.

constitutes a threat to liberal democracy. Hardt thus writes that the two main characteristics of populism, anti-elitism and anti-pluralism, result in the rejection by populists of central values of constitutional democracy. He argues that populists in particular "deny the legitimacy of democratic opposition (since they represent the will of the people, which is the only legitimate instance) and thereby democratic pluralism as such. It follows from this logic of populism, that it tends to reject institutions and legal rules that stand in the way of unfettered majoritarian democracy, including parliamentarianism and constitutional limits on government power. When in power, constitutional governments can therefore be expected to undo the legal and constitutional safeguards that entrench constitutional democracy." The objective of this edited volume was, amongst others, to investigate this claim with regard to various national legal systems.

What is interesting to note at this point is that this does not necessarily seem to be the conclusion of all contributions in the volume. Thus, not all authors arrive at the determination that populism per se constitutes a danger to liberal democracies. Quite to the contrary, Hans-Joachim Lauth and Christoph Mohamad-Klotzbach conclude in their article about political parties in democracies that right-wing populist parties are more linked to democratic backsliding than left-wing populist parties, which have shown integrative movements that can, as a matter of fact, even revive democracy. Tjitske Akkerman comes to a similar conclusion, stating that left wing populist parties endorse indeed also (the) other values of democracy and the rule of law, such as equality and fundamental rights. Juan Antonio Chinchilla Peinado and Mónica Domínguez Martín, on the other hand, in their chapter on Spain, do not prescribe to an analysis based on such a right-left dichotomy. Instead, in the Spanish context, they find that populist parties at national level generally "assume the rules of the game of the democratic system configured by the Spanish Constitution". For them the difference in nature rather lies in the different between populist parties at national level and populist movements at sub-national level, such as the Catalan independence movement.

This edited volume contains a variety of highly interesting and well analysed case studies about how national constitutional safeguards were successful, or not successful, in preventing the rise of populism in the various national legal systems, in addition to the more thematic chapters about populism as a contemporary phenomenon as such. It is not possible to do full justice here to all of the different approaches and analyses provided by the authors, but we nevertheless believe that some common concluding remarks can be made regarding the function of constitutional designs as protective shields for liberal democracies and their values.

2 Liberal democracies – what makes them resilient?

2.1 *Vulnerability – An essential feature of liberal democracies?*

One of the paradoxes of liberal democracies is that by their very nature and definition they are more vulnerable to attempts at destroying or limiting their scope and essence than other political systems. Liberal democracy is based on the principle of free and fair elections and majority rule, including a well-functioning public sphere where information can be exchanged freely, which, however, at the same time is accompanied by constitutional rules to safeguard the protection of minorities. And furthermore, democracy is very much intertwined with rule of law notions and mechanisms that limit the discretion of simple majorities in order to protect the open nature of civil society and the state. Democracy is therefore not simply majority rule but also about restricting majority rule and ensuring that majorities are not excessive nor abusive towards opposition, minorities and non-mainstream adherents.

The argument here is furthermore that the more open to newcomers in elections – thus the more liberal democratic – a political system is, the easier it is for populists with an illiberal agenda to rise into power. Democracy also includes the inherent notion that others, meaning non-majoritarian opinions and groups, must also have the opportunity to be heard, to be taken seriously and to be able to have an imprint and to become a majority. Conversely, the less open the system is for new ideas and new political actors, the more it will be protected against populism but also the less it will adhere to liberal democratic standards. This is even more so the case, one might argue, where liberal democratic systems are designed specifically to keep populists out that claim to be the true voice and the only true representatives of a large segment of the people. Is a liberal democracy still a liberal democracy when it does not allow those into power that – truthfully or not – claim to represent both the explicit and implicit will of the electorate? Or when it hinders policies made by those representatives, albeit based upon the claimed will of the (silent) majority?

On the one hand, under the concept of liberal democracy, it would seem inherently paradoxical to discriminate against certain ideas, opinions or groups unless their objectives are inherently anti-democratic or anti-rule-of-law. On the other hand, democracies, and also liberal democracies, do have the right to defend their existence and their fundamental characteristics. To that purpose they have, in quite a few variations, installed various features and defensive mechanisms, that are at the same time part of their existence as well as paradoxical defensive tools. Part of their existence are aspects such as rule of law, horizontal and vertical separation of powers, rigid constitutions, independence of institutions such as judiciary, agencies, public prosecutors, the media, constitutional review, protection of human rights, ombudsmen, parliamentary powers, election systems and others. Paradoxical defensive tools are election systems that limit proportional representation and therefore make it hard for new parties to enter parliament (through for instance imposing high thresholds for entering parliament); limits in political powers for small groups of parliament; limitations of parliamentary powers, favouring the executive; possibilities to ban parties; judicial review of legislation and preference for human rights protection and others.

Limitations on liberal democratic characteristics, in the form of defensive tools as described above, is therefore not an impediment to liberal democracy. Rather, such limitations and defensive tools are part and parcel of liberal democracies: they define a liberal democracy and serve to keep the latter both alive and workable. But they must at the same time be exercised in such a way that they do not lead to impediments of essential liberal democratic features, such as the ones we have described. We will return to this double-sided sword aspect later.

2.2 *The (false) democracy claims of populists*

This edited volume uses the definition of populism by Jan-Werner Müller, which focuses on the rise of populism where an appeal is made to the people, whose views are allegedly not represented by the political elites in power, by using emotions over rational arguments in the political debate, thereby often simplifying complex political issues. Populist groups thus have in common their claim to represent the silent majority of the people, implying that such majority support prevails over all other features of the liberal democratic system, in which they operate. Leaving aside the question of whether such claims are truthful, two more practical conflicts arise here. Firstly, a democracy, and in particular a liberal democracy, is not only characterised by taking the wish of a majority (50% + 1) of the electorate as the basis for any kind of decision-making. Instead, the focus is on an open public debate as well as the protection of individuals against the majority, in addition to binding the legislature to a set of legal rules (rule of law), as Tjitske Akkerman rightly points out in her contribution. Secondly – and this is particularly important where populists are already in power – election systems may, in fact, distort majority calculations. Some election systems thus create 'fake' majorities by enabling a (large) minority to still have a majority of the seats in parliament. Indeed, such an election system is itself not a violation of the democratic principle. Instead, it should make those claiming to represent a majority of the electorate, as well as those believing such claims, aware of this flaw in their claims of being representatives of the majority. Moreover, the majoritarian argument is all the riskier since, as Paul Blokker indicates in his chapter on East-Central Europe with respect to Romania and Slovakia, a too strong majority rule, i.e. a one-party rule or rule by nepotism and a small elite, can also relate to corruption. Lord Action's statement is still accurate: power tends to corrupt and absolute power tends to corrupt absolutely. Therefore, working on defensive mechanisms in favour of liberal democracies, it is good to also build anti-corruption agencies or institutions and establish incompatibility of functions, to be enforced by anti-corruption agencies with a clear mandate. This is all the more important where election systems do facilitate large majorities in parliament even if they do not correspond with majorities of the votes. But even where they do correspond, it is imperative to ensure effective other mechanisms to prevent such majorities from turning into abusive or overwhelmingly powerful entities. Shielding courts from political influence is in such a case the more relevant: where majority appointments of judges might be acceptable in election systems with coalition government and shifting majorities, a similar procedure would be risky and not acceptable in systems with strong and stable majorities in parliament. And similarly, it can be argued that media and media control ought to be more strictly protected against majority interference in essential one-party majorities.

2.3 Efficiency or stability as a protective tool against populism?

Democracies that have as their main objective the efficiency of the system often favour a strong government in lieu of long deliberative processes in parliament. Strong governments, and specifically those who also command a majority in parliament, may be potentially tricky from the point of view of liberal democracies as it puts them in a strong position to push through policies that might undermine core liberal democratic characteristics such as minority protection. The reason speaking in favour of a strong government, however, is that it serves to establish and maintain a government and to have its policies adopted, implemented and shielded against opposition groups and other perspectives. Some democracies therefore make such a stable majority government a central feature of constitutional law by seeking to trim the election system in such a way that it generates stable majorities and thus governments (examples would include the United Kingdom, Germany, and France). A parallel trend hereto is that, at the same time, executives have increasingly taken control of their parliaments by, e.g. (largely) controlling the agenda of parliament or possessing tools to force legislation through parliament. While this ensures an effective government, this goal is achieved possibly to the detriment of other values such as consideration of minority views, acceptance by civil society, or ignorance of the fact that not necessarily all policy proposals of a government/majority in parliament are supported by a majority of the population. In particular the latter might create an experience of a loss of ownership and control by the electorates; especially where this is coupled with increasingly technocratic policymaking. Imposing a percentage for state debt, a percentage for fiscal deficit, a percentage for the reduction of emissions and other environmental hazards and climate change might be efficient; at the same time it also creates a – perceived or real – democratic deficit by significantly limiting the room for manoeuvre of parliament and democratic majorities.

When effectiveness is key in those circumstances, much relies upon other guarantees and checks and balances. Precisely then, and because of that, a liberal democracy does require relevant counterweights. These do not exist to frustrate effective government, but to serve the principles of a liberal democracy: to keep the channels of decision-making open; to keep rule of law and human rights guarantees intact; and to ensure independent institutions and agencies to do their work. However, such counterweights may also be weak or considered to be giving in, as Dante Gatmaytan describes in his chapter about the Philippines, in which he demonstrates that the Supreme Court has problematically deferred to the executive and deferred from functioning as a counterbalance. At the same time, George Karavokyris' chapter about Greece notably shows that even the strong majoritarian model in Greece does not necessarily lead to a serious threat of the liberal and democratic acquis. Quite to the contrary, Matteo Bonelli argues in his chapter on Italy that the constitutional safeguards constructed to prevent a return to authoritarian forms of the past in Italy have turned the government so inefficient and unable to provide for swift decision-making that it has, in fact, facilitated the rise of populism by "giving to the citizens the impression that traditional parties and institutions are inefficient and thus useless".

2.4 Independent courts – An indispensable component of liberal democracies?

Many of the chapters in this edited volume agreed that one of the most important tools in protecting liberal democracies are constitutional courts, which in quite a few instances can, and do, contribute to the legitimacy of a state and its institutions by being independent and impartial, occasionally controlling public decisions when these are disproportionate to citizens, and operating in open court with public arguments and counterarguments and a reasoned decision. For the same reasons, they also constitute an obvious target for populist attempts to erode the state of liberal democracy: judges are independent, often appointed for life, with tools to nullify statutes and administrative decisions. And indeed, the more tools they have the likelier it is that politics might sense frustration with regard thereto. And still constitutional courts cannot be said to be indispensable: both the United Kingdom and the Netherlands operate without a probing form of judicial (constitutional) review and still qualify as well-functioning liberal democracies. This aspect shows the complex nature of the issue at hand. There is indeed much more than legal features, and much more than having or not having a constitutional court: the more is the total sum of all existing mechanisms and checks. Some of these are indeed also custom or fair play or decency or integrity. The less constitutional conscience of all actors in a given model, the more legal tools we may need, all the while exercising due care and realising that courts may also not be strict or may be too lenient or giving in or forced to give in or being packed by the executive. This problem of court-packing was also specifically identified by Petra Gyöngyi in her chapter as an issue for liberal democracy in Hungary. Interesting though, courts can occasionally also be seen as strengthening parliaments by imposing upon them duties which they must exercise, and when limiting the exercise of powers by parliaments, to frequently enjoy confidence among the electorate. Since they do so whilst protecting individual rights and liberties, and also do so with open arguments and counterarguments and independent and impartial reasoning. And even countries without constitutional courts can be seen to provide extensive protection of individual rights and parliaments which do abide by general perceived notions of rule of law and human rights as the UK practice under the Human Rights Act may show.

2.5 Constitutional law and constitutional fair play: A balancing act

And it is exactly the point made above with regard to constitutional courts that can also be made in a more general manner for the functioning of constitutional safeguards in a liberal democracy. On the one hand, we do have a variety of legal rules and tools available to us to protect liberal democracy against populists. On the other hand, how such legal rules and tools work out in practice is an entirely different thing. The argument can be made that in the absence of any legal rules fair play may determine the framework under which actors in a political system will act, which sometimes might lead to more desirable outcomes than a rigid legal and constitutional system, which is not adhered to in practice. This can perhaps be better described by a traffic law analogy. There has been evidence that in a street crossing, in which buses, cars, bikes and pedestrians meet, it might be better to not have any traffic rules on who gets priority over whom at all. By relying on the common sense and sense of fairness of all traffic participants, it can lead to the latter also showing more awareness and displaying more careful behaviour. On the other hand, we can also design very elaborate roundabouts, in which the rules are clear as to who receives priority over whom. These are effective and run smoothly as long as all drivers behave according to the rules; but as soon as there is one or many outliers that do not follow the rules, chaos normally prevails, and traffic will slow down because traffic participants will start blocking each other. Both examples show that sometimes rules are not needed, and that sometimes they are ineffective. It all depends on the custom and practice surrounding the existence of such rules and the level of fair play involved. This conclusion is also relevant in constitutional law and in the context of populism in liberal democracy.

Constitutions in liberal democracies are, in essence, a balance between three interests: (1) the (continued) existence of the state and its essential features; (2) democracy and sovereignty, in the sense that the electorate is at the basis of the state and has a say over its course and most important policies; and (3) the rule of law and human rights, in the sense that abuse of powers is to be prevented and penalized, and that the rights of the citizens are protected. When the objectives of efficiency or effectiveness prevail, democracy or rule of law may be in danger; in a similar vein, when democracy, understood as majority rule, prevails, the rule of law or effectiveness may be at stake; and when the rule of law prevails indeed effectiveness or democracy may become too limited. And on top of these balancing acts there is also civil society to be taken into the equation: the stronger the civil society and the free press and NGOs and the more transparency exists in a system, the more difficult it might be for a political system to become unbalanced or for populists to take over.

In many of the case studies we note that authors describe a deficient, or perhaps flawed, constitutional design when it comes to their objective of protecting the state of liberal democracy; and yet such a flaw has never (until now) proven to be an issue, simply for the reason that an abuse thereof has never occurred either because the idea of fair play prevailed or because some practices are simply considered to be not done. The catchpoint of this line of argument is, of course, that once the perception that certain practices are not done changes – or possibility never existed in some systems – the existence of legal rules becomes indispensable. And it is likewise indispensable that such rules are enshrined in a relatively rigid manner at constitutional level, where possible safeguarded by a strong constitutional court, so as to avoid that they are simply dispensed with by a populist majority through an ordinary legislative procedure once they have risen into power. We will discuss some suggestions for desirable constitutional safeguards to protect liberal democracies against illiberal populism in the next section.

3 Constitutional safeguards to protect liberal democracies in times of populism and their limits

3.1 *Independent courts*

We have mentioned above the importance of independent courts in a liberal democracy. They constitute an impartial instance that can control public decisions and improve deliberative democracy by operating in open court with public arguments and counterarguments and a reasoned decision. However, because by their very nature – independent, often appointed for life, with tools to nullify statutes and administrative decisions – they are often targeted by populists in an attempt to erode liberal democracy. Indeed, the more tools they have the likelier it is that politics might sense frustration with regard thereto. Be aware when ministers and politicians complain about courts as independent supervisors and reviewers of what politics do: this is usually a sign that they feel untouchable and claim to be untouchable, whereas democracy is about being vulnerable, transparent and accountable. The role of courts in protecting liberal democratic values are two-fold: on the one hand, they must have strong powers to exercise their role as guardians of the constitutions, by, for example, being able to annul undemocratic laws even against the political will of the majority. Such power may also be combined with the participation of citizens. Maria Bertel, in her chapter about Austria, thus calls the people 'guardians of the constitution' where they access the Constitutional Court. This is because the Austrian Constitutional Court, while the direct guardian of the constitution, in most instances may not act *ex officio*. At the same time, the they must themselves be sufficiently protected against attacks by populists. Rosa Ristawati and Radian Salman in their contribution about Indonesia in that respect argue that the Indonesian constitutional court has in their opinion in some cases leaned too much towards satisfying populist majorities. To use the Italian example, as described by Matteo Bonelli in his chapter, there has been so far no attempt of court-packing or undermining the independence of judges in Italy, which he attributes to the Italian constitutional framework. He writes in this regard: "First, the constitution requires an agreement between parties for the election of the five judges selected by parliament. In this manner, and providing that there is no supermajority of one party (or a coalition of), it is very difficult, if not impossible, to create a completely unbalanced court. Second, even in the case in which the parliament pushes forward controversial nominations, the fact that other judges are chosen by other actors make any packing plan even more complicated. A Hungarian or Polish situation in which the constitutional court becomes the expression of the political majority seems thus unlikely. In contrast to those experiences, thus, the Italian model could be a suitable candidate for export." We would tend to agree with especially the latter statement.

3.2 Electoral systems

Electoral systems can contribute both to the rise of populist parties and be a safeguard against it. They may enable populist movements to obtain a majority in parliament without possessing a majority of the votes through specific calculation methods; or they can make it very difficult for extreme or populist groups to obtain seats, let alone a sufficient amount of seats to form a government. In Greece, for example, as George Karavokyris explains in his contribution, a system of enhanced proportional system was in place until 2016. Specifically, the law provided for the direct election of 250 out of 300 members of parliament, with the last 50 seats being granted to the majority party, in order to ensure the governmental stability. This of course can greatly benefit any party, including populist parties, that wish to form the government without necessarily having acquired a majority of electoral votes to do so. Conversely in France the electoral system has arguably contributed to preventing populist parties from coming into power until today. This feature became apparent in the contribution about Indonesia written by Rosa Ristawati and Radian Salman. And, in the chapter on France, Diane Fromage and Sébastien Platon look into the question as to why no populist party has so far managed to come into power in France. They, amongst others, attribute this to the two-round uninominal majority system, under which a second round of elections must be organised, unless one of the candidates obtains an absolute majority of the votes cast representing at least 25% of the registered voters, a second round must be organised. In that case, the candidate obtaining a relative majority of the votes cast is elected, but only those candidates which have obtained the votes of at least 12,5% of the voters legally registered may participate in the second round. Fromage and Platon write in this regard that "[t]his second condition has certainly contributed to limit the *FN*'s rise as elections with three candidates in the second round are particularly rare: in most cases, a right-wing candidate is competing with a left-wing candidate. Some have noted in fact that, more than the type of voting system in place (i.e. uninominal or majority system), what matters is the fact that there is more than one round." Another factor identified by them are the rules governing campaign financing in France. Thus, financial support for political parties by the State are dependent on, among other things, the results obtained in the latest legislative elections, which means that it often "tends to freeze the composition of the Parliament, to a certain extent, by providing more money to the parties who already fared well in previous elections", thereby making it harder for political outliers to enter parliament.

3.3 Rigid decision-making procedures

We have touched upon the idea that rigid decision-making procedures can contribute to preventing the rise of populism above. The idea is that any constitutional safeguard, no matter how effective, becomes irrelevant if it can be easily dispensed of by a populist majority through an ordinary legislative procedure once they have risen into power. Therefore, we would argue that the creation of a type of law such as the organic laws in France, which must go through special procedures for adoption because they deal with aspects that are fundamental to the democratic state under the rule of law, would be very beneficial to the safeguarding of liberal democracies.

Related to the issue of rigid decision-making procedures is also the question of whether to allow the holding of referenda in a political system or not, though always with the qualification that some issues such as the rule of law, human rights, and democracy itself cannot be the subject thereof. Thus, referenda can be seen as a tool of populism, as Alison Young indicates in her chapter on the UK, but we can also note that referenda may also act as an outlet for frustration or dissatisfaction when this outlet function (letting off steam) may not be a general feature of the parliamentary system since the referendum issues are in the eyes of the electorate not well considered or met by the parliamentary parties, and making them part of parliamentary debate is hard due to the elections system or the way parliament functions. Young specifically points at this double-sided feature of referenda: they can both suppress democratic deliberation and be the outcome of deliberative democracy. This is also in line with what Ilker Gökhan Sen argues in his chapter about the conflicts between referenda and democratic constitutionalism. He thus writes that in particular the all-or-nothing character of referenda can lead to social polarization and damage pluralism and democratic elements in a society. At the same time, however, he argues that referenda can also be a tool of liberal democracy, in particular where it serves as a way to protect minority interests by constituting a veto tool against unwanted policy changes. The difficult question here is therefore perhaps how to ensure that referenda will indeed serve as a tool for deliberative and liberal democracy rather than against it. Our suggestion here is to seek ways to make referenda less one-dimensional: focus less on the yes/no element and rework them as tools to not only ask pro or con, but also for alternatives. For example, the question should not just be "Brexit – yes or no?"; but also include a question asking "if yes, would you opt for any Brexit or only within certain conditions; and if you no, what would you recommend if Brexit were to take place.?" Such referendums may show splits in society, but also serve as compromising tools for a consensus and reflexion.

3.4 *Strong accountability mechanisms*

We would also suggest the introduction of mechanisms into the political system, which enable parliaments and minorities in it to exercise their powers and scrutinize the government and give parliamentarians the tools to effectively propose legislation and follow up on criticism in society. Democracy must be done and must be seen to be done. Indeed, one thing electorates expect is that politicians not only quarrel but also deliver and fix what is wrong; also, they expect that their voice has an impact upon those in power in that the political elite is responsible and accountable. Democracy is about majorities and minorities and about peaceful transitions of power and transitions of politicians. An ineffective parliament at some point becomes a focal point for criticism; if even a parliament is not capable of voicing public sentiment, democracy is truly at risk. Therefore, ensure to enable them to voice those sentiments, to follow up on them by scrutinizing the government and proposing different policies. Too often members of parliaments consider it their prime duty to keep the majority government in power (and themselves in parliament), and undeniably that is one of the functions of parliament. But the other is to represent the people and the electorate. The phrase representative democracy indeed has to mean something in real life and cannot be equated with supporting the government till the very end. Bonds do have to exist (in parliamentary systems) between government and parliament, but parliament must also be empowered to represent concerns of the electorate and to table them and be seen to translate them in policies.

3.5 *Democracy as a common project*

Democracy is a multi-faceted description of a variety of societies. But what they all have in common is an attitude and a recognition that it is about respect for different opinions, for compromise, for fair play and minorities, transparency and open government, and individual rights and freedoms. It is so complex that it deserves maintenance, discussion, education, study, protection and continuous assessment: how are we doing? Do we treat all citizens fairly and with due respect? Are the channels of communication open? Do the politicians in charge listen and communicate and are they responsive to the citizens and the needs and anxieties of society? Do all players play by the rules of fair play and do we make them responsive to the whole people whom they are supposed to represent? Institutions like the Ombudsman, or courts, or other bodies where citizens may address their complaints, do indeed serve as lines of communication or tools through which the malfunctioning of a democracy may be addressed. Officially also members of parliament are supposed to have such a function, and indeed members of parliament do exist who take that function very seriously and thereby contribute to the quality of democracy. However, here it might be recommendable to build an (again independent) institution which may assess the quality of democracy, which measures citizen's satisfaction and confidence, and which analyses the quality of debates as well as how parliament addresses major issues and fulfils its representative function. Such an independ.ent institution should, moreover, also make data available about and publish analyses about parliament, and transparency and thereby, on a policy and structural level, enhance the effectiveness of all other actors. It can also be asked to supervise democracy projects in schools. In short: we suggest to create an independent committee or institution which has as its duty to critically assess the quality of democracy and rule of law; with regular reporting and with such reports in turn feeding into political and societal debate.

3.6 *Respected/authoritative representative figure*

As the Italian example has shown, even the role of a (to a large extent ceremonial, but still – or maybe therefore – authoritative) function as President (which is also visible in Germany) may also play a role in mitigating policies that go against the grain of liberal democracies. Similarly, this can hold true for other authoritative and well-respected institutions such as a Senate, as for instance the House of Lords, which has in common with largely ceremonial but well-respected presidents that they must rely upon persuasion and well connectedness to the general public. In short, we believe that the existence of institutions with possibly less political power, but with powers of persuasion, who are attuned to the quality of politics and the needs of society, and who can be approached by citizens with concerns, and who at their own initiative can pick up signals from society, can be highly beneficial for the state of liberal democracy. And when things run out of hand, they may resort to the few powers they have, such as blocking legislation, refusing to appoint a minister, or going public in a televised address. They would, essentially, constitute a sort of insurance policy that in serious circumstances a signal can be given.

3.7 Ensuring strong civil society and increasing information literacy

In addition to the present checks and balances and constitutional safeguards that can be found in liberal democracies, both the strengthening of civil society and the strengthening of information literacy of the people is indispensable if we want our liberal democratic systems to be resilient against populist threats in the long-term. If, as Hoai-Thu Nguyen argues in her chapter about populism in times of social media, we can no longer rely on journalists to filter information and to put that information into a larger (political) context for us due to the gradual replacement of traditional mass media such as press, television and radio by social media, then such a task necessarily falls to each individual citizen themselves. The problem, however, seems to be that there is a growing number of people who are no longer simply uninformed, but in fact disinformed, meaning that they form their preferences based on inaccurate factual beliefs – a development that is further exacerbated by the way we share and consume information in the digital age. And furthermore, there is ample psychological research showing that humans tend not to believe information that is contrary to their beliefs and are even inclined not to want to be confronted with such information. Here is a task for education and upbringing to make people aware of that tendency and confront them from early age on with antagonist opinions and information. In the same manner, a strong civil society with a strong scientific background can contribute to the quality of the public discourse by holding to account populists for spreading fake or disproportionate claims and even by perhaps taking over some of the fact-checking tasks, that in traditional media would fall to journalists, themselves in social media.

There is however a paradox here as well: if populism is also, or largely about sentiments (will of the majority, sovereignty, nationhood, anti-elite) and about political sentiments, it might be difficult to pronounce a plea here for a more rationalised debate, based upon figures and data and research. The obvious response from an electorate would be: these data do not sit well with us, so they must be false. And yet, it seems to us it is the only way forward: introduce the relevance of data in education and strengthen civil society with information about policy and data and argumentation. If that was a function of newspapers and traditional media, and that function becomes less relevant through their relative demise, it is important to build new similar institutions, which are independent from political majorities (and minorities) and can serve as transparent feeders for decision-making and public debate. And who can by doing so stimulate and enable debate between antagonists.

4 Some concluding remarks about the structurally limited bite of laws

Overall, we have seen in this edited volume that strong constitutional safeguards can indeed contribute to the prevention of populist parties rising into power and to erode essential features of liberal democracy. In this chapter we have tried to bring the arguments together and advance some modest suggestions of our own that are based on the various experiences in the different national legal systems and our observations enriched from comparative constitutional law. The obvious drawback of these suggestions, is however, that of course they depend on the political actors to use them in accordance with their objective – namely to protect the liberal democracies. Where populists, however, have come into power with a sufficient majority to adopt laws or even constitutional amendments, any of such safeguards will be toothless. Independent courts can be packed with partisan judges; powerful courts can be curbed in their competences; electoral systems and financing campaigns can be amended to benefit the parties in power. Matteo Bonelli's contribution makes a good reading in this perspective. His conclusion on the Italian system might also well serve as a conclusion to our edited volume on how to protect liberal democracies against populism: any optimism in this regard "needs also to acknowledge the inherent fragility of any legal safeguard against raw political power." However, this is not to say that we will not have to try and protect the fragility of any such legal safeguards nonetheless and to raise awareness about the importance of liberal democracies amongst the wider public and about what we may stand to lose if majorities were, in fact, given free rein in trampling upon the notion of democracy and rule of law.

Appendices

Appendix 1

Fig. A1: Trust in politicians

Fig. A1 Trust in politicians in Europe (2002-2016); Data: ESS Round 1-8; mean scores; missings excluded; some countries had been surveyed not in every round on this topic.

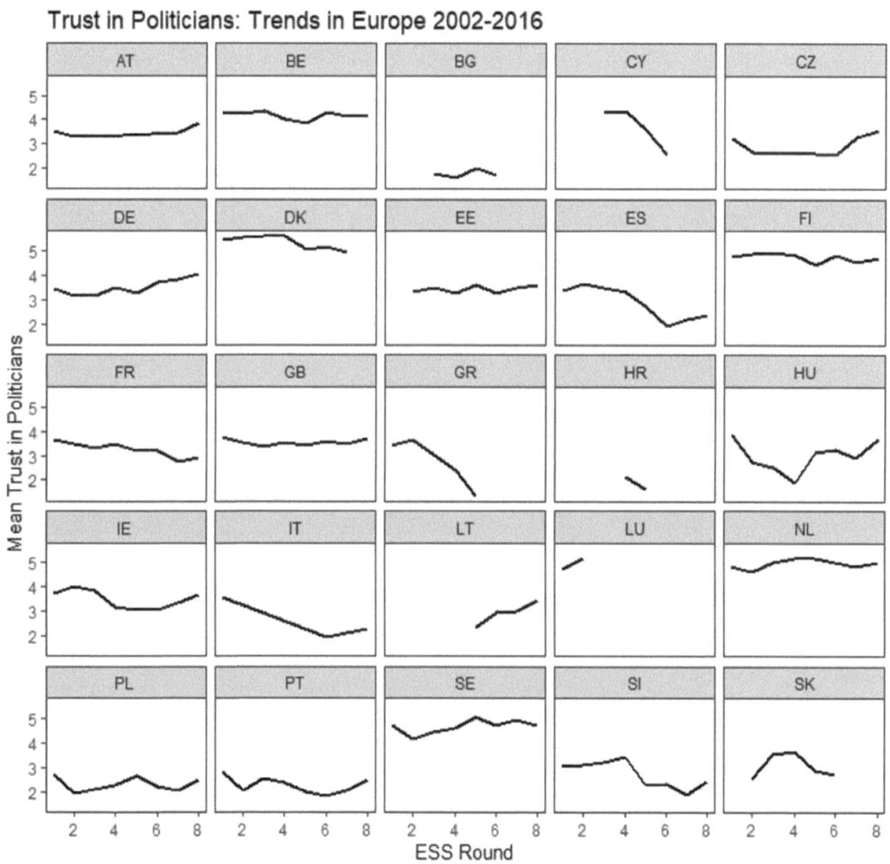

APPENDIX 2

Basics of liberal democracy.

1. Equality before the law and individual and minority rights
   a. Is this principle endorsed or questioned explicitly?
   b. To what extent do policy proposals endorse or restrict equality before the law?
   c. To what extent do policy proposals extend or restrict fundamental rights?
   d. To what extent do policy proposals endorse or restrict access of citizens to justice?

1. Judicial constraints on executive power
   a. To what extent do policy proposals endorse or restrict the independence of the judiciary?

1. Legislative constraints on executive power
   a. To what extent do policy proposals weaken or strengthen legislative control of the executive?

Appendix 3

List of Election Manifestoes

Partij voor de Vrijheid, Nederland weer van ons! Concept-verkiezingsprogramma PVV 2017-2021. http://pubnpp.eldoc.ub.rug.nl/root/verkiezingsprogramma/TK/pvv2017con.

Partij voor de Vrijheid, Hún Brussel, óns Nederland: verkiezingsprogramma 2012-2017. http://pubnpp.eldoc.ub.rug.nl/root/verkiezingsprogramma/TK/pvv2012.

Socialistische Partij, #PakDeMacht: programma voor een sociaal Nederland voor de verkiezingen van 15 maart 2017. http://pubnpp.eldoc.ub.rug.nl/root/verkiezingsprogramma/TK/sp2017.

Alternative fur Deutschland, Unser Programm zur Bundestagwahl. April 2017. https://www.afd.de/wahlprogramm.

Die Linke, Die Zukunft für die wir kämpfen. Langfassung des Wahlprogramms zur Bundestagswahl 2017. https://www.die-linke.de/fileadmin/download/wahlen2017/wahlprogramm2017/die_linke_wahlprogramm_2017.pdf.

Rassemblement National, Les 144 engagements présidentiels. Marine 2017. https://rassemblementnational.fr/pdf/144-engagements.pdf.

France insoumise, L'avenir en commun. Le programme de la France insoumise. https://laec.fr.

9 789490 947231

Printed by Libri Plureos GmbH in Hamburg,
Germany